"Surprise, when it happens to a government, is likely to be a complicated, diffuse, bureaucratic thing. It includes neglect of responsibility, but also responsibility so poorly defined or so ambiguously delegated that action gets lost. It includes gaps in intelligence that, like a string of pearls too precious to wear, is too sensitive to give to those who need it. It includes the alarm that fails to work, but also the alarm that has gone off so often it has been disconnected. It includes the unalert watchman, but also the one who knows he'll be chewed out by his superior if he gets higher authority out of bed. It includes the contingencies that occur to no one, but also those that everyone assumes somebody else is taking care of. It includes straight-forward procrastination, but also decisions protracted by internal disagreement. It includes, in addition, the inability of individual human beings to rise to the occasion until they are sure it is the occasion—which is usually too late . . . Finally, as at Pearl Harbor, surprise may include some measure of genuine novelty introduced by the enemy, and possibly some sheer bad luck."

Thomas C. Schelling, from the foreword to *Pearl Harbor: Warning and Decision* by Roberta Wohlstetter (Stanford University Press, Stanford, Calif. 1962)

THE INTELLIGENCE
WAR

Penetrating the secret world of today's advanced technology conflict

THE INTELLIGENCE WAR

**Penetrating the secret world of
today's advanced technology conflict**

Introduction by
Dr. RAY S. CLINE

Chief author and consultant
COLONEL WILLIAM V. KENNEDY

Co-authors
**Dr. DAVID BAKER
COLONEL RICHARD S. FRIEDMAN
LIEUTENANT-COLONEL DAVID MILLER**

a Salamander book

Published by Salamander Books Limited
LONDON

Published by
Salamander Books Ltd.,
Salamander House,
27 Old Gloucester Street,
London WC1N 3AF,
United Kingdom.

© Salamander Books Ltd., 1983

ISBN 0 86101 1473

Distributed in the United Kingdom by
Hodder & Stoughton Services,
P.O. Box 6, Mill Road,
Dunton Green, Sevenoaks,
Kent TN13 2XX.

Credits

Editor: Ray Bonds

Designer: Mark Holt

Maps and diagrams: TIGA
(© Salamander Books Ltd., but see individual
source credits)

Photographic research assistance: John and
Diane Moore, and Picture Research (USA)

Filmset by Modern Text Typesetting Ltd.

Colour reproduction by Rodney Howe Ltd., and
Bantam Litho Ltd.

Printed in Belgium by Henri Proost et Cie

In the course of the preparation of this book
a great number of people and institutions have
been of assistance to us. Many of them cannot be
named for security reasons, and it is not
possible here to name them all. However, we do
record our gratitude to them all, for without
their help this book would not have been possible.
In particular we gratefully acknowledge the
assistance of the following distinguished
authorities in the international intelligence
field who helped by reviewing all or parts of
the manuscripts, and/or who gave helpful
information and advice.

Dr. Ray S. Cline (see introduction).
Mr. Spencer Davis, US Senate Select Committee
on Intelligence.
Professor John Erickson, Professor of Politics
and Director of Defence Studies, University of
Edinburgh.
Col. Richard S. Friedman, US Army (co-author).
M. Pierre Galante, *Paris Match.*
Lt. General Mordecai Gur, Israel Defence
Forces (Ret.).
Colonel Chaim Herzog, former Chief of Aman
(Israeli Military Intelligence Service), and from
May 1983 President of Israel.
Dr. Richard Kiessler, *Der Spiegel.*
Vice-Admiral Sir Louis Le Bailly, RN (Ret.),
formerly Chief of Defence Intelligence, United
Kingdom.
Hon. Clare Boothe Luce, formerly US Ambassador
to Italy, member of President's Foreign
Intelligence Advisory Board.
Mr. Chapman Pincher, author, formerly
correspondent of *The Daily Express,* London.
Capt. Tom Richards, US Navy Reserve, Professor
of Photography, Syracuse University, New York
and London.
Rear Admiral Robert W. Schmitt, US Navy (Ret.),
Director for Intelligence and Space Policy, Office
of the US Under Secretary of Defense for Policy.
Herr Carl Schopen, formerly Defence
Correspondent, *Frankfurter Algemeine Zeitung.*
Col. Joseph E. Sites, US Army (Ret.).
Maj. Gen. R.J.G. Weeks, Canadian Forces (Ret.),
formerly Chief of Intelligence, North Atlantic
Treaty Organization (NATO).

Special thanks are due, also, to Mr. Scott
Armstrong of *The Washington Post,* to Col.
Seiichi Soeda, Japan Air Self-Defense Force (Ret.),
Special Assistant to the Managing Director,
Foreign Press Center, Japan, for having made
available important source material, and to
Mr. Douglas Richardson, Editor of *Defense
Materiel* and formerly Defence Editor of
Flight International for much technical advice.

In addition, the publishers have had much
appreciated assistance from many international
government departments, manufacturers,
photographic agencies and individuals, and
would like to thank them all, and in particular
Mr. Edward A. Michalski, Ms Bettie Sprigg,
Mr. Robert A. Carlisle and Mr. William Rosemund.

Ray Bonds, Editor

Chief author and consultant:
COLONEL WILLIAM V. KENNEDY,
Armor, US Army Reserve, formerly Intelligence
Officer with the US Air Force and enlisted
servicemen in the US Army (Regular).

Col. Kennedy has had the unusual experience
of completing an intelligence assessment,
of bringing that assessment to national
and international attention through competitive
open publication and then of participating in
the strategic assessment by which his findings
were translated into action.

Along the way he saw, first hand, the
administrative blockages, the bureacratic
rivalries and the suffocating committee-style
intelligence processing that often defeats the best
efforts of competent intelligence operatives
and analysts.

As an intelligence officer in the US Air Force
Strategic Air Command, 1953-55, Kennedy
produced an analysis, drawn entirely from
unclassified sources, of Soviet vulnerabilities in
Asia. He brought these findings to public
attention through articles in the military and
commercial press over a period of more than 20
years. As a faculty member of the US Army
War College in May, 1979, he was invited
to present a proposed North Pacific strategy to
a meeting of Defense and State Department
planners in the Pentagon. In 1982 he had the
satisfaction of seeing the first elements of that
strategy put into effect with the announcement
that two squadrons of USAF F-16 fighters are
to be stationed in Northern Japan while
simultaneously a major US Navy exercise was
conducted along the Aleutian Islands. The Soviet
Union validated the strength of the new Allied
deterrent strategy by responding more
aggressively to that exercise—including the
first ever sorties by Backfire bombers against a
US naval task force—than against any such
exercise to date elsewhere in the world.

At a time when official assessments were still
sunk in a muddle of committee politics, Kennedy,
as an Army Reserve Colonel, published in
Army Magazine and The Atlanta *Journal* and
Constitution an assessment of Allied interests in
Northeast Asia that, through the efforts of a
prominent Atlanta attorney, began the process
by which a misguided Carter Administration
effort to withdraw the US 2nd Infantry Division
from Korea—and thereby destabilize the
entire region—was reversed.

It is this pattern of success, outside of and
often in spite of the official intelligence and policy
bureaucracy, that has led Kennedy to the
conviction that the US Central Intelligence
Agency is a bureaucratic disaster and that it
should be replaced by a more open, more
individually based system of analysis. From an
analysis of Soviet, British, French, West German,
Israeli and other important intelligence systems
he proposes a programme of intelligence reform
that would give the Western alliance and Japan
a more effective, far less costly and more
honourable means of fighting the worldwide
"Intelligence War" against the KGB and its
appurtenances in the Warsaw Pact. Colonel

Contents

Kennedy's military career has included service in Japan, China and the United Kingdom. Beginning with participation as a student editor in the debate that led to US entry into the North Atlantic Alliance, Kennedy's analyses and commentaries have appeared in the military, commercial and religious press of the United States, Europe and Asia. He is co-author of *The Chinese War Machine* (Salamander, 1979) and of *The Balance of Military Power* (Salamander, 1982), and a contributor to several compendia of academic papers, most recently, *China, the Soviet Union and the West* (Westview, 1982).

Co-authors
Dr. DAVID BAKER. A frequent broadcaster and lecturer in space sciences and astronautics, David Baker has enjoyed a long association with NASA and has qualifications in manned flight planning operations. His professional qualifications include BSc in Astrophysics, PhD for work on Evolution of the Solar System, and a diploma in Astronautics, all read at Rice University, Texas. He is currently tutor in Astronomy at Nottingham University's Department for Extra Mural Studies. A Fellow of the British Interplanetary Society, and regular contributor to many technical aerospace journals and the national press, Mr. Baker is author of the books, *The Shape of Wars to Come* and *The Rocket*.

COLONEL RICHARD S. FRIEDMAN, Military Intelligence, US Army. Colonel Friedman first entered military service during World War II in which he served as a Sergeant assigned to the Office of Strategic Services (OSS) in the European, African and Middle Eastern Theatre of Operations with the US Army. As a commissioned officer, Colonel Friedman has served in a variety of assignments, most recently with the US Army General Staff in Washington, as Defense and Army Attache in Budapest, Hungary, and on the International Military Staff of NATO Headquarters. Colonel Friedman was graduated from the US Army Command and General Staff College and the US Army War College.

LIEUTENANT-COLONEL DAVID MILLER. A serving officer in the British Army, Lt. Col. Miller has served in Singapore, Malaysia and Germany, and has filled several staff posts in Army headquarters. He has been an officer in the Royal Corps of Signals and commanded a regiment in the United Kingdom. He is currently serving at the Ministry of Defence in London. He has contributed numerous articles to technical defence journals on subjects ranging from guerrilla warfare to missile strategy. He has been co-author of a number of books, including Salamander's *The Vietnam War* and *The Balance of Military Power*. Lt. Col. Miller's father was an officer in the Royal Navy, hence the interest in maritime matters, which includes his recent book for Salamander, *An Illustrated Guide to Modern Submarines*, and the chapter in this book, "Intelligence and the war at sea".

*The views of Col. Kennedy and Col. Friedman do not purport to reflect the positions of the Department of the Army or the Department of Defense of the United States.

Introduction

Dr Ray S. Cline
Senior Associate, Center for Strategic and International Studies, Georgetown University; former
Deputy Director for Intelligence, the Central Intelligence Agency; and former Director of the Bureau
for Intelligence and Research, the US Department of State.

IF World War III ever breaks out, even before missiles fall on targets in the United States and Europe, the first Soviet blows will be aimed at destroying American intelligence satellites, the silent sentries orbiting in space. So crucial to ferreting out the dimensions of military threats and giving early warning of attack are overhead electronic and imaging sensors that they must stand at the top of the target list in Moscow's command centres.

Thus in modern times the nature of hostilities highlights the eternal high priority of intelligence in deterrence of war and defence against surprise attack.

The ancients fully understood this fact long before the technology of intelligence reached the skies, let alone space. Sun Tzu's "The Art of War" nearly 2,500 years ago pointed out, "the reason the enlightened prince and the wise general conquer the enemy . . . is foreknowledge." Further, Sun Tzu continues, this knowledge "must be obtained from men who know the enemy situation". Finally, it is observed, "An army without secret agents is exactly like a man without eyes or ears."

The clashes of armies around the globe are governed, or in happy circumstances prevented, by the findings of strategic intelligence systems employing both highly sophisticated technical devices and also the classical, historical human resource, the espionage agent. In fact battles are often preceded by secret warfare between the intelligence services of major nations in search of superior foreknowledge that may predetermine the outcome of the struggle for international power and influence, sometimes even forestalling military showdowns before the actual fighting begins. The "darkling plain" on which the intelligence armies wage these secret wars is a battlefield little understood by the people of the nations whose security depends on the skills brought into play on their behalf.

Understanding the intelligence machine and the role it plays in protecting free societies is indispensable for all who want to grasp the nature of the world of the 1980s and to cope with the endemic strategic conflicts of this era.

Charged with the collection and evaluation of information about foreign strengths, motives, and plans, the intelligence officer stands in the first rank of national defence to deter moves designed by hostile powers for their own advantage and to guide the planning of defensive efforts if actual hostilities come. He serves the policy-maker in developing an effective picture of strategic stakes and risks before it becomes necessary to call upon military forces in a violent act of persuasion. If war breaks out, the intelligence officer follows, taking a prominent place behind the lines sizing up the ebb and flow of contending armies in the ultimate arbitration of the battlefield.

Great Britain and the United States, intimate collaborators in intelligence in World War II and ensuing international conflicts, have led the way in creating the intelligence machine that does as much or more than military weapons and forces to protect the way of life and the national interests of the democratic states. This network, with its strategic partners in West Europe and Asia, is on constant watch.

The intelligence adversaries are the tightly integrated totalitarian state security services of every Communist nation, particularly Cuba, East Germany, and the USSR. The all-powerful Soviet service, some 500,000 strong, upon which the Cubans and East Germans depend, was founded after the Bolshevik triumph in 1917 by Lenin, who said, "revolution is only worth anything when it knows how to defend itself".

It is not always possible for the US Central Intelligence Agency (CIA) to forecast with confidence the interplay of move and counter-move within the Communist sphere, but awareness of the risks, and a sense of the results, in peacetime and in war, is the goal of the well-informed intelligence service.

It is not an easy goal. Political revolutions, guerrilla insurrections, and Soviet-sponsored "wars of national liberation" abound in every quarter of the globe. While the US intelligence services can literally photograph and count every ICBM launcher in the Soviet Union, in regional struggles for spheres of influence accurate information that has to come from human sources on the ground often lags far behind the spread of disorders and confusion. Although it established beyond doubt Communist involvement in the recent revolutionary upheavals in Nicaragua and El Salvador, the American intelligence machine could not easily and definitively determine exactly how much the trouble was basically internal or external. Intelligence gaps were wide, particularly while agent resources were redeployed.

When the Falkland Islands suddenly rose in prominence as a policy issue, seemingly out of nowhere in a 150-year-old dispute, intelligence attention shifted to a remote region and type of warfare far from the space age. At the same time details were urgently needed on the Soviet military campaign to suppress fearless Afghan resistance fighters in high Asian mountains and passes where ancient rifles were bringing down modern helicopters. In Southeast Asia it was necessary to comprehend the incredibly complicated political arrangements to stitch together armed opposition to Vietnamese military occupation of Kampuchea, which transformed this suffering land into a proxy battleground between China (PRC) and the Soviet Union.

On the other side of the world Soviet pressure forced Polish police and armies to restrain the Solidarity workers' movement, while a trail of circumstantial evidence from St. Peter's Square in the Vatican through Sofia to Moscow cried out for intelligence confirmation both of the linkage between Poland and a Polish Pope and possible complicity or foreknowledge of Soviet leader Andropov and the KGB in the 1981 assassination attempt against Pope John Paul II.

Yes, these times bring plenty of problems for the intelligence machine. In the early 1980s the intelligence agencies worked with inadequate resources, too modest a backlog of data and insights concerning places like El Salvador, Kampuchea, and Poland—in short an intelligence overload.

When precise and definite information is available, it is one of the most thrilling moments in the lives of the clandestine operator, who succeeded in his quest, and the analyst, who benefited from the search. Just such an occasion was the Cuban missile crisis. In 1962, the Soviet Union tried to gain the strategic upper hand by secretly deploying medium and intermediate-range missiles in Cuba—only a few minutes flight from American cities and military targets. After a systematic search of several months to find out what was going on in Cuba, a U-2 pilot flying 70,000 feet (21,335m) over a field near San Cristobal snapped the single photograph that revealed the whole story. His target had been pinpointed by two observant Cubans on the ground working for the CIA. One was a classical espionage agent who reported through secret channels; the other was a refugee who, when he reached Florida, told CIA interviewers what he had seen before he left. One had noticed unusual military activity at a place near San Cristobal, and the other made an accurate drawing of a Soviet missile, shrouded with canvas, being transported toward San Cristobal. The sketch showed the number of axles and wheels on the trailer so as to identify it unmistakably as carrying a medium-range Soviet missile.

Understanding the intelligence machine and the role
it plays in protecting free societies is
indispensable for all who want to grasp the nature
of the world of the 1980s and to cope with the
endemic strategic conflicts of this era.

Because President Kennedy knew about the missiles and Krushchev did not know that the knew, the USSR withdrew its missiles in the most crucial strategic retreat of the era. At the end Vasiliy Kuznetsov, Soviet foreign service chief, said the USSR would never again enter such a strategic contest at such a disadvantage.

The U-2, a high-flying aircraft invented by the CIA, and its camera capable of taking pictures from altitudes 15 miles (24km) above the Earth, permitted analysts to recognize objects on the ground at San Cristobal with dimensions as small as 12 inches (300mm). It was the U-2 also that had pinned down with the same precision missile facilities at the Soviet satellite launching sites at Tyuratam, Kapustin Yar, and Plesetsk. From this time forward, overhead photographic reconnaissance of the Cuban missile crisis supplemented the traditional discipline of electronic signals and analysis and espionage.

The truth is that only a very small percentage of intelligence operations produce such exciting results. Few involve dangerous and secret adventures. Most of the work consists of humdrum tasks of sorting, sifting, mulling over, and describing data files. The excitement for intelligence analysts is in reality in separating the wheat from the chaff, the signals from the noise. The reward for all the unsung heroes and heroines of the intelligence profession is in the private satisfaction of bringing to light pieces of information and insights to be passed to top officials of the nation. The technical and human collectors of intelligence pile up the raw data. The analysts reduce it to meaningful ideas related to national security. Occasionally intelligence officers feel they may have helped their political leaders to make a sound decision and thus have struck a small blow for liberty in the defence of their country.

During the past few decades the conventional sources—press reports, foreign radio broadcasts, foreign publications, and reports of diplomatic and military attachés—have been supplemented by a vast flood of technical data gathered from photographic imagery and electronic signals. Mountains of research materials are now available for these sources. The range of the coverage and the bulk of the data have revolutionized the profession of the intelligence officer. The intelligence machine will never be the same. Yet these satellites and electronic intercept systems are enormously complex and costly. They can be afforded only by the United States and the Soviet Union, which followed the American path into high technology intelligence, lagging just a few years behind in each new development.

From the early 1960s on, US reconnaissance from space has made the Iron Curtain and the Bamboo Curtain irrelevant, much to the annoyance of the two closed societies where secrecy is highly prized. This technical miracle has greatly reduced the burden on the secret agent. Lives need not now be risked in gathering facts that can easily be seen by the eye of the camera.

Instead the agent concentrates on gathering ideas, plans, and intentions, all carried in the minds of men and to be discovered only from their talk or their written records. Nobody has yet taken a photograph of what goes on inside people's heads. Espionage is now the guided search for the missing links of information that other sources do not reveal. It is still an indispensable element in an increasingly complicated business.

Even though the intelligence machine has become complex and costly, modern intelligence analysis and strategic decision-making cannot get along without its contribution. Nor could arms control agreements and defence policies be fashioned without the precise knowledge of the strategic weapons systems involved that only the intelligence professionals can supply.

Though the USSR rivals the United States and spends more money and uses more manpower, American intelligence has remained first in the field. The United States has shared its skills with the United Kingdom, a trusted partner in secret intelligence since World War II, and has passed at least some of the vital knowledge derived from the intelligence machine to friendly governments around the world. All of the NATO countries and other bilateral treaty partners of the United States in the Mideast and West Pacific, ranging from Japan to Australia, benefit from the security that good intelligence gives.

In turn, in lesser regional contexts and with more emphasis on traditional intelligence collection methods, these friends and allies supplement the holdings in the data bank of the American intelligence system.

Sheer volume and bold risk-taking is a strength on the Soviet side in the intelligence wars. On the other hand, the innovativeness in technology and objectivity of intelligence analysis in a free society suggest that the United States, the United Kingdom and their allies have the best intelligence machine in the world.

January 1983

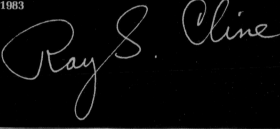

Chapter one

What is intelligence?

IN LATE 1981 or early 1982, the US destroyer *Caron* moved into position off the coast of Nicaragua and El Salvador. Equipped with an array of specialised electronic gear, the *Caron*'s mission was threefold: to monitor radio traffic that would keep US intelligence agencies abreast of diplomatic developments in Central America; to monitor guerrilla radio traffic in El Salvador and any cross-border traffic between the guerrillas and possible supporters in Nicaragua; and to observe, by radar, coastal traffic to determine if supplies were moving from Nicaragua to the guerrillas in El Salvador.

At almost the same time that the *Caron* was moving into position, four Japanese nuclear experts were temporarily overcome by gas injected under the door of a railway compartment while they were travelling between Moscow and Leningrad. Although the technical papers they were carrying appeared not to have been disturbed, there was ample time for the papers to have been photographed while they were unconscious.

And, all the while, the *Caron* and the train traffic between Moscow and Leningrad—even the movement of guerrilla patrols in El Salvador—were almost certainly being recorded by cameras in satellites or reconnaissance aircraft.

Yet, according to US Senate investigators, the most important of all intelligence—that indicating the direction of future political and economic policy—was coming from the most ancient of all sources: that is, from diplomats and military attaches accorded open diplomatic status. The elaborate, enormously expensive technical means of modern intelligence-gathering, say the Senate investigators, do nothing more than supplement the work of the diplomats in this vital area of political intelligence.

Indeed, an intelligence flow of major influence on ultimate US and European government policy toward Central America was not coming from governmental sources or through government channels at all, but from the village priests and missionaries of the Roman Catholic and other Christian churches living and working among populations on both sides of the civil wars in the region. Based on this information, Christian churchmen throughout the Western world were urging the US Government to stop military aid to all sources in the El Salvador conflict—a powerful, combined voice that could not be ignored.

Not only in Washington, but in Moscow, Tokyo, London, Bonn, Paris, Copenhagen and Singapore the same high government officials who were trying to make some sense out of the Central American situation were being bombarded by a massive flow of information from many other directions.

In Britain, for example, an organization called rather innocuously "Government Communications Headquarters (GCHQ)" (which in 1982 achieved notoriety as information on alleged leaks was made public) was pulling out of the airwaves the same sort of government-to-government and intra-government messages that the USS *Caron* was collecting off the coast of Central America. The progenitors of GCHQ had monitored the deployment of the Imperial German High Seas Fleet during the Battle of Jutland in 1916. The organization operates today in the technical tradition of the electronic wizards who made possible the fantastic "Ultra" code-breaking operations in World War II. Similar organizations in most other major nations gather political, military, economic and even personal messages and deliver these to various government departments, chiefs of state or intelligence agencies.

Only a few years ago it could be said that collection of information was the major problem confronting governments. A massive technical revolution in information-gathering means has brought about a drastic change in that situation. Today *analysis* of the ocean of information available is by far the most difficult problem with which the users of intelligence must contend. Indeed, buried in the mass of data being collected from Central America in early 1982 was a snippet of information about the use of Argentinian "counterinsurgency" specialists by the US Central Intelligence Agency to "destabilize" the leftist Sandinist government in Nicaragua. Who among the world's intelligence analysts suspected that the Argentinians might interpret that—the latest in a long history of ultmately disastrous CIA "covert action" ventures—as licence to seize the Falkland Islands? In addition, the term "users of intelligence" must now be broadened to include industrial and internal political groups.

Italian, West German and other European counter-terrorist operations are based, of course, on classic intelligence-gathering means, supplemented and expanded by exotic modern technology. Spectacular success was achieved by the Italian police in penetrating the notorious Red Brigade organization, making possible the release of US Brig. Gen. James L. Dozier and other kidnap victims. Such penetration is accomplished by inserting police agents into the

1 ▲

2 ▲

The intelligence process is the collection of information, its collation, analysis and dissemination. These simple words cover an operation that is complicated, thrilling, manpower-intensive and very expensive. It is also the life-blood of the diplomatic and military machines.

1 USS *Caron,* a Spruance class destroyer, of the US Navy, was deployed to the coast of Nicaragua and El Salvador in 1981/2 and used in an electronic surveillance role, for which her equipment was ideal.

2 Soldiers of the El Salvador army being given instruction by a member of the US Special Forces. The US involvement in Latin America is increasing gradually but inexorably; something they may come to regret.

3 Brigadier-General James L Dozier, the senior US Army officer on NATO service, who was kidnapped by the Italian Red Brigade. His release was due to a very determined and successful clandestine operation by the Italian intelligence services.

3 ▲

terrorist organization, by gaining the co-operation of disgruntled or disillusioned members of the organization, or by a combination of these means. Wiretaps and electronic monitoring that can penetrate masonry walls are also involved, as are highly sophisticated cameras and lenses.

So rapid is the advance in the new technology that it is becoming increasingly difficult for any government to keep secret even a slight "leading edge" in collection capabilities. A striking example is the Nikon FM2 camera. With a shutter speed of 1/4,000 second, the camera makes possible quick, high-resolution photography by agents on the ground to verify and supplement satellite and aerial photography. In the past such ground photography often was distorted by camera vibration—the inevitable product of haste and slow shutter speeds, or of the agent's position on a train, aircraft or other moving platform. Since the FM2 is made in Japan, and Japan is the acknowledged world leader in such technology, it is quite likely that this commercial development is, in fact, ahead of what is now available to any of the world's intelligence agecies. This is due to the fact that

Japan imposes no security limitations on its industry, moving into the worldwide commercial market as soon as new developments are proven sound. This freedom from "security" restrictions is undoubtedly a major asset for Japanese industry in worldwide competition, since Japan's major industrial competitors must often restrict their leading technology to classified military purposes.

Cameras in space

The same technology that made the FM2 possible is used in the most secret reconnaissance satellites. Over 400 types of glass are available from which to mix, by computer, the combination of optics necessary for sharp definition of objects on the earth's surface thousands of miles below the orbiting or stationary satellite. The photographs acquired by this means are so sharp that analysts have been able to observe Soviet soldiers decontaminating their vehicles in Afghanistan—a strong indication that chemical warfare is in progress.

Night and bad weather obscure even the

most sophisticated optical lenses. Infrared photography partly fills this gap, and in some way goes a dimension beyond the best optical photography. For example, it is now possible to determine from infrared photography that a particular aircraft type was located at a particular airfield several hours earlier, and even the extent to which the fuel tanks were filled. This wizardry is the product of the heat "signature" left by the several components of the aircraft and their relative heat density.

Commercial enterprise intrudes into this sophisticated world of intelligence in two ways. First, as advances in ground photography indicate, it is now often commercial rather than government research that produces the most important technological advances. Second, commercial enterprises are now making use of intelligence methods and technology to steal the secrets of their competitors.

Nowhere is this interplay of government intelligence requirements and civilian research illustrated more dramatically than in the hypersensitive world of cryptology—the design and breaking of codes. Where once the cryptographer could look only to govern-

ment as a possible purchaser of research products, now a far more lucrative field has opened up in the protection of computers and their linkage with other computers. This had led to an attempt by the US counterpart of Britain's GCHQ—the US National Security Agency (NSA)—to censor cryptographic research in American universities, *before* the products of that research are offered to the government or the commercial market. The scholars concerned have fought this intrusion and a less adversarial relationship appears to have been worked out, whereby researchers will discuss their work "informally" with NSA representatives to determine if open publication of results might jeopardise government codes and code-breaking.

Philip H. Dougherty, advertising columnist of the New York *Times*, reports that advertising agencies spend millions of dollars per year on what are essentially intelligence functions—gathering and analyzing data about consumers, competitors and prospective clients. Former British Prime Minister Edward Heath has been hired to head an "international advisory council" to a company, International Reporting and Informa-

tion Systems, built around a computer such as is used by the US Central Intelligence Agency to store data that can then be retrieved by analysts studying specific trends—in this case in the international business community. The computer will be fed by 96 correspondents deployed throughout the world. Their reports will be assessed by some 33 analysts under a former US State Department official.

Of somewhat longer standing is a "Defence Marketing Service" that provides "market intelligence" for arms manufacturers. This, in essence, is a classic military intelligence operation in commercial form. The pressure of competition has already resulted in the use by some commercial enterprises of sophisticated intrusion and copying devices that were once the province only of the police or government intelligence services.

Can busy executives in the commercial world properly assess the information flowing in to them from such "intelligence" sources? The fact that International Reporting and Information Systems could find a place in the marketplace indicates that they cannot—that some intermediary organi-

zation, an "intelligence agency", is needed to sift out meaningful data from the mass of information that becomes available daily.

For government, this process of assessment is being made more urgent and more difficult by a revolution that is taking place in the "national means of surveillance"—the satellite reconnaissance systems—upon which mutual verification of successive arms control treaties largely depends.

Strategic aerial reconnaissance

These overhead means of surveillance first became available in the 1950s, on a strategic scale, with the development of the U-2 (U = "Utility") aircraft. For the first time it became possible to photograph huge sectors of an entire continental-size country, such as the United States or the Soviet Union. A considerable time-lapse occurred, however, between the time the aircraft took its pictures and the time these could be recovered after landing, transported to analysis centres, developed and examined.

High-altitude satellites vastly expanded —but did not replace entirely—the coverage provided by the U-2 and a later recon-

1 To the untrained eye this is a picture of an army lorry. To a military expert it is a Soviet Army ARS-14 chemical decontamination vehicle with special filtration apparatus above the cab, and sealed windows/vents. But this picture was taken in Afghanistan, and so an intelligence expert sees it as evidence of Soviet use of chemical agents there and would at once start looking for collateral confirmation.

2 Further evidence is another picture of Soviet troops in Afghanistan. Chemical troops are using standard Soviet decontamination equipment to clean down armoured troop carriers. It is not likely that the Soviet Army has the time or opportunity in Afghanistan to hold exercises so the only possible explanation must be that they have been using chemical agents for real. The picture is building up.

3 The Nikon FM2 camera and its long focal length lens attachment are ideal for intelligence use. The camera has a shutter speed of 1/4,000th second which enables high resolution pictures to be taken without worrying about camera vibration leading to distortion—the inevitable result of haste.

4 In the past, night and bad weather have given shelter from the camera; but this is no longer so. Infra-red photography will not only "see" through darkness, but can also record the heat pattern of a target (such as these Saab Viggens) *after* it has left the scene.

naissance aircraft, the SR-71. Both of these aircraft types continue to serve the US Air Force. The quality of their relatively low-altitude photography (both aircraft have a "ceiling" of over 80,000ft, 24,380m) continues to be superior in certain situations and against certain "targets" to that obtainable from satellites.

Even with the satellites, recovery of film continued to impose a significant limitation. The United States, for instance, relies on aircraft equipped to snag packages of film ejected by satellites over ocean surfaces and slowed in their final phase of descent by parachute. Now "real-time" satellite photography is becoming available by use of electronic scanners that translate film image instantaneously to telemetry and relay this information through companion communications satellites for immediate production of photographs at ground stations.

Here again, what is known of commercial development tells us much of what is available in the "classified" military sphere. The most advanced of the commercial systems is the General Electric Company's Landsat D programme under development for the US National Aeronautics and Space Agency (NASA). Although it gathers its information by analysis of seven radiometric bands monitored by its sensors, rather than from optical photography alone, the comparison of Landsat D with earlier stages in Landsat development indicates the amazing progress under way.

Earlier Landsat systems were limited to a ground resolution of just over 262 feet (80m). Landsat D will provide a resolution of about 98 feet (30m), at least as good as the earliest military surveillance systems. But far beyond the capability of those early military systems, Landsat D will be able to supply photographs "assembled" from telemetry within 48 hours or less of transmission from the satellite. Further, "electronic enhancement" of the satellite data now under development by General Electric enables analysts to sharpen images of such "targets" as roads, airfields and railroads by mathematical emphasis of bands of data in the computers.

As concerns the military systems, the photography becoming available through "real-time" transmission is expected to be at least 10 times more accurate than the satellite photography available during the 1970s and early 1980s.

Inevitably, this elaborate array of surveillance and intrusion devices has spawned an almost equally complex array of counter-measures designed to protect a nation's or a business enterprise's vital secrets. These countermeasures are broken down into two major categories — "security" and "counter-intelligence". Security is the protection of information and finished intelligence by *passive* measures, such as safes, codes, electronic "sweeping" of rooms to detect listening devices, etc. Counter-intelligence is protection through *active* measures, such as penetration of subversive groups, expulsion of diplomats thought to be spies, the "turning" of a spy into a "double agent" against his or her original sponsor, etc. The term "counter-espionage" pertains to such active measures against spying ("espion-

age"), and is included in the larger term, "counter-intelligence".

Although its potential counter-intelligence role is never so much as mentioned in official US Government publicity, probably the single most important counter-intelligence device coming into operation today is the Space Shuttle, of which the *Columbia* is the prototype. With its apparent ability to intercept, examine and capture the satellites of a foreign power, the Space Shuttle is, in effect, an anti-satellite, anti-reconnaissance interceptor. In this role it far surpasses anti-satellite technology developed to date by the Soviet Union.

Such a manned "spaceship" is especially important because it is extremely difficult to intercept and jam the electronic "reports" by which satellite photography can now be transmitted almost instantaneously to earth. Those signals are sent out in concentrated, high bursts of energy along an extremely narrow beam. The jamming or intercept ground station must be precisely within the beam width to intercept or interfere. Just as aerial combat began, in World War I, with combat between reconnaissance aircraft, so the outline of future "space wars" can be seen in this beginning of anti-satellite interception.

A cruder but effective means to blind all satellite reconnaissance over a particular country would be to explode a high-yeild nuclear device in the region below that "patrolled" by the satellites. Electromagnetic pulse from such an explosion would "blind" the satellites for perhaps 24 hours or longer, but it would be a sure signal of hostile intent. Infrared photography can be "blinded" by a much simpler device — simply setting off a railroad flare in the vicinity of a "target" known to be the subject of infrared reconnaissance.

The analyst's assessment

At the receiving end of this "intelligence war" is the analyst. Often recruited straight out of college and with little or no direct experience with the countries, peoples and military systems that are the subjects of his studies, the analyst may or may not be able to "see" through this confusing mass of information, often fragmented and distorted by counter-intelligence measures. Even if he does make a timely, accurate assessment, that assessment still might be rejected by high officials because it contradicts strong, often emotional preconceptions.

The New York *Times* observed in a recent editorial, for example, that the British Government has consistently underestimated the strength of Irish nationalism. Yet the British intelligence services have been able to penetrate every aspect of Irish society virtually at will throughout most of 800 years of invasion and conquest. Indeed, it is apparent from British Army assessments captured by the Irish Republican Army and published extensively abroad that British Military Intelligence had made a correct assessment, yet top British officials and the British Information Service continued to portray an opposite assessment. Plainly, the facts developed by competent intelligence analyses simply were not acceptable

1 ▲
1 First flight of the SR-71 was 21 years ago, but it retains a unique photo-reconnaissance capability.

2 The potential intelligence and counter-intelligence capabilities of the Space Shuttle are never officially mentioned, but far exceed anything the USSR possesses.

3 An early U-2, which entered service in 1957. Developments are the U-2R/TR-1 and real-time down-link is now fitted.

4 Satellite camera system. US Landsat D has cameras with a resolution of about 98ft (30m); military satellites have higher performance equipment with electronic enhancement to reveal the finest detail.

5 Satellite picture of Washington DC. To the layman a picture such as this seems of little value, but to the intelligence analyst it is a positive mine of information. Satellite photography can now show individual people.

2 ▲

3 ▲

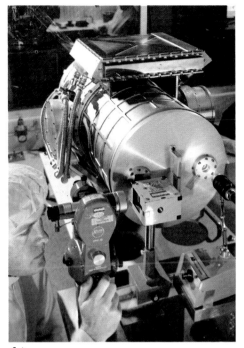

4 ▲

5 ▲

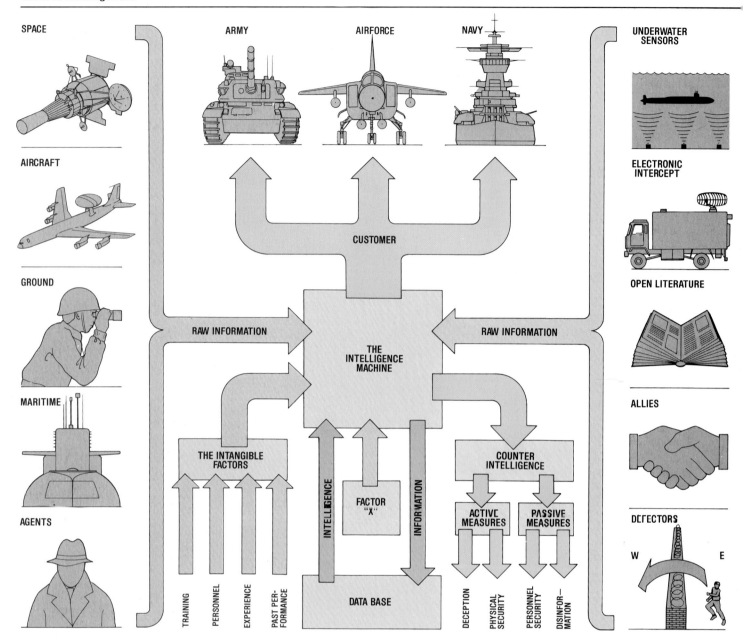

SPACE

AIRCRAFT

GROUND

MARITIME

AGENTS

ARMY

AIRFORCE

NAVY

UNDERWATER SENSORS

ELECTRONIC INTERCEPT

OPEN LITERATURE

ALLIES

DEFECTORS

CUSTOMER

RAW INFORMATION

RAW INFORMATION

THE INTELLIGENCE MACHINE

THE INTANGIBLE FACTORS

COUNTER INTELLIGENCE

INTELLIGENCE

FACTOR "X"

INFORMATION

ACTIVE MEASURES

PASSIVE MEASURES

TRAINING · PERSONNEL · EXPERIENCE · PAST PERFORMANCE

DATA BASE

DECEPTION · PHYSICAL SECURITY · PERSONNEL SECURITY · DISINFORMATION

W · E

THE INTELLIGENCE MACHINE

The military intelligence machine is a very expensive business, which in the more important countries is active every hour of every day of the year. The fuel of these mighty machines is raw information, which is sucked in from many sources, most of which are illustrated here.

Space is currently the intelligence man's dream, with sensors able to roam at will over every country, unfettered by fences or frontiers; there are no "no-go" areas for satellites. Known in political circles as "national technical means", satellites bring/send back information as detailed as the first flight of a new aircraft, or the accuracy of a missile, or even whether the calibre of a new tank gun is 123mm or 125mm.

Aircraft like the AWACS have radar and other sensors which can see far into hostile territory, and which can feed the "take"

down to their bases as it is received, i.e., in "real-time". Although at first sight they appear vulnerable, they are able to detect threats early and to organise counter-measures to ensure their own protection.

Ground sensors range from radars and remote sensors, such as the ADSID, to the soldier with a pair of binoculars. The major problem is range limitations, due to terrain and weather, which is why so much emphasis is placed upon airborne recce.

Maritime surveillance includes both surface ships and submarines. Mounting a multiplicity of sensors, these ships can range over the world's oceans, limited only by the extent of "territorial waters".

Agents are the traditional source of the most vital information, because they are able to penetrate right into the heart of a hostile system. This frequently

enables them to gather not only cold facts (how many tanks, what type of ships, etc) but also the "feel" and methods inside the heart of the enemy camp and the leadership's future intentions. Thus, for many years, the Soviet spy Kim Philby was able to give the KGB information on morale, organisation and personalities inside the British Secret Intelligence Service (SIS). Such information is simply not available by other means.

Underwater sensors now cover large areas of the ocean floor, particularly in the "choke points". They are designed to give information not only on ship and submarine movement, but also on the ocean itself.

Electronic warfare is today one of the most important means of gathering information in both peace and war. Radio intercept can provide raw information from insecure radio links, but can also

build up pictures of deployments, tactical dispositions, individual idiosyncracies (of both commanders and operators) and equipment utilisation. Such intercept activities cover radio, radar, microwave, and other electromagnetic transmissions.

Open literature is a source which is sometimes overlooked. All nations produce vast amounts of paper on military subjects (newspapers, magazines, pamphlets, books) as well as films and videos. These are valuable not only for the factual information they give away, but also for the insight they give into thought processes and moral influences on commanders and staffs.

Allies are frequently a valuable source of information and also help to spread the load in this very expensive undertaking. Unfortunately the traffic on such "two-way streets" does not always flow with

equal freedom in both directions.

Defectors are invaluable prizes to intelligence services, because, like the better agents, they can give information in depth about their specialised area.

Data Base is the pool of knowledge built up by the intelligence machine over the years, which enables every new bit of information to be analysed properly. It is rather like a jig-saw puzzle where each piece is fitted in using a combination of the fragment of a picture and the shape of the sides, with each new piece making completion slightly easier and slightly more inevitable.

Intangible Factors also contribute to the effectiveness of the machine. These include the standard of training, the quality of the people in the organisation, the collective experience of the machine, and its past performance.

Factor X is an important aspect possessed by some

organisations. It is the ability to be in the right place at the right time, to know who has a certain piece of knowledge, and sometimes just to be lucky.

All these disparate elements have to be welded together and processed, leading finally to an output—intelligence. This is then handed over to the operator—military or political—who must then decide what to do with it.

Counter-intelligence is the protection of this vast machine. This includes active measures, such as deceiving the enemy and the use of disinformation. The passive measures are mainly a matter of security: physical and personnel. The former is becoming an increasingly expensive and technology-oriented task as the threat becomes more and more sophisticated. The latter (personnel security) is an endeavour to protect against leaks, but this will never be totally foolproof.

1 An SAC B-52 crew "scrambles" on a simulated alert. Intelligence must provide the warning which ensures that US forces are given the maximum possible notice of an incoming strike; a 24 hours-a-day, 365 days-a-year commitment.

2 The penalty of failure by the intelligence system of either side could possibly be an all-out nuclear war. It is thus essential that national leaders have the best possible intelligence service and that their assessment of intelligence reports is accurate.

emotionally and politically to those who wished to continue the British military occupation.

More than ever before, the lives and fortunes of the individual citizen and his or her family depend upon an accurate understanding of how this intelligence process works, and of its very serious limitations.

Strategic importance of intelligence

So what is "intelligence"? The word "intelligence" has become almost hopelessly confused with things that it is not.

Intelligence is *not* the subversion of a foreign government or political party. Intelligence is *not* the kidnapping or murder of foreign (or one's own) statesmen or agents. Intelligence *is* the gathering of information that can enable a government (or a business concern, or an individual) to gain advantages over rivals or competitors, or at least to survive. Intelligence *is* the *processing,* or *analysis,* of information to determine how much of it should be passed on as useful and reliable.

Understanding the intelligence function is now more important than at any time in the history of the human race. For the first time since the 1950s, the concept of a surprise strategic nuclear attack ("first strike") now dominates the international security debate.

Although obscured through the 1960s and 1970s by what former US Secretary of Defense James R. Schlesinger calls an academic "theology" about nuclear weapons, the concept of a "first strike" has been central to modern war since the American "first strike" by nuclear weapons against Japan in 1945.

Because no one knows what will happen after the first nuclear weapons are used in a future conflict, every statesman who has nuclear weapons at his disposal will be tempted to "pre-empt" the use of such weapons by a real or supposed enemy. Such a nightmarish decision would be made, of course, only in circumstances in which a nuclear-armed statesman became convinced that the survival of his country, or perhaps only of his fellow party members and himself, depended upon this last, desperate choice. Elaborate command and control bunkers dug into mountains and hillsides testify to the belief that there is some margin of chance for survival by the leadership that strikes first and with overwhelming force.

A second influence driving intelligence to the forefront of international concern is the powerful thrust of the Soviet Union toward superiority over the Western world in strategic nuclear armament.

As pointed out by Prof. William R. Van Cleave, Director of Defense Studies at the University of Southern California and a delegate to the SALT-1 talks, "US strategic planners always have tended to assume that, based on a superior intelligence capability, the United States would have advance strategic warning of an enemy nuclear attack. Up until the mid- and late-1970s US strategic nuclear power was so secure that even if the assumption of such a superior intelligence capability had been incorrect, the United States could have absorbed a surprise attack and still have responded with overwhelming force. We have permitted severe vulnerabilities to develop in our strategic forces, and in our command, control, communications and intelligence capabilities as well. The result is that we are making our forces more and more dependent on that assumption of intelligence superiority and effective strategic warning at the very time that assumption itself is more and more questionable."

Because the military situation is so dangerous, and because the outcome of a strategic nuclear war is so doubtful, more emphasis than ever before is being placed by rival powers on economic and political moves designed to destroy an opponent short of war. An efficient intelligence system is essential to defend against such actions.

Intelligence versus operations

Unfortunately, at the very time when there is a greater need than ever before for a clear understanding of what intelligence can and cannot do, the intelligence function has become befogged and besmirched by activities that have nothing to do with intelligence, as such. That is, assassination plots against national leaders, subversion of governments, propaganda and psychological warfare—all of which are totally foreign to the intelligence function. To the extent that they have any legitimacy at all, such functions are properly described under the heading of political and military "operations". The mischief lies in failing to maintain a distinct organizational boundary. In short, intelligence is one thing; operations are something else.

The distinction, as shown in figure 1, emerged during the development of the military staff system during the 18th and 19th centuries. Thus, the intelligence officer at successive staff levels is mainly concerned with gathering, analyzing and disseminating information of use to the command and to the echelons above and below it. His focus is on the enemy or, in time of peace, on foreign forces in general, in particular those that might pose a future threat, or which might become allies.

The operations officer is the staff agent who literally operates the forces of the command. Using intelligence reports of the enemy situation as presented to him by the intelligence officer, he designs forces and courses of action to protect the command and to accomplish its mission.

In a representative military staff system all of this, of course, goes on through the commander, or by his delegation; that is, the intelligence officer describes the enemy situation to the commander; the operations officer presents alternative courses of action to deal with the enemy, and the commander either approves of one of those courses of action or designs one of his own. The commander is free to accept, reject or put a different interpretation on the estimate given to him by the intelligence officer.

One of the great virtues of separating these functions is that it prevents or at least discourages the operations officer—always the dominant staff officer in a strong staff—from designing an "enemy situation" to

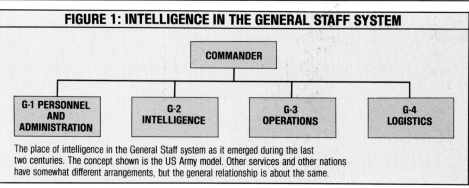

FIGURE 1: INTELLIGENCE IN THE GENERAL STAFF SYSTEM

The place of intelligence in the General Staff system as it emerged during the last two centuries. The concept shown is the US Army model. Other services and other nations have somewhat different arrangements, but the general relationship is about the same.

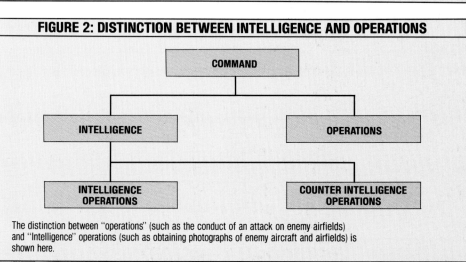

FIGURE 2: DISTINCTION BETWEEN INTELLIGENCE AND OPERATIONS

The distinction between "operations" (such as the conduct of an attack on enemy airfields) and "intelligence" operations (such as obtaining photographs of enemy aircraft and airfields) is shown here.

1 ▲

2 ▲

3 ▲

4 ▲

1 Former US President Carter with King Hussein and the late Shah of Iran. Due to a failure to appreciate the distinction between intelligence and operations the CIA has repeatedly become involved in Iranian affairs, usually with disastrous consequences. It certainly appears also to have wrongly assessed events in Iran.

2 Brezhnev and Castro. The accurate and timely detection of the missile build-up in Cuba was a prime example of good intelligence; the "Bay of Pigs" was an example of the worst type of misuse of an intelligence organization. The alleged CIA/Mafia association showed a total confusion of values and priorities.

3 Captain Seth S. Searcy, commander of the aircraft carrier USS *Essex* during the "Bay of Pigs" fiasco, one of the incidents that have made intelligence a "dirty word". The involvement of military forces in intelligence-planned and -led covert operations has never been successful and has produced some very unhappy situations.

4 A committee room in Washington DC set up to play the notorious "Watergate Tapes" in 1974. Nixon's downfall was brought about by some very shady characters who had been involved in covert actions on behalf of the intelligence community, an admixture which must be avoided.

favour a preconceived course of action. Within the overall heading of "intelligence" the general staff concept recognizes such actions as obtaining photographs of a new foreign aircraft as an "intelligence operation". How this is distinguished from "operations" in the more general sense is shown in figure 2.

On the Soviet side of the "intelligence war", the intelligence function was obscured by the gradual merging into one department—*Komitat Gosudarstvennoi Bezopasnosti*, KGB ("State Security System")—of a number of activities peculiar to the nature of the Soviet state, several of which bear no relation to the original concept of intelligence. Among these are the administration of border troops, and the domestic secret police with their elaborate system of prisons and "labour camps". The logic for this appears to have been that, since certain aspects of intelligence-gathering and processing require secrecy—"security"—the people who operate the intelligence services are the sort of people who should operate everything that has to do with "security" of the state. This was the extension of a necessary, but distinctly subordinate, intelligence activity—counter-intelligence—to a degree that virtually inverted the normal relationship.

The tail that wags the dog?

Since it is essentially a negative activity, counter-intelligence seldom produces information that is of value to the central intelligence-gathering activity. Placed under the same administrative "roof" as the intelligence-gathering agencies, the counter-intelligence staff becomes a competitor for funds. The more people and material resources the counter-intelligence part of the agency controls, the more likely its operators are to gain the upper hand in the agency as a whole and so to create a "tail-wagging-the-dog" situation. From public discussions by counter-intelligence specialists at a consortium conducted by the National Strategy Information Center, Washington, in 1979-80, and from investigations by committees of the US Congress, it is apparent that just such a situation occurred in the Central Intelligence Agency during the 1950s and 1960s. Ultimately it was necessary to force a decentralization of counter-intelligence functions in the Agency and to dismiss large numbers of agents to prevent the counter-intelligence staff from smothering the analytical function. To what extent this same sort of bureaucratic rivalry affects the overall efficiency of the KGB is not clearly known in the West. It is certain, however, that the KGB includes many activities that are more properly included under the heading of "operations", or at least administration, than under intelligence in its traditional sense.

Because of the nature of the Communist system, by which only Communist governments and Communist law are considered to have legitimacy, the Soviet Union and its associated governments have been much bolder in intermixing intelligence-gathering and counter-intelligence *operations*. The latter have included kidnappings and

murder of foreign agents and defectors from the Communist governments, although these activities were largely suspended, at least in the Western nations, because of adverse publicity from defections of KGB assassins, notably Bogdan Stashynsky who confessed to the murder of anti-Soviet exiles Lev Rebet and Stefan Bandera in the 1950s.

A particularly brutal series of KGB political murders occurred in Afghanistan in the 1970s, leading up to the Soviet military takeover in December 1979. In the case of the Afghanistan operation and similar activities, it is apparent that the KGB apparatus built originally to ensure the internal security of the Soviet state has emerged as a method of political-military activity much closer to traditional, if unsavory, diplomatic and military operations than to intelligence, as such.

This linkage within the same agency of intelligence-gathering and production with a vast military and police operational capability (in particular with their power of arrest and judgment) has, at times, made the predecessor agencies now incorporated into the KGB a threat to the state and party that created them. Stalin made use of this system to create and maintain a monstrous personal dictatorship. Only quick action by Stalin's successors, in 1953, prevented the operator of the "State Security System" of that day, Lavrenti P. Beria, from seizing Stalin's mantle.

By an entirely different historical process, this intermingling of operations and intelligence also occurred within the principal adversary of the KGB—the American Central Intelligence Agency (CIA) and to a lesser, or at least less obvious, degree in West European intelligence agencies—Britain's in particular.

The progenitor of the Central Intelligence Agency was the World War II Office of Strategic Services (OSS). Apparently because no one knew where else to put it, there was inserted into the OSS structure a "Directorate of Operations", the principal functions of which were subversion, propaganda and the spreading of false rumours (later to become known by the Soviet term, "disinformation").

These functions—properly described as "operations" rather than "intelligence"—were absorbed into the Central Intelligence Agency when it was created in 1947. Virtually all the activities that, in the words of US Senator Daniel P. Moynihan, have made intelligence "a dirty word", are the product of this merging of what are clearly operations functions (now known as "covert action") into the intelligence structure. The best known examples to date are the disastrous attempt to invade Cuba at the Bay of Pigs in 1961; the overthrow of the Mossadeq Government in Iran and the restoration of the Shah in 1953; the overthrow of a left-wing government in Guatemala in 1954; implication at least in the undermining of Salvadore Allende's government in Chile in the 1970s; preparations to assassinate Patrice Lumumba in the Congo in 1960; and plots to assassinate Fidel Castro of Cuba in the early 1960s, apparently in league with the American organized crime syndicate (the "mafia"). To this unhappy record must now be added reports of Argentinians employed by the CIA in Central America and the encouragement this gave to an Argentinian ruling junta that even senior US State Department aides now describe as "a bunch of thugs". Agents trained in such "covert action" activities figured prominently in bringing about the Watergate crisis that led to the resignation of President Richard M. Nixon in 1975, and in organizing and supplying international terrorist activities of the Libyan Government, including Libya's direct military intervention in Chad during the early 1980s.

Less extensive in scope but no less notorious were some of the activities carried out by the counter-intelligence staff of the Central Intelligence Agency. A series of bizarre and in some cases criminally tragic experiments was conducted by CIA counter-intelligence agents on unsuspecting American citizens during the 1950s and 1960s, involving the use of drugs. The intent was to develop means of interrogating captured foreign agents or preventing our own from being interrogated. This tragic episode culminated in the suicide of Dr. Frank Olson of the US Army Biological Center, Fort Detrick, Md., in 1953, several days after having taken, unknowingly, a CIA-administered dose of the drug LSD. Others were enticed to CIA "safe houses" on the basis of chance encounters with agents in bars and administered various drugs so that their behaviour could be observed. Whatever the properties attributed to such drugs in fiction, they were found to be useless for any purpose other than destroying the physical and mental health of the victim, something any policeman or doctor who had dealt with drug addicts already knew.

In sum, none of these disreputable actvities had anything to do with the intelligence function, as such: that is, with the gathering, analysis and dissemination of accurate and reliable information.

An additional burden borne by both of the principal contending intelligence agencies is their own large bureaucratic structures. When the present vast intelligence bureaucracies were created in the aftermath of World War II there was no evidence that such elaborate, highly centralized structures could be counted upon to improve the quality of intelligence available to the world's statesmen.

Certain it was that the collection of information had to be expanded and systemized. There was no body of experience, however, to show that a highly centralized structure would be superior to a decentralized system (that is, separate military, economic and political components operating under the appropriate ministries) with a small staff, such as that of the US National Security Council, to synthesize reports for the chief of state. In fact, the British experience, on which the OSS and subsequently the CIA were supposedly based, indicates that just such a decentralized system, with a small coordination and assessment staff at the top, is the most efficient approach.

Performance to date in successive post-World War II military crises indicates that

the principal intelligence agencies are about as good at anticipating and "covering" such events as the better civilian journalistic enterprises. That comparison is not made lightly, as the following incident illustrates.

As a young lieutenant, serving in a unit of the US Strategic Air Command, the author was careful to read the New York Times' foreign and military coverage with great care each day. Simply stated, the Times, even a day or so late by mail, presented a clearer and more comprehensive understanding of what was going on in the world than did what the unit received from the national intelligence agencies. Invariably, whatever the intelligence agencies got around to relating of a given topic, usually much later than the Times' coverage, did little more than confirm what the Times had reported. Most of the senior staff officers of the unit refused to believe that this was so, even when presented with the documentary proof. They simply would not believe anything that was not marked "secret". One who was not afflicted with the disability, Lt. Col. Lionel Proulx, later became intelligence officer of a major Strategic Air Command Headquarters, the Eighth Air Force.

"You know," Colonel Proulx told me later, "I became convinced that you were right about the Times' coverage. I have been reading it carefully every day, and when the Suez Crisis was building up (1956) I became convinced from reading the Times that we had better get ready for an alert. So I took a deep breath, went down to General Sweeney's office and told him that he ought to take preparatory measures for a command alert, and why I thought so. He accepted that advice and put the command in a status just short of an official alert.. Three days later we got a message from SAC Headquarters to put our units on alert. To SAC's astonishment, we were able to reply almost instantly that the command was on full alert. General Sweeney then directed my office be moved right next door to his."

Why, despite their great technical advantages, the official intelligence agencies should be only the equal of, or worse than, the best of civilian journalism and scholarship came to light during the US Senate hearings in January and February 1981, relative to appointment of Wiliam J. Casey and Vice Admiral Bobby R. Inman as Director and Deputy Director, respectively, of Central Intelligence. The disparity, said Admiral Inman, is traceable to "the lack of depth in our understanding of individual countries".

In fairness to the intelligence agencies, some of what the major newspapers report, particularly from capitals such as Washington, London, Paris and Bonn, does in fact come from intelligence sources.

Current intelligence

In essence, experience of the past 30 years has shown that the big intelligence bureaucracies are fairly good at describing what is going on at any given moment. Their technical surveillance means can convey in hours information about the movement of forces and the apparent intent, or at least direction, of those moves — information that once took days or weeks to assemble. As

1 ▲

1 Newspapers, magazines, books and TV are frequently sources of information more up-to-date, and possibly also more accurate, than that provided by the intelligence services. The latter are usually fairly good at describing what is going on at any particular moment, but all too often seem unable to produce accurate long-range intelligence forecasts, especially where the assessments are produced by committees. The often more open-minded journalist is usually free of such constraints and his news/analysis is printed substantially as recorded on the spot. However, some "news" is leaked by intelligence sources.

2 Homer Lea (1877-1912), a US citizen who played an important role in Sun Yat-Sen's revolution in China. Lea wrote two remarkable books which described the essential elements of all the major campaigns which have occurred in this Century. Such amateurs are invariably heartily disliked by intelligence professionals.

3 Mrs Clare Boothe Luce, wife of the proprietor of Time-Life, who rediscovered the works of Homer Lea and ensured that his main books, The Valor of Ignorance (1909) and The Day of The Saxon (1912) were republished. Mrs Luce was subsequently appointed to the President's Foreign Intelligence Advisory Board.

concerns the crucial "first strike" decision, the statesmen concerned are apt to have fairly accurate information that an enemy attack could occur at any moment. This category of intelligence is generally known as "current intelligence".

The principal weakness of the modern intelligence bureaucracies, publicly acknowledged recently by US Senator Barry Goldwater, Chairman of the Senate Select Committee on Intelligence, is the production of accurate long-range intelligence—precisely the form of intelligence that statesmen need in order to avoid ever finding themselves driven into the "first strike" or "pre-emptive strike" nightmare.

What we know essentially is that, in this century at least, the best long-range estimates were made by individuals and the worst by the sort of committees on which the intelligence bureaucracies currently are based. We also know that the strength of these long-range assessments were, with a single exception, in direct proportion to the freedom of the estimator from bureaucratic control.

Foresight of Homer Lea

The most remarkable of the 20th century long-range assessments, as verified by subsequent events, are those of the American military writer, Homer Lea. In *The Valor of Ignorance,* published in 1909, and *The Day of the Saxon,* published in 1912, Lea described the essential elements of all of the major conflicts that would occur during the succeeding decades of the 20th Century, even, in *The Valor of Ignorance,* going as far as identifying the landing beaches over which the Imperial Japanese Army would eventually invade the Philippine Islands.

Born a cripple and further limited by increasing frailty and the onset of blindness by the time he died at the age of 35, Lea was precluded from acquiring direct experience in his own country's military establishment. He overcame this by joining the entourage of Dr. Sun Yat Sen during the Chinese Revolution. That he managed to drag his twisted, failing body through it all and produce his books in the process is magnificent testimony to the power of the human intellect and spirit.

By the late 1930s the American military establishment had so far forgotten Lea's work that he was no longer mentioned in instruction at the United States Military Academy, at least in the memory of graduates of that era. Long out of print, his books were saved from oblivion by, of all people, a professional playwright who also happened to be the wife of Henry Luce, chief of the vast Time-Life publishing empire. Thanks to the wealth and influence of Mrs. Clare Boothe Luce, Lea's works were republished. Although his work is not taught at the Military Academy to this day ("Probably because the faculty thinks it is 'too controversial,'" says a recent graduate), the US Government had the good sense to recognize Mrs. Luce's great contribution by appointing her to the President's Foreign Intelligence Advisory Board.

More narrow in scope and of shorter time range than those of Lea, but no less pres-

2 ▲

3 ▲

cient, were the assessments of Maj. Gen. J. F.C. Fuller and Capt. B. H. Liddell Hart of Britain, and then-Col. Charles de Gaulle of France, in regard to the future development of mechanized war. All had at least one thing in common: they were regarded as "troublemakers" by their own military bureaucracies.

Liddell Hart was wounded in World War I and invalided out of the service. At a time when George S. Patton, Jr., and Dwight D. Eisenhower were being silenced in the US Army for advancing similar assessments, Liddell Hart's pensioner status enabled him to go on publishing and fighting the Army "establishment"—something he could not have done as a serving junior officer, or as a junior officer forced out prior to retirement because of his views. Fuller and Charles de Gaulle also both fought running battles with the leadership of their respective armies.

Only the German Army saw, with spectacular results, the validity of the 1920s and 1930s assessments made by Liddell Hart, Fuller and de Gaulle—not exactly what any of them intended.

There is only one generally known instance in this century in which the validity of a long-range assessment by an individual serving member of a government was recognized instantly and put into effect by high authority to the subsequent great benefit of the nation he served.

The Ellis estimates of future war

In 1921, then-Major Earl H. "Pete" Ellis of the US Marine Corps developed an estimate of a future war for control of the Western Pacific. Whether by accident or foreknowledge, Ellis' estimate was an extension and refinement of the concepts advanced by Homer Lea. Ellis presented his estimate to the Commandant of the Marine Corps, Maj. Gen. John A. Lejeune, in the form of a 30,000-word operations plan. Lejeune approved the plan on July 25, 1921. It became the foundation and guide for the successful World War II American amphibious campaign in the Pacific.

"Pete" Ellis was far more a true "troublemaker" than any of the authors of the long-range estimates cited earlier. He was, in fact, an out-and-out neurotic, eventually succumbing to a combination of neuroses and alcoholism during an attempt to gain first-hand knowledge of Japanese military preparations. It was to Lejeune's everlasting credit that he had the insight and the sense of proportion to recognize the genius in Ellis, and then deal with the neuroses as best he could so that Ellis could pursue his work. That may have been possible only in the small, close-knit Marines of the 1920s.

As indicated earlier, the accurate, long-range estimates of the much less "troublesome" Patton and Eisenhower got nowhere in the Army until World War II swept away most of the traditionally mediocre peacetime Army leadership. Whether Ellis could have survived in the larger, and inevitably more bureaucratized Marine Corps of the present day is questionable.

The vast bureaucratization and centralization of intelligence that occurred in the United States after World War II and that

had been occurring all along in the Soviet Union goes against the grain of the compelling evidence that individuals, not committees or "study groups", produce competent long-range assessment.

The impact of this process was described in vivid terms by US Senator Walter D. Huddleston during February 1981 hearings on CIA appointments:

"Few things have contributed so to the danger that this country now finds itself [in] as the CIA's faulty national estimates over the last decade and a half [1965-81]. When the Soviets were beginning the greatest strategic buildup of all time, the CIA said the Soviets were unlikely to try to match us in numbers of missiles. When the Soviets approached our numbers, the CIA said they were unlikely to exceed it substantially. When they exceeded it substantially the CIA said that the Soviets would not try for the capability to try to fight and win a war against us. And now that the Soviets have nearly achieved such a capability, the CIA's estimates tell us the Soviets cannot be sure it will work."

Even more disturbing is the growing belief among observers of the intelligence scene that the US Government misread Soviet intentions entirely during the 1962 crisis over deployment of Soviet nuclear-capable missiles in Cuba. For nearly 20 years, the dominant self-assessment in the United States has been that the administration of President John F. Kennedy went to the "brink" of nuclear war to force Soviet Premier Nikita S. Krushchev to "back down" and withdraw the missiles. Then, supposedly as a way of enabling Krushchev, Castro and company to "save face", the United States agreed to take some of its missiles out of Britain and Turkey, and at least informally pledged not to invade Cuba.

Briton's alternative theory

It always seemed rather odd that the Soviet Union would be adjudged willing to risk its Russian homeland to save the likes of Castro's Cuba. It also seemed strange that a Soviet "withdrawal" from Cuba has been followed by a steady increase in Soviet air, land and naval strength on the island—including the capability to launch nuclear weapons from Soviet surface ships and submarines sheltered in Cuban ports.

Now British journalist Chapman Pincher has formed the opinion, from close contacts in the British intelligence services, that the true Soviet intention may have been to gain the guarantee of Cuban security that President Kennedy eventually granted. In support of this reassessment, Chapman Pincher and his sources set forth the possibility that the "defection" of Soviet intelligence Colonel Oleg Penkovsky in 1961 was, in fact, a Soviet "plant" and that information Penkovsky conveyed was deliberately intended to mislead the United States in regard to the Soviet missile deployment then taking place in Cuba.

Dr. Ray S. Cline, then Deputy Director for

1 Major Earl H. "Pete" Ellis, USMC, a neurotic and eventually alcoholic Marines officer who in 1921 produced an assessment and campaign plan so accurate that it was used virtually unchanged for the American amphibious war in the Pacific. Ellis's intelligence estimate was very close to that of Homer Lea, but whether he borrowed from the earlier work is not known. He was, as so often, a flawed genius.

2 Major-General Commandant J. A. Lejeune, 13th Commandant of the US Marine Corps, July 1, 1920-March 4, 1929. General Lejeune was the essential complement to Major Ellis—a commander who listened to his intelligence expert, knew he was right, and acted accordingly. Too often, when intelligence experts have actually been correct their assessments have been ignored or misinterpreted by their operational commanders.

3 Nikita Krushchev addressing the 15th session of the United Nations General Assembly in October 1960. Only two years later the Cuba missile crisis was thought to take the world to the brink of nuclear war as a result of a grave misjudgement by the Soviet leader.

4 President John F. Kennedy delivering his State of the Union message where he warned that "troubled waters" lay ahead for the US. Careful reappraisal of the missile crisis suggest that it could have been Kennedy who was misled, and Krushchev the ultimate victor.

5 The Soviet vessel *Labinsk* carrying missiles to Cuba on November 9, 1962. A victor in military terms is he who remains in command of the field. Before the missile crisis the Soviet position in Cuba was precarious; since then it has been secure. Who was the winner?

1 ▲

2 ▲

3 ▲

4 ▲

LABINSK

5 ▲

1 Mariel Naval Port in Cuba photographed from a low-flying USAF reconnaissance aircraft on November 2, 1962. Three Soviet ships are being loaded with missile erectors, fuel and oxidiser trailers, and missile launch rings, indicating that the crisis was over.

2, 3 Details from the same reconnaissance mission show the impedimenta of missile launch sites being assembled prior to re-loading on the ships. This picture and the enlarged boxed areas (**3**) show the main complex and trailers in great detail, indicating that only the most naive could expect to hide military activity from determined and well-equipped intelligence organizations, such as the USA's.

4 At a storage site some 3½ miles (5.6km) north of Mariel Port lie more elements of the Soviet missile units with another freighter loading in the background. Such low-level pictures are very clear and detailed, but are only possible when there is no counter-air threat as was the case over Cuba.

Intelligence in the CIA, disputes the view that Penkovsky was a "plant".

"Penkovsky delivered vast amounts of doctrinal literature," Dr. Cline recalls, "—a category of information the Soviets hold very close. Also, he gave us much information about military technology, enabling us to identify the missiles in Cuba".

The end result cited by Chapman Pincher is difficult to refute: "Castro and the Communist regime are still in power and *all* American cities are threatened by Soviet missiles."

Whether the American misreading of Soviet purpose (if that was the case) was due to a faulty intelligence assessment or to a "mindset" on the part of the President and his principal advisors—notably his brother, Robert—may never be known.

Soviet weaknesses

Difficulty in producing reliable long-range estimates is not confined to the Western intelligence agencies by any means. Impossible though it seems in Western eyes, there is substantial evidence that at least some parts of the Soviet Government believe in the possibility of a NATO attack on the Warsaw Pact nations. (One distinguished Western specialist on Soviet affairs says, "They believe that because they *must* believe it.") Whatever the reason, there is a continuous effort by Soviet intelligence agencies to try to determine how and when such an attack might occur.

It is fascinating to speculate about the effect it would have in the NATO chancelleries were they to receive an announcement

from their Supreme Allied Commander that, "We are thinking about having a go at the Russians next Tuesday morning—before breakfast."

There is an impression from all of this of giants bumping up against one another in the dark, doomed to such confrontations by inability to make use of the human intelligence (small "i") that history has shown is often available to them.

A horrifying summary of the forces that could push a statesman into a pre-emptive "first strike" was published in November 1981, by Dr. Herbert L. Abrams, a professor of Radiology at Harvard Medical School, in the *New England Journal of Medicine*. A surprise nuclear attack on the United States, Doctor Abrams wrote, could result in 86 million deaths, some 40 percent of the US

5 The Soviet merchant ship *Anosov* leaving Cuba on November 6, 1962, with 8 missile transporters, each with a canvas-shrouded missile. Pictures like these set the seal on the apparent American triumph; President Kennedy and his brother Robert gained great political prestige from this episode.

6 Colonel Oleg Penkovsky, the high-ranking KGB officer who was executed in 1963 for treason. He is alleged to have passed many valuable secrets to the West over a period of two years, but the whole story has been queried by the distinguished British journalist/author Chapman Pincher.

7 MiG-23 aircraft recently supplied by the Soviets. A line-up of Soviet-supplied MiG-23 aircraft of the Cuban Air Force. The inescapable fact is that Soviet influence in Cuba is as strong as ever, and many thousands of their troops are stationed on the island, giving them an invaluable springboard into Latin America, the United States' own backyard.

5▲ 6▼

7▼

population, within minutes. For the survivors, he paints a hellish world of disease and an animalistic struggle for food and the other necessities of life.

Confronted with such a prospect for his country, would a US President forego a pre-emptive "spoiling attack" against the vulnerable and brittle Soviet command and control system—the system without which no successful. coordinated Soviet strike could be launched? The example of the Israelis in repeated pre-emptive strikes against neighbouring countries thought to be preparing attacks—most notably against an Iraqi nuclear reactor in June 1981— indicates that almost beyond question the decision would be to pre-empt.

But how would the President or any other statesman in a similar situation know for certain that an enemy attack was imminent? Information flows in around the clock from all the sources described in the chapters that follow. The quality of the "intelligence" that emerges is dependent, above all, on the quality of the people who collect, analyze and present the processed intelligence to the chief of state or prime minister. Far better it would be if governments could find a way to make use of the long-range estimates of a Homer Lea, a B. H. Liddel Hart or a Charles de Gaulle. Then statesmen might avoid being trapped into that terrible "first strike" decision. But history shows that the chances of having a Lejeune or a Guderian at the right place, at the right time and on the right side are very, very slim.

Since there is no known way of developing and using reliable long-range estimates that

governments will pay any attention to, the production of timely and accurate current intelligence can be seen as being all the more important.

The statesman who makes that fateful "first strike" decision may have no more than 15 to 20 minutes in which to decide to act. That decision will be a product of the intelligence, good or bad, formal or informal, he has received throughout a lifetime. Above all, it will be a product of the intelligence organization through which must come most, or all, of the intelligence indicators that will force him to confront the possibility of an enemy attack.

In a very real sense, then, the lives of every man, women and child on earth depend on how well or poorly those intelligence organizations function.

Chapter two

The world's intelligence organizations

AS THE BLANK spaces in figure 2 indicate, the world's intelligence establishments try to hold close all information about their internal organization, budget, etc. It is all the more remarkable, therefore, that there became available, in February 1982, an authoritative document describing in detail the internal structure of one of the most modern and efficient of all the world's intelligence organizations, that of Israel.

The document is nothing less than the official US Central Intelligence Agency assessment of the Israeli services entitled, "Israel: Foreign Intelligence and Security Services", published in March 1979, under the most stringent security restrictions. The CIA assessment was among documents stolen from the US Embassy in Iran following its takeover by a mob subsequent to the January 1979 Iranian Revolution. What a document of that sensitivity was doing in so exposed a location is difficult to understand. The "ill wind" of its theft, however, offers the general public an insight into the *modus operandi* of one of the world's most modern intelligence organizations.

The importance of the CIA assessment lies not only in what it says about the Israeli services, but in the light it sheds on the US and British secret services as well, for the Israeli services were created essentially on the model of the British services and of the Office of Strategic Services, World War II progenitor of the present US central intelligence organization. The founders of the Israeli services served in the British and US organizations or had the advice of some of the highest members of those services.

Dual allegiance of Jews

This sense of dual allegiance on the part of many Jews, worldwide, to their own country and to Israel continues to provide Israel with sources of information and assistance that go far beyond what a country of that size could expect to achieve from its own resources. However, the CIA assessment notes that many non-Israeli Jews have a clear sense of primary loyalty to their own country and that there have been instances in which they have reported to their own security services Israeli efforts to recruit them as agents.

What emerges from the CIA assessment, supplemented by interviews with Western intelligence officials who have observed Israeli intelligence work at first hand, is a picture of an efficient system, but one which is so utterly ruthless in the pursuit of

what are perceived to be immediate Israeli interests as to jeopardize much more important long-term interests.

This is apparent, in particular, in the Israeli attack on the USS *Liberty,* a plainly marked US Navy electronic surveillance ship operating in the Eastern Mediterranean during the 1967 Middle East War. An accumulation of evidence published by survivors and other authors in the US Naval Institute *Proceedings* during recent years makes it seem apparent that the length and violence of the attack, spread over a period of several hours and resulting in the death or wounding of many members of the *Liberty*'s crew, could not have been other than a deliberate "counter-intelligence" strike approved at least by the leadership of the Israeli Defence Forces. The growing conviction that the attack on the *Liberty* could not have been an accident is undoubtedly a factor in the increasing estrangement between the United States and Israel at a time when, more than ever, Israel is almost totally dependent upon the United States for its survival.

As shown in figure 1, the Israeli services follow in their general structure a pattern common to other national intelligence organizations. at least in the West. There is an organization oriented primarily to the collection of foreign political, economic, scientific and technological information (Mossad), a military intelligence system (Aman), and an internal security service (Shin Beth).

Unlike Britain and the United States, which have separate electronic information-gathering agencies, but similar to the West German services, it is the military intelligence system within the Israeli Defence Forces that is primarily concerned with gathering electronic intelligence. Shin Beth has an important share in electronic eavesdropping, however, in that all the telephone communications in Israel can be monitored from a switchboard in Shin Beth headquarters without the tell-tale "patching" of wires or the location of elaborate monitoring equipment in the neighbourhood of the surveillance "target".

Unlike the case with most other modern intelligence systems, the preparation of Israeli national intelligence estimates is assigned to the Defence Forces, reflecting

1 The US hostages return from Teheran to a heroes' welcome. Some effects of the incident are still being felt, such as the loss to the Iranian mobs of the very highly classified CIA handbook "Israel: Foreign Intelligence and Security Services", since made public. Also lost were US "listening posts".

1 ▲

The activities of the world's major intelligence services are unremitting and relentless, and often in contradiction to the apparent political realities. Covert operations against friends, and help to those in "another camp", all happen regularly in the twilight world of the intelligence war.

the almost constant military state of alert since independence in 1948. But there are separate research and evaluation centres in the Ministry of Foreign Affairs and Mossad to provide the Government with viewpoints independent of the military.

The remarkable performance of the Israeli services in enabling Israel to survive the war for independence, in 1948, and to achieve spectacular "first strike" successes in subsequent wars in 1956 and 1967 were the products of a superior intelligence system that used every means from elec-

tronic monitoring to the use of Oriental Jews who could pass as Arabs to infiltrate the societies and governments of the neighbouring Arab states. The CIA assessment attributes initial Israeli setbacks in the 1973 "Yom Kippur" War to increased Arab awareness of the importance of communications security, and to the failure of the Israeli intelligence services properly to assess information it was receiving from its long-established system of agents and its bi-lateral relationships with the intelligence services of other countries.

Why were the Israeli services able to act with such efficiency in 1948, 1956 and 1967, but not in 1973? As the CIA assessment emphasized, the Israeli services were organized and led for those first 20 years of independence by a collection of brilliant and daring men assembled from the very top levels of advanced societies throughout the world. The fact that these men had been willing to risk life, fortune and the safety of their families to come to Israel when they did, often quite late in life, set them apart as a truly exceptional group. Alertness, fast

1▲

2▲

3▲

1 Israel has fought a remarkable battle for survival over the past 35 years, in which the intelligence services have played as vital a part as combat troops.

2 These Israeli reservists in the Sinai in 1973 epitomise the tradition of their army. Now the generals are getting plump and the intelligence services becoming bureaucratic and hidebound.

3 Former Egyptian President Sadat and Israeli Prime Minister Begin in a friendly moment at Camp David, September 12, 1979. Their intelligence services have been at each other's throats for 3½ decades and such public displays of political comradeship do not necessarily indicate any lessening of the private battle in the shadows. The Egyptian service should not be underrated.

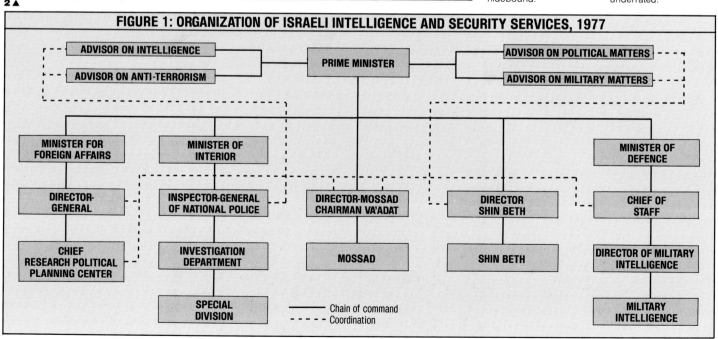

FIGURE 1: ORGANIZATION OF ISRAELI INTELLIGENCE AND SECURITY SERVICES, 1977

ADVISOR ON INTELLIGENCE
ADVISOR ON ANTI-TERRORISM
PRIME MINISTER
ADVISOR ON POLITICAL MATTERS
ADVISOR ON MILITARY MATTERS

MINISTER FOR FOREIGN AFFAIRS · MINISTER OF INTERIOR · MINISTER OF DEFENCE

DIRECTOR-GENERAL · INSPECTOR-GENERAL OF NATIONAL POLICE · DIRECTOR-MOSSAD CHAIRMAN VA'ADAT · DIRECTOR SHIN BETH · CHIEF OF STAFF

CHIEF RESEARCH POLITICAL PLANNING CENTER · INVESTIGATION DEPARTMENT · MOSSAD · SHIN BETH · DIRECTOR OF MILITARY INTELLIGENCE

SPECIAL DIVISION · MILITARY INTELLIGENCE

——— Chain of command
- - - - Coordination

response to warnings and a willingness to risk being wrong were second nature to such a group, developed in a hard school of personal survival.

The CIA assessment records a significant change as this early generation of Israeli intelligence officers began to be thinned by time. The original intelligence cadre began to be replaced by students recruited directly from secondary school, or while serving their mandatory period of military service. Yet, as the CIA notes, the intelligence services have not been able to pay enough to retain the most enterprising of the recruits. Also, the brightest potential recruits tend to shy away from the anonymity of intelligence work. Indeed, it is apparent that advancement has come to be based to a considerable extent not on performance but on acquisition of advanced degrees. In short, a process of bureaucratization set in.

The CIA assessors failed to see that this gradual stifling of initiative and imagination —the inevitable result of the bureaucratic process—was the only significant change between the successes of 1948-67 and the failures of 1973. Why? Because the CIA itself is one of the world's supreme examples of bureaucratization, with the results cited by Senator Huddleston in chapter one.

Some part of the 1973 problem may also have been due to a complacency born of the fact that Israeli intelligence had for so long outclassed the Arab intelligence services. The Arabs, however, never have been able to capitalize on such vulnerabilities despite superior resources.

In a conversation with the author on November 30, 1982, Lt. Gen. Mordecai

FIGURE 2: THE PRINCIPAL INTELLIGENCE AGENCIES

COUNTRY	AGENCY	FUNCTIONS					CONTROL[3]	SIZE OF STAFF[5]	BUDGET[5]
		MILITARY INTELLIGENCE	STRATEGIC INTELLIGENCE	ELECTRONIC INTERCEPT	DOMESTIC[1] COUNTER-INTELLIGENCE	FOREIGN[2] COUNTER-INTELLIGENCE			
France	DGSE (Direction Generale de la Securité Exterieure), formerly SDECE	●	●	●		●	Prime Minister		
	Deuxieme (2d) Bureau	●					Minister of Defence		
	DST (Bureau for Defence and Surveillance of the Territory)				●		Minister of the Interior		
Czechoslovakia	STB (State Secret Security)						Minister of the Interior		
E. Germany	SSD (Ministry for Security and Intelligence	●	●	●	●	●	Politburo		
W. Germany	BND (Federal Intelligence Service)	●	●	●		●	Chancellor	6,000	$90,000,000
	MAD (Military Intelligence)	●		●			Minister of Defence		
	Bfv (Counter-Espionage)				●		Minister of the Interior		
Israel	Mossad (Office of Intelligence and Special Missions)		●			●	Prime Minister	1,500-2,000	
	Aman	●	●	●			Chief of Staff, Defence Forces	7,000	
	Shin Beth				●		Prime Minister	1,000	
United Kingdom	The Secret Service (MI6)	●	●			●	Foreign Minister		
	Defence Intelligence Service	●					Minister of Defence		
	The Security Service (MI5)				●		Home Minister	(Publication impermissible)	
	GCHQ (Government Communications Headquarters)			●			Foreign Minister	10,000	
United States	CIA (Central Intelligence Agency)	●	●		●	●	President	15,000	$1,500,000,000
	DIA (Defense Intelligence Agency)	●	●				Secretary of Defense	7,000	$9,000,000,000 (includes NSA)
	FBI (Federal Bureau of Investigation)				●		Attorney General		
	NSA (National Security Agency)			●			Secretary of Defense		
	Bureau of Intelligence and Research		●				Secretary of State	325	$12,500,000
USSR	KGB (Ministry of State Security	●	●	●	●	●	Politburo	25,000 (Intelligence) out of 400,000 total	Unknown[4]
	GRU (Chief Intelligence Directorate, General Staff)	●		●			Ministry of Defence	25,000	

[1]Responsibility for counter-espionage within borders of its own country.
[2]Responsibility for counter-espionage beyond borders of its own country.
[3]The Government official to whom the chief of the agency reports.
[4]Barron states in *KGB* that "it may be that no one in the Soviet Union knows exactly how much the KGB costs the nation," because of the use of resources throughout the entire Soviet system.
[5]Figurers shown are estimates compiled by journalists or interpolated from various government documents. While the figures for any one country or agency are approximations only, they do serve to illustrate the relative size and budget of the expenditures on Intelligence by the several nations.

Gur, Chief of Staff of the Israeli Defence Forces from 1974 to 1978, cited two principal continuing weaknesses in Arab intelligence, one strategic, the other tactical, "They never have been able to put together the 'big picture,'" General Gur said of the strategic failure. "They continue to operate solely on a national basis, never putting together the pieces each nation obtains to form a full mosaic."

In the tactical sphere, General Gur cites an inability of the Egyptians to proceed from carefully pre-planned operations to identification of targets of opportunity. "The failure of the Egyptians to exploit their initial success after they breached our positions on the Suez Canal in 1973 is a case in point. We had many weaknesses at that time, but either Egyptian military intelligence was not able to identify those points of weakness once the situation became fluid, or their operative staffs were not able to exploit them if, in fact, good intelligence was provided."

Intelligence is a key factor in maintaining Israeli technological superiority in the Middle East, demonstrated most recently by the precise bombing attack on an Iraqi nuclear reactor thought to be preparing material for nuclear weapons.

British intelligence penetrated

The "grandfather" of most of the principal intelligence services outside of the Communist world is Britain's Secret Intelligence Service (SIS), often referred to as "MI6", a designation it bore for a time after reorganization of British intelligence in 1905.

From its beginnings in Elizabethan times until very recently the SIS and its predecessors were truly secret, in that very little was known about them even within the upper echeons of the British Government. British laws and perhaps even more effective informal pressures precluded any but the most peripheral press coverage. Ultimately, however, freedom from public scrutiny and informality of internal arrangements proved to be disastrous. Beginning in the 1930s and continuing until the 1960s and possibly longer, British-born agents of a foreign power (the Soviet Union) not only penetrated MI6 but actually operated it on behalf of their foreign masters. They were able to accomplish this because of an incredibly naive assumption that anyone born of a particular British background and educated in its best universities was *ipso facto* loyal beyond question.

The investigations and publicity that followed defection or confession by some of the principal traitors shattered probably forever the concept of an SIS that would be but a shadow perceived only dimly in the recesses of the Foreign Office. Today the leadership and general nature and duties of the SIS are widely known among the British public and tracked by journalists to a degree considered unthinkable a few years ago.

The great strength of the SIS lies in its worldwide sources developed during the period of the British Empire and retained in the Commonwealth system and in other more informal connections maintained as the former colonies became independent.

1 ▲

2 ▲

3 ▲

4 ▲

1 Donald Maclean died on March 6, 1983, in his Moscow flat—alone, and racked with nostalgia for England, just over 31 years after defecting to the Soviet Union, which has honoured him as a hero.

2 Kim Philby, most ruthless and coldblooded British traitor, almost became head of the British SIS. He has betrayed people all his life, even stealing Maclean's wife in Moscow.

3 Officers of Britain's West Mercia police force who led the investigation into the traitor Geoffrey Prime. In front of them are items given to Prime by his Soviet masters for communication. The "Prime case" did great harm to Anglo-US relations in the intelligence sphere.

4 Mrs Thatcher seen with US Secretary of Defense Caspar Weinberger is, as Prime Minister, responsible ex officio for the British intelligence services, one of the largest and most important parts of which is the Government Communications Headquarters (GCHQ) at Cheltenham

(**5**). The Prime case was a grave embarrassment both to GCHQ and to Mrs Thatcher, although it should not be forgotten that the USA has also suffered from some disastrous spy scandals, including two in the National Security Agency (NSA), the US counterpart to GCHQ. But if men like Prime can hide for so long, how many more are there?

5 ▲

The Government Communications Headquarters (GCHQ) at Cheltenham with its worldwide electronics collection capability now supersedes the Secret Service as Britain's primary source of raw information for intelligence analysis. By no means to the joy of its directors, a considerable amount of information became available about GCHQ when one of its former employees, Geoffrey Arthur Prime, was arrested in April 1982, and was later convicted as a long-term Soviet spy.

First of all, the size of the organization turned out to be much greater than had been suspected. Although it was not possible to pin down a precise figure, the total seems to be somewhere between 6,000 and 10,000. That this clearly is in excess of Britain's reduced worldwide requirements is obvious. The "extras", it turned out, are accounted for by much greater American, Canadian and Australian participation than had been known heretofore. This multinational involvement also would seem to account for the extensive damage to Allied as well as British interests reported by Prime Minister Thatcher when she described the Prime case to Parliament on November 10, 1982.

The Prime case brought demands from the US Central Intelligence Agency for greater participation in GCHQ operations and internal security. Conveniently forgotten was the fact that two "closet" homosexuals had defected to the Soviet Union from the National Security Agency—US counterpart to GCHQ—with cryptographic information apparently at least as important as that which Prime delivered.

Despite wild reports to the effect that NATO was "in tatters" as a result of Prime's disclosures, the truth seemed closer to the assessment by former CIA Deputy Director Bobby Inman. "My own guess," said Inman, "is that it's not a Kim Philby-scale case, which was the most damaging of the postwar era . . . Allegations of the kind of information Prime passed . . . I can't believe a language translator had access to." Inman's assessment was supported by US Secretary of Defense Weinberger. From their remarks and corollary remarks by Senator Daniel Moynihan of the US Senate Intelligence Committee, it seems as though the Prime case involved much less serious damage than the earlier betrayal of satellite secrets by two young Americans.

The pattern in both cases seems to have been the same—"defection in place", at least initially in the NSA case, resulting from character deterioration *after* basic security checks had been completed. That sort of character deterioration almost always is accompanied by development of an ability to lie so convincingly that the subject no longer distinguishes between truth and falsehood, and so makes such "scientific" gadgets as the polygraph worthless.

MI5, the Internal Security Service, has been reorganized and considerably strengthened by new procedures, principally more thorough background investigations, following revelations in the past two decades that British traitors had used their social and educational connections successfully to penetrate MI5 as well as the SIS.

The British armed forces continue to operate intelligence systems primarily for the collection and dissemination of "operational", that is tactical, intelligence. These are combined at the ministerial level under a Director of Military Intelligence whose staff also produces economic, scientific and technical intelligence.

Joint Intelligence Committee

The work of all British agencies—MI5, MI6, GCHQ and Defence Intelligence—is co-ordinated by a Joint Intelligence Committee (JIC) consisting of the chiefs of each of the intelligence services with representatives from the Foreign Office and other "civilian" agencies operating under the general supervision of the Cabinet Secretary, a civil servant whose six-to-eight-year tenure is intended to reduce partisan political influence.

The most important feature of the British intelligence system, as seen by Allied intelligence officers who have gained an insight into its operation, is its method of assessment. Assessment of a highly specialized subject might be made entirely within one intelligence agency—such as the GCHQ in the case of a new foreign code. That assessment must then undergo scrutiny by the JIC as a whole before it is transmitted to higher Government officials as "approved intelligence". The fact that the reputation of the chief of the agency concerned is directly at stake in this examination by his peers is seen as an excellent "quality control" mechanism.

A more complex subject, such as, say, an emergent crisis in the Middle East, requires the participation of the best that all agencies can supply. The crucial task of combining all of this information into a brief, clear and, above all, accurate and timely analysis is assigned to a very small team—perhaps no more than four or five people—detailed to the assessment task for a period of time from their "parent" agencies. One of those team members assumes responsibility for the analysis, based on background and experience. That analyst then has authority to call for information from any part of the Government. Upon completion, his assessment goes to the JIC for final review.

The Allied observers from whom this description was obtained expressed the view that the ideal combination would be the sophisticated US space and electronic collection system and the British assessment system.

The JIC's assessments, based on long-term intelligence estimates and short-term day-to-day assessments by Current Intelligence Groups, are reported to the Cabinet's Overseas and Defence Committee, whose membership is kept secret, though the Prime Minister is known to chair it and other members include senior Cabinet and ministerial committee officials.

The JIC's assessment process came under scrutiny during 1982, following the Falklands conflict, and critical comment was published in the official "Falkland Islands Review" prepared by Lord Franks and five other Privy Councillors. Better known as the "Franks Report", and published in January 1983, the review addressed itself to two basic questions: could the Thatcher Government have foreseen the Argentine invasion of April 2, 1982, and could the Government have prevented the invasion?

Much to the surprise of many, including Falkland Islanders themselves, the report gave a negative response to both. But between July 1981 and March 1982, according to evidence quoted in the report, the Joint Intelligence Committee's Latin America Current Intelligence Group met 18 times without once discussing the Falkland Islands, although the Islands had been discussed twice during JIC weekly meetings held during that time by the head of the assessments staff, and on several other occasions consideration was given to the need to update the latest assessment which had been made in July 1981. On each occasion up to March 1982 it was decided that there was no need to revise the assessment.

Only two days before the invasion, on the morning of March 31, a new assessment was made and (quoting from the Franks report), "In its conclusion it expressed the view that, while the possibility that Argentina might choose to escalate the situation by landing a military force on another dependency or on the Falkland Islands could not be ruled out, the Argentine Government did not wish to be the first to adopt forcible measures."

No help from US intelligence

In its comment on the JIC assessment process, the Report stated: "There was no coverage of Argentine military movements within Argentina, and no advance information was therefore available by these means about the composition and assembly of the Argentine naval force that eventually invaded the Falklands. There was no intelligence from American sources or otherwise to show that the force at sea before the invasion was intended other than for normal naval exercises. No satellite photography was available.

"The British Naval Attache in Buenos Aires reported the naval exercises when he became aware of them *mainly on the basis of Argentine Press reports.*" (*Emphasis added* —Editor.) "We are not sure that at all important times the assessments staff were fully aware of the weight of the Argentine Press campaign of 1982. As a result it seems to us that they may have attached greater significance to the secret intelligence, which at that time was reassuring about the prospects of an early move to confrontation . . . The changes in the Argentine position were, we believe, more evident on the diplomatic front and in the associated Press campaign than in the intelligence reports."

The Report drew conclusions that a review should be made of the arrangements for bringing to the Joint Intelligence Organisation's attention information other than intelligence reports, and also of the composition of the Joint Intelligence Committee itself; and, on January 25, 1983, Prime Minister Thatcher announced that she intended to act on the Franks proposal that an official of the Cabinet Office be appointed chairman of the JIC, engaged full

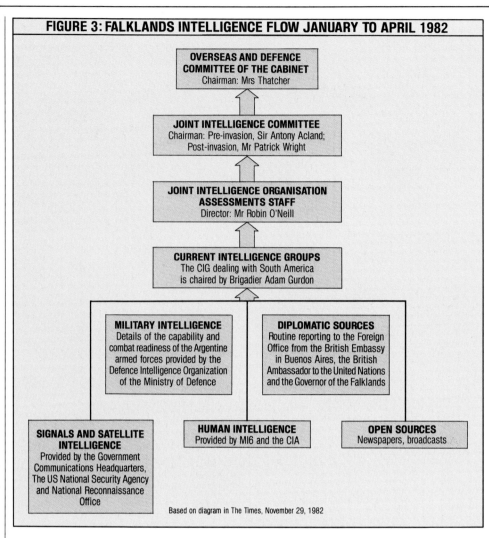

FIGURE 3: FALKLANDS INTELLIGENCE FLOW JANUARY TO APRIL 1982

OVERSEAS AND DEFENCE COMMITTEE OF THE CABINET
Chairman: Mrs Thatcher

JOINT INTELLIGENCE COMMITTEE
Chairman: Pre-invasion, Sir Antony Acland; Post-invasion, Mr Patrick Wright

JOINT INTELLIGENCE ORGANISATION ASSESSMENTS STAFF
Director: Mr Robin O'Neill

CURRENT INTELLIGENCE GROUPS
The CIG dealing with South America is chaired by Brigadier Adam Gurdon

MILITARY INTELLIGENCE
Details of the capability and combat readiness of the Argentine armed forces provided by the Defence Intelligence Organization of the Ministry of Defence

DIPLOMATIC SOURCES
Routine reporting to the Foreign Office from the British Embassy in Buenos Aires, the British Ambassador to the United Nations and the Governor of the Falklands

SIGNALS AND SATELLITE INTELLIGENCE
Provided by the Government Communications Headquarters, The US National Security Agency and National Reconnaissance Office

HUMAN INTELLIGENCE
Provided by MI6 and the CIA

OPEN SOURCES
Newspapers, broadcasts

Based on diagram in The Times, November 29, 1982

2 ▲

3 ▲

1 The British aircraft carrier HMS *Hermes* returns from the South Atlantic, intact and afloat despite many Argentine claims that she had been sunk. The greatest failing of Argentine intelligence was to underestimate the British reaction to the invasion, and the despatch of the Task Force came as a great surprise, its use even more so!

2 The Argentine destroyer *Rosales* on a joint exercise with the US Navy. The British Naval Attaché in Buenos Aires reported pre-invasion exercises from reports he read in the Press.

3 The Argentine destroyer *Espora*. During the war, the Argentine Navy was pretty well bottled up in port, fearing submarines, especially after *Belgrano* was sunk.

time on intelligence matters and have direct access to the Prime Minister in the same way as the heads of security and intelligence agencies.

French intelligence

The most difficult of the principal West European intelligence services to describe or assess are those of France.

The post-World War II French Intelligence and Security services are an amalgam of elements dating from the first Napoleon and a parallel system organized by Gen. Charles de Gaulle during World War II as leader of the Free French, first in London and later in Algiers.

From the end of World War II until 1981, the primary French Intelligence service was known as the Service de Documentation Exterieure et de Contre-espionage (SDECE), called colloquially "The Pool". That is, it was a "pool" of pre-World War II civilian and military services staffed by service members and civilians.

With the inauguration of President Francois Mitterand in 1981 there was a substantial revision of the Gaullist structure. The SDECE became the Direction Generale de la Securité Exterieure (DGSE), but its functions remain substantially the same. These are carried out by three directorates, one responsible for collection and analysis of foreign intelligence, one for counter-espionage outside of France, and an "action" directorate that plans and conducts political-military operations abroad. Most of the latter have been concerned with maintaining French influence in former French African colonies. To assist in this purpose the action directorate has assigned to it the 11th Airborne Division, based near Toulouse — paratroopers used in Chad and Zaire in recent years as a means of shoring up governments friendly to France or at least protecting French interests from disruption.

In various French administrations the SDECE and its successor have reported to the Minister of Defence, the Minister of the Interior or direct to the President.

Internal security is the responsibility of the Directorate for Surveillance of the Territory (DST) operating in conjunction with the Sureté, the overall police system. Both the DST and the police report to the Minister of the Interior. In general terms their roles are analogous to those of MI5 and Scotland Yard in Britain. DST counter-espionage activities resulted in the expulsion in April 1983 of 47 Soviet officials for spying, a suggestion being that prime targets were the Hades and Exocet missiles, and France's neutron bomb developments. These expulsions, and others recently from Britain, Italy, Spain, Belgium and Holland, indicate the usefulness of the information gleaned during 1982-83 from a KGB agent who defected to American agents in Europe.

French military intelligence generally has been known as the "Deuxieme Bureau". The term describes a staff function ("G-2" in American parlance) rather than a separate organization. There is, for example, a Deuxieme (Second) Bureau at battalion level consisting of one officer and successively

larger "Deuxieme Bureaux" up to the level of the Army General Staff. The Navy and Air Force have their own intelligence services. Collectively, however, French military intelligence generally is known as the "Deuxieme Bureau". It performs many of the same functions as "The Pool" and it is between these two groups that the overlapping and obscurity of functions and missions occurs that non-French NATO officers find so puzzling. In the view of knowledgeable observers of the French services, Vladimir Volkoff's novel, *The Turn Around,* presents an accurate picture of the duplications and rivalries inherent in the French system.

This problem has been compounded by the establishment under various French administrations of special intelligence and security organizations designed to serve the special interests of a ministry or the President himself.

Until its disestablishment by the Mitterand administration, France operated a special "Court of State Security" to govern intelligence operations, including the "action" department of the DGSE. The feeling of the Mitterand administration seems to be that this court was being used by the intelligence services to obtain judgments against people who were not otherwise chargeable in the French judicial system.

As is the case with the British SIS, the SDCE benefits from well established contacts in France's former colonial empire. Also, as with the British services, Allied observers believe that there has been extensive Communist penetration of the French intelligence services as a result of the ideological ferment in Europe since the end of World War I. Whatever damage may have occurred, the French services are credited with continuing competent service. As an example, the American columnist Jack Anderson and others credit the French services with making an early, accurate assessment of the revolutionary situation in Iran in the late 1970s and of passing that information along to the United States, but to no avail.

A special military counter-intelligence unit established in 1961 appears to have stirred the ire of the Socialist Party that took power in 1981. Plans were announced by the new Socialist Defence Minister to re-organize the unit and to change its focus from an alleged concern with political viewpoints of armed forces members to maintaining security of equipment and documents.

Few such counter-espionage units in any country have been able to avoid such entanglements for long. Also during 1981, even the highly respected Royal Canadian Mounted Police came under investigation and criticism by the Canadian Government for having exceeded its authority in dealing with the separatist movement in Quebec Province. The police unit, said a government commission, "did not adequately distinguish between legitimate dissent and genuine threats." A common threat in all such recent investigations — incuding those in Britain, Israel and the United States — is that such units tend to develop an extreme *esprit de corps* that can easily deteriorate into a belief that they are a law unto themselves. The CIA assessment of the Israeli services concluded that, "If the government requested the execution of a certain task, legal and illegal, it would be accomplished." The danger that a government might use such misguided loyalty to destroy the democratic process makes all the intelligence services, especially those engaged in counter-espionage, a double-edged sword.

That concern plainly worried the Canadian Government as it sought to establish a new intelligence agency, combining both foreign intelligence and internal security. The new agency is to operate directly under cabinet supervision and will be headed by a senior civil servant.

German intelligence

In the final weeks of Hitler's Third Reich, in April and May 1945, Maj. Gen. Reinhard Gehlen, Chief of Department 12 (intelligence, Eastern Front), Germany Army General Staff, managed to move his staff and its superb files into the Western zones of occupation. First under the auspices of US Army intelligence and then as a department of the new Federal Republic of Germany, General Gehlen and his staff formed the nucleus of what is today the Federal Intelligence Service (BND).

The BND seems to be the most truly centralized intelligence service of any NATO nation. It includes such basic military functions as the gathering of order-of-battle information, using members of the military detailed to BND for that purpose. BND is also primarily responsible for strategic electronic intelligence. Even the interrogation of prisoners would be conducted by BND in time of war. Assessment is left entirely to the political leadership. The Military Intelligence Service (MAD) confines itself to tactical intelligence only; that is, only the sort of intelligence that would be gained from direct contact with an enemy—apart from the key prisoner interrogation function. All of this reflects General Gehlen's efforts to avoid the mistakes made by World War II German intelligence, which was seriously undermined by rivalries among competing bureaucracies.

The German internal security service (Bfv) also reflects hard-learned lessons from the 1930s and World War II. Instead of the highly centralized Gestapo of nightmarish memory, the Bfv functions as a decentralized system in which the several German states retain significant responsibility for internal security.

At the same time that West Germany was building this new intelligence structure, the Soviet Union was busily organizing an intelligence service under a so-called "German Democratic Republic" created by a cadre of German Communists returned from exile in Russia or who emerged after the Nazi defeat.

Until 1961, the BND and its sister MAD and Bfv services were "reinforced" by some 300 agents of the East German services who defected over the relatively open border. Even after the building of the Berlin Wall and the "death zone" along the rest of the border, 30 additional East German agents managed to get across to join what they regarded as a more truly "German" service in the West.

For most of the past 30 years, the focus of the rival German intelligence services was on each other. As the German economy recovered, with spectacular success in the West and then slowly in the East after the imprisonment of the entire East German population in 1961, the focus of these agencies has shifted to a broader scene.

Today the intelligence services of West and East Germany rub shoulders in an increasing number of overseas stations. Economic intelligence is clearly the primary target for the BND as West Germany seeks to maintain and expand its position as one of the world's industrial powerhouses. East German intelligence also seeks economic information, but its primary focus remains political and military. Particularly in the "Third World" nations of Africa and Latin America, the East German SSD has proved to be a valuable servant of its KGB masters.

The expanding scope of the West German intelligence services is indicated by revelations in the German magazine *Konkret* in March 1982 that an attempt was made to recruit an "agent of influence" in the official family of US President Richard Nixon, apparently in 1970, for the purpose of reaching Nixon "with German points of view". Allegations were stated in the same report that Hans Langemann, then apparently an agent of either BND or the internal security service, Bfv, succeeded in gaining US Central Intelligence Agency cooperation in suppressing documents implicating Nazi connections of former German Chancellor Kurt Georg Kiesinger.

Italian intelligence

The spectacular success of the Italian internal security agencies in rescuing US Brig. Gen. James L. Dozier from Red Brigade terrorists came at a time when Italy's Office of Intelligence Coordination was in great disarray owing to the arrest of high civilian and military officials in connection with the activities of a Masonic lodge thought to be establishing a right-wing "state within a state". That the Italian services can perform effectively when free of such involvement was demonstrated not only by the Dozier episode but also by the successful detection of what apparently was a Soviet nuclear submarine intruding on Italian Navy manoeuvres off Taranto in March 1982, and the pursuit of the submarine to international waters.

The smaller West European nations depend largely on their diplomatic services, including the military attache component, membership in the North Atlantic Treaty Organization and bi-lateral arrangements with larger countries to gain needed intelligence.

Japanese intelligence

Japan developed an efficient intelligence system based on the British model after the Meiji Restoration of the latter 19th century, which saw Japan's transformation from a mediaeval to a modern state. The intel-

1 ▲
1 All smiles as former West German Chancellor Helmut Schmidt chats with Soviet President Brezhnev in 1980. Behind the diplomatic niceties, however, the secret intelligence battle is waged remorselessly: Schmidt knew that his predecessor, Willy Brandt, had an East German espionage agent in his private office.

2 A valuable intelligence target, this IBM 0.22in (5.7mm) square chip has the same processing power as the IBM 1401 ADP system in background.

3 Technological espionage is widespread and in June 1982 18 Japanese "businessmen" were caught trying to steal secrets from IBM.

2 ▲

ligence services along with just about everything else went down to ruin in World War II. During the long period of military occupation US and Allied powers took responsibility for security of the Japanese homeland. During this same period, however, Japan collected openly through diplomatic, business and academic sources an enormous amount of political and economic information that was, in effect, processed into high-quality intelligence by the Foreign Ministry, the Ministry of International Trade and Industry and the large industrial conglomerates. It was this intelligence system, although not designated as such, that enabled Japan to identify potential markets, analyse them in great detail and then design and produce high-quality products with spectacular success. None of the other major industrial powers has demonstrated this capacity to adapt the intelligence function so effectively to economic requirements.

Indications that Japan has begun to rebuild a clandestine service came to light in June 1982, when the US Government charged 18 Japanese businessmen with an attempt to steal confidential computer information from the US-based International Business Machine Corporation. The charges followed a "sting" operation by an undercover FBI agent who offered the IBM documents and tapes in exchange for $622,000 dollars, a princely sum in terms of international espionage. This case, in which the names Hitachi and Mitsubishi Electric Corp. were allegedly involved, stirred the US CIA, DIA, FBI Customs Service and Postal Service into setting up a "Critical Technology Task Force" which would use computerised information banks to identify which US hardware and programming might be the target of foreign industrial espionage and, through the CIA and DIA, ensure that products requested by foreign companies were really needed for legitimate activities and not for military purposes.

Japanese military intelligence

Post World War II Japanese military intelligence has developed very slowly in the face of public hostility to any hint of a resurrection of the militarism that brought Japan to ruin in World War II. This fear of a revived militarism is reflected to the present day in the refusal of the Japanese Diet (Parliament) to authorize a document security system. The Japanese military intelligence system exists at present as offices for specific geographic areas in the civilian bureaux of the Defense Agency, in the J-2 (Intelligence) section of the small Joint Staff, and in the intelligence sections of the Ground, Air and Maritime Self-Defense Forces—the euphemism imposed for "Army, Navy and Air Force" under the no-war restrictions of the Japanese Constitution. A small corps of highly trained, multi-lingual intelligence officers is being developed in each of these organizations. Also, the Japanese genius for electronics is producing an expert electronic intercept service. It was this service that monitored fighting on the Sino-Soviet border in 1969, producing tapes of Russian tactical radio

3 ▲

33

traffic through which it was possible to identify the precise point (a request for corps-level artillery support) at which the government in Moscow intervened to limit the fighting.

The Japanese intelligence and military capability overall has developed to the point where Japan can keep an accurate track of Soviet air and naval operations in the vicinity of the Japanese archipelago. Of special importance is Soviet naval traffic through the three straits—the Soya (La Perouse), Tsugaru (between Honshu and Hokkaido) and Tsushima (between Japan and Korea) —through which most of the Soviet Pacific Fleet must pass to gain the open ocean. This activity is reported in the annual Japanese Defense White Paper, as shown in the map.

Chinese intelligence

The People's Republic of China is heir to one of the oldest intelligence systems in the world. How much of that system it was able to wrest from the Nationalists before they decamped to Taiwan and how efficiently it operates today are unknown. Virtually all that is known is that the Communist Chinese intelligence service is organized as one of the 13 secret departments among a total of 30 operated by the Central Committee of the Communist Party. That would appear to put intelligence at a considerably lower level than is the case in the Soviet Union and other Communist governments but, as in the USSR, what shows in organizational charts may not reveal the actual influence of intelligence chiefs operating under another title in the top organs of government.

Intelligence of the non-aligned

Throughout the increasing family of emergent "non-aligned" nations there is increasing awareness of the situation described by Charles Proteus Steinmetz, one of the founders of Israeli intelligence: "There will come about an age of small and independent nations whose first line of defence will be knowledge."

About all that most of these emerging nations are able to do is keep track of events in neighbouring countries. Membership of the United Nations provides a vast and relatively cheap expansion of this nascent intelligence interest and capability. By trading off bits of information about their own immediate area, UN representatives of these small nations can obtain from counterpart representatives of the larger nations information about regional and worldwide developments.

Several small, independent countries that were "underdeveloped" only a few years ago are moving into the class of fully developed industrialized nations and their intelligence capability is growing apace with economic and political development. This process is taking place mainly around the rim of the Pacific Ocean and includes to date South Korea, Taiwan, Singapore, and Malaysia.

Australia and New Zealand, of course, already possess advanced intelligence organizations with worldwide connections through their membership in the British

Commonwealth and by treaty links with the United States. The Australian services consist of the Australian Security Intelligence Organization (ASIO) and an Office of National Assessments (ONA). As was done in the United States, the key responsibility for national intelligence assessments was shifted from the military to a separate civilian agency (the ONA) after WW II.

The most advanced intelligence organizations in Africa are those of Egypt and South Africa. Both are focused not only on neighbouring countries but on the superpowers as well, for both are major targets of superpower politics. In the case of South Africa the effort by the United States, Britain and other Western nations to bring about abandonment of its racist *apartheid* policy limits the amount of information the South African services could otherwise expect to receive. As a result, South Africa has been reduced to such embarassing escapades as attempting to infiltrate its Chief of Military Intelligence, Lt. Gen. P. W. van der Westhuisen, into the United States under a false identity, only to have him promptly recognized and ejected on March 15, 1981, together with compatriots Admiral Willem Duplessis (a former defence attache in Washington apparently previously expelled in April 1979) and Brigadier Nels van Tonder, after they had visited the Defense Intelligence Agency in the Pentagon, an official of the US National Security Council, and the State Department.

Superpower intelligence activities

To one degree or another all of the intelligence organizations discussed thus far are participants of the titanic struggle for information that goes on between the only two intelligence organizations that possess a full array of modern collection capabilities. These are, of course, the intelligence organizations of the United States, loosely combined under the chief of the Central Intelligence Agency, and those of the Soviet Union.

The initiative in world power politics since World War II clearly has been with the Soviet Union. Any consideration of the "intelligence war" waged during these past three decades must begin, therefore, with the operation of the Soviet intelligence agencies, for the Soviet initiatives are based on or are influenced by the information supplied by those agencies. There are two of them: the "Committee for State Security" (KGB), and the military intelligence service —the GRU (Main Intelligence Directorate of the General Staff).

The Soviet KGB

How the Soviet intelligence agencies relate to the other principal intelligence agencies of the world is shown in figure 2. Figure 4 portrays the place of the Soviet intelligence agencies in the Soviet Government.

Membership in the Defence Council and the Politburo itself—the ruling body of the Soviet Union—gives the chief of the KGB far greater influence than is exercised by any of the other principal intelligence agencies.

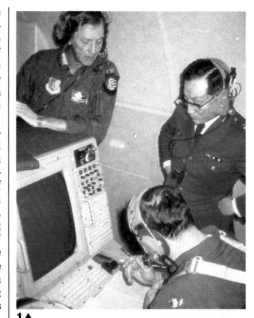
1▲

2▲

3▲

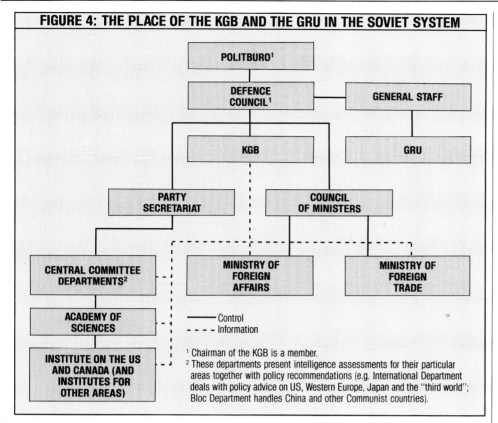

FIGURE 4: THE PLACE OF THE KGB AND THE GRU IN THE SOVIET SYSTEM

POLITBURO[1]

DEFENCE COUNCIL[1]

GENERAL STAFF

KGB

GRU

PARTY SECRETARIAT

COUNCIL OF MINISTERS

CENTRAL COMMITTEE DEPARTMENTS[2]

MINISTRY OF FOREIGN AFFAIRS

MINISTRY OF FOREIGN TRADE

ACADEMY OF SCIENCES

INSTITUTE ON THE US AND CANADA (AND INSTITUTES FOR OTHER AREAS)

——— Control
- - - - Information

[1] Chairman of the KGB is a member.
[2] These departments present intelligence assessments for their particular areas together with policy recommendations (e.g. International Department deals with policy advice on US, Western Europe, Japan and the "third world"; Bloc Department handles China and other Communist countries).

1 Japan learns a lot on defence from the West, especially the US. Here the "sensitive" AWACS is demonstrated.

2 Caspar Weinberger and his Japanese opposite number, Ito, continued the US-Japanese dialogue on defence matters in 1982.

3 An "old boys" gathering with a difference as former Soviet chief delegate at the UN, Arkadiy Shevchenko, attends the 1981 convention of the US Association of Former Intelligence Officers. He was the highest defector for years.

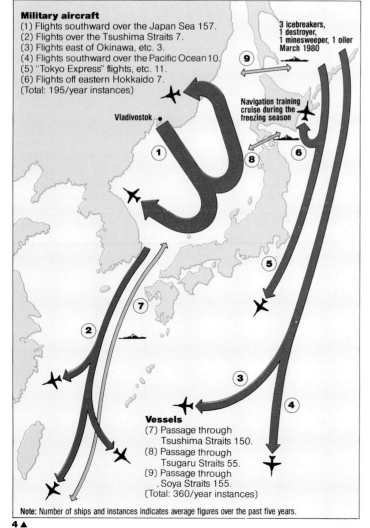

Military aircraft
(1) Flights southward over the Japan Sea 157.
(2) Flights over the Tsushima Straits 7.
(3) Flights east of Okinawa, etc. 3.
(4) Flights southward over the Pacific Ocean 10.
(5) "Tokyo Express" flights, etc. 11.
(6) Flights off eastern Hokkaido 7.
(Total: 195/year instances)

3 icebreakers, 1 destroyer, 1 minesweeper, 1 oiler March 1980

Navigation training cruise during the freezing season

Vladivostok

Vessels
(7) Passage through Tsushima Straits 150.
(8) Passage through Tsugaru Straits 55.
(9) Passage through Soya Straits 155.
(Total: 360/year instances)

Note: Number of ships and instances indicates average figures over the past five years.

4 ▲

4 The relationship between Japan and Russia has been an uneasy one for centuries Successive annexations of Chinese territory in 1858 and 1860 brought Russia to the Sea of Japan. Joint Russian/Japanese control of Sakhalin, set up in 1867, led to a deal in 1875 when Russia took total control in return for Japan assuming responsibility for the Kurile Islands. After the Russo-Japanese War of 1904-05 Japan annexed half of Sakhalin. In 1945 the Russians had their revenge and not only took back all of Sakhalin, but also the Kurile Islands as well. Despite this Soviet resurgence Japan still sits firmly astride the routes which the Russians need for air and sea egress from the Seas of Japan and Okhotsk to the open waters of the Pacific. These exits are through the Tsushima Straits in the south, the Tsugaru Straits between Hokkaido and Honshu, and the Soya Passage between Hokkaido and Sakhalin. As a warning to the West, Japan issued this map showing that in 1980 there were 360 ship movements through these three straits and some 195 flights. In addition the Soviet Far East Fleet uses the Sea of Okhotsk as a safe haven for its SSBNs.

Controlling a powerful force of internal security troops and, above all, with information flowing from agents throughout the Soviet system, the chief of the KGB participates in the *selection* of the Soviet chief of state and sometimes goes beyond that.

In 1953, the last of Stalin's internal security chiefs, Lavrenti Beria, made a grab for power and was shot for his troubles. Yuri V. Andropov, chief of the KGB for 15 years, succeeded where Beria failed by adroitly leaving the KGB in time to "launder" himself just six months before the death of Leonid Brezhnev in November 1982. By all accounts, however, the KGB and the military were the powers that brought Andropov to the top. As an example of how this worked, western newsmen report that Andropov was able to use KGB communications to call his subordinates and supporters to Moscow at the time of Brezhnev's death, circumventing the Communist Party channels in the hands of his rivals.

Subsequent to the Beria incident, the Party chiefs sought to keep the KGB under control by delegating selection and promotion of KGB personnel to one of the departments which serve as the staff of the Communist Party Central Committee. How that system will work now that the KGB has, in effect, taken over the Party remains to be seen.

As shown in figure 4, the KGB enjoys a major bureaucratic advantage over the Soviet military intelligence service, the GRU, in that the chief of the KGB operates at the very top levels of the Government, while the chief of the GRU is represented only indirectly in those councils by the Defence Minister.

Except for business and personal contacts—severely limited in the tightly compartmented Soviet system—the KGB controls not only foreign intelligence but also the domestic information that reaches the greater part of the Soviet Government. Only the General Staff, through the GRU, has an independent source of overall foreign intelligence. The Party Secretariat has an independent source of political intelligence through its overseas Party contacts, but it lacks the comprehensive sources of the KGB and GRU.

The government institutes

Of special interest in recent years has been the emergence of governmental and quasi-governmental intelligence-gathering "research institutes" in both the non-communist and Communist worlds. The prototype was established by the US Air Force in the early post-World War II era as what is now known as the RAND Corporation. Although nominally private academic institutions, none could survive without some form of direct or indirect government subsidy, if only in the form of tax exemptions.

As shown on the left side of figure 4, the Soviets have adopted the "institute" idea in recent years. Their Institute on the US and Canada is only one of an array of such organizations dealing with research on major geographic regions and functions. In fact they are intelligence agencies for both

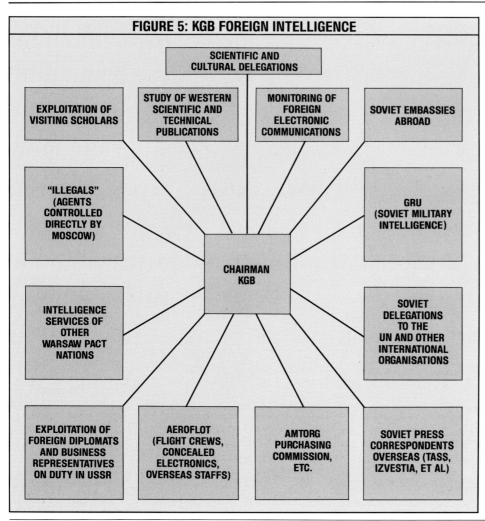

FIGURE 5: KGB FOREIGN INTELLIGENCE

SCIENTIFIC AND CULTURAL DELEGATIONS

EXPLOITATION OF VISITING SCHOLARS

STUDY OF WESTERN SCIENTIFIC AND TECHNICAL PUBLICATIONS

MONITORING OF FOREIGN ELECTRONIC COMMUNICATIONS

SOVIET EMBASSIES ABROAD

"ILLEGALS" (AGENTS CONTROLLED DIRECTLY BY MOSCOW)

GRU (SOVIET MILITARY INTELLIGENCE)

CHAIRMAN KGB

INTELLIGENCE SERVICES OF OTHER WARSAW PACT NATIONS

SOVIET DELEGATIONS TO THE UN AND OTHER INTERNATIONAL ORGANISATIONS

EXPLOITATION OF FOREIGN DIPLOMATS AND BUSINESS REPRESENTATIVES ON DUTY IN USSR

AEROFLOT (FLIGHT CREWS, CONCEALED ELECTRONICS, OVERSEAS STAFFS)

AMTORG PURCHASING COMMISSION, ETC.

SOVIET PRESS CORRESPONDENTS OVERSEAS (TASS, IZVESTIA, ET AL)

1 ▲   2 ▼

collection and analysis. The US Federal Bureau of Investigation recently identified Georgi Mainedov, a representative of the Institute for the USA and Canada in Washington, as a KGB agent whose primary focus was on SALT arms limitation treaties. The intelligence columnist Robert Moss also cites a "recent defector from the Institute, Miss Galina Orionov'a," as stating that many staff members of the Institute are KGB agents. According to Harrison E. Salisbury, former New York *Times* correspondent in Moscow, "Georgi A. Arbatov, founder and director of the Institute . . . has been a close associate of Mr Andropov (then KGB director) since the early days of the Institute". The Institute on the US and Canada, and similar institutes for other areas of the world, serve, in addition, as effective channels for Soviet propaganda to non-Communist academic institutions and even into non-Communist governments. This is accomplished by an astute exploitation of academic and bureaucratic rivalries in other countries.

Particularly during the past 10 to 15 years, access to sources within the Soviet Government has come to be seen as a prized advantage by members of the Western academic community in and out of government who are seeking to gain status as "Sovietologists". Long before the "institutes" came into existence, individual Western and Japanese scholars had gained such entrées as the product of deep expertise and persistent work. The institute idea capitalized very effectively on the eagerness of those who sought to bypass the tedious and often lifelong persistence of the true experts ("scholars", perhaps being the better term; there being no "experts" outside of the Soviet Politburo). Recent experience has shown that the directors of the Soviet Institute on the US and Canada, in particular, have become adept at forcing Western academic visitors to vie among themselves for the time and attention of the Institute's hierarchy. Who in that hierarchy a visitor gets to see and how much time is spent with that person has become a sort of Western academic "pecking order". The "who" and "how long" of it, of course, are allocated on the basis of how much information the visitor supplies and how well he or she relates the Soviet message through publications and other channels. It is an amazingly simple formula, but it works. It is a short step from that process to offering financial support for academic research, and that is now taking place.

By following exactly this pattern the North Korean Government produced at Arizona State University in February, 1976, an American participant (an associate professor at the Eastern US Villanova Catholic university!) who faithfully and passionately presented the North Korean view of world affairs, probably better than any North Korean diplomat could have done. It would have been a simple matter to reinvite the professor concerned to a similar "symposium" in Pyongyang and to obtain thereby a detailed report of the participants at the Arizona State gathering and their presentations.

Thus an important new intelligence-gathering channel has been opened up. It is not confined to civilian academic institutions. In appreciation for the "hospitality" of the Soviet Institute on the US and Canada, Soviet and East European "scholars" have been given entrée to American governmental institutes (notably the Strategic Studies Institute at the US Army War College) in which classified documents are visible on desk tops and classified information is being discussed. The Soviets are by no means so liberal in entertaining their guests.

Scant wonder that Cord Meyer, formerly of the US Central Intelligence Agency, and other Western intelligence officials regard the work of the Soviet "academic" institutes as among the most effective in the entire Soviet intelligence network. The Western visitors who are making this possible are not traitors, in the main, but they are most certainly naive.

The KGB's sources

In addition to this new channel, the sources of foreign intelligence available to the KGB are vast, as indicated by figure 5. The most important source of information for the KGB and for any intelligence organization staffed to exploit it is the worldwide "information explosion". The pace of technological development is such that it is impossible for any government to restrict it

3 ▲

4 ▲

5 ▼

1 Former CIA agent Cord Meyer has given grave warnings about the determined efforts being made by Soviet intelligence agents to take advantage of the gullibility and naivete of some Western academics and institutions.

2 Edith Road, London W4, one of the homes of known KGB/GRU agents in the British capital. The Soviet intelligence assault on the UK since World War II has been intense, indicating that they estimate the country to be be a high priority target.

3 The Aeroflot offices in London, part of a growing network belonging to the Soviet national airline. All Aeroflot and other Soviet commercial staff are valuable KGB sources of information, unwitting or not. Several Western countries have found it necessary to expel Aeroflot staff for espionage activities, the most recent being Italy. Italian arrests were related to the alleged plots to kill the Pope, an international scandal the full details of which have yet to be revealed. Aeroflot is rapidly acquiring a dubious reputation for some of its activities.

4 An Ilyushin Il-86 airliner of Aeroflot. Civil flights in the West give the USSR some excellent opportunities for espionage, a recent example being the overflight of the Electric Boat Company submarine yard at Groton, where US SSBNs are built.

5 Another Soviet tentacle is the news agency — Tass; this is its London office. In addition, the KGB controls the intelligence services of the other members of the Warsaw Pact; the effort is, to put it bluntly, on a very broad front, and successful.

to "classified", that is, secret, channels. Indeed, any government that attempts to do so will cripple its own progress by denying its own scientists and engineers the means to interact with the ideas and discoveries of their colleagues throughout the world. This is also why non-governmental journalistic enterprises when properly organized and staffed can do as well as the governmental intelligence agencies, or better, in identifying future trends and likely developments in many areas.

A principal means available to the KGB to exploit the "information explosion" are the institutes of the Academy of Sciences. As described earlier, these draw on the information supplied by visiting foreign scholars. Their main work, however, is to sift through the thousands of publications available in many languages describing the work of scholars, scientists and engineers worldwide.

Soviet scientific and cultural delegations visiting foreign countries provide an ideal means to gather information openly on new developments in the non-Communist world. Because such delegations are controlled entirely by the government it is an easy matter to include trained KGB agents and to "debrief" *all* members in detail on their return.

Although it rivals the KGB in some respects, the lower position of the GRU — Soviet military intelligence — in the governmental hierarchy makes it an essentially supplemental service to the KGB. Since KGB agents are located throughout

the armed forces command structure, as part of the KGB internal security function, it would seem very difficult for the armed forces to hold back information desired by the KGB.

The Soviet official airline, Aeroflot, offers a variety of means to gather information, both openly and clandestinely. By their normal flight functions, Aeroflot crews gather large amounts of information about foreign airfields and navigation systems. Since they have far more extensive access to non-Communist flight facilities than foreign airlines have to Soviet facilities, this is a major "plus" for Soviet intelligence. For undercover, or clandestine, gathering of information, Aeroflot offers a variety of ways to insert KGB agents into air crews and among overseas clerical and business staff. Possibly more important, there are many ways to conceal cameras and electronic devices aboard Aeroflot aircraft. Normal flight patterns permit extensive gathering of photographic and electronic intelligence. "Accidental" overflights of forbidden zones, as occurred in the United States in October 1981, permit blatant intrusion over key defence installations since it is unlikely that non-Communist countries would shoot down an airliner known to be filled with passengers. Penalties can be imposed after the fact, but where a high-priority intelligence "target" is concerned the price may be well worth the information gained.

The control of "illegal" agents — that is, agents who assume a false foreign identity —

and the operation of spy rings from Soviet embassies abroad are aspects of a world-wide system of espionage that is described in greater detail in chapter 4. Although such spying is the most dramatic of intelligence activities, and still occasionally produces spectacular results, the most important clandestine spying by the Soviet Union or any other nation is the interception of electronic communications.

The KGB has full control of the intelligence services of all other Warsaw Pact nations with the possible exception of Rumania, which pursues a dangerous quasi-independent course from Moscow. This control of non-Soviet agencies has been especially beneficial to the KGB when Soviet operations and presence in a given country must be reduced, as when Britain and Egypt in recent years ordered all or a large proportion of the Soviet "diplomatic" staff out of the country. In these instances, the intelligence services of Czechoslovakia and Poland have proven adept at carrying out Soviet missions. In Britain, in particular, numerous Soviet penetrations or attempted penetrations of sensitive British security areas have been found to be under Czech or Polish direction. East Germany's intelligence service is an especially important asset to the KGB because of that country's scientific and technological competence. This provides entrée for East German agents where Soviet agents would not be welcome, particularly in "Third World" countries.

Similar intelligence assistance is obviously forthcoming from non-Warsaw Pact friends of the Soviets, such as Afghanistan, Cuba (whose adventures in Africa and Central America have been orchestrated and largely funded by the Kremlin), and also from Vietnam, to a lesser degree: there cannot be much happening in the Communist-controlled Southeast Asian countries and their neighbours that the KGB is not privy to or not had an instrumental hand in.

The United Nations and other international organizations provide infinite means of access, open and covert, to "target" countries. Here again the Soviets enjoy a major advantage since the Soviet Government controls absolutely all of its nationals who join such staffs, whereas in many cases non-Communist governments make no attempt to determine the ideology of their citizens serving on such staffs and establish no assignment or reporting procedures for the gathering of information.

Background of the KGB

The nature of the "intelligence war" between the KGB and its principal rival, the American CIA, is shaped by history and national background. The KGB evolved from the Bolshevik "Cheka", Lenin's secret police. Although there have been several changes in name and organization since (GPU, OGPU, NKVD, MGB), the agents of the KGB still are referred to in the Soviet Union today as "Chekists". From the days of Ivan the Terrible through Lenin's Cheka to the present, the Soviet Government has been obsessed with internal security. As indicated earlier, this is reflected in the massive KGB resources devoted to internal security compared with the gathering and analysis of foreign intelligence (375,000 in the KGB internal security departments, compared with 25,000 in the foreign intelligence departments).

Even though its original orientation was inward toward Russian society rather than outward toward foreign countries, history provided the KGB with major advantages over its current rivals. For one thing, the KGB has been in continuous existence in one form or another since 1917, whereas the US CIA did not come into existence until 1947. Most important of all was the advantage given to Soviet foreign intelligence by the internationalism of the original Communist philosophy.

Thousands of non-Russian idealists throughout the world were caught up in the announced ideals and goals of the Russian Revolution. The motion picture "Reds", which has been on recent international release, describes this in vivid terms. Many of them continued to be carried along even after the Bolsheviks subverted those early aspirations and established a new and even more terrible class system, for which the original Cheka provided the execution squads, the torture chambers and what would become known as the "Gulag Archipelago" of slave labour camps.

The system of Communist parties formed from the nucleus of early Communist idealists provided a ready-made worldwide intelligence network. Emotionally committed to the ideals of international revolution, those early Communists felt themselves duty-bound to warn the Soviet Union of what they conceived to be threats to its safety, and to obey the orders of the Communist International (Comintern) established in Moscow.

Nothing of that sort was available to the principal non-Communist nations. It was only when disillusionment began to set in with the Trotsky-Stalin split and grew worse with the Hitler-Stalin Pact of 1939 and the revelation of the scope of the Stalinist terror by Soviet Premier Krushchev that the old network of Communist idealists began to collapse. Increasing high-level defections from the Soviet Union and other Communist nations then began to counterbalance the advantages Soviet intelligence had enjoyed for more than 30 years.

The Warsaw Pact allies

The East European Communist parties that were placed in power by the Soviet Army after World War II provide the KGB with a convenient alter ego. Since each of these captured nations is able to maintain its own embassy the effect is to multiply Soviet centres of communications and espionage control. When restrictions are imposed on the Soviet Embassy, operations are often simply switched to one of the Soviet "allies". When, for example, severe travel limitations around London were imposed on Soviet attachés by the British Government following Soviet aggression in Afghanistan, in December 1979, the Soviets simply sent Czechoslovak and Polish attachés to attend open military events that ordinarily would have been attended by themselves. How closely controlled the "allies" are in this sort of activity was demonstrated when a British military publication with offices outside the limit began receiving Polish and Czech visitors in place of Russians, then suddenly began to be visited by Russians again when, for administrative reasons, it happened to move its offices back nearer London.

The US intelligence agencies

Had Stalin himself defected in the 1930s, the United States scarcely would have known what to do with him. It had no intelligence service other than those of the Army and Navy—assignment to which was regarded in both services as the death knell of a career. The small US code-breaking service that had been established in the US State Department during World War I was dismantled in 1929 as "ungentlemanly".

Lacking any means to make use of the long-range "strategic" intelligence provided by such writers as Homer Lea (even the work of Lt. Col. "Pete" Ellis of the Marines was confined to a relatively low level), or to respond in time to the tactical ("current") intelligence of the incoming raid itself, the United States was stunned by the Japanese attack on Pearl Harbor, Hawaii, in December 1941.

"Hadn't the Americans ever heard of our successful surprise attack on the Russian Fleet at Port Arthur in 1904?" one of the planners of the Pearl Harbor raid asked in wonderment. They had, of course, but they

1 ▲

2 ▲

1, 2 The Warsaw Pact work as one, under the control of the KGB. Thus, when Soviet attaches were limited to a radius of 25 miles from London staff from the Polish (**1**) and Hungarian (**2**) embassies simply took their place.

3 President Truman signs the National Security Act on July 26, 1947, setting up the Central Intelligence Agency, the successor to the wartime Office of Strategic Services (OSS). The CIA has often carried out a difficult task admirably, but has sometimes tarnished its image.

4 Set up in 1961, the main task of the DIA is collecting and producing intelligence for the Secretary of Defense and the Joint Chiefs.

5 The original mandate for the CIA confined it to true intelligence functions, but the onset of the Cold War led to covert operational tasks as well.

6 The CIA building. The CIA is by no means the only intelligence agency in the USA, but its director is the only adviser in this field with direct access to the President.

3 ▲

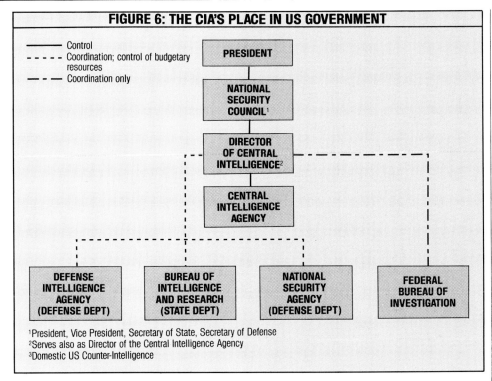

FIGURE 6: THE CIA'S PLACE IN US GOVERNMENT

—— Control
- - - - Coordination; control of budgetary resources
– – Coordination only

PRESIDENT

NATIONAL SECURITY COUNCIL[1]

DIRECTOR OF CENTRAL INTELLIGENCE[2]

CENTRAL INTELLIGENCE AGENCY

DEFENSE INTELLIGENCE AGENCY (DEFENSE DEPT)

BUREAU OF INTELLIGENCE AND RESEARCH (STATE DEPT)

NATIONAL SECURITY AGENCY (DEFENSE DEPT)

FEDERAL BUREAU OF INVESTIGATION

[1]President, Vice President, Secretary of State, Secretary of Defense
[2]Serves also as Director of the Central Intelligence Agency
[3]Domestic US Counter-Intelligence

4 ▲   5 ▲

6 ▲

had no way to put the knowledge to use.

The World War II US Office of Strategic Services (OSS) was a hasty effort to build a central intelligence system. As their model, the designers of the OSS turned to Britain's security services, the principal features of which, as discussed earlier, were sparse, efficient use of manpower and an ability to stay out of the news.

The Central Intelligence Agency

The British looked on in amazement as the Americans produced, first in the OSS and later in the CIA, bureaucratic giants that would be almost constantly in the news —in recent years almost always as "bad news". A former chief of one of the British intelligence services commented, "We never expected anything like that."

The burgeoning of the CIA bureaucracy might have been averted if the "Cold War" between the United States and the Soviet Union had not broken out so soon after the creation of the CIA in 1947.

The original Congressional mandate for the CIA covered true intelligence functions only. Psychological warfare and political "covert actions" had been included in the wartime OSS structure. There was no legal provision, however, for incorporation of these "operational" activities in the new central intelligence structure. These activities were inserted into the nascent CIA by former OSS "covert action" agents whose old wartime activities were given a new lease of life by the "Cold War".

The place of the CIA in the US Government is shown in figure 6. As indicated, its creation did not supplant the intelligence and counter-intelligence agencies of other US Governmental departments. Centralization of control did occur, however, in the priority given to the Director of Central Intelligence (and chief of the CIA) as the only intelligence adviser with direct access to the President and the National Security Council. Also, the Director of Central Intelligence, at least nominally, allocates the overall governmental foreign intelligence budget.

The DIA and State Department

The US Army, Navy, Air Force and Marine Corps retained intelligence staffs directly related to combat operations, but relinquished many functions to the Defense Intelligence Agency (DIA) in 1961. DIA operates the military attache system. It duplicates much of the military analysis conducted by CIA. Although DIA cannot present its analyses direct to the National Security Council, the Secretary of Defense can, if he chooses, present DIA estimates that differ from those of the CIA.

The extent of the rivalry between CIA and DIA is indicated by the fact that, over 20 years after the event, both agencies are still supplying newsmen with rival claims over whose photo interpreters "found" the Soviet missiles in Cuba that resulted in the celebrated Cuban missile crisis.

The State Department's Bureau of Intelligence and Research is concerned mainly with political and economic matters. Additional specialized intelligence flows to CIA from the Department of the Treasury, which controls a worldwide narcotics investigation bureau, and the Department of Commerce, which conducts studies of worldwide economic conditions.

Internal structure of the CIA

The internal structure of the CIA is shown in figure 7. Almost all of what the world public has heard about the CIA derives from the activities of the "Directorate of Operations", formerly known as the "Directorate of Plans". This is the directorate that plans and conducts "covert actions", such as the overthrow of the Mossadeq Government in Iran in 1953, the Bay of Pigs invasion of Cuba in 1961, the attempted assassination of Patrice Lumumba in the Congo in 1960 and cooperation with the US organized crime syndicate in the early 1960s plans to assassinate Fidel Castro of Cuba. This Directorate got into the news again in the early 1980s when its Director, Max C. Hugel, was fired for questionable business practices and when US Secretary of State Alexander Haig accused the Soviet Union of organizing terrorist activities in Libya only to find to his great embarrassment, and that of the United States, that it wasn't only the Russians, but former agents of the Directorate of Operations, CIA, apparently in league with officials still serving in the agency, who were training the Libyans and supplying them with sophisticated explosives and other technology. So involved was the situation that the US Army blundered into supplying a Special Forces master

sergeant on active duty to assist in the Libyan terrorist operation, an episode that no one in the US Government seems able to explain to the present day.

The administration of President Ronald Reagan seemed to interpret its election, in 1980, as licence to get back into the business of CIA undeclared wars, suspended following revelations of successive CIA disasters in the mid-1970s. Old "covert action" warriors were called back from retirement and, sure enough, promptly produced yet another diplomatic and public relations disaster—this time by mobilizing discredited Argentinian and former Nicaraguan National Guard thugs to "destabilize" the quasi-Marxist Sandinist Government in Nicaragua. More sophisticated Americans, led by Catholic and Protestant churchmen and *Newsweek* magazine, seem to have been able to intervene in time to prevent another "Bay of Pigs" fiasco.

The Directorate of Intelligence and the Directorate of Science and Technology perform the true intelligence functions of the CIA. The Directorate of Administration, of course, deals with the usual internal tasks of management. It is in the Directorate of Intelligence and the Directorate of Science and Technology that the laborious work goes on of sifting through the vast quantity of information our world produces every day for those items that must be quickly identified, assessed and passed on to the leadership of government to guide policy or to provide early warning of danger. As with the information collected by the KGB, most of the CIA's data comes from non-govern-

ment, "unclassified" sources. Indeed, in regard to these "open" sources, both agencies are working from substantially the same information. As concerns "covert", or secret sources, the KGB seems to rely more heavily on human sources (Humint) while the US agencies rely more heavily on technological collection. The difference in what they produce, however, is largely determined by quality and speed of assessment and dissemination.

Tucked away with "covert action" in the CIA Directorate of Operations are the counter-intelligence staff and the true "spies", the traditional undercover operatives still necessary to verify and clarify information gained from cameras and electronic listening devices. Although it has many successful operations to its credit—notably the exposure, beginning in 1951 and continuing into the 1970s, of Soviet agents who had infiltrated the British security services—the CIA's counter-intelligence staff has brought upon itself much the same sort of unpleasant publicity that the "covert action" staff seems to produce with almost predictable regularity. It was the counter-intelligence staff that ran the bizarre and tragic illegal drug experiments of the 1950s and 1960s. No sooner did the publicity from that unsavoury programme die away than the counter-intelligence staff got back into the news again with another of its periodic "raids" on the domestic counter-espionage responsibilities of the Federal Bureau of Investigation. In the 1950s this rivalry produced at least one comic-opera episode in a Washington restaurant when CIA agents and FBI agents mistook each other for the

1 Intelligence work seems to be increasingly equipment-oriented, with men and women fiddling with ever-more-sophisticated gadgets, like these USN sailors with their high-powered microscope for photo-interpretation. Accurate and timely assessments and useful reports still depend upon the quality of the people, however.

2 CIA intelligence operator studying a large-scale aerial photograph. Intelligence work is mainly a matter of endless routine drudgery, with only the occasional and unexpected dramatic breakthrough. Aerial photography remains one of the most accurate and detailed surveillance methods used by the CIA and DIA.

3 A CIA operative making a relief model, possibly for a special operation. Such actions are not normally part of "intelligence" work.

4 The constant monitoring of the airwaves is an activity undertaken by every intelligence agency in the fight for ever more information.

1 ▲

FIGURE 7: INTERNAL ORGANIZATION OF THE US CENTRAL INTELLIGENCE AGENCY

- **DIRECTOR**
  - **DIRECTORATE OF INTELLIGENCE**
    - **OFFICE OF POLITICAL RESEARCH**
    - **OFFICE OF STRATEGIC RESEARCH**
    - **OFFICE OF CURRENT INTELLIGENCE**
  - **DIRECTORATE OF SCIENCE AND TECHNOLOGY**
    - **NATIONAL PHOTOGRAPHIC INTERPRETATION CENTER**
    - **OFFICE OF ECONOMIC RESEARCH**
    - **IMAGERY ANALYSIS SERVICE**
  - **DIRECTORATE OF ADMINISTRATION**
  - **DIRECTORATE OF OPERATIONS**
    - **COVERT ACTION**
    - **COUNTER INTELLIGENCE**
    - **COVERT COLLECTION**
    - **OFFICE OF GEOGRAPHIC AND CARTOGRAPHIC RESEARCH**

(Based on report of the US Senate Select Committee on Intelligence)

KGB, got into a fist fight and were hauled off to jail—and onto the front pages of the Washington newspapers.

Undeterred, the CIA's counter-intelligence staff seemed to be seeking from the new Reagan Administration a signal for renewing this internecine warfare. Although the CIA counter-intelligence staff did not get all it was seeking, a directive issued by President Reagan on December 4, 1981, seemed to open the door to new CIA incursions on the FBI's "turf".

In the meantime, the genuine CIA intelligence staffs do their best to carry out their work amidst the seemingly endless, highly publicized, small wars and empire-building of the "covert action" and counter-intelligence staffs.

According to William Casey, CIA Director, quoted in the New York Times in January 1983, the Agency's intelligence-gathering and covert operations were severely curtailed during the decade prior to Ronald Reagan's election in 1980. But from a 40 per cent cut in funding for America's intelligence agencies in the 1970s and a 50 per cent reduction in staff, the increase in the CIA's budget for fiscal year 1983 is apparently 25 per cent, compared with 18 per cent for the overall Department of Defense.

New York Times correspondent Philip Taubman commented that Mr Casey ". . . is overseeing the biggest peacetime build-up in the American intelligence community since the early 1950s. At a moment when the Reagan Administration is forcing most government agencies to retrench, the CIA and its fellow intelligence organisations are enjoying boom times."

All this, according to Taubman, presents prospects of a career in the once-tarnished CIA in an appealing new light to university graduates who, in the 1970s, might have been put off by the Agency's abuses of power at home and abroad.

As was the case with mid-1970s Congressional investigators, Taubman found that Casey is preoccupied with a revived "covert action" capability rather than with the true intelligence aspects of the agency.

How well do KGB/CIA perform?

How well do these vast organizations serve the purpose for which they were created, at least as concerns the timely, accurate production of foreign intelligence?

When Soviet Premier Leonid Brezhnev visited German Chancellor Helmut Schmidt in the German capital of Bonn in November 1981, Brezhnev spoke with expert knowledge of the concerns expressed by Europeans who had been demonstrating for several months previously against nuclear arms. Some students of Soviet Union affairs say that this came less from good intelligence collection and analysis than from prior orchestration of the demonstrations by the International Information Department of the Soviet Central Committee. (A "masterpiece of social and political action" in the opinion of respected Edinburgh University Professor John Erickson.)

The consensus seems to be that only with such foreknowledge could Brezhnev have exploited the situation so readily. That is, most students of Soviet intelligence believe there is extreme compartmentation in the Soviet intelligence system with very poor coordination "between the boxes" in the Soviet organizational chart. That, of course, corresponds very well with the known behaviour of bureaucracies and bureaucrats everywhere, as is illustrated by the following.

Again an incident from the author's personal experience, illustrating an acute and unresolved problem of compartmentation in the American services, suggests both the seriousness of the defect and that it probably is far more acute in the Soviet services where the rivalries involve personal safety as well as bureaucratic advantage. Early in 1980, military officers assigned to the Study and Analysis Gaming Agency (SAGA) of the US Joint Chiefs of Staff were preparing a political-military war game involving some of the highest officials of the US Government. The locale was Northeast Asia, an area on which the planners of the war game had very little good information. Having just completed three extensive trips through the region in about as many years, and with over 10 years of close study of developments there, the author, then on duty at the US Army War College, was able to offer the background the war game planners needed. No sooner did the Director of Academic Affairs at the War College hear about the effort, however, that he ordered it stopped on the grounds that it was not a completed and fully approved "study". As a nicely wrapped up "study", the information would not be available until months after it was needed by the war game planners. And so, information that was badly needed and which had cost the American public several

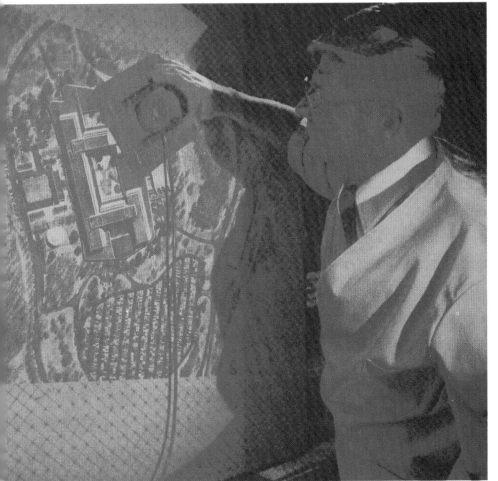

2 ▲

3 ▲

4 ▲

thousand dollars to accumulate disappeared into an academic dustbin.

In democratic societies such sequestering of the information needed to produce accurate, timely intelligence is the stuff of petty bureaucratic politics, or simply of minds hopelessly ensnared in administrative "red tape". In totalitarian societies information is not only power, but may be the means of personal survival in a terrifying physical sense.

Prof. John Erickson, one of the very few really competent students of the Soviet system, believes that information is not only highly compartmented in the Soviet Government, but poorly disseminated as well once refined into intelligence. This is carried to such extremes that the Warsaw Pact "allies" of the Soviet Union in Eastern Europe have been forced to invite in Western scholars to brief them on the Soviet order of battle!

The rivalry between KGB and GRU

The sequestering of information and finished intelligence in the Soviet system is compounded by an intense rivalry between the KGB and the GRU (Military Intelligence). There are indications, for example, that the KGB has "allies" within the East Asian Institute of the Soviet Academy of Sciences while the GRU's strong suit is with "allies" in the African Institute. This rivalry extends to academic sources in the non-Communist world. That is, factions within the rival intelligence agencies and other sectors of the Soviet Government seek out Western academic sources that will support a particular point of view and then use these sources to "prove" their case in Moscow.

The long and short of it seems to be that the Soviets are quite good at gathering vast quantities of information and of using adroitly the finished intelligence produced therefrom in support of carefully planned campaigns—such as the anti-nuclear campaign in Europe in 1981.

Because of the rivalries, the tight compartmentalization and the jealous withholding of important information and intelligence the Soviets appear to do much more poorly in making accurate assessments of fast-moving situations. Considering this weakness it is conceivable that the Soviet leaders could panic if there was to be a coincidence of several events—such as an uprising in Eastern Europe coupled with Chinese aggressiveness in border clashes and markedly increased dissidence within the Soviet Union—that led them to believe a vast conspiracy was in motion against them, a situation they are preconditioned to believe by their own ideology and propaganda. Professor Erickson and some US State Department observers believe something of that sort precipitated the Soviet invasion of Afghanistan in December 1979.

CIA performance

How well does the US Central Intelligence Agency perform in comparison? The end result of the entire intelligence process is the "national estimate". How that estimate is developed in the US system is shown in figure 8.

59942   Federal Register / Vol. 46, No. 235 / Tuesday, December 8, 1981 / Presidential Documents

Part 1

Goals, Direction, Duties and Responsibilities With Respect to the National Intelligence Effort

1.1 *Goals.* The United States intelligence effort shall provide the President and the National Security Council with the necessary information on which to base decisions concerning the conduct and development of foreign, defense and economic policy, and the protection of United States national interests from foreign security threats. All departments and agencies shall cooperate fully to fulfill this goal.

(a) Maximum emphasis should be given to fostering analytical competition among appropriate elements of the Intelligence Community.

(b) All means, consistent with applicable United States law and this Order, and with full consideration of the rights of United States persons, shall be used to develop intelligence information for the President and the National Security Council. A balanced approach between technical collection efforts and other means should be maintained and encouraged.

(c) Special emphasis should be given to detecting and countering espionage ~ ~ts and activities directed by foreign intelligence services ~ ~ment, or United States corpora~~ ~ estab-

1 ▲

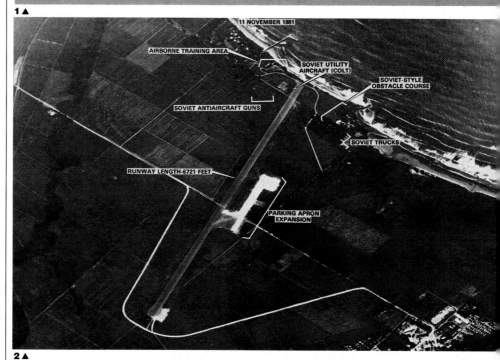

2 ▲

FIGURE 8: PRODUCTION CYCLE OF THE US NATIONAL INTELLIGENCE ESTIMATE (NIE)

President or his Assistant for National Security Affairs, or Director, CIA, states requirements

Director Central Intelligence refines requirement and assigns tasks to collection agencies (CIA, DIA, NSA, etc.)

National Foreign Intelligence Board reviews draft and forwards final NIE

Intelligence agencies collect and analyze data, prepare draft National Estimate

3 ▲

4 ▲

1 December 4, 1981, was the date of issue of Executive Order 12333 in which President Reagan defined the goals, duties and conduct of the national intelligence effort. A similar charter for the KGB or GRU has yet to be published!

2 The US Press refused to believe executive reports that there was Communist involvement in Nicaragua. Eventually the US Government had to release these previously classified U-2 aerial photographs of Montelimar Airfield to prove such involvement quite conclusively. The CIA's record in such current intelligence activities is relatively good; indeed, considering the resources at its disposal, it ought to be. It is in the area of long-range forecasting at strategic (and often tactical) levels where it has proved to be weak. All too often the open Press has been wiser and more accurate.

3 Lunching with President Reagan are National Security Adviser William Clark (left) and Secretary of State George Schultz (right). These are the three men with overall responsibility for intelligence matters, although detailed control is at a lower level. The CIA has direct access to the President.

4 US Secretary of State Schultz with Ambassador Rabb, whose name was found on a Libyan terrorist "hit-list" by CIA clandestine operatives. It has been suggested that some former CIA agents now working for the Libyan Government may be acting for both sides; a somewhat hazardous occupation!

5 President Truman had a notice in his office: "The buck stops here". The White House is still the final authority and also holds the final responsibility for decisions made from intelligence assessments.

5 ▲

The establishment of "requirements" is a crucial part of the intelligence process in any system. The available information is so vast and the resources, even for such large agencies as KGB and CIA, are so limited that great care must be taken in defining and prioritizing what must be learned.

In the Soviet system, the right to establish requirements is thought to be limited to a small number of people at the very top of the Soviet hierarchy. One of the advantages of the US system—characteristic of other democratic nations as well—is that civilian and military officials down to very low echelons can state intelligence requirements and obtain support from high-level agencies as resources become available.

In theory, the US intelligence process begins when the President or one of his principal aides states a requirement. In actuality there are few direct requests from the President, most requirements being established by lower ranking officials in anticipation of events likely to attract Presidential attention. Thus there is a continuing surveillance in process in most key areas. When special requirements do arise the Director of Central Intelligence (who is also Director of the Central Intelligence Agency) assigns tasks to the appropriate agency which prepares a National Intelligence Estimate (NIE). The draft NIE is then reviewed by a National Intelligence Co-ordinating Council. If approved, it is sent to the President and distributed to other officials deemed to have a "need to know". This process can be completed in a few hours if the need is urgent.

To provide for emergencies, a "Watch Committee" composed of CIA and DIA officers stands by throughout the day and night. When important indicators begin to show up these officers can prepare in a matter of hours or minutes what amounts of an ad hoc "National Intelligence Estimate" on the probability of imminent hostilities. This is sent to the most senior intelligence officials and the White House. It is probably this "Watch Committee" that would make the crucial assessment that an enemy attack was about to occur, and it is this quickly assembled data that would confront a President possibly shaken out of a deep sleep in the early hours of the morning and required to decide the fate of the world in the next 15 to 20 minutes.

Inadequate communication

When time is available, the NIE appears as a formally published document distributed to Government officials and allies on a "need-to-know" basis. If the "need to know" is defined too narrowly, operating agencies and individuals essential to success of an operation could be excluded. Something of that sort happened, apparently, in the Iran rescue raid as actually attempted.

Also, the best intelligence in the world can be rendered useless by inadequate or incompetent planning, or by confusion and delay induced by poor command structures. Those elements of failure were apparent in 1968 when North Korean gunboats succeeded in capturing the US Navy ship *Pueblo* from under the noses of what were

then clearly the most powerful navy and air force in the world. Much of the blame for "intelligence failures" heaped on the CIA and the other US intelligence agencies in recent years should have been directed, therefore, to this continuing weakness in the US military planning and command system.

As discussed in chapter 1, the overall record of the CIA and the American intelligence system in general during the past 30 years indicates that it is not as good, in terms of long-range "strategic" intelligence, as that of the best journalism and scholarship in the non-Communist world. In short, the record shows that there is enough information on the public record at any given time to enable the trained observer to make a judgement about long-range national interests, objectives and policies that is at least as good as the judgement of the intelligence agencies.

The CIA's record in regard to current intelligence is somewhat better, as indeed it should be considering the technical resources available. The United States apparently was able to warn Israel in 1973 of an impending Egyptian attack, but the warning was ignored. The much-maligned CIA clandestine service, also apparently was able to warn US diplomats in 1981 of possible Libyan terrorist attacks, leading one to wonder if the former CIA agents in Libya's employ are "working both sides of the street".

Although it dealt with operational data—that is, "friendly" forces information rather than intelligence of enemy forces—the blockage cited earlier of Army War College information badly needed by the US Joint Chiefs of Staff indicates that compartmentalization and sequestering of information occurs in the American system as well as in the Soviet system. In fact, a senior European intelligence officer feels that, in meeting with senior US intelligence officials, "part of my job seems to be giving information from one US intelligence service to another since otherwise the information might not filter through quickly enough".

Supposedly disagreements in the development of National Intelligence Estimates are recognized by permitting dissenting agencies to record their views in footnotes. In practice those who have examined the US estimates over the years believe that they are characterized by the bland mediocrity typical of all bureaucratic committee work. Worse, once published, US intelligence officers throughout the system tend to regard the NIEs as "gospel truth". Indeed, to challenge them is to challenge the judgement of the high intelligence officials who wrote the estimates, and they are the same people who promote or demote. For many years, for instance, those in the CIA who challenged the prevailing judgement that the Sino-Soviet conflict did not present a serious, long term threat of war were simply denied promotion.

In spite of this suffocating bureaucratic burden a former chief of NATO intelligence credits individual American intelligence officers with "brilliant performance". Hopefully the system will someday be revised to assist rather than hinder such performance.

Chapter three

The world-wide intelligence exchange

SELDOM DOES a single item of information delivered to a single military or political agency emerge as "approved intelligence" on which governmental or military policy or action can be based. Usually thousands, even millions, of bits of information that flow in from the array of sources discussed in this book must be sifted and compared by the organizations described in the previous chapter before any meaningful picture begins to emerge.

This process is further complicated by the fact that only two nations—the United States and the Soviet Union—possess the full array of modern collection capabilities. Even with those nations, no single agency possesses all the means necessary to collect and properly assess the mass of data available. By some means or other, therefore, there must be a sharing of information among nations and among agencies within nations.

There are two broad categories of intelligence sharing—formal and informal. Formal sharing of information and of finished intelligence *within* each nation is the product of how well or how poorly the government is organized and, in the military sphere, the extent to which the armed services are able to overcome inherent rivalries and jealousies. At the international level, formal intelligence sharing is governed by treaties among coalitions, or as bilateral arrangements between one nation and another.

Far more important are the informal relationships. These spring from friendships between diplomats or military attaches, from mutually profitable working relationships between intelligence agencies of different countries and from agreements approaching the nature of a secret treaty.

An insight into the scope and importance of these informal relationships is provided by the information that recently has become available, by capture and publication of documents stolen from the US Embassy in Teheran, Iran, concerning Israeli intelligence relationships (as described in the previous chapter). Both Mossad (the foreign intelligence service) and Shin Beth (the internal security service) are shown in these documents to have had close working relationships with the Turkish, Ghanaian, Japanese, monarchist Iranian, Spanish, Portuguese, Austrian, South African, Singapore, Indonesian, Taiwanese, Thai, South Korean, Kenyan, Zairean and Liberian services. In addition, Israel is identified as a member of the "Kilowatt" group, "an organization which is concerned with Arab terrorism and is comprised of West Germany, Belgium, Italy, the United Kingdom, Luxembourg, Netherlands, Switzerland, Denmark, France, Canada, Ireland, Sweden and Norway". And then there is, of course, the vast and intimate intelligence relationship with the United States, very little of it based on formal treaty agreements.

The American-Israeli "connection" came about because of the role of the United States and the American Jewish community in establishing Israel as an independent nation. A common interest in combating terrorism gave birth to the Kilowatt group. Other relationships came about through invitations to Israel to train the security services of newly independent nations, such as Ghana and Liberia. Relationships with Iran and Turkey were sought "to break the Arab ring encircling Israel".

Strangely enough, the emergence of what may be the world's most extreme Muslim government, in Iran, did not eliminate Mossad connections with Iran. Israel, it now turns out, is one of the major arms suppliers for the post-Shah Iranian government, providing a continuing, albeit much more limited, intelligence link. One purpose of this seemingly inexplicable link, according to Western intelligence sources quoted by the New York *Times,* is "to weaken the Iraqi Government and army by keeping Iranian armed forces in the field and fighting". In short, Mossad's true intelligence capability through its connection with the Shah's government was lost, only to be replaced by a relationship involving its operational "covert action" arm. The latter relationship, however, implies a net loss of information—the difference between mutual confidence and a hard-eyed, buyer-seller exchange.

Israel, South Africa and Taiwan see a mutuality of interest as the world "pariahs". Afraid that it is being betrayed into the hands of its mortal enemies by American infatuation with new-found friends in Peking, Taiwan plainly is establishing its own worldwide intelligence network. Both Israel and South Africa have similar apprehensions, although for different reasons. They see a common interest in trading intelligence as a matter of mutual survival.

The importance of intelligence sharing is illustrated most vividly, perhaps, by the

1 Israeli Prime Minister Begin with US President Reagan. The USA has gained a vast amount of intelligence from Israeli sources which may help explain the latitude given by the US to its frequently wayward Mid-East ally.

1 ▲

Most countries have a greater thirst for intelligence than can
be satisfied by their own agencies. They therefore
set up networks of cooperation—both formal and informal—
with other countries, agencies and even individuals,
which can lead to some very curious relationships.

Israeli relationship in Lebanon. The Christian militiamen provide Israel with advance warning of Palestinian and Syrian moves that endanger Israel, and the Israelis provide the Christian communities with intelligence about intra-Arab developments, as well as other support, that could be obtained from no other source.

Israel's intelligence relations with France have varied with the shifts of government in France. As with the United States, however, Israeli access to French Government and society depends less on governmental agreements than on the sympathy of Jews and of non-Jews who feel a sense of guilt over Hitler's persecution of the Jews. Detailed Israeli knowledge of the Iraqi nuclear reactor, attacked by Israeli warplanes in June 1981, almost certainly came from French technicians who were working on the reactor, possibly relayed through personal, informal channels. Israel's own nuclear weapons programme is based entirely on such relationships.

Out of this network of informal intelligence relationships, therefore, Israel has been able to operate on a worldwide scale on the basis of small national intelligence investment.

The capstone of this worldwide Israeli network supposedly was access to US satellite intelligence which was gained, according to Gen. Sharon, former Israeli Defence Minister, as a result of one of Israel's few formal intelligence agreements, part of the "strategic cooperation pact" signed by Israel with the United States in March 1981. Whether the access survived Israeli Prime Minister Begin's cancellation of the cooperation agreement in December 1981 is not known.

Brutal Israeli methods

It is apparent from the attack on the USS *Liberty,* cited in the first chapter, and from Israeli efforts to penetrate US diplomatic and security services, cited in the Teheran documents, that the extensive formal and informal intelligence-sharing arrangements are not seen as any reason by the Israelis to spare the United States from the sometimes brutal Israeli intelligence-gathering and counter-intelligence methods. Whether that is wise in the long run remains to be seen.

Following publication of the Central Intelligence Agency analysis of the Israeli services, Richard Beeston, Washington correspondent of London's *Daily Telegraph,* established from diplomatic sources that the counter-terrorism intelligence-sharing organization "Kilowatt" was established to trade information about Libyan as well as Palestine Liberation Organization groups—acting "as a centre for banks of information on terrorist organizations, operatives, methods and links", much as Interpol acts as an international clearing house for information on ordinary criminals.

The United Nations provides an almost infinite means of informal intelligence-sharing, benefiting, in particular, the many nations too small or too poor to support a worldwide, or even a regional intelligence service. As indicated earlier, it is in this major "mart" for intelligence-sharing that

1 ▲

2 ▲

3 ▲

1 Israel's pursuit of her national interest is totally uncompromising, and when the USS *Liberty* got too close for comfort in June 1967 Israeli aircraft struck without warning to force her to leave the area.

2 US Defense Secretary Weinberger speaking to the Press as US Marines disembark in Beirut in late 1982. US reactions in the Lebanon have been due, at least part, to a desire to be seen by Americans and others to limit violent Israeli actions.

3 Top Warsaw Pact generals at a post-exercise review, accompanied by General Castro-Ruz of Cuba (left). All appears friendly on the surface and the Pact has a veneer of mutual cooperation between equals. In fact, the USSR controls the Pact forces with a rod of iron, especially their intelligence services. The intelligence flow tends also to be one-way, towards the Soviet Union, with the KGB/GRU apparently allowing little to flow in the other direction.

4 A Soviet Air Force Bear strategic reconnaissance aircraft being "intercepted" by a USAF F-14 just off the eastern coastline of continental USA. The Soviet Air Force uses Cuban airfields regularly for such "snooping" missions.

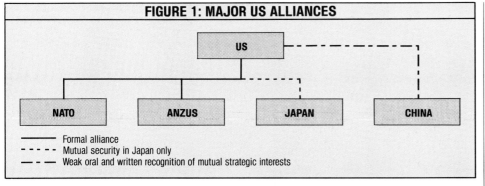

FIGURE 1: MAJOR US ALLIANCES

US

NATO — ANZUS — JAPAN — CHINA

——— Formal alliance
- - - - Mutual security in Japan only
— — — Weak oral and written recognition of mutual strategic interests

FIGURE 2: SOVIET COMBINED FORCES PEACETIME ADMINISTRATIVE AND INTELLIGENCE LINKAGES

Central Committee
Communist Party of the Soviet Union

General Staff

Military Districts (Western USSR) — Soviet Military Representation in the Middle East, Africa and Asia — Warsaw Pact Countries — Sino-Soviet Border

(Based on Brig. J. Hemsley's *Soviet Command and Control.* p 335).

4 ▲

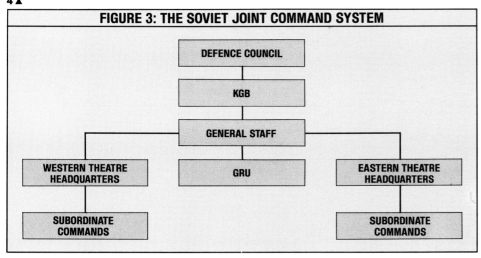

FIGURE 3: THE SOVIET JOINT COMMAND SYSTEM

DEFENCE COUNCIL

KGB

GENERAL STAFF

WESTERN THEATRE HEADQUARTERS — GRU — EASTERN THEATRE HEADQUARTERS

SUBORDINATE COMMANDS — SUBORDINATE COMMANDS

the small nations can trade-off bits of important information about their immediate neighbours for intelligence that the larger nations have gathered about worldwide or regional developments.

By some fashion or other, formal or informal, all nations must somehow gain access to the worldwide intelligence available only from the United States or the Soviet Union. The most obvious way of accomplishing this would seem to be through direct alliance (figures 1 and 2). It is not, however, as simple as all that—the nature of those alliances being the determining factor.

The difference between the two sets of alliances that shapes all intelligence relationships is that the system headed by the Soviet Union is in most, but not all, cases an imposed system of alliances, while that headed by the United States is in all cases a matter of free association. There are strengths and weaknesses on both sides. To understand these, it is first necessary to understand how intelligence is shared *within* the two major systems concerned.

By and large, the Western nations and Japan permit a relatively free flow of intelligence throughout their governmental structures. Although controlled in all cases by a "need to know", very little information is restricted only to a few people at the top. Operating on the belief that the entire structure functions best when its parts are fully informed, the greater part of what these nations learn is rather freely circulated. In general, there are far more *bureaucratic* obstacles to information in the Western and Japanese democracies than obstacles of true security "classification".

As described earlier, there are two principal intelligence-gathering agencies in the Soviet Union—the KGB and the GRU. As an arm of the Intelligence Directorate of the General Staff the GRU receives information from a worldwide network of agents directed by Soviet military attaches abroad and, also, from the intelligence staffs of the Soviet Army, Navy and Air Force (figure 3). Tactical intelligence gathered by Soviet Army units in combat against guerrillas in Afghanistan, for instance, is relayed up the military chain of command to the General Staff. Soviet Tu-95s flying reconnaissance missions out of Cuba along the East Coast of the United States might report through naval channels to the General Staff, or direct to the naval branch of the GRU in Moscow.

The principal feature of the Soviet intelligence system is tight compartmentation. In the totally bureaucratized Soviet state, where information is often the substance of personal as well as official survival, this compartmentation can be carried to such extremes that often only a few people at the top have all of the pieces necessary to make sense out of a particular development. During one of the Strategic Arms Limitation Talks (SALT) meetings, for example, a US delegate was asked by a Soviet delegate not to speak too openly on information about Soviet strategic weapons, since some of the Soviet delegation were not cleared to know such details!

Students in NATO and elsewhere of the Soviet system warn, however, that the tight control of intelligence at the top of the Soviet pyramid can be loosened when it is deemed necessary to provide for more rapid, local analysis of regional developments. These observers confirm that the normal channels of Soviet intelligence are rigid and compartmented, represented by family tree lines in figure 4. They believe, however, that the Soviets can and do link those primary channels at whatever level is necessary, maintaining such linkage only as long as is necessary to cope with the immediate situation.

It has long been open knowledge, confirmed most recently by a KGB defector, Vladimir Kuzichkin, that the KGB "ran the show" in Afghanistan through successive regimes beginning in 1973 and culminating in the installation of Babrak Karmal in 1979. While the KGB continues to occupy a central role, the occupation of Afghanistan by Soviet forces and the resultant guerrilla war would have necessitated some form of intelligence sharing at the local level, as represented by the lower band in figure 4. Possibly more portentious, however, is the linkage that emerged in 1979 in the Soviet Far East.

From US and Japanese sources it is now possible to establish that the Soviets established at Chita on the Sino-Soviet border what amounts to a theatre headquarters, combining control of the Soviet Pacific Fleet with the land and tactical air forces of the Transbaykal and Far East military districts stretching across 1,000 miles (about 1,600km) of the frontier. Only twice before in their history had the Soviets established such a headquarters—once to control the Soviet assault on Japanese forces in Manchuria in 1945 and again, in 1947-1953, during and immediately after the Chinese Civil War.

That the Soviets were anticipating immediate military operations during the 1947-53 period, as well as in 1945, is apparent from information that subsequently became available in the West. It is now known, for example, that the Soviets made an offer to the Nationalistic commander in Sinkiang in 1949 to set him up as an independent Nationalist entity backed by Soviet forces, but the Chinese commander was not able to clear this with the Nationalist government, by then in Canton, before he was overwhelmed by the Chinese Communist forces. Furthermore, the Chinese Communists themselves have acknowledged that Kao Kang, a Communist chieftain in Manchuria, was in active consultation with the Soviets looking toward the establishment of an indepedent Manchurian state, during precisely the years up to 1953 that the Soviet theatre headquarters was being maintained.

Soviets in Far East

On August 3, 1981, according to Gregory C. Baird, reporting in the *US Naval War College Review,* the Chinese called the reestablishment of the Soviet Far East command structure a "war zone command headquarters". Thus was formed the upper level band shown in figure 4, plainly, as the NATO observers have indicated, in response to

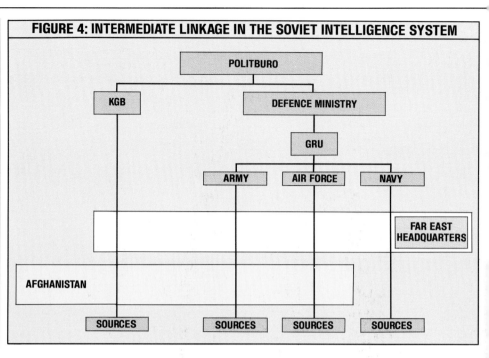

FIGURE 4: INTERMEDIATE LINKAGE IN THE SOVIET INTELLIGENCE SYSTEM

1 Soviet SA-4 Ganef surface-to-air missile launcher and its crew alongside the main runway at Kabul airport in Afghanistan. The photograph was taken through the window of a civil airliner as an "opportunity" target.

2 New Soviet leader Yuri Andropov was previously head of the KGB, which ran the Soviet operation in Afghanistan from 1973 onwards, an involvement the Russians now believe is their "Vietnam". Was this an intelligence failure on their part?

1 ▲

2 ▲

what seems to be perceived by the Soviet leadership as a dangerous situation.

The Soviet ground forces officer who commands in the Far East and his deputy, the commander of the Soviet Pacific Fleet, probably control the military intelligence assets of the forces under their command, including the naval reconnaissance aircraft, submarines and surface ships that constantly patrol the international waters around Japan and sometimes intrude into Japanese territorial waters as well (see the map in chapter 2). The communications assets under their command are more than adequate to monitor communications traffic throughout Northeast Asia. Less certain is the degree of access the Soviet military command at Chita has to reports from GRU attaches and agents operating in Tokyo and other Asian capitals.

As is the case throughout the entire Soviet system, all of the information available to the military command headquarters at Chita is also available to the KGB, either directly through formal liaison channels or indirectly from the political officers, in effect KGB agents, at all levels in the Soviet military structure. The military has no such pervasive access to KGB information. It gets what the KGB thinks may be needed to perform a carefully circumscribed mission, and nothing more.

There are two Soviet allies in Northeast Asia—North Korea and Mongolia. Mongolia is totally under Soviet control with several Soviet divisions on Mongolian territory along major invasion routes into China. It is likely that there are local intelligence linkages between these Soviet units and the local Mongolian security and intelligence units. Through their own Asian population the Soviets have the means to penetrate the Mongolian services and to assure themselves that they are receiving every item of intelligence the Mongolians produce. The Mongolians may be able to pry out some information by a reverse use of such Asian ethnic channels, but what they get from the Soviets is mainly what the Soviets think they need to know.

The Soviet relationship with North Korea is considerably more complex. Although they were once as totally under Soviet control as are the Mongolians today, the North Koreans have been able to wriggle out from that control to a considerable degree by playing off the Chinese against the Russians, and vice versa, much as Marshal Tito in Yugoslavia played off the West against Russian dominance.

In recent years, the North Koreans have been seeking to wriggle further from under the Soviet net by indicating to the United States that they would like to end their present dependence on the Soviet Union *and* on China by seeking some sort of as yet ill-defined neutrality. Obviously, each step along this path has influenced the intelligence-sharing relationships with the Soviet Union and with China as well. The present situation can best be described as "byzantine". Distrusted by all and mistrusting all, North Korea pursues its own intelligence objectives aided by relationships it has managed to develop with other renegades, notably Libya and Iran, through arms sales

and service agreements such as pilot training programmes. Both the Soviet Union and China still gain some benefit from North Korean intelligence but the primary focus of the North Korean effort appears to be directed to finding a way to avoid being trampled if the two giants on its northern border go to war.

Cuba's intelligence relationship with the Soviet Union is somewhat analogous to that of Mongolia in that Cuba's communist government is totally dependent upon Soviet largesse for survival. Distance, however, and a cultural background totally foreign to that of the Soviet Union or any of its parts, enable Cuba to maintain intelligence channels of its own developed through guerrilla movements in Central and South America and the Cuban military presence in Africa. Agents implanted in the Cuban omigré population in the United States provide some information, but the strategic intelligence upon which the survival of Cuban Communism depends can come only from the Soviet collection capability, much of it based in Cuba but under Russian control.

Vietnam occupies a unique position in that it is dependent upon Soviet intelligence and other Soviet support only to the degree that it wishes to pursue its design for conquest of all Indochina and perhaps contiguous areas. It was that self-generated dependence that caused Vietnam to join the Soviet economic system and to grant the Soviets important electronic intelligence facilities at Da Nang, as well as landing rights for Soviet naval intelligence aircraft. A decision by a future Vietnamese government to seek peace and prosperity through association with the Association of Southeast Asian Nations (ASEAN) and Japan could produce a radical change in this situation, affecting Soviet intelligence operations throughout Southeast Asia.

Warsaw Pact input

Compared to the complexities of its intelligence situation in Asia, Soviet intelligence relations with its "partners" in the European Warsaw Pact are simple indeed. The Soviets simply demand and get any information that the East European nations obtain, and they make sure of this by implanting KGB and GRU agents quite openly within the "allied" intelligence agencies. Rumania is perhaps an exception to this since it has managed to distance itself somewhat from Soviet policy. It is very doubtful, however, that Rumanian intelligence is able to obtain or hold on to much that the Soviets don't learn from other sources or from agents within the Rumanian government itself.

"Sharing" is scarcely the word to describe the Warsaw Pact intelligence relationship. As indicated, the Soviets take everything the East European services produce. They give so little in return that the East European "allies" have been reduced to such bizarre expedients as inviting Western academic specialists on the Soviet military establishment to brief their military staffs on the Soviet order of battle. This totally lop-sided relationship is sustainable, of course, only because the East European Communist governments are acutely aware that they were carried into power on Soviet bayonets and are sustained there only by the reality, or the threat, of Soviet intervention.

There could scarcely be a more extreme contrast with this tightly controlled Soviet system than the "intelligence show" produced by the US State Department on March 9, 1982, in which the products of US aerial reconnaissance over Central America were put on display in the interest of gaining public, Congressional and Allied support for US Government policy in the region. Yet the essential human intelligence resources necessary to verify and supplement such technical sources were not all under the control of the US Government. As noted earlier, the best of these belong to private religious and charitable organizations which not only do not consider themselves necessarily as allies, much less servants, of the US Government, but which consider themselves to have been seriously damaged by past association or implications of association with the US Central Intelligence Agency. Anyone—including the US Government itself—wishing to arrive at a reasonably accurate assessment of the situation in Central America, therefore, would be obliged to consider not only what the Defense Intelligence Agency pictures showed, but also what the churches and other private agencies operating in the region had to say.

Much the same thing could have been said about French Government intelligence and policy during the last years of its African empire and of British Government policy in Ireland in more recent years. In short, no Western government can monopolise, even in wartime, the flow of information necessary to produce accurate intelligence to the extent to which this is done routinely in the Soviet sphere.

Is this a weakness or a strength? The answer to that question would seem to lie in an assessment of the relative efficiency with which intelligence is handled in the North Atlantic Treaty Organization (NATO) compared with the methods of its opposite Soviet organization, the Warsaw Pact.

In contrast to the Warsaw Pact arrangement, any of the 16 NATO members is free to withhold from the organization any or all of the information produced by its own intelligence services, all of which are as independent from one another as the nations they serve.

The several NATO headquarters shown in figure 5 exist in peacetime as planning organizations only. The NATO budget is notoriously austere, to the extent that the NATO headquarters might never be employed as such in actual operations, the respective commanders being more likely, at least in some instances, to rely on their better equipped national headquarters.

The NATO intelligence staffs, as such, are similarly austere. Their principal function is to gather what the 16 participating nations choose to make available for development of a common planning base. One of the important effects of this system is to provide an honourable means for the small NATO nations to gain an insight into regional and world problems without going cap-in-hand

to one of the larger members solely on a bilateral basis.

The NATO arrangement does not preclude bilateral arrangements and there are many such arrangements in existence. One of the closest of these is that between Canada and the United States, deriving obviously from the fact that both occupy the same land mass in direct line of fire across the polar region from Soviet bombers and missilry. There has been an intimate sharing of US and Canadian intelligence in the North American Air Defense Command for decades, enshrined in the Distant Early Warning (DEW) line of radar and related missile warning stations stretching across the arctic regions of Alaska and Canada.

The so-called "special relationship" between Britain and the United States that emerged during and following World War II has produced very close collaboration between the intelligence services of both countries, producing a continuous exchange of information in all areas. The arming of British submarines with Polaris and (as planned) Trident missiles, for example, implies the furnishing of US-produced target materials obtainable only from satellite sensors. Collaboration between the British Secret Intelligence Service and the Central Intelligence Agency, and between the British Internal Security Services and the US Federal Bureau of Investigation, is rooted in the World War II Office of Strategic Services relationship with the counterpart British services.

British intelligence in Ireland

The Northern Ireland problem has strenuously exercised British intelligence activities —which have included the age-old methods of assessment of reports from paid informers, detailed warnings of terrorist activities from specially trained Army personnel perilously living the life of undercover agents, evaluation of uniformed Army street patrols, through to the use of sophisticated reconnaissance equipment, day and night, especially at large crowd gatherings such as funerals of slain guerrillas or political meetings, when the familiar slap of helicopter rotor blades indicates that high resolution photography is being undertaken to establish the identity or presence of known guerrilla organization members who appear for propaganda purposes.

In addition to British Army intelligence units, the "Troubles" have drawn in the services of British espionage and counterespionage services, in Ireland and also in England, in attempts to counter guerrilla activities. Also involved have been the intelligence agencies of the Irish Police (Garda) and Army, of the United States (in respect at least of tracing the sources of captured weapons, reports of potential purchases of weapons for the outlawed Irish Republican Army—IRA—and in supplying information on the activities of Noraid, the fund-raising institution in North America), of West Germany (following bomb raids by the IRA on British bases in Germany), of other NATO nations with regard to tracking of IRA arms purchases abroad, and even, according to at least one report, of

1 ▲

1 The British intelligence services have been operating in Ireland for centuries, as English politicians have struggled to find answers to the "Irish problem". Here IRA gunmen man a Creggan estate roadblock during the heyday of the "no-go" areas which were ended in Operation Motorman on July 28, 1972.

2 The entrance to NORAD's command HQ deep in a mountain in the USA. The air defence of northern America clearly involves both the USA and Canada, and both countries work closely, sharing both operational tasks and intelligence responsibilities, a good example of a bilateral relationship.

3 NATO political leaders at one of their regular meetings, with Secretary-General Luns in the centre flanked by President Reagan and Mrs Thatcher. NATO has only a small intelligence staff of its own, with no collection ability at all. It depends, instead, on what the 16 participating nations care to contribute from their own operations, a flow which varies from one country to another. At meetings such as this there is an opportunity for top-level exchanges of intelligence tidbits which may have been held back, for nationalistic or bureaucratic reasons, at the lower operating levels. However, there is also concern about KGB "penetration" of NATO.

2 ▲

3 ▲

FIGURE 5: NATO ALLIED COMMAND EUROPE

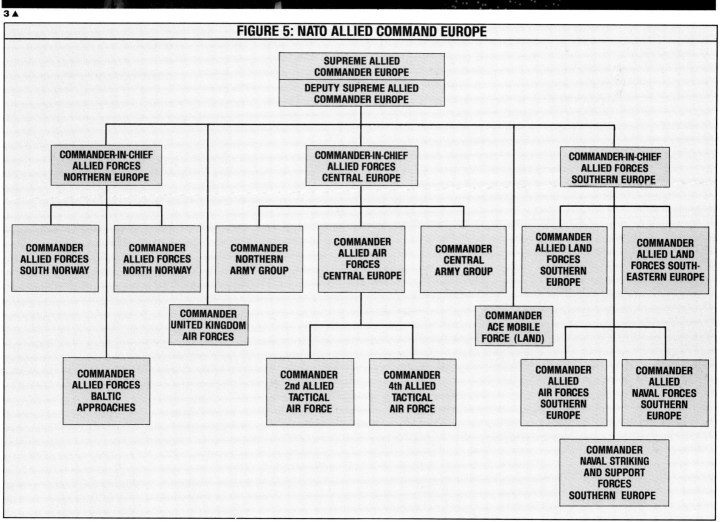

SUPREME ALLIED
COMMANDER EUROPE

DEPUTY SUPREME ALLIED
COMMANDER EUROPE

COMMANDER-IN-CHIEF
ALLIED FORCES
NORTHERN EUROPE

COMMANDER-IN-CHIEF
ALLIED FORCES
CENTRAL EUROPE

COMMANDER-IN-CHIEF
ALLIED FORCES
SOUTHERN EUROPE

COMMANDER
ALLIED FORCES
SOUTH NORWAY

COMMANDER
ALLIED FORCES
NORTH NORWAY

COMMANDER
NORTHERN
ARMY GROUP

COMMANDER
ALLIED AIR
FORCES
CENTRAL EUROPE

COMMANDER
CENTRAL
ARMY GROUP

COMMANDER
ALLIED LAND
FORCES
SOUTHERN
EUROPE

COMMANDER
ALLIED LAND
FORCES SOUTH-
EASTERN EUROPE

COMMANDER
UNITED KINGDOM
AIR FORCES

COMMANDER
ACE MOBILE
FORCE (LAND)

COMMANDER
ALLIED FORCES
BALTIC
APPROACHES

COMMANDER
2nd ALLIED
TACTICAL
AIR FORCE

COMMANDER
4th ALLIED
TACTICAL
AIR FORCE

COMMANDER
ALLIED
AIR FORCES
SOUTHERN
EUROPE

COMMANDER
ALLIED
NAVAL FORCES
SOUTHERN
EUROPE

COMMANDER
NAVAL STRIKING
AND SUPPORT
FORCES
SOUTHERN EUROPE

China with regard to the exposure of Libyan-IRA arms transactions.

Among the European members of NATO there is a skein of intelligence relationships reflecting all of the complex elements of ancient and modern European history. These range from the traditional ties of Britain's "Old Alliance" with Portugal to personal friendships based on the accident of whether a particular German intelligence officer was captured in 1945 by the British or the Americans, and, in at least one case, deriving from a lifelong friendship that grew up between a French prisoner of war and the aristocratic German family to whose farm he was assigned as a labourer.

In contrast to the tightly compartmented Warsaw Pact system, therefore, there is an enormous lateral flow of often highly technical military information through all elements of not only the NATO military structure but throughout the societies of the NATO nations. Not the least significant aspect of this relatively free flow of information is that much of it is picked up and published or broadcast every day by the news media, heard or read by citizens and military alike.

Because he or she is exposed literally from birth to these cross-currents of information it can be argued that the NATO intelligence officer does not need the support of a large, formal staff to arrive at an accurate planning assessment. Indeed, the deliberately small British national assessment system suggests that this is the case.

The NATO intelligence staffs cannot afford to rely, of course, on what they happen to hear on the television newscast or read in the morning newspaper. What, then, is the reliability of the "approved intelligence" that they receive from NATO's national intelligence staffs? NATO officers familiar with this flow of intelligence are firm in their belief that NATO never has lacked the intelligence necessary to carry out its assigned planning function in a timely and competent manner. In each case, of course, that evaluation is made not only on the basis of what the officer concerned knows of NATO intelligence but, also, in the light of his own national intelligence.

French intelligence and NATO

One of the most interesting aspects of NATO intelligence is the role played by France. Although France placed greater public emphasis on the fact that it was withdrawing from the *military* rather than the *political* NATO bodies, it is in the military rather than the political field that French intelligence has been most cooperative. French assessments arrive carefully written to "disembody" the information conveyed from any particular intelligence agency. The result, however, is that the French services participate fully and effectively in the overall NATO effort.

Practical results of this cooperative NATO intelligence effort have become so commonplace as to be accepted as the norm by the peoples of the Western democracies. A Turkish strategic assessment in December 1981, for example, warning of increasing tension in the dangerous Erzurum-Tbilisi-Tabriz triangle of Turkey, the Soviet Union and Iran, was consciously written as a NATO document, providing effective strategic warning in a manner difficult or impossible to achieve through cumbersome diplomatic channels. Released to a visiting British journalist, John Bulloch of London's *The Daily Telegraph,* the document served to warn the civilian populations as well.

This depth of information about the most sensitive strategic problems, in contrast to the paucity of such information outside of official channels in the Soviet bloc, is the great strength of the NATO system in contrast to the Soviet system of alliances, at least over the long term. That is, it is through the sharing of this information—much of it true "hard" intelligence—that the Western peoples arrive at the consensus needed to maintain a stable alliance.

The strength of the Soviet system is that it serves to create, but it does not guarantee, the best possible conditions for surprise —diplomatic, economic or military. Its great weakness lies in the brittleness of its imposed structures and ruthless exploitation. Also, the sequestering of information among a relatively small group greatly increases the danger of confusion and panic if the initial surprise fails or goes awry and, in particular, if the governing group is destroyed or dispersed.

Non-NATO US allies

There are extensive and important intelligence relationships outside of NATO, but with an important relationship to that alliance. The oldest and most formal of these is that of ANZUS (Australia, New Zealand and United States) involving a military alliance among these three countries. This relates directly to NATO in that the alliance supports and expands Australian surveillance of the Indian Ocean, the Arabian Sea and the Persian Gulf. Intelligence documents are circulated routinely among the ANZUS members. Each nation retains special markings for documents that are not to be shared with allies. In the United States the marking is "NOFORN" ("no foreign distribution").

The United States has a number of other important intelligence-sharing arrangements outside of NATO, each one a reflection of the nature of the overall diplomatic relationship. Although the United States and South Korea are members of a "Combined Military Command", the relationship is uneasy because of the refusal of successive South Korean military governments to permit a return to a fully democratic society and because of the imprisonment and other mistreatment of South Koreans fighting for such rights. Despite this, there is generally full sharing of military intelligence related to the security of South Korea, but a much more cautious sharing of political intelligence.

Even though the United States has agreed to sell a major intelligence system—the Airborne Warning and Control System (AWACS)—to Saudi Arabia, and is providing its own US Air Force AWACS aircraft in the interim, the Saudis have told the United States they will not share intelligence they

1 NATO officers chatting in the corridors. Even the best of Allies supplement the official channels by individual contacts both on and off duty, and at all levels—a useful form of communication.

2 Lord Carrington, former British Foreign Secretary, whispers into the ear of a fellow NATO Minister. Both political and military intelligence is exchanged in this way, and more likely to be trusted.

3 The USA is selling AWACS aircraft to Saudi Arabia, but the Saudis have said that once they have taken over the operation they will not share with the USA any intelligence gained from the aircraft.

4 Vessels of the NATO Standing Naval Force Atlantic (STANAVFORLANT). Such close cooperation in peacetime will lead to more effective operational and intelligence activities in war. Many members of NATO forces can, however, serve for years without actually meeting or working with other NATO partners.

5 A delegation from the Chinese People's Republic inspects the Space Shuttle. Sino/US ties are growing ever closer and there is a lot of cooperation in intelligence matters. A large monitoring station has been set up in NW China, replacing the US station in Iran which was lost in the Shah's fall.

4 ▲

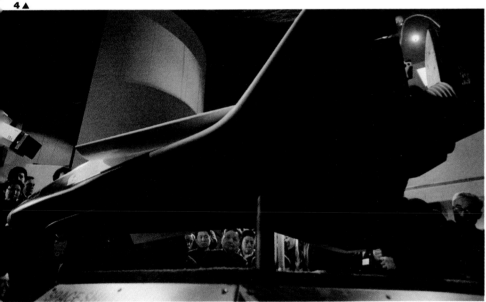

5 ▲

gather once they are operating their own AWACS aircraft. It is a relationship uncomfortably close to that which prevailed in US-Iranian intelligence relations prior to the fall of the Shah.

The CIA assessment of Israeli intelligence, published by the Iranian militants, makes it plain that there is a growing intelligence relationship among the Arab states surrounding Israel. There are improved communications security measures among the Arab states and an improved mutual sharing of the results of a growing Arab intercept capability. Very little of this, however, is shared with non-Arabs.

Following the fall of the Shah and the loss of important US communications and missile testing monitoring stations in Iran, the United States was successful in arranging for establishment of substitute stations in China. At first it appeared that the Chinese would agree only to accept and operate the equipment and pass on to the United States only what it pleased the Chinese to pass on. Subsequent press reports indicate that the stations are functioning, possibly with American technicians.

The entire question of intelligence-sharing between China and the United States is clouded by US suspicions of possible Chinese rapprochement with the Soviet Union and doubts about the stability of the post-Mao Chinese regime. On their part, the Chinese have made no secret of the fact that they consider the United States as "enemy No. 2" and that they intend to humiliate the United States by forcing it virtually to turn over Taiwan to Chinese Communist control —not a prescription for the sort of mutual trust and confidence that encourages full sharing of intelligence, or anything else.

There would be a US-Japan intelligence exchange fully on the scale of that with the NATO and ANZUS partners were it not for the fact that the Japanese have no laws for securing classified documents. A substantial interchange does occur, but under obvious limitations.

China has proven itself adept at gaining a vast amount of free military and technical intelligence from the industrialized nations by talking about large-scale future purchases of one sort or another. The designer of the excellent Japanese Type 74 tank was invited to Peking and is known to have held extensive discussions with Chinese military leaders. Chinese military delegations have "shopped" throughout Europe and the United States. Possibly more important, they have used student exchange arrangements as a means to penetrate Western and Japanese technical institutes while limiting Western and Japanese students in China largely to the humanities. Out of all of this they have obtained, free of cost, literally tons of technical data that would have cost a Western or Japanese customer very substantial fees.

Of great long-term significance is the quiet sharing of intelligence that has been growing steadily since the mid 1970s among Japan, South Korea and Taiwan. It was obvious that key military and civilian defence officials interviewed by this writer in all three countries in 1978 were well acquainted and shared a common base of

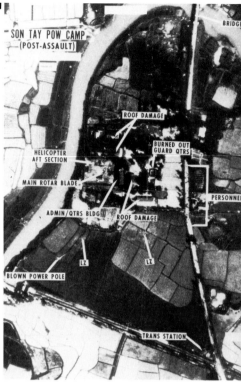

2 ▲

1 A Soviet trawler which does not appear to be devoting much effort to fishing. An alert officer at Strategic Air Command noted one day that there was a clear relationship between the positions of such trawlers and the routes SAC bombers would take to attack targets in the USSR. Further checks showed the trawlers were using EW radars.

2 A US force carried out an air assault on Son Tay PoW camp on November 30, 1970. Much was known about the camp (**3**) but on arrival it was found to be empty. The raid was commanded by Colonel Arthur 'Bull' Simons (**4**), a great fighting soldier (centre right). Afterwards the Government salved its conscience by handing out medals (**5**).

information. Unless war or some political catastrophe occurs, such as the successful subversion of Taiwan by Peking, it seems virtually certain that this quiet intelligence exchange will mature eventually into one of the world's key regional security systems. A similar system is already in existence in Southeast Asia where ASEAN, organized initially as an economic grouping among Indonesia, the Philippines, Malaysia, Thailand and Singapore, has taken on increasing military significance with a regular exchange of political, economic and military intelligence.

It would be a mistake to conclude that the nature of intelligence-sharing is governed entirely, or even primarily, by the nature of structural or diplomatic arrangements. How powerfully the human factor can influence these arrangements, even when there is no question of release of information to a foreign country, can be seen in the following incident.

Some years ago, an intelligence officer of a US Air Force Strategic Air Command heavy bomber wing noticed a report from the US Navy that Soviet fishing trawlers were operating in waters directly under the routes bombers from the unit would fly en route to targets in the Soviet Union. From photographs in the Navy report, the Electronic Countermeasures Officer of the bomber unit was able to determine that the

Soviet trawlers were equipped with early warning radar. It was immediately apparent that Soviet fighter-interceptors would receive warning of the precise track of the American bombers well over a thousand miles — and well over an hour — before the bombers would be picked up by Soviet continental radars, assumed up to then to be the first warning the Soviets would receive of the attacking bombers.

A message was sent through the intermediate Air Force headquarters to Headquarters, Strategic Air Command, asking for continued surveillance and more information from the Navy.

"You are in the Air Force," came back the reply. "Let the Navy run their business and you run yours."

Nevertheless, the trawlers were plotted on the Air Force unit's operations and intelligence maps. Some months later, one of these maps was used by the commander of the wing to brief Maj. Gen. John B. Montgomery, then commanding the wing's next higher headquarters.

"Say, Bert," General Montgomery asked of the briefer, "what are those little boats you have pasted there?"

When their significance was explained to him, Montgomery exclaimed "Dear God!", and agitatedly asked his intelligence officer, "Did you know anything about this, Rocky?" A greatly embarrassed Rocky knew all about

it, since the messages had passed through his hands and he had deemed it discreet not to question the judgement passed down from Strategic Air Command, or even to report it to Montgomery. The upshot of it all was that for years thereafter those "little boats" appeared on maps showing the Soviet threat to US Air Force wartime operations. So the information finally got through to everybody who "needed to know", but only after months of delay.

Dangerous jealousies

Inter-service jealousies exist not only among the military services of a particular country but among their civilian intelligence and security services as well. In his several books on the infiltration of the British security services by Communist agents, the British journalist Chapman Pincher cites numerous instances in which service pride prevented full investigation of suspicions, leading to enormous damage and even loss of life through betrayal of agents by traitors in high places who could otherwise have been identified and prosecuted long before.

Even the integration of several services, such as illustrated in figure 3 as concerns the Soviet services, does not provide a guarantee against human tendencies to concentrate on the "trees" rather than the "forest". The US "Joint" command structure,

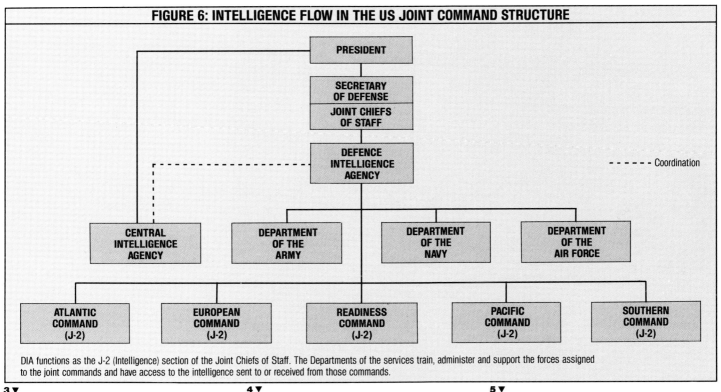

DIA functions as the J-2 (Intelligence) section of the Joint Chiefs of Staff. The Departments of the services train, administer and support the forces assigned to the joint commands and have access to the intelligence sent to or received from those commands.

3 ▼   4 ▼   5 ▼

combining Army, Navy, Air Force and Marine components in particular geographic areas (figure 6), was intended specifically to improve the flow of information.

As concerns the West, at least, integration of services under "joint" arrangements have proven to be no panacea. Charges of "intelligence failures" have been raised about a succession of major operations, in particular the 1970 American raid on Son Tay, North Vietnam, to rescue prisoners of war thought to be held there, the 1979 attempt to free American hostages in Iran, and the 1982 Falklands War between Britain and Argentina.

A great many factors contribute to the success or failure of complex operations like the Son Tay or Iran raids. Far more are involved in a decision by two nations to go to war, declared or undeclared. Care should be taken, therefore, in addressing the question of how these alleged "intelligence failures" came about.

If there was an "intelligence failure", was it a failure of collection, analysis or dissemination? If there were true "failures" in any or all of those components of the intelligence process, were there mistakes and failures in other aspects of planning and decision-making that compounded failures of intelligence, or which were so gross as to make the deficiencies in intelligence irrelevant?

Thanks to the work of Benjamin F.

Schemmer in *The Raid,* we have a reasonably clear picture of the events leading up to the raid on Son Tay and the conduct of the raid itself. Far from an "intelligence failure", the record shows a stunning success, in that the American prisoners were able to transmit through the US reconnaissance system, by arrangements of clothing on wash lines and spoil from building projects, not only that 55 American prisoners were at Son Tay—a small camp 23 miles (37km) west of Hanoi —but that six of them were in need of immediate medical attention!

Prompt decisions needed

That information was received and confirmed by American authorities in May 1970. On July 14, 1970, the Son Tay camp was evacuated to avoid flood waters. When the raid on a "dry hole" was conducted in November, US authorities knew that the camp had been evacuated and then re-occupied, but there was no evidence that it was in use again as a prison camp.

Intelligence, in particular of the sort transmitted by the prisoners at Son Tay, is not something that can be put into storage and then taken out fresh and viable months later when it is finally "convenient" to put it to use. There must be a prompt decision to act or not to act. If the decision is affirmative, action must follow decision in a matter of

hours or, at the most, days. For that sort of speed the authority and the means to act must be near at hand.

In the case of Son Tay the decision was delayed by authorities in Washington. Two weeks were wasted right off the bat, briefing Pentagon staff agencies. Another 10 days were lost because the US Joint Chiefs of Staff were engaged in a round of "retirement ceremonies, speeches and welcoming parties". With half a million US troops in Southeast Asia, the Joint Chiefs proceeded to organize a Joint Army and Air Force raiding party from scratch *in the United States.* More time and effort was consumed by arranging for special permission for the raid commander to be admitted to Vietnam because he was not a war college graduate and the Vietnam command had ordained that only colonels who were war college graduates could serve in the theatre as combat commanders.

As it turned out, the non-war-college graduate conducted a brilliant raid. Although foredoomed to failure—at least as concerns its primary purpose—by transfer of the prisoners, the raid forced a concentration of prisoners that produced a dramatic improvement in their condition and shook the military authorities not only of North Vietnam but also of China and the USSR.

In the case of the Iran raid intelligence again was not the problem. The general

1 ▲

2 ▲

1 A USAF F-16 fighter-bomber deploys to Korea as part of a plan to place two squadrons of these aircraft within striking distance of the major Soviet Navy base at Vladivostok. This deployment took place as a result of an individual's initiative and after a major rearguard action by a territorial commander a very determined team.

2 The daring Entebbe raid is described at a Press conference by Israeli chief-of-staff Lt. Gen. Mordecai Gur. The Israeli's intelligence is not that much better than anyone else's; their success stems from an ability to put that intelligence to rapid and effective operational use in a sound, simple and workable plan.

3 ▲

3 RH-53 helicopters in desert camouflage rehearse aboard USS *Nimitz* for the raid to free the US hostages from the Embassy in Teheran when the mission failed in a desert collision, eight Americans lost their lives. The Iranians ensured US humiliation in a disgusting publicity display.

4 Shortly afterwards a sad, chastened President Carter announces the failure of the operation. The USA had voluminous intelligence on Iran as a result of decades of cooperation with the Shah's military and civil authorities. The raid appears to have failed through unsound operational plans and poor passage of information rather than through any major deficiencies in intelligence.

4 ▲

location of the prisoners was known. From visits by clergymen, other foreigners and possibly from clandestine channels as well the location of every American hostage within the Teheran Embassy compound may well have been known with exactitude. Former President Jimmy Carter has stated in his memoirs that agents disguised as a photo-documentary team managed to get into Teheran. These or other US agents were able to organize a covert network within the country sufficient to produce a fleet of trucks and other essential logistic support. From decades of close association with the Iranian armed forces, the United States had ample reliable intelligence on every usable landing area, the city of Teheran itself and other relevant data. The likelihood of sandstorms at certain times of the year certainly was no news to the US Air Weather Service that had been represented in Iran for years. Yet it appears that such forecasts *were not provided to the operators of the raid,* or at least to the helicopter pilots who were to participate.

The Iran raid ended in disaster at a desert assembly area in Iran—the final stopping point preparatory to the attack. The decision to cancel had nothing to do with lack of intelligence, except as concerns failure to disseminate the weather data which in turn resulted in the loss of the inexplicably thin margin of helicopter support needed to complete the operation.

The collision between an Air Force C-130 and a Marine helicopter at the desert assembly site, which resulted in the loss of eight American lives and subsequent bitter recriminations in the press between un-named Army and Marine "sources", also had nothing to do with an "intelligence failure". But it did symbolize and drama-tize failures in high-level strategic assess-ment, excessive centralization of authority, incompetent high-level planning and uncon-trolled bureaucratic competition.

Although laundered ("whitewashed" if you will) by a subsequent Joint Chiefs' inquiry, enough information is now on the record from journalists such as Drew Middleton of the New York *Times* and high officials of President Jimmy Carter's admini-stration to confirm that the Iran failure, and the crippling delay of the Son Tay operation, are the products of a deeply flawed US military command and planning process.

How deep these flaws go can be seen in the following incident. As a member of the US Army War College faculty, in 1980, this writer initiated a study of means to exploit the relatively favourable US strategic posi-tion in the North Pacific to restrain Soviet actions in such areas of Soviet superiority as the Persian Gulf. Two US Marine Corps officers, then students at the War College, offered to participate. Just as one of those officers was to depart on a trip to the Aleutian Islands to gain a first-hand impres-sion of the operating area, the trip was cancelled by order of the US Pacific Command (PACOM)—the US joint command responsible for the entire Pacific.

Later it was learned that the Deputy Commander of PACOM had heard that the North Pacific study might include consider-ation of a "Northeast Asia Command" long proposed by US Army sources as a means of preventing further disasters such as the loss of an intelligence-gathering ship, the USS *Pueblo,* to the North Koreans in 1968. A Northeast Asia Command would be carved out of the PACOM domain. The mere mention of the thought was enough to get the Aleutians study cancelled. The War College simply lacked the gumption to override the PACOM interference. Fortu-nately, I was able to interest a military advisor to the incoming Reagan Admini-stration in the results of that and previous inquiries into the subject. A North Pacific strategy was inaugurated in September 1982, with a major US Navy exercise near the Aleutians and a concurrent announcement that two squadrons of US F-16 fighter-bombers are to be stationed within striking distance of Vladivostok. That success was achieved, however, only by circumventing the established planning process.

In an article published in the New York *Times* Magazine on November 7 1982, Gen. David C. Jones, then just recently retired as Chairman of the Joint Chiefs of Staff, confirmed the basic planning weaknesses described here.

The Entebbe raid contrast

This shabby record of what is supposedly one of the world's "superpowers" contrasts with the performance of the Israeli Defence Forces (IDF) in the July 4, 1976, Entebbe raid by which a planeload of hostages were freed. The IDF raid on the Ugandan airfield was conducted over a distance twice as great as the Iran raid and five times greater than the Son Tay raid.

In an interview with the author on November 30, 1982, Lt. Gen. Mordecai Gur, Chief of Staff of the IDF at the time of Entebbe, declined to comment directly on the Son Tay and Iran raids—except as concerns the latter—"The results speak for themselves". From his description of the available intelligence, however, it is clear that the Israelis had no better intelligence than the Americans as concerns either the Son Tay prison camp, at least initially, or the hostage situation at Teheran. The differences are entirely in the realm of organization, planning and execution— "operational", not intelligence matters.

"From the time of the rebuilding of the Israeli forces after the Yom Kippur War in 1973," General Gur stated, "we created a capability to conduct such a long-range operation. We did not create a single specialized force. What we used at Entebbe was drawn from four different sources. Each of those elements, however, was responding to a common plan and worked at developing capabilities that would support the plan."

Those separate elements were fused into a single force in 24 hours. "Although they were from separate commands," General Gur said, "the leaders all knew each other, and I knew what each of them could or could not do. Throughout the operation they could recognize each other by voice and I, also, could identify them by their voices over the radio."

General Gur emphasized the importance

of understanding the difference between Israel as a small, beleaguered nation accustomed to thinking of threats in terms of seconds, and the United States with a size and population that enables it to think and act more slowly.

With that distinction kept in mind the position General Gur occupied as overall raid commander at IDF Headquarters equates more to that of the Joint commander in a US overseas theatre. In the case of the Son Tay raid authority never was delegated to the theatre commander, and in the case of the Iran raid only fragmentary authority was delegated to the naval commander in the Indian Ocean. It was as though a national command authority in Rome or Paris had retained control of the Entebbe raid, cutting General Gur's headquarters out of the picture. The result, as shown earlier, is that it took months to assemble, train, equip and transport the Son Tay raiders to an assault position—a process completed by the Israelis in 24 hours. In the Iran raid cohesion never was achieved. Communications in both American raids were a major problem, although the US forces were operating with vastly greater resources than were available to the Israelis. In the case of the Son Tay raid, at least, that was a direct product of introducing an overall joint raid commander

into a theatre communications network that he could not possibly have mastered in the time available.

In short, the information now on the public record leads to the conclusion that the Washington military bureaucracy is so smothered in its own red tape and bureaucratic rivalries that it is incapable of making use of the intelligence available in a timely and competent manner or of delegating authority to someone who can and will so act. Worse, in the case of the overall disaster in Vietnam and of the almost humiliating failure of the Iran raid, the Washington defence bureaucracy demonstrated that it is unable or unwilling to provide top civilian authority with an accurate assessment of risks, or, in the case of the military chiefs, to resign when those warnings are ignored.

All of this was portended in 1968, when a National Security Agency warning that the North Koreans planned to seize the *Pueblo* was "lost" on a Defense Intelligence Agency clipboard for three weeks while the military command structure in Asia waited for its "letter from the Pentagon" before acting to protect the ship and its crew—repeating the entire "Pearl Harbor" process in miniature.

Except for the DIA bumbling in the *Pueblo* incident and the failure of weather data

dissemination during the Iran raid, all of these successive disasters point squarely to failures of planning, strategic assessment and military-political coordination at the highest levels, rather than to "intelligence failures".

Talk of an "intelligence failure" in regard to the Falklands War of 1982, also, will not stand close analysis. The fact that Britain retains responsibility for its citizens and property in Hong Kong, the Falkland Islands, Gibraltar and other distant locations is "confirmed intelligence" to any schoolchild who can read a geography book. The decision to orient the Royal Navy entirely towards its North Atlantic Treaty commitments, scrapping or selling the aircraft carriers essential to defence of far-flung residual sovereignty, had everything to do with budgets and nothing at all to do with intelligence.

For their part, the Argentinians ignored the history of at least a thousand years in concluding that Britain would acquiesce to blatant aggression against the Falklands and, in particular, to the extension to the population of the islands of a military regime that has apprehended without due process and tortured and murdered thousands of its own citizens. For one thing, it was as if the Argentinians had not the slightest notion of

1 ▲

2 ▲

1 Argentinian marines returning to a US Navy LST at the end of a joint exercise (UNITAS) in 1981. The following year UK intelligence failed to appreciate what the Argentines intended, despite several clear signals; equally Argentina totally underestimated British reactions, ignoring the lessons of history.

2 A machine-gun mounting on the side rail of a British ship during the Falklands War. There has been no shortage of warning about the threat posed by modern attack aircraft but the Royal Navy found itself short of early-warning and of close-in defences. Perhaps these are now being put right.

3 The Royal Navy's destroyer HMS *Cardiff* returns in triumph from the Falklands War. The British success was remarkable and well-deserved, but it was also in many ways the result of what Wellington had referred to at Waterloo as "a damned close-run thing". For the Argentines it was an almost total national disaster, and extremely humiliating. It is, however, debatable as to how much influence intelligence has in such an emotionally-charged atmosphere as that of Argentina in late 1981/early 1982. It is to be hoped that wiser counsel now prevails. There can now be no doubt about Britain's reaction to further Argentinian military aggression.

3 ▲

the place the Spanish Inquisition enjoys, if that is the word for it, in British memory and mythology.

On both sides these were failures of strategic assessment, not of intelligence.

Once the war began, what properly should be termed intelligence omissions rather than "failures" began to emerge. It became apparent, early on, for instance, that surveillance by satellite is not as comprehensive as the viewers of television news and the readers of Sunday supplements have been led to believe. To support its British allies, the United States found it necessary to reorient its surveillance satellites to provide more effective coverage of the South Atlantic. If some press reports are to be believed, the Soviets did have good surveillance of the British Fleet and provided this to the Argentinians. Such information could have been produced, however, by submarines and fishing fleets or by penetration of British military intelligence. The latter possibility emerged in November 1982, with the arrest of Lance Corporal Philip Aldridge of the British Army Intelligence Corps, alleged to have had unauthorized contacts with the Soviet Embassy in London during the Falklands War.

Whatever the exact details, the Falklands experience served to emphasize that "resources" continue to play a crucial role in intelligence and that the greater Soviet investment in this regard may help it to overcome to some extent the technological advantage of the West in terms of satellites and related communications intelligence.

The loss of the British destroyer HMS *Sheffield* to an air-delivered Exocet missile during the Falklands campaign was clearly the product of the omission of wide-ranging electronic reconnaissance and countermeasures aircraft normally assigned to a fully capable aircraft carrier, but unavailable in the South Atlantic because of the faulty strategic assessment by the British Government cited earlier.

Anglo-American relations

Overall, the Falklands campaign demonstrated the importance of effective combined Anglo-American intelligence and operational planning on the one side, and, on the other, the inadequacy of ad hoc Argentinian measures to begin such relationships with whomsoever it could find after hostilities began. The long-established Anglo-American relationships were an important factor in enabling Britain to put together the largely unseen but vitally important command, control and logistical system that made it possible to regain the Falklands and to administer a humiliating defeat to the Argentinians in the process.

Although questionable in concept and flawed in execution, the American Iran raid also demonstrated the value of effective combined intelligence and planning relationships. From what now appears on the public record it seems obvious that an informal combined forces relationship with Egypt and Israel and a more formal relationship with Turkey made possible the deployment of US C-130 aircraft and plans for post-strike recovery with in-flight monitoring and assistance from Israel. Support also may have been provided directly by Saudi Arabia, although the presence of US AWACS aircraft in that country, capable of monitoring in-flight progress and communications on their own, may have obviated the need for direct support by the Saudis.

In general, it can be concluded that most nations with strong joint and combined relationships are able to obtain the intelligence needed for policy planning, but that errors of analysis and administrative blockages often defeat the best of the collection efforts. What might be done to avoid such assessment and planning failures is discussed in chapter 10, "The importance of coping with intelligence".

Chapter four

Espionage and counter-espionage

ESPIONAGE—spying—has been an aspect of human affairs since society began, so much so that when formal diplomacy was established aspects of espionage were given the protection of international law. The military attache system by which uniformed representatives of foregin military establishments are permitted to "spy" openly in the countries in which they are stationed is the most open expression of this curious arrangement.

The "extraterritoriality" granted by nations to each other's diplomatic delegations, by which the premises they occupy become an extension of their own country's "territory", makes such places a natural centre not only for the "open spying" of legal diplomacy but for all sorts of secret, illegal spying. This is a constant source of difficulty and embarassment to the professional diplomatic service, but there is no way of getting away from it—if it is assumed that such illegal activity is necessary and justified. This derives from the simple fact that only in the "extraterritoriality" of the embassy can there by any hope for maintaining secure communications with the homeland. This then sets the pattern by which all of modern espionage is conducted, that is, by extension of spy networks outward from the embassy with communications patterns of various sorts back to the embassy for retransmission to the homeland. Such retrans-

mission is accomplished by "diplomatic pouch"—mail supposedly protected from host nation search—or by coded radio or cable messages.

Unless hand-carried by diplomatic courier there is, in fact, no assurance that the privacy of the diplomatic pouch will be honoured. China, for example, has continually infringed the US diplomatic mail system from the time relations were re-established in 1979. All major nations make elaborate efforts to intercept and decode diplomatic communications as well as internal electronic communications of other nations.

Figure 1 summarizes the levels of espionage in descending order from open diplomacy at Level 1 to the illegal world of the spy in Level 3.

Until World War I considerable discretion was exercised to prevent espionage from interfering with accepted diplomatic activity. The deterioration of all social relationships that occurred as a consequence of that conflict—in particular, the ideological assault on the established social and international order by the Bolshevik government in Russia—led to a much more blatant usurpation of diplomatic privilege.

KGB espionage operations

No nation in history has made such extensive use of the diplomatic "cover" for espionage as has the Soviet Union. Indeed, it is generally believed that KGB agents account for as much as 70 per cent of the staffs of Soviet embassies in various "Third World" countries. At various times in Mexico and other Latin American and African countries the ratio of the Soviet "diplomatic" representation to the representation of those countries in Moscow has been as high as five to one. Among the industrialized nations, Britain has found it necessary, in 1971 to expel as many as 105 Soviet "diplomats" at one time. The US Federal Bureau of Investigation estimates KGB representation in Washington at about 50 per cent of the Soviet Embassy staff.

When it is considered that the KGB controls the espionage organizations of Poland, Czechoslovakia, East Germany and other Warsaw Pact countries, the total KGB representation in such capitals as Washington, London and Paris is truly amazing. To that total must be added, of course, the

FIGURE 1: THE LEVELS OF ESPIONAGE

LEVEL 1
DIPLOMACY
Social events, visits by scientific and cultural delegations, travel by military attaches, study of host nation newspapers, books, periodicals.

LEVEL 2
QUASI-OFFICIAL
Voluntary or involuntary reporting by businessmen, tourists, journalists and other travellers to home-country intelligence agencies. Recruitment of bona fide journalists, scholars, missionaries, etc., as continuing part-time intelligence sources.

LEVEL 3
THE SPY
Illegal insertion of agents to pose as bona fide citizens of the "target" country. Recruitment of foreign nationals to betray secrets of their home country. Encouragement of military and civilian government employees to defect openly with valuable information.

1 The embassy of the Soviet Union in London. The "extra-territoriality" granted by nations to each others' embassies makes them a natural centre for both the open "spying" accepted by all—but also, in some cases, for subversion.

1 ▲

Espionage is an unavoidable activity for most states, even
though politicians prefer to pretend that
they know nothing about it. Counter-espionage, part of
counter-intelligence measures, is simply
the unavoidable corollary of espionage itself.

representatives of Soviet Military Intelligence (GRU) and its alter egos in the "allied" Warsaw Pact embassies, as well as the KGB staffs in the Soviet and East European United Nations delegations and in airline, commercial, press and other "unofficial" areas of the Communist governments.

The Soviets' intelligence allies

As shown in chapter 3, the intelligence support the Soviet Union gets out of its other "allies," such as Vietnam and Cuba is determined by the nature of the overall Soviet political relationship with those countries and by geography. Cuba is undoubtedly a prime source of support throughout Latin America and in those parts of Africa where Cuban troops or advisers are deployed. Most of what the Soviets get from the Vietnam connection, however, probably comes from the direct access to the area accorded Soviet technicians. Still lower down the list for both reliability and comprehensive coverage would be the information the Soviets are able to obtain by virtue of working partnerships with Libya and Syria. Even if it is true, as reported in the press, that East Germans are running the Libyan intelligence and security service it is difficult to think of any nation that would be considered with more suspicion than Libya by virtually the entire international diplomatic community, a severe limitation on what the Libyans can produce.

The effect of the "padding" of Soviet Embassy staffs with intelligence agents is plain in the total numbers of Soviet diplomatic delegations to the major nations as compared to reciprocal representation in the Soviet Union. Generally it has run 2:1 or more in favour of the Soviets.

The Soviet embassies are nominally under the control of the Foreign Ministry. In fact, Soviet ambassadors are known to have been "co-opted" by the KGB so that to all intents and purposes the KGB rather than the Foreign Ministry is in charge. Whether or not under the nominal control of the Foreign Ministry, all intelligence operations in the Soviet embassies, including ultimately those of the GRU, come under the control of the First Chief Directorate of the KGB in Moscow. The organization of that directorate is shown in figure 3.

The KGB embassy staff

The chief of the KGB apparatus in each embassy is known as the "Rezident". He controls operations through five subordinate sections. Their collective headquarters in each embassy is known as the Refentura —the secure room or suite containing codes, communications means (primarily radio, with "scramblers" on each end to complicate the decoding problem even further) with Moscow and where plans and reports are prepared.

As indicated in figure 3, the KGB appears to make no attempt to distinguish between the gathering of intelligence and subversive operations. Both appear to be conducted under the same embassy staff officer (the chief of the Rezident's Section 1), and carried out by the same intelligence agents.

Section 2 is responsible for security of the embassy itself and for counter-intelligence operations against the host nation's internal security system. Section 3 collects information available in the open scientific and technical press and arranges for other aspects of open collection, such as participation by Soviet scientists in host nation conferences, visits to universities and laboratories, etc. Presumably this section either dispatches its own agents or arranges with Section 1 for collection of information the host nation attempts to keep secret.

The term "illegal" as related to Section 4 refers to Soviet agents who have been implanted illegally in the host country by use of false identities. These do not enter the host country through the embassy and indeed seek to avoid any direct contact with the embassy. The support provided by Section 4 is in the form of currency left at predesignated locations and specialized equipment provided by similar means, as for instance by deposit in a luggage locker of a railway station or airport. In some cases, the "illegal" may have his own direct communications with Moscow by means of compact radio transmitters capable of sending messages in concentrated bursts so as to foil host nation direction finding equipment. Specialized receivers, also, may enable the "illegal" agent to receive coded instructions direct from Moscow. Such equipment is, of course, a major liability, since if discovered, by its mere presence it could destroy the years of work spent constructing the spy's elaborate false background.

FIGURE 2: SOVIET BLOC MILITARY/CIVILIAN ADVISERS IN MID-EAST AND AFRICA

COUNTRY	SOVIET	CUBAN	EAST GERMAN
MID-EAST AND NORTH AFRICA			
Algeria	8,500	170	250
Iraq	8,000	2,200	160
Libya	2,300	3,000	–
North Yemen	475	–	5
South Yemen	2,500	800	325
Syria	4,000	5	210
SUB-SAHARAN AFRICA			
Angola	700	18,000	450
Congo	850	950	15
Ethiopia	2,400	5,900	550
Guinea	375	280	125
Madagascar	370	55	–
Mali	635	–	20
Mozambique	500	1,000	100
Tanzania	300	95	15

Source: US Sec. of Defense Weinberger's Report to Congress, Fiscal Year 1983

1 One likely operation in the early days of any future conflict is raids by small parties of "civilians" on NATO airfields; planning and reconnaissance goes on in peace. Only the British Royal Air Force Regiment is trained and organised to defeat such a threat.

2 The Soviet Trade Delegation's building in London, which was apparently "penetrated" by British counter-intelligence using a double-glazing worker to plant listening devices, take clandestine photographs and help establish that Soviet espionage activities had taken place, leading to the expulsion of Soviet diplomats.

3 Among the "agents" exposed in this way were Vladimir Chernov (shown), a civil service translator "asked" to leave the country in January 1983, Victor Lazine, second secretary at the Soviet embassy, Vladimir Zadneprovskiy, trade diplomat, and Zhotov (see below).

4 Soviet Captain Anatoly Zhotov, told to leave Britain in December 1983 for spying, apparently on Falklands Task Force ship repairs. Also kicked out, in April 1983, was his colleague, assistant air attache Col. Gennadiy A. Primakov, a frequent visitor to the editor's offices. A few days later France expelled 47 Soviets for spying in the military sphere.

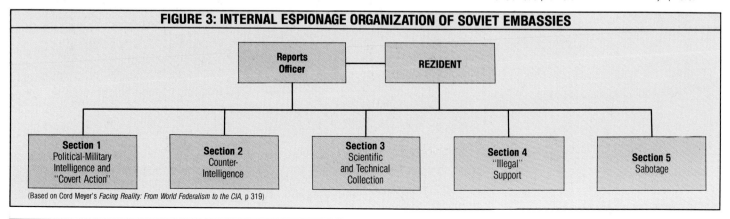

FIGURE 3: INTERNAL ESPIONAGE ORGANIZATION OF SOVIET EMBASSIES

Reports Officer

REZIDENT

Section 1 Political-Military Intelligence and "Covert Action"

Section 2 Counter-Intelligence

Section 3 Scientific and Technical Collection

Section 4 "Illegal" Support

Section 5 Sabotage

(Based on Cord Meyer's *Facing Reality: From World Federalism to the CIA*, p 319)

A much safer method of communication for the "illegal" as well as for other agents is the letter drop or prearranged meetings in third countries lacking effective counter-intelligence organizations.

For Western countries, the work of Section 5 is perhaps the most dangerous of all activities conducted through the Soviet embassies. The damage that a handful of terrorists such as the Bader Meinhoff Gang in Germany and the Red Brigades in Italy can do, even in the face of well organized police surveillance, is all too apparent from a long succession of bloody episodes.

The Communist Party of each of the Western nations provides a far broader base of support than is enjoyed by any of the fanatical terrorist groups. Even though, as in the United States and Italy in particular, the Communist core may have dwindled to a few thousand members this still provides fertile ground for the organization of five- or six-person squads to carry out specified, carefully pre-planned sabotage operations in the event of war or some crisis short of war. Except for Britain's Royal Air Force Regiment, for instance, there is virtually no military organization especially tasked and trained to defend air bases. The intelligence necessary to exploit such vulnerabilities can be gathered by native Communists posing as hunters, fishermen or tourists over a period of months or years without arousing suspicion. It is the job of Section 5 to organize such a capability and to direct collection of the intelligence necessary to support it. Here again, as in Section 1, there is no distinction between the gathering of information and the planning and conduct of what are, in effect, covert military operations.

In the larger embassies the Reports Officer has the job of collecting the information gathered by the operating sections and relaying it to Moscow. In smaller embassies the *Rezident* might be his own Reports Officer.

Methods of operation

Where they can get away with it, Soviet intelligence agents assigned to the embassies do not hesitate to operate in the open. The senior "civilian" member of the military attache's office of the Soviet Embassy in Washington, for instance, has shown up regularly at meetings of the American Association for Asian Studies — with China specialists from Moscow in tow — recording by written note or tape recorder everything that was said at the conference about China.

Against less accessible "targets", the embassy-based agents, and the "illegals" as well, work hard at recruiting nationals of the host country as surrogate agents. Indeed, there is evidence from defectors that KGB "staffers" in the embassy are assigned quotas from such recruitment.

Although they have suffered many defeats, such as the mass expulsion of agents from Britain and Egypt (in the late 1970s), the Soviets have achieved spectacular success in their recruitment operations, far outweighing whatever losses they have experienced. Consider the following:

1. The penetration of Britain's Secret Service (MI6) and Internal Security Service (MI5) to the extent that for a number of years before, during and after World War II the KGB appears effectively to have *operated* those services.

2. The gaining of access to the depository for US contingency plans and cryptographic documents entering or leaving Europe, due to the treachery of US Army Sergeant Robert Lee Johnson in the 1960s. For just a few thousand dollars, Johnson, while "guarding" the US Army's vault at Orly Field, Paris, regularly removed codes and other documents for copying by KGB agents.

3. Theft over the mid-1970s of what news accounts cite as KH-11, reportedly the most highly classified of all US satellite surveillance technology. This was accomplished apparently by two juvenile delinquents, John Boyce and Andrew Daulton Lee, who, like the British traitors cited above, were able to use family connections as entrée to secret work simply by promising to "behave".

Profile of potential recruits

From their long and often successful experience in achieving such penetrations the Soviets clearly have established profiles of potential recruits. This is reflected in a document, "The Practice of Recruiting Americans in the USA and Third Countries", acquired by Western intelligence agencies

1 ▲

2 ▲

3 ▲

4 ▲

and reproduced as an appendix to John Barron's book, *KGB*. From such Soviet sources and from the work of Western journalists such as Chapman Pincher of Britain and Robert Lindsey of the United States it is possible to draw up similar profiles of "targets" for KGB recruitment.

The amoral government employee

Figure 4 could well be US Army Sergeant Robert Lee Johnson, the traitor mentioned above, who, from December 15, 1962, to April 21, 1963, obtained for KGB agents virtually all of the US contingency plans and cryptographic documents that were deposited for safekeeping by US couriers passing through Orly Field, Paris.

The Johnson type unhappily is the reverse image of freedom in democratic, in particular American, society, for the same freedom that permits and encourages the individual to reach his or her full potential can breed a rootlessness that degenerates into irresponsibility. In each of the recent American wars (Korea and Vietnam), "Johnson types" were identified among American prisoners of war and were exploited by their captors to betray their own comrades and to make propaganda against the United States.

The spoiled brat

Figure 5, "The Spoiled Brat", could be represented by John Boyce, who with Andrew Daulton Lee, betrayed to the Soviets some of the most sensitive of all US satellite surveillance technology. This sort of "target" is distinctly the product of post-World War II American affluence in which parents who had experienced the desperation of the Great Depression of the 1930s resolved that "My kids are not going to have it as tough".

Insulated throughout their childhood from their country's desperate, unresolved social and economic problems, many of the children of this generation were shattered when they came up against those problems as young adults. In many cases, they correctly saw a dichotomy, even hypocrisy between their parents' espoused political and religious ideals and what they finally learned of their parents' indifference to those ideals in practice. The less stable among them, and they are numbered in at least tens of thousands, all too easily saw the moral failures of the parents as failures of the principles and ideals themselves. They became prey to all of the "pied pipers" that have ever appeared to lead humans astray—most vicious among them the purveyors of a new drug "culture". All the while these well-educated, well-connected children of affluence retained the ability to re-enter the mainstream of American society any time they chose to conform to its greatly loosened structures. The moral and psychological dependencies that had led them into the "drug culture" were made to order for KGB recruitment.

The disaffected intellectual

Figure 6 could be represented by Britain's Anthony Blunt, who was the archetype of the disaffected intellectual. With Guy Burgess, Harold Kim Philby and others from respectable British backgrounds, he was among the traitors who used family and educational background to secure influential positions in the British security services and betray those services to the Soviets from the 1930s into the 1950s. Some of these people were genuine utopians who thought they saw in the Russian Revolution the salvation of mankind. For all of that, they were willing to disregard successively the mass starvation of the Russian peasantry, the Hitler-Stalin Pact of 1939 and the Stalinist terror.

The disaffected intellectual recruited today by the KGB is likely to be a scruffier type, however, usually from the fringes of Western or Japanese academe and therefore susceptible to the sort of psychological and material blandishments the KGB can offer—invitations to the Soviet Embassy, audiences with successively higher officials of the Soviet Institute on the US and Canada and similar Moscow "institutes", paid travel to the Soviet Union, North Korea and other Communist nations, subsidisation of research and surreptitious financial assistance for publication.

The conviction of two Soviet agents—Geoffrey Prime and Prof. Hugh Hambleton—in Britain in 1982 indicates some residual appeal in the Soviet "dream", but also the extent to which that appeal has run thin.

Prime admitted to volunteering his service to the Soviets in 1964 while serving as an electronics intelligence specialist in the Royal Air Force. "I needed to believe in something," Prime told his interrogators. From what has now become known, however, it appears that this was less an attraction to Soviet ideology, per se, than a reaction to a tragic childhood and youth that left him resentful of his own background and susceptible to any "something" that might serve as a substitute. Hambleton did not admit to intellectual attraction, but stated, "I still tend to identify with the Soviet officer class," as curious an ideological attraction as is likely to be found.

The lonely secretary

As disillusionment with the Communist "solution" to the world's ills has spread, the KGB has directed its recruitment efforts more and more to the outcasts and the lonely of "target" societies. In several instances it has achieved notable results by focusing on relatively well-to-do, but desperately lonely single women working as secretaries in Western governments.

Figure 7 could be represented by one of the most tragic of these recruitments, a German woman suborned by a marriage to a KGB agent, Heinz Sütterlin, and pressured into delivering sensitive documents from her job in the West German Foreign Ministry by threats from Sütterlin that he would leave her. When she found out, after capture in 1967, that Sütterlin had married her only on orders from the KGB she hanged herself.

The "lonely secretary" extends to many different sorts of people who suffer from the same problems of loneliness or alienation whether inflicted by circumstance, society or themselves. In the words of the KGB Gen. Paul Anatolevich, quoted by John Barron,

1 ▲

3 ▲

Figure 4 KGB target No. 1, the amoral government employee (military or civilian).

Virtually no sense of guilt when caught

Little or no record of selfless service to other individuals or groups (church, community, etc.).

Unwilling or unable to complete in open civilian society.

Self-gratification a primary motivation — tendency to promiscuity, alcoholism.

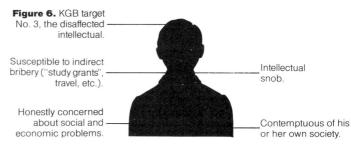

Figure 6. KGB target No. 3, the disaffected intellectual.

Susceptible to indirect bribery ("study grants", travel, etc.).

Honestly concerned about social and economic problems.

Intellectual snob.

Contemptuous of his or her own society.

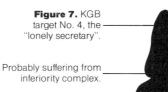

Figure 5. KGB target No. 2, the spoiled brat.

Excess of parental indulgence.

Easily detached from early standards and family background.

Insulated by privileged surburban or ex-urban upbringing from problems of race, poverty and disease.

Alienation from sacrifice as a means to attain goals.

Figure 7. KGB target No. 4, the "lonely secretary".

Probably suffering from inferiority complex.

Typical of those sought out by ruthless KGB system preying on weak, the dissaffected, the vulnerable.

1 Anthony Blunt, the English art expert, who spied for the Soviet Union during his World War II service with Britain's MI5. According to Chapman Pincher (in his book, "Their Trade is Treachery"), Blunt "was one of the most damaging spies ever to operate in Britain", having informed the Russians about the American intelligence organization OSS, among other things. Those who had campaigned for years to find the traitors behind Burgess, Maclean and Philby were finally vindicated when it was revealed that Anthony Blunt was the notorious "Fourth Man". Here seen giving a Press conference following his public exposure in 1981, Blunt had not followed the other three by escaping to Moscow, and died, shamed and stripped of honours and titles, in England on March 26, 1983.

2 The tools of a spy's trade, including Soviet-made "tonal decoder", list of dead letter box locations, pad for "invisible" notes, and the necessary chemicals for revealing them. These are some of the items used by Professor Hugh Hambleton, a Canadian academic sentenced in London in December 1982 to 10 years imprison-ment for espionage. Although efforts were made at his trial and in Canada to give the impression that he was a "Walter Mitty" character, it is nevertheless concluded that he was very important to Soviet intelligence. He claimed that he had never been a Communist, but that he was attempting to keep the peace between the two superpowers. His treach-ery came to light during interrogation of one of his Soviet "handlers", Rudi Herrman, captured follow-ing a joint FBI/Canadian Mounties operation.

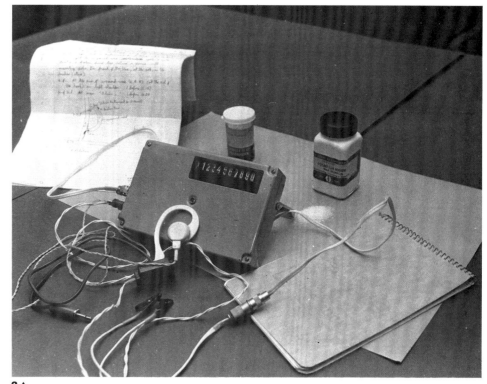

2 ▲

3 ▲▶

3 David Bingham was a sub-lieutenant in the Royal Navy when he was ensnared into espionage activities by his wife, Maureen. Bingham had risen from junior seaman in 1956 to petty officer in 1964, and in 1968 he went on an officer's course where he won the Sword of Honour, a record of which anyone could be proud. In February 1970 Mrs

Bingham just walked into the Soviet embassy and offered her husband's services; it was as simple as that. He was given the usual impedimenta of the trade: letter codes (above), letters wrapped in string and coated to look like stones and films (right). Eventually, increasing demands and death threats from the Russians, and financial pressures from his wife, broke him.

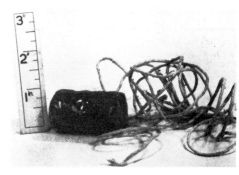

"Go search for people who are hurt by fate or nature — the ugly, those suffering from an inferiority complex, craving power and influence but defeated by unfavourable circumstances . . . . The sense of belonging to an influential powerful organization will give them a superior feeling over the handsome and prosperous people around them."

To say, of course, that every homely, unhappy or lonely person in Western society is vulnerable to KGB recruitment would be an absurdity. Indeed, two of the men cited in chapter 1 who made lasting, momentous contributions to their country's long-range intelligence would fit into one or more of those categories. As with the rich, the talented and the beautiful, however, there is a fringe of people in all of these "vulnerable" categories who cannot balance human frailty or misfortune with some compensating strength and who are prime prey for the espionage exploiter.

Dissatisfied US civil servants

There is in the KGB training document republished by John Barron a glimpse of yet another KGB "target profile". Among the factors the KGB lists "as a basis for recruiting employees of government institutions" is "Dissatisfaction with the rigid policy of the US Government toward civil servants — infringement on the rights of the individual". For the KCB to cite "the rights of the individual" is surely a case of the Devil quoting Scripture, considering its treatment of millions of Soviet citizens in its prisons and labour camps. But the "dissatisfaction" of which the training manual speaks does exist and it is serious enough and widespread enough to suggest a vulnerability that the US Government has yet to recognize.

While serving as an Army staff officer in the Pentagon, the writer once delivered six coordination copies of a document marked "Secret" to as many staff agencies, obtaining a receipt from each. A few minutes after returning to my office I received a call from a civil service employee who stated, "I have something here with your name on it. I suggest that you come down and get it." He had found one of the six "Secret" papers stuck behind the toilet paper in a w.c.

From my receipts I was able to determine that the chief of a Directorate (an infantry colonel) next door to the civil service employee, but in a different staff agency, had signed for the "lost" copy. From the elapsed time it was obvious that the colonel must have been on the way to the men's room when he signed for the document, and absent-mindedly left it there, and that the civilian who now had it in his possession was the next person to see it. Also, like at least 90 per cent of the "classified" documents that circulate in the US Government, there was nothing at all "secret" about the paper. Yet it was only with the greatest difficulty that I managed to persuade the civilian to return the document to the colonel without forcing me to file a formal report of a "security violation", with possibly grave and totally unjustified consequences to the officer. From beginning to end in that discussion it was apparent that the civilian had been waiting for many long years for the

1 ▲

2 ▲

1 A conference in progress at NATO headquarters in Brussels. There are large numbers of officers, NCOs and civilians working in NATO and its subordinate HQs. These are prime targets for the Soviet secret services.

2 Herr Willi Brandt the popular and respected West German Chancellor who developed an "Ostpolitik" to reduce East-West tensions. The East Germans responded by planting a spy in his private office; Brandt had to resign.

3 The hustle and bustle of the hallway of the Pentagon building in Washington, DC. Although superficially efficient and happy, there are great stresses and strains in this organization especially between the military and civilians.

4 Many Third World countries seem paranoid about spies, and arrest people on the flimsiest of excuses. One such victim could have been Michael Borlace, held in a Zambia jail for 15 months on charges of spying for S. Africa.

3 ▲

4 ▲

opportunity to have a senior military officer at his mercy, and that he relinquished the opportunity with bitter reluctance.

The source of such bitterness lies in considerable part in the contemptuous attitude of many members of the military services, not only in the United States, deriving from a feudal tradition whereby there must always be an underclass to validate the "superiority" of the chiefs. With the spread of egalitarianism and enhanced respect for individual civil rights in Western societies, that assumption of inherent military superiority has steadily eroded, leaving the civil servant as the last "humble retainer", expected to accept pay grades significantly below those of less qualified military counterparts and to maintain an attitude of self-effacing humility in the presence of their military "superiors".

The fact that some service-employed civilians are more technically competent than their military counterparts only exacerbates resentment toward civilians who do not "know their place". The continuation of this foolish resentment undermines overall defence efficiency, but that warning is a long way from being accepted by the US military, as the KGB have discovered.

The "dissatisfaction" noted by the KGB can become particularly acute in the lower civil service pay grades, where the standard practice during a period of contraction is to release, or lower the grades of, the lowest ranking female employees as the group least likely to resist.

Deep penetration of US Government?

The fact that the KGB has known of this extensive dissatisfaction for years and has been methodically exploiting it, while the US Government indicates not the faintest glimmer of recognition that it exists, suggests that the government may have been penetrated far more extensively than anyone has yet realized. Indeed, the ingrained ability of the career civil servant to hide his or her true feelings and to act out the charade expected provides ideal "cover" for the "recruited" agent.

During the administration of President Jimmy Carter, a "Civil Service Reform Act" was passed that, as often happened during that period, produced the opposite effect to that intended. That is, the law greatly reinforced military intimidation and retaliation against the civil servant who dared, in terms of the KGB manual, to assert the "rights of the individual".

Where once it was necessary to prove in an open hearing that an employee should be dismissed, it is now possible for a military (or civilian) administrator to dismiss any civilian under his jurisdiction on the flimsiest of charges, to place the cost of defence entirely on the employee—by then without income—and, even when subsequent hearings are resolved in the employee's favour, to string out endless appeals until the employee is financially broken or gives up and seeks other employment. If all of this fails, or if failure is anticipated from the beginning, the Department of Defense empowers any administrator to make charges of psychiatric "instability" against an employee—exactly as the KGB does in the Soviet Union—and to force the employee into psychiatric consultations which, in American society, constitute permanent damage in such crucial matters as future employment and even purchase of insurance policies. No matter that any and all of such charges eventually may be proven false or malicious, or both, the military administrator is held in no way accountable for such character assassination and will almost unquestionably have disappeared into some distant assignment or retirement by the time the tortuous appeals process is completed.

From observation of this system in the Department of the Army at least it is apparent that military lawyers and civilian personnel officers often can force an employee with an "individual rights" complaint—in particular the often abused lower ranking female employee—to the point of a nervous breakdown simply by threatening to put him or her through this administrative, legal and medical gauntlet. Small wonder that the latent hostilities cited by the KGB are fertile ground for dissidence and worse.

Interestingly enough the Central Intelligence Agency has protected itself against this gaping vulnerability by arranging for its employees to be excepted from the ordinary civil service system. As a result, CIA employees are often as much as two pay grades above military and civilian employees of other agencies performing identical or more complex duties.

In December 1981 US columnist Jack Anderson revealed that KGB agents in the Soviet Embassy in Washington routinely received from US civil service employees lists of classified documents produced by the General Accounting Office, the auditing arm of the US Congress. According to a GAO investigator interviewed by television newsmen after appearance of the Anderson report, the classified documents themselves are being handed out. Plainly, although less clearly defined than the others shown in figures 4, 5, 6 and 7, the KGB "profile" of "dissatisfaction" in the US civil service seems to be well grounded, and very, very productive.

British and American examples are cited in the vulnerable "types" discussed here because the very openness of those societies permits close inspection even when it is necessary to keep some evidence secret. That these types exist in other countries, although not in such sharp relief, is apparent from the flow of news, day by day.

What do we make, for instance, of reports in 1980 and 1981 of the arrest of allegedly Russian agents in the crucially important Northeast frontier region of China? One of them apparently was a Eurasian member of that desperately lonely and vulnerable Russian and Eurasian population that was isolated in Manchuria by the Russian Revolution and the Chinese Civil War. He would certainly seem to fit in exactly with General Anatolevich's "people who are hurt by fate or nature". A Chinese, Yue Zhonglie, age 28, apparently crossed the frontier and offered his services to the Soviets. A dissatisfied civil servant?

More difficult to "type" are people such as Michael Borlace, a British-born former

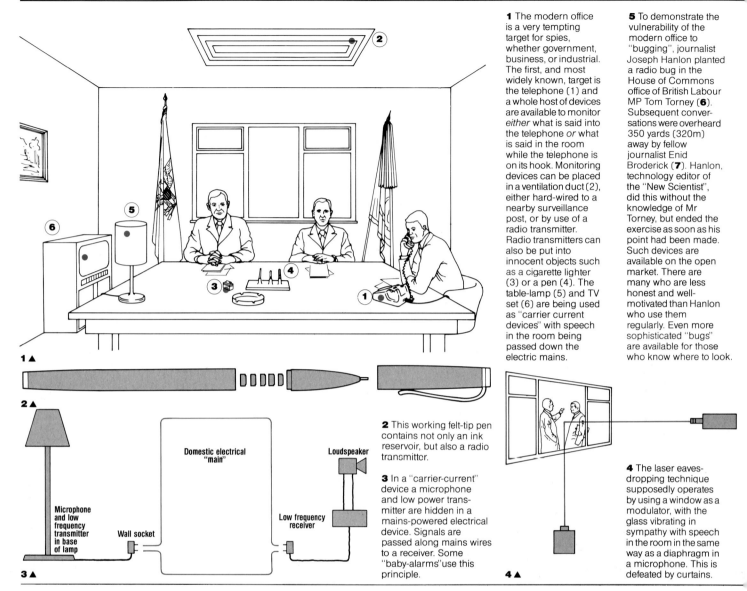

1 ▲

2 ▲

3 ▲

4 ▲

1 The modern office is a very tempting target for spies, whether government, business, or industrial. The first, and most widely known, target is the telephone (1) and a whole host of devices are available to monitor *either* what is said into the telephone *or* what is said in the room while the telephone is on its hook. Monitoring devices can be placed in a ventilation duct (2), either hard-wired to a nearby surveillance post, or by use of a radio transmitter. Radio transmitters can also be put into innocent objects such as a cigarette lighter (3) or a pen (4). The table-lamp (5) and TV set (6) are being used as "carrier current devices" with speech in the room being passed down the electric mains.

5 To demonstrate the vulnerability of the modern office to "bugging", journalist Joseph Hanlon planted a radio bug in the House of Commons office of British Labour MP Tom Torney (**6**). Subsequent conversations were overheard 350 yards (320m) away by fellow journalist Enid Broderick (**7**). Hanlon, technology editor of the "New Scientist", did this without the knowledge of Mr Torney, but ended the exercise as soon as his point had been made. Such devices are available on the open market. There are many who are less honest and well-motivated than Hanlon who use them regularly. Even more sophisticated "bugs" are available for those who know where to look.

2 This working felt-tip pen contains not only an ink reservoir, but also a radio transmitter.

3 In a "carrier-current" device a microphone and low power transmitter are hidden in a mains-powered electrical device. Signals are passed along mains wires to a receiver. Some "baby-alarms" use this principle.

4 The laser eavesdropping technique supposedly operates by using a window as a modulator, with the glass vibrating in sympathy with speech in the room in the same way as a diaphragm in a microphone. This is defeated by curtains.

Rhodesian helicopter pilot who was released after 15 months imprisonment in Lusaka, Zambia, in July 1980. If his accusers are believed, it could be surmised that he was either a crass "amoral" type employed by South Africa to maintain white supremacy by espionage against South Africa's black neighbours, or a pure idealist, a reverse image of the earliest Communist type, following the dictates of a misguided conscience. However, Borlace claimed on release that for five of the 15 months in prison he was tortured in an attempt to make him confess to spying charges.

Methods of recruitment

How does the KGB, or any intelligence agency, go about recruiting the weak, the disaffected and the resentful into its service? Some recruits literally "walk in" to the Soviet Embassy. These, however, tend to be greatly mistrusted if for no other reason than that countries with strong internal security systems almost certainly photograph and identify the "walk-in" as soon as he or she appears at the embassy gate.

Despite the vast publicity given to KGB methods and purposes over the past half century and more, many citizens of non-Communist countries apparently think nothing of establishing extensive social

relationships with representatives of the various Soviet embassies, the Soviet delegation at the United Nations, or such "cover" agencies as Aeroflot and the TASS news agency, even though the majority of employees of those agencies are known to be agents of the KGB and GRU. There seems to be even less reluctance to socialize with the KGB's surrogates from Poland, Czechoslovakia, Bulgaria and other East European nations. In recent years, such free and easy socializing has included employees of US Government agencies.

During the past 20 years the KGB has moved some distance from its old practice of deploying obvious thugs in ill-fitting "New-Style-Soviet-Man" suits as its intelligence agents abroad. The new breed of KGB overseas agent is likely to be well educated in the culture and history of the "target" nation as well as his or her own country and to be dressed in the Western style suits that are, curiously enough, now the hallmark of success in the Soviet and East European "New Class".

Given the naivete of so many in the open, democratic societies it has become increasingly easy for the KGB to contact and evaluate potential recruits simply by moving about openly at social, educational and other professional gatherings. This sort of work continues to be supplemented by the

network of Soviet and East European "illegals" who operate under cover of false identities and conduct their own recruiting. However the new traitor is recruited, it is the *Rezident* or a higher official in Moscow who determines whether the new recruit is to be "controlled" by an "illegal" or directly by an agent from the Embassy.

CIA espionage operations

In contrast to the vast KGB espionage system, the US espionage network is overshadowed (some would say smothered) by the vast US technical collection apparatus and perhaps even more so by the creeping and increasingly disreputable "covert action" bureaucracy. "Covert action" as indicated earlier is the US term for subversion of foreign governments, attempts on the lives of foreign leaders, the planting of rumours and the whole unsavoury lexicon of "dirty tricks" that have come to be associated in recent years as "intelligence" functions when, to the extent that any of them have legitimacy in war or in peace, they are properly defined as "operations" functions.

It is apparent from the US Congressional investigations of the mid-1970s that "covert action" effectively dominates the CIA. It also is apparent from the reports of those

investigations that technical means of collection dominate the DIA—as was displayed to the world in the intelligence "show and tell" of March 1982 on Central America. The State Department's Bureau of Intelligence and Research employs no agents abroad and works almost entirely from open sources.

What there is of an American espionage system, therefore, is to be found in the Central Intelligence Agency's Directorate of Operations (see figure 7, page 40) where it competes—not very successfully it seems—with "covert action". These two elements—espionage and covert action—constitute what is referred to darkly as the "clandestine services". The extent to which the "camel" of "covert action" came to dominate the intelligence "tent" in the CIA should be instructive to any nation seeking to build an effective intelligence service.

Strangely enough there was no authority in the CIA's basic "statutory charter"—the National Security Act of 1947—for "covert action". In short, the CIA was to be just what the name implies—an intelligence agency only. "Covert action" was introduced, according to the Senate investigators, by decree of the National Security Council without reference to Congress, much less to the public. "We do not believe," said Lawrence Houston, former General Counsel

of the CIA, "that there was any thought in the minds of Congress that the CIA . . . . would take positive action for subversion and sabotage."

By 1961, the Senate Committee reports, "clandestine activities [that is, covert action] had overtaken intelligence analysis as the CIA's primary mission . . . . As in the previous decade, operations dominated policymakers' perceptions of the Agency's role. In the subsequent decade, what is now the Directorate of [Clandestine] Operations averaged 52 per cent of the CIA budget and included 55 per cent of Agency personnel, the greater part of them involved in covert action."

Inevitably, the Senate investigators found, this heavy emphasis on "covert action" meant that it would become the principal "track" of advancement in the Agency. This was confirmed when two "native sons" of the Agency emerged as Directors of Central Intelligence. Both of them (Richard Helms and William E. Colby) were "covert action" careerists.

It was only natural that these "home-grown" Directors would patronize the part of the Agency from which they had emerged, even further enshrining "covert action" as, in the words of the Senate investigators, "the pre-eminent activity within the organization". Even a Director from outside the Agency found that "90 per cent of his total

time" was taken up with covert action.

As concerns the Defense Intelligence Agency, the Senate Committee found that 87 per cent of its resources were spent on technical means of intelligence collection, and only 13 per cent on all forms of "human intelligence". Considering that the entire US Defense Attache system is funded from that 13 per cent, not much is left for espionage by human agents!

When it completed its review of all the US intelligence agencies, the Senate Committee concluded that, "The reporting of the Foreign Service, together with that of the military attache system, based on firsthand observation and especially on official dealings with governments, *makes up the most useful element of our foreign intelligence information. Clandestine and technical sources provide supplementary information.*" (Emphasis added.)

US espionage abroad

As would be expected, the organization of what espionage capability the US does possess abroad would reflect the obsession with "covert action" that dominates budget, staff and policymaking in the "home office". The CIA counterpart to the KGB *Rezident* in embassies abroad is called a "Station Chief". The staffing of US embassies, whereby many of the jobs used by the KGB as "cover" for its agents are assigned by the United States Foreign Service to foreign nationals, makes it pretty obvious that the CIA Station Chiefs enjoy nowhere near the staff support of the KGB *Rezidents*. Nor, of course, would the CIA chiefs get very far attempting to give orders to British, French, or West German intelligence officers, or those of other US allies.

There is however, often good voluntary cooperation among those agencies. For example, an agent of Britain's MI6 is reported by Japan's Kyodo News Agency as having assisted CIA in encouraging the defection of a Soviet fighter pilot with his aircraft to Japan. This resulted in the delivery to Japanese and Western intelligence agencies of a MiG-25 interceptor and the opportunity to study the aircraft in detail before it was returned to Soviet control.

Since the State Department is firmly in control of all US embassies, there is no chance of the CIA Station Chief "co-opting" an ambassadorship, as in the Soviet system. Further, there is sometimes an uneasy relationship between the US State Department and CIA representatives in the embassy, deriving from two factors: first, what appears to be a considerable pay differential in favour of CIA employees; and second, the seemingly unending series of disasters and humiliations for US foreign policy produced by the CIA "covert action" staffs.

The finding by the Senate investigators that the work of the Foreign Service officers and the military attaches is by far the most valuable intelligence the United States receives should have greatly encouraged those groups, unfairly overshadowed for many years by the publicity (for good or ill) generated by the CIA's activities.

The one area in which the CIA's "clandestine services" seem to have done consistently outstanding work is in the handling of defectors from the Soviet Union and its "allies". Such defectors are unquestionably the principal US source of covert information about what goes on in the USSR, the size and budget of the US espionage services obviously precluding any large-scale attempt to insert or support "illegals" in the Warsaw Pact nations.

The FBI and Soviet agents

John Barron's *KGB* provides a fascinating glimpse of the information these defectors have provided and of the contribution the Federal Bureau of Investigation has made by encouraging and exploiting the defection of Soviet agents in the United States.

One of the most interesting cases Barron brought to light is that of Kaarlo Tuomi. American-born but returned to the USSR at 16 by his Finnish Communist stepfather, Tuomi had the ideal background for an "illegal" in that he had already lived in the "target" country and could speak its language. After two years of intensive training by the KGB's top instructors, Tuomi was sent to the United States through Canada. On March 9, 1959, scarcely two months after his arrival, Tuomi was arrested by the

US Federal Bureau of Investigation. Within the first few hours of interrogation, Tuomi realized that he had been identified and under continuous surveillance probably from the moment he landed in Canada. How Canadian and US counter-espionage agencies learned of Tuomi's true identity and purpose, apparently while he was still in the bosom of the KGB, remains one of the Cold War's most fascinating mysteries.

On the "other side of the coin", however, it seems apparent from the published work of Harry Rositzke and other former CIA officials that Western penetration of the Soviet Union by "illegals" ended in the early 1950s with the reimposition of KGB internal USSR controls that had been disrupted by World War II.

Other non-Communist operations

The legacy of the British and French empires is a vast network of personal, political, economic and military overseas contacts that provide for those governments a flow of information, largely for free, that equals or surpasses what the Soviet Union spends huge sums to obtain through the KGB. Because of their worldwide economic contacts, West Germany and Japan, also, obtain large amounts of information once thought to be the province only of the spy. A West German manufacturer called in by the Egyptian Government, for instance, to repair surface-to-air missiles obtained from the Soviet Union was able to give a business associate at a cocktail party an accurate estimate of the state of the Soviet electronics industry. That business associate was a retired officer of the German Army, and NATO was the ultimate beneficiary of the intelligence gained. The cost to NATO: zero.

For a time the British Secret Service (MI6) fell into the "covert action" trap that has so greatly damaged the CIA's efficiency and reputation. MI6, it turns out from the work of Chapman Pincher, was a full partner with the CIA in what ultimately proved to be one of the worst disasters ever produced by "covert action"—the overthrow of the Mossadeq Government in Iran in 1953 and the restoration of the Shah. That effectively blocked a gradual transition for Iran from the monarchy to a more broadly based government, thereby setting the stage for extremism. And that, of course, led directly to the orgy of anti-Westernism that accompanied and followed the fall of the Shah in 1979 and to the humiliation of the United States in the overrunning of its Embassy and the year-long imprisonment of the Embassy staff.

Recognizing, in Chapman Pincher's words, that "misfortune seemed constantly to dog the Secret Service's attempts to help resolve Britain's international problems", Sir Dick White put a stop to such practices when he became Chief of the Secret Service in 1956. Today, MI6 operates in its traditional role, supplementing the work of the British Foreign and Defence representatives abroad, but tightly controlled by the Foreign Ministry and, unlike the CIA, possessing no separate link to the national capital by which to circumvent the ambassador.

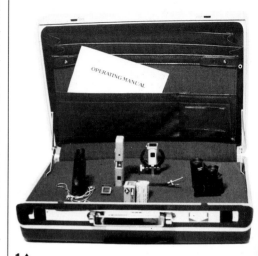

1 ▲

2 ▲

4 ▲

4, 5 The borescope utilises fibreoptics to see "through" objects such as walls and doors. A small hole is required through which the borescope is inserted, and viewing is then done either with the naked eye or with a TV monitor. Such techniques can also be used to see into barrels suspected of containing explosives, envelopes, petrol tanks on cars, and so on. The technology was developed for industrial and medical use by the British company Keymed Industrial.

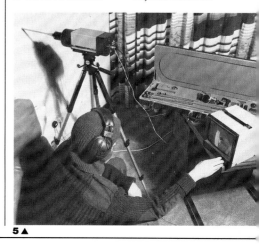

5 ▲

Three cases, all commercially available from CCS Communication Control Inc., packed with espionage, security and communications devices. The sort of equipment designed specifically for use solely by secret security services can only be imagined.

1 The CCS II Covert Camera Spy System includes photographic equipment specially designed for undetected photography missions, allowing long-distance or close-up (8in/203mm) pictures to be taken, and can even "shoot round corners".

2 Designed for detecting deception during a face-to-face or telephone conversation, this is a voice stress analyzer, which apparently displays a simple numerical read-out instantaneously.

3 This case presents a long-range wireless security/communication system. Item (1) lets you know if the person you are talking to is lying while you record the conversation with a six-hour tape machine (2). A special detector (3) shows whether *he* is recording *you,* while another device tells you if a bug is operating (4). There is a radio transceiver (5) and a radio telephone (6) with a built-in scrambler (7). Physical protection includes a non-harmful spray (8), a super-sensitive bomb sniffer (9) and a bullet-proof lining to the case that gives protection against .357 Magnum bullets (10). If someone should try to steal this case from you there is a built-in siren alarm (11).

6, 7, 8 The pictures show how borescopes can detect the contents of a room in a situation such as a terrorist "siege". The borescope can be fitted to a variety of lenses to give the desired field of view in the target room. A general view (**7**) will enable the number of occupants to be counted, identifications to be made, and the general situation assessed. Different lenses enable weapons to be examined in detail (**8**). Darkened rooms are viewed using TV cameras with low-light capability.

Borescope equipment was thought to have been used by Britain's security services during the London Iranian Embassy siege in 1981, to reveal information on terrorists' weapons and positions, and the disposition of hostages.
Uses of technology such as these are gradually bringing the terrorist menace under control, but presumably they will respond by using technology to counter the security forces' devices. This is a battle in which the government forces must remain well ahead.

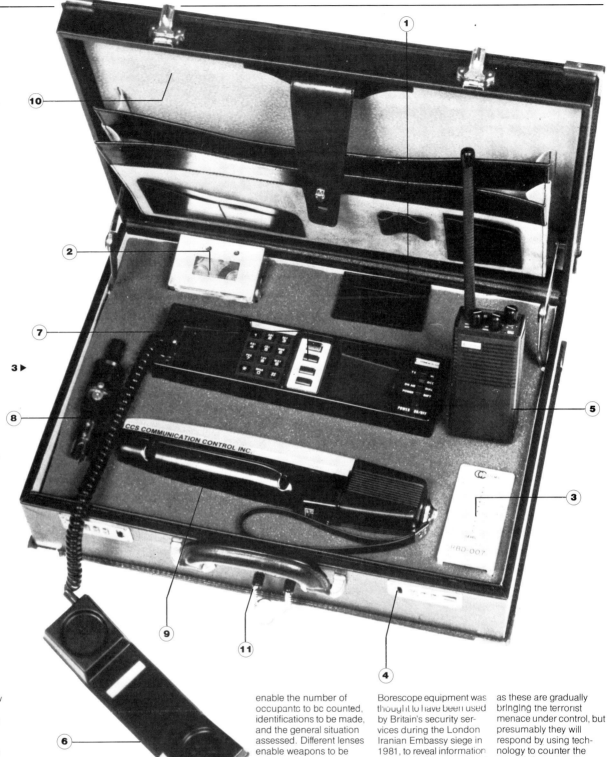

6▲

7▲

8▲

1, 2 Remote camera release by radio (here a Nikon F3) has created a number of surveillance possibilities. The diagram shows a doorway in a suspected building with a transmitter placed in the lintel which is triggered each time the door is opened. The transmitter sends a signal to the receiver which, unmanned, can be in a building across the road. The shutter is released, following which the motor-drive winds the film on. Thus, each time the door is opened a photograph of visitors or occupants is taken and a hard record obtained.

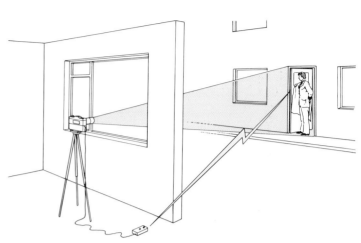

1 ▲   2 ▲

4 ▲   5 ▲

6 ▲

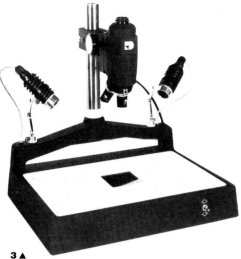

3 ▲

3 The CCS Infrared Counter-espionage System can detect alterations in documents and even "read" burned or stained letters.

4 Sometimes intelligence experts can trip themselves up. The photograph was actually taken by an agent in 1958. As the picture was of necessity taken from a considerable distance the impression was given of short length and a very high nose-up attitude, whereas the aircraft was some 185ft (56.2m) long, with 83ft (25.3m) span. The aircraft, a Soviet M-50 Bounder bomber, never got beyond the proto-type stage. The picture was declassified in 1978 (**5**), something which would probably not happen today.

6 One of the most notorious espionage dirty tricks was the installation by Soviet agents of a "bug" in the American Eagle in the US Embassy in Moscow, in 1952. The device was apparently a small capsule measuring 8 inches (203mm) in diameter, operating with a 9in (227mm) long antenna. Today equipment is available to detect the existence of "bugs". When the incident was descibed to the UN Security Council some members of the USSR delegation (at left of picture) seem to have had difficulty in keeping a straight face.

7 The US Embassy in Moscow had long been a major target for Soviet electronic monitoring and bugging; a cause of endless complaints.

7 ▲

The French and German services operate in much the same manner and, to judge by their ability generally to stay out of the headlines, apparently with the same quiet efficiency.

By far the most consistently successful espionage operations of a non-Communist nation are those of Israel. The capture and transportation to Israel for trial of the Nazi war criminal Adolf Eichmann, the purloining of atomic material for nuclear weapons manufacture, the classic espionage as well as electronic intelligence operations that accompanied the Entebbe raid in 1976, and the precise technical intelligence that made possible the successful air raid against an Iraqi nuclear plant in 1981 would constitute in themselves a "how-to-do-it" manual of espionage if the full story of those operations could be made known.

Beyond these strictly "Israeli" intelligence operations it is generally recognized in the West that Israel possesses some of the best information available about what is going on within the Soviet Union. This derives, of course, from the steady flow of Soviet emigrants to Israel. One such immigrant turned out to be an expert on Soviet warship powerplants. Another, Boris Rabbot, was a personal adviser to then-Soviet Chairman Leonid Brezhnev. Rabbot's report that the Soviet Union is primarily concerned with China rather than Europe still has not sunk in in the West, a prime example of how information that goes against prevailing "wisdom" can be ignored entirely because of cultural orientation or emotion.

Here again, as with the British, French, German and Japanese "espionage" operations, Israel's ability to operate on a world-wide basis derives from a very low budget and special circumstances. Whether from Jews who retain a passionate ethnic or religious attachment, people who feel a collective guilt over the holocaust of the Hitler era, or simply people who admire Israel's dogged determination to survive and prosper, Mossad and other Israeli intelligence services are able to obtain at little or no cost information and active cooperation that could, and does, cost the "superpowers" huge amounts of money and effort to obtain.

Counter-espionage measures

Counter-espionage involves all measures taken to prevent disclosure of information. As such it is part of the overall subject of "counter-intelligence". The most effective of all counter-espionage measures are those passive measures which avoid drawing the attention of would-be intruders to sensitive areas, documents and persons. Guards, fences, safes, vaults, coloured papers marking sensitive documents, all attract attention, saying, in effect, to the intruder, "Here it is. See if you can get it."

Active, or offensive, measures of counter-espionage involve the seeking out of the would-be intruders and physically barring or removing such agents from protected areas, places and persons. The conversion of a spy into a "double agent" and the "feeding" of false information to a known spy also constitute "active" measures.

Countering the KGB

Part of the reason why the Soviet Union deploys such large numbers of KGB agents to "target" countries is to overwhelm the internal security services of those countries. For every foreign agent introduced into a country, several members of that country's security force must be employed full-time or part-time for surveillance and other pro-tective measures. That was a factor in Britain's mass expulsion of Soviet agents in 1971. With Britain's security force being somewhat limited, the large infusion of Soviet and East European agents was plainly an attempt at saturation. By getting rid of 105 assorted KGB agents, Britain effectively reduced the work load on MI5.

Physical intrusion into known centres of espionage for the purpose of identifying agents, stealing codes or implanting listening and photographic devices is a standard method of counter-espionage in all nations, but it is an especially difficult and risky process in democratic societies. The United States, in particular, has great difficulty in controlling such intrusions. The burglary that set off the "Watergate" crisis and the rifling of a psychiatrist's office in the Daniel Ellsburg "Pentagon Papers" case in 1971, although not conducted by persons then on the government payroll, were certainly the work of people conditioned to such practices by past association with the "covert action" programmes of the Central Intelligence Agency. The US Government became directly involved when Federal Bureau of Investigation agents were used in the service of the racial prejudices of the then-Director of the Bureau, J. Edgar Hoover, in electronic surveillance of the civil rights leader Dr. Martin Luther King.

In 1981 the counter-espionage unit of Canada's Royal Canadian Mounted Police also became involved in difficulties when a Commission of Inquiry found that it had overstepped legal bounds in permitting surveillance of possible subversives to lap over into surveillance and harassment of legitimate political activities. The surveil-lance was of Quebec separatists. The unit transgressed in failing to distinguish between legal and illegal means of achieving political objectives. As noted in chapter 2, France has had a similar experience with a counter-espionage unit. In both the French and Canadian cases the units were disestab-lished and their duties transferred to agencies thought to be more easily controlled and less susceptible to political excursions.

Unfortunately, in the case of the FBI and the RCMP, controversy over infractions has obscured somewhat the brilliant accom-plishments of both services in countering foreign espionage. A particularly impressive example of the FBI's performance is recorded in chapter XII of John Barron's *KGB*, "The Spy Who Changed His Mind".

It must be kept in mind, also, that the work of such counter-espionage organiza-tions is virtually the only sure way of countering sabotage units organized from among local Communists by Section 5 of the KGB embassy staffs. The FBI has been particularly effective in managing to infil-trate the American Communist Party and thereby keeping track of its activities.

Britain has managed to keep MI5 out of "hot water" by a rather ingenious strategem. MI5 never has been legally established as a Government department. Never having been "legalized", it is somewhat difficult to determine which of its activities are "legal" and which "illegal". Nevertheless, Britain carefully controls authority for wiretapping by requiring warrants from the Home Secretary or Foreign Secretary, depending on whether British citizens or foreign diplomats are involved. Such warrants must be justified on a month-to-month basis. Neither MI5 nor any of the British governmental agencies responsible for their own internal security is permitted the power of arrest. That power is reserved to the police under surveillance of the Attorney General and the courts.

The KGB and its East European branches know full well the limitations placed on the internal security services of the democratic nations and they exploit them to the full.

Admiral Bobby R. Inman, testifying before the US Senate in January, 1981, cited the lead of the US and other democratic societies "in the computer field" as a major advantage in countering the KGB. MI5, for example, maintains at its offices in Curzon Street, London, a computerized filing system that cross-references several million files on persons and other aspects of security-related data.

Soviet counter-espionage

In contrast to the elaborate legal safeguards imposed by democratic societies on their internal security agencies, the KGB and its allied agencies have virtually no legal limitation on their methods. Expediency, however, sometimes establishes such limits.

From its beginnings as Lenin's counterrevolutionary Cheka, murder on a vast scale has been the hallmark of what is now the KGB. It required no great moral or legal adjustment, therefore, to make use of killing as a "final solution" to foreign espionage. Also, as stated earlier in the chapter, the KGB makes no attempt to separate intelligence-gathering from "covert action". As a result many of the KGB's most brutal actions have often been attributed to "intelligence" when, in fact, they have nothing to do with espionage or the broader aspects of intelligence.

The one aspect of KGB terror in foreign countries that does relate to counter-espionage is the kidnapping or murder of defectors. Since these victims usually already have told what they know to the countries granting asylum, the aim of the KGB retribution squads is to discourage future defections. Despite this, defectors at all levels of Soviet and East European society continue to come forward.

Aside from the limited budgets devoted to penetration of Communist societies by US and allied intelligence services, the prospects for success historically have been very slender. This is attributable, of course, to the KGB's pervasive surveillance of every aspect of life in the Communist countries. History also indicates, however, that once

the KGB apparatus is disrupted by foreign military invasion or internal upheaval deepseated resentments by sectors of the Soviet population against the Communist regime provide extensive opportunity for espionage within the Soviet Union.

By far the greatest success of the KGB in recent years seems to have been the betrayal by Boyce and Lee ("the spoiled brats" referred to earlier) of CIA satellite technology. According to Sen. Daniel Patrick Moynihan of the US Senate Intelligence Committee in an interview with CBS News on November 22, 1982, the betrayal and the loss of verification it entailed was the major reason why the United States did not accept a second Strategic Arms Limitation Treaty (SALT).

"Basically," Senator Moynihan stated, compromise of the satellite system "made them temporarily at least useless to us because the Soviets could block them . . . . *Nothing quite so awful has happened to our country as the escapade of these two young men.*" (Emphasis added—*Editor.*)

Almost equally important technology was betrayed in the late 1970s by William H. Bell, a Hughes Aircraft Company employee, who sold vital "Stealth" bomber technology, F-15 interceptor "look-down-shoot-down" radar data and information on the US Navy's Phoenix air-to-air missile for the price of a down payment on a California condominium.

According to a CIA summary published in April 1982, the Soviet Union directly, or indirectly through its East European satellites, has been successful in purchasing technology that US and other Western firms have been eager to sell regardless of the strategic consequences. Where open purchase was not possible the Soviets in at least one instance acquired an entire integrated circuit processing plant by commercial transactions under a West German "cover".

In one of the strangest of all such operations in recent years, two West German businessmen, Ernest Ries and Helmut Willinger, were accused by German authorities in August 1982, of selling information to the Soviets, not from governmental sources, but from what is ostensibly a commercial operation—Defense Marketing Services of Greenwich, Connecticut. The "marketing service", it developed, is handling documents that are restricted by some form of governmental controls to Western governments and defence contractors.

At least one other KGB business "deal" went awry when US agents intercepted a corporate jet on which an American firm was attempting to send to the Soviet Union a multispectral scanner used by reconnaissance aircraft and satellites to intercept voice communications. KGB agents waiting for the aircraft in Switzerland received only an assortment of sand bags. The president of the firm attempting the shipment promptly left the United States for parts unknown.

Disinformation

"Disinformation" is an aspect of KGB operations that has received considerable publicity in recent years but, like "covert action", it has very little to do with intel-

1 Occasionally Western counter-espionage forces overstep the mark and have to be brought back into line. This happened with the "Mounties", whose counter-espionage role has been taken away, after harassment of Quebec separatists.

2 A uniformed KGB Border Guard represents only a small visible part of a huge organisation. KGB operatives are literally everywhere in the Soviet Union to ensure permanence for the CPSU.

3 The FBI building in Washington, DC. The FBI has had a troubled history, with J.Edgar Hoover its lengendary head being both the hero and the villain, using the FBI to harass Martin Luther King, prompted by his own racial prejudices.

4 Computer tapes (these are FBI's) are now the life-blood of virtually every intelligence organisation. No other method could cope with the vast volume of information and the need for rapid processing.

1 ▲

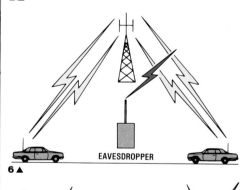

2 ▲

EAVESDROPPER

6 ▲

EAVESDROPPER

7 ▲

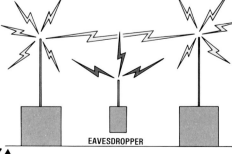

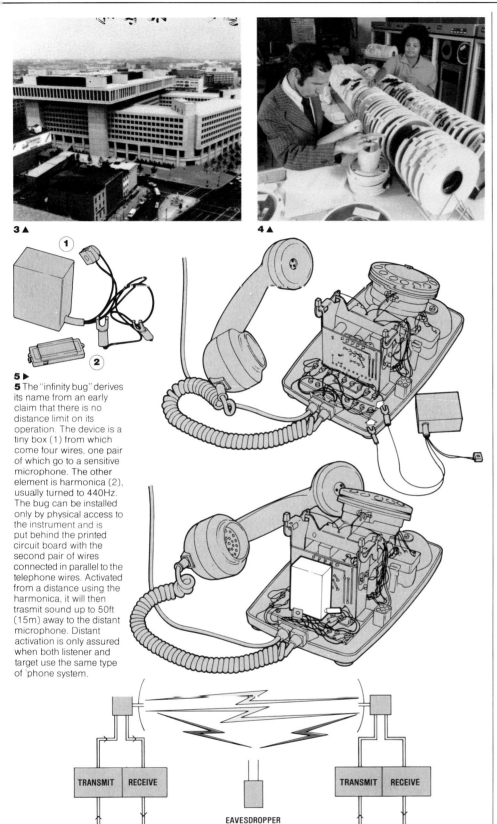

3 ▲

4 ▲

5 ►

5 The "infinity bug" derives its name from an early claim that there is no distance limit on its operation. The device is a tiny box (1) from which come four wires, one pair of which go to a sensitive microphone. The other element is harmonica (2), usually turned to 440Hz. The bug can be installed only by physical access to the instrument and is put behind the printed circuit board with the second pair of wires connected in parallel to the telephone wires. Activated from a distance using the harmonica, it will then trasmit sound up to 50ft (15m) away to the distant microphone. Distant activation is only assured when both listener and target use the same type of 'phone system.

8 ►

TRANSMIT | RECEIVE

MULTIPLEXER

CIRCUITS

CIRCUITS

EAVESDROPPER

TRANSMIT | RECEIVE

MULTIPLEXER

CIRCUITS

CIRCUITS

6 VHF communications, eg, mobile system, use relays and have "line-of- sight" characteristics. The eavesdropper must be within sight of one station.

7 HF radio links use one frequency for send and receive. An eavesdropper can tune into the frequency some distance (even up to thousands of miles) from the transmitters.

8 Modern trunk systems use microwave links (UHF) with many circuits over each link. The circuits are fed into a multiplexer which stacks them electronically, and feeds them over

one pair of wires to the transmitter. At the far end the process is reversed. Eavesdropping into this system is commonplace. The eavesdropper must be between the towers.

ligence or counter-espionage as such. A form of "disinformation" by which false information is transmitted through spy networks with or without the cooperation of "double agents" can properly be described as counter-espionage. The use of false press reports, rumours and the like, however, is a form of psychological warfare and has nothing to do with intelligence or counter-espionage although it depends upon accurate intelligence for success.

The balance sheet

Unless they intend to convert themselves into police states on the Soviet model, the democratic societies must contend with the fact that the KGB will continue to be relatively more successful in penetration of those societies than the non-Communist countries will be in penetration of the Soviet Union and its "allies". Experience has shown, however, that the police state itself produces such extreme pressures on its citizens that many of them will risk family, social and economic status and life itself to defect. Although there have been defections in both directions the balance is heavily on the side of the free societies. Whether that, in turn, equalizes the loss of such vital technology as that betrayed to the Soviets in the Boyce-Lee case (KH-11 satellite surveillance system) is impossible to tell at this stage.

Even when it has purloined important Western and Japanese technical advances, however, the Soviet Union has not always been able to exploit them due to inadequacies of manufacture. Japanese cameras and miniaturized electronic components on the open market, for example, generally are thought to be well ahead of anything the Soviets can produce on their own.

The Soviet espionage effort in the West and Japan does not depend on sophisticated technology. Most of what the Soviets have obtained has simply been carried out and handed to them in its original form. The age-old human frailties of greed, lust and uncontrolled resentment against a private or government employer seem to provide ready access to government offices, research laboratories and manufacturing plants.

Ironically, Western and Japanese technological superiority is of little use to the West in the field of earthbound espionage because the tight internal controls of the Soviet and East European system make penetration difficult in Eastern Europe and virtually impossible in the USSR. In short, the elaborate surveillance technology so fascinating to readers of spy fiction produces next to nothing in the real world of intelligence. Its primary use is in police work, of which counter-espionage is, of course, an important part.

The West and Japan are almost entirely dependent upon the space and electronic interception technology discussed in chapters 5 and 6. There lies the true Western and Japanese advantage, expanded by the contributions of Soviet defectors. Those advantages, reflecting as they do a fundamentally healthier society and economy, more than offset Soviet advantages based on relatively free access.

Chapter five

Intelligence and the electronic battlefield

ON MAY 4, 1982, a British Type-42 destroyer, HMS *Sheffield*, was destroyed by a sea-skimming, French-built Exocet missile during the Falklands campaign. It was an incident which puzzled many, since the Type-42 destroyer was designed to be part of a layered air defence system to protect the main body of the British fleet.

In the late Spring and early Summer of 1982, a concerned world watched as Israeli Defence Forces invaded Lebanon in a major conflict against military elements of the Palestinian Liberation Organization (PLO) and the regular forces of Syria. By mid-June, Israeli military leaders claimed to have destroyed 86 Syrian aircraft including Soviet built Mikoyan MiG-23 fighters and five French-built Aérospatiale Gazelle attack helicopters. The Israelis claimed that they had lost only two helicopters and one US-built A-4 fighter-bomber. In another report, it appeared that 19 Soviet built Syrian SAM-6 surface-to-air missiles in the Bekaa Valley area had been destroyed by the Israeli Air Force (IAF) without losses. In all of these reports, electronic warfare was a decisive factor.

These two examples serve to illustrate the vital and central role played by electronic technology in every aspect of modern warfare. Success in combat is related directly to a battle for *time*. Reduced to its basic elements, *electronic warfare is fought entirely on the battlefield of time,* frequently measured in seconds or even micro-seconds. Just as any commander must concentrate his forces to attack the enemy at some vulnerable point, an attacker on the electronic battlefield must use his intelligence *and* operational resources to deny or minimize the defender's capability to react in a timely way.

This chapter focuses mainly on the role of electronics as applied to intelligence, but it must be kept in mind that electronic technology is now employed in a wide range of military activities and this range, while not always related directly or specifically to intelligence, cannot be ignored.

In the Bekaa Valley example, the Israeli forces employed remotely piloted vehicles (RPVs), such as their Mastiff, as well as "drones" to ascertain the radio frequencies used by the Syrian SAM-6s. (An RPV is a platform which is under remote but direct control, while a "drone" functions without remote control.) Two Israeli Grumman E-2C Hawkeye aircraft obtained electronic bearings on Syrian missile radar systems to plot their exact location. Tactical electronic

computer links then identified details concerning the weapons systems while Israeli aircraft destroyed the SAM-6 sites with electronically guided rockets. In the case of the Syrian fighter aircraft, the Israelis positioned E-2C aircraft off the coast of Lebanon where their radars could detect Syrian jets taking off from their bases. After the Syrian planes were airborne, the Israelis then jammed their ground-control radio links, leaving the Syrian pilots without guidance, while the Israeli fighters were quickly directed to advantageous intercept points. This example illustrates the vital interface of current intelligence, as well as basic intelligence (acquired over a longer time), with tactical operations.

Inadequate "intelligence" means defeat

The loss of HMS *Sheffield* points up yet another facet of modern electronic combat. This type of destroyer is supposed to constitute a main fleet defence against air attack in concert with airborne early warning aircraft to detect low-flying enemy aircraft. Unfortunately for *Sheffield,* there were no airborne early-warning radars and fighter air protection was inadequate. When the Exocet missiles were sighted close-in, the Sea Dart missile system on *Sheffield,* designed to engage aerial platforms at a distance, simply was unable to get on target in time, because of the slower reaction time of Sea Dart. The lack of adequate intelligence (e.g., early warning radar) coupled with an insufficient operational capability (fighters and proper countermeasures) resulted in a tactical defeat.

Because the term "electronic warfare" (EW) has gained such common acceptance it is used throughout this chapter; however, the term is somewhat inaccurate since electronic warfare, for the most part, is not some means of combat using electrons as a weapon, but rather it is a form of conflict which uses the entire spectrum of *electromagnetic radiation* as a battlefield. The standard NATO definition, for instance, states that electronic warfare is: "That division of the military use of electronics involving actions taken to prevent or reduce an enemy's effective use of radiated electromagnetic energy and actions taken to ensure our own effective use of radiated electromagnetic energy."

1 Lit up like a beacon, a radome in the early warning chain demonstrates that it is, like so many other electronic surveillance systems, working 24 hours a day, 365 days a year to prevent a "worst-case" surprise attack.

1 ▲

Electronic warfare is a relatively new but utterly
deadly battlefield, where victory or defeat
may come in a matter of seconds or even microseconds.
Electronic intelligence is vital to survival
in this struggle.

The origins of electronic warfare are to be found in the military employment of electric telegraphy during the Crimean War in 1855. The only recorded countermeasures taken in these early days were, unwittingly, by British soldiers who discovered quickly that the gutta-percha "plastic" used for insulation could be used as a replacement for broken pipestems. Electronic warfare during the American Civil War (1860-1865), the Franco-Prussian War (1870-1871), and the Boer War (1899-1902) consisted mainly of efforts to intercept or interrupt enemy telegraph transmissions. With the development of wireless telegraphy, advances in interception and interference techniques provided a means of rudimentary countermeasures, and 1903 the US Navy had developed a primitive programme for interfering with enemy signals by "jamming" them with a signal transmitted on the same frequency.

During the Russo-Japanese War (1905) there were several instances in which Russian forces attempted to "jam" or interfere with Japanese fleet signal communications. The results were mixed. In one case, a Russian shore-based operator prevented Japanese vessels from successfully ranging their guns in an attack on Port Arthur. In another instance in the Battle of Tsushima, radio operators on the Russian cruiser *Ural* blocked signals from the Japanese ships tracking her flotilla movements. The final outcome of the battle suggests this effort was not completely effective.

World War I communications

By the time of World War I electronic communications had improved in technology and were in wider use. The importance of secure communications, interception techniques and cryptanalysis grew. Newer applications for electronic technology began to appear in areas other than for communications. British, French and American forces fighting in Europe were able to use signals transmitted by German forces for direction finding and target location. In cases in which messages could not be read or deciphered, Allied intelligence officers were able to analyze patterns of signal transmissions and accurately predict enemy activity. By 1916, the German High Command had established a central organization for the same purpose. Wireless signals were also employed by both sides as an aid to navigation of aircraft and naval vessels.

Electronic warfare quickly achieved a pre-eminent position during World War II and advances in technology accelerated at a very rapid rate. The significance of electronic warfare during this period would be difficult to over-emphasize. As Winston Churchill commented in his war memoirs:

"This was a secret war, whose battles were lost or won unknown to the public, and only with difficulty comprehended, even now, to those outside the small high scientific circles concerned. Unless British science had proven superior to German, and unless its strange, sinister resources had been effectively brought to bear in the struggle for survival, we might will have been defeated and destroyed."

Because of the long lead time for system development, the successes and victory described by Churchill could never have been achieved unless the foundations had been laid at an earlier date. The first steps were initiated when the Royal Academy of Science of Great Britain asked Sir Robert Watson-Watt if radio rays could be employed as a weapon against an enemy aircraft. In an amazingly prophetic response, Sir Robert replied that this was not yet possible, but that technology could be developed to locate the aircraft. It was Sir Robert Watson-Watt's now famous "Death

1▲

2▲

1 Although designed for carrier use, the E-2C Hawkeye AEW aircraft has acted as a major force-multiplier in recent Israeli actions.

2 In the Beka'a Valley raids the Israelis were able to destroy many of these SA-6s using sophisticated ECCM techniques.

3 Soviet-made Fan Song radar is the target acquisition and fire control radar for Egyptian SA-2 Guideline surface-to-air missile.

4 An Egyptian SA-2 Guideline missile base in the desert near Cairo. The missiles are grouped in a circle around the Fan Song radar.

5 The most feared low-level air defence weapon—the Soviet-made ZSU-23-4. Its valve-technology radar is simple, reliable and very effective. The Israelis fell foul of this system when they tried to fly low to avoid Egyptian SAMs.

3▲

4▲

Ray Memorandum" that inaugurated the research that produced early radar-controlled air defence systems. Early radar systems functioned by transmitting radio pulses which, when they reached a reflecting surface, produced an echo. The radar receiver used the echo to locate and identify the target surface. Modern radars, although more sophisticated, use this same principle.

World War II marked the major turning point for the development of EW and specialized related equipment and it is to these early programmes that Churchill referred in the statement quoted above. During the air battle over Britain in 1940 the German Luftwaffe had to rely on radio navigational aids or "beams" to guide their bombers to their targets. The Germans employed a series of stations in France transmitting beams which the bombers could follow to London. This beam system, known as Lorenz, was countered by the British with a countermeasure called "Meaconing" (masking beacon) which retransmitted the German signal and, in the process, "bent" the signal to lead the bombers away from the targets. As soon as the Luftwaffe discovered the countermeasure, they developed a new system of beams. The British concluded that they could either jam the new system or employ deception. Intelligence indicated that deception offered immediate results and the deception system selected was successful.

In the air battle in Europe during World War II, the "battle of the beams" played a most significant role, and the losing side in the EW battle lost the air war as well. Experiences in air battles during the Korean conflict and by US forces in Vietnam continued to provide examples of the increasing impact of EW in intelligence as well as in combat operations, particularly in the air.

EW in 1973 Mid-East war

It remained for the 1973 Middle East War to demonstrate a broad spectrum of EW employment since most of the then-latest Soviet SAM and anti-aircraft artillery were in action against the Israeli Air Force (IAF) which used US and French-built aircraft systems. Arab forces used the high-altitude SAM-2 with its Fansong-B radars, as well as the SAM-6 at lower altitude, together with Straight Flush radar. At medium altitudes, the Arab forces used the SAM-3 and its Low Blow radar. For close-in air defence, the Arabs had the portable SAM-7 and the very effective ZSU-23-4 Shilka self-propelled, quad-mounted 23mm cannon system direc-

ted by its own Gun Dish radar. When the IAF sought to avoid the high and medium altitude SAMs, they fell victim to the AA and SAM-7 fire. After initial heavy losses, during which the IAF collected new intelligence, the Israelis were able to adopt suppressive countermeasures and operate effectively. However, the lessons of the 1973 conflict were not lost on other nations, and these lessons initiated today's continuing trend towards extensive development of new systems.

Looking more closely at the 1982 example of the IAF action taken against the Syrian SAM-6 sites in Lebanon, it becomes clear that the Israeli action followed the description categorised below under Electronic Support Measures (ESM). That is, the IAF intelligence searched for and found the SAM sites by locating the source of radar emissions (ELINT). By then analyzing the collected data, they could identify the type of equipment and associated weaponry. At this point, previously acquired intelligence was used concerning the characteristics of SAM-6 (for example, range, accuracy, capabilities and vulnerabilities). With the intelligence process completed, the IAF commander could then make a decision whether to attack and destroy the missiles, or perhaps bypass or avoid them. This example again

1 ▲

2 ▲

3 ▲

THE ELECTRONIC BATTLEFIELD

A diorama of an EW battlefield based on a Middle East setting. The advancing force on the right has an HQ (1) and numerous radio links and electronic sensors. The links include: from the main HQ to subsidiary HQs (2), infantry to tank (3), recce HQ (4) to foot patrols (5), and artillery observation post to gun lines (6). Electronic sensors include radars for air defence (7) and ground surveillance (8).

For the defending force on the left the first priority is to use Electronic Support Measures (ESM) to build up the picture of the enemy Electronic Order of Battle (EOB). ESM consists of airborne radar detection and analysis (9), ground monitoring (10), and SIGINT activities (11). Once the EOB has been established, the nature of the retaliatory action must be decided. For example, there are occasions when greater results will be gained from monitoring a radio net than by jamming it. In the latter case a variety of mobile jammers can be deployed (9, 12, 13) depending upon the terrain, locations and frequencies involved. Alternatively, the ESM-derived

information can be used to provide targets for artillery (14) or other means of fire support. Finally it is absolutely vital that the ESM and ECM battle is carefully controlled and coordinated (15), as haphazard and uncoordinated EW will lead to chaos and a waste of effort. The potential fruits of successful EW are great, since every modern army is trained and equipped to depend entirely on the use and availability of telecommunications. If the links are broken, however, the flow of information will cease, orders cannot be issued, and tactical cohesion will break down totally within hours.

(Source: Based on information from IAI Elta Industries Ltd.)

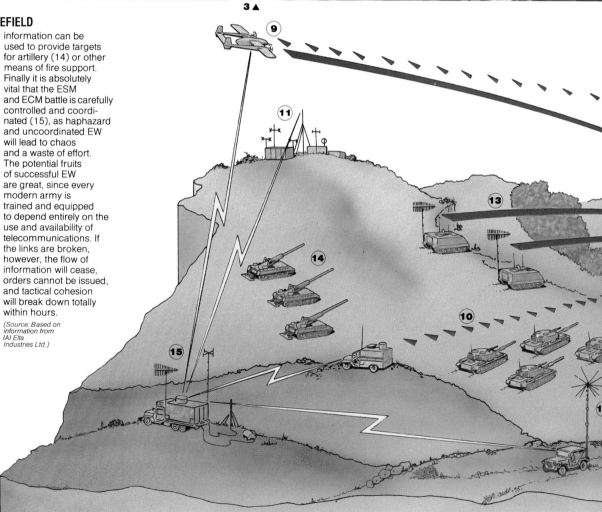

illustrates the direct inter-relationship in conflict between intelligence, air and air defence combatants. A somewhat similar process is involved in the case of the land or sea battle as well.

All of the many facets of electronic warfare can be conveniently incorporated into the three broad categories:

Electronic Warfare Support Measures (ESM);
Electronic Countermeasures (ECM); and
Electronic Counter-Countermeasures (ECCM).

The essential elements of these categories are described in the table below.

CATEGORIES OF ELECTRONIC WARFARE

Category	Description	Purpose
Electronic Warfare Support Measures (ESM)	Actions taken to search for, intercept, locate, record and analyze radiated electromagnetic energy for the purpose of exploiting such radiations in support of military operations, (direction finding of radios and radars is an ESM technique).	Intercepting Identifying Analyzing Locating
Electronic Countermeasures (ECM)	Actions taken to prevent or reduce the enemy's effective use of the electromagnetic spectrum. (ECM includes jamming and electronic deception).	Jamming Disrupting Deceiving
Electronic Counter-Countermeasures (ECCM)	Actions taken to ensure friendly use of the electromagnetic spectrum against electronic warfare despite the enemy's use of countermeasures	Protecting

In any discussion of electronic warfare, one is invariably confronted with a question as to which element or category of EW is of primary importance—what are the systematic priorities? It would appear obvious that, since for every system, every measure, there is, or will be, a countersystem or countermeasure, EW must be taken as a composite of all of its elements. While this is an accurate statement, military commentators frequently give pride of place to operational systems, that is to those systems which provide direct, immediate or destructive effect against enemy forces, such as electronic guidance systems for weapons delivery, or perhaps air defence or artillery target acquisition systems, naval gunfire systems or anti-submarine detection and destruction systems. There is no question but that these elements, together with navigational, reconnaissance, and various sensors, occupy first place in military use of radiated electro-magnetic energy. However, it is important to recognize that military communications, the second major user of electronics, because of its dominant role in command, control and intelligence, remains of fundamental—perhaps primary—concern in this discussion.

The accompanying chart displays the electromagnetic spectrum subdivided by military use. If one examines only the High Frequency (HF); Very High Frequency (VHF) and Ultra-High Frequency (UHF) bands it is

4▲

1 Boeing E-3A AWACS coming in to refuel. The permanent deployment of airborne EW platforms such as this has introduced a totally new element in the electronic battle.

2 This Circularly Disposed Antenna Array (CDAA) is one of a number of US stations around the world. These monitor from HF to UHF and have DF accuracies between 3° and 5°.

3 An American soldier operating a Piranha radio jammer. Jamming is not a simple task, and must be controlled; indiscriminate jamming will cause chaos on *both* sides.

4 C50 radio relay detachment of the British Army. Such highly directional UHF systems are very difficult to monitor, but airborne EW platforms may change such immunity.

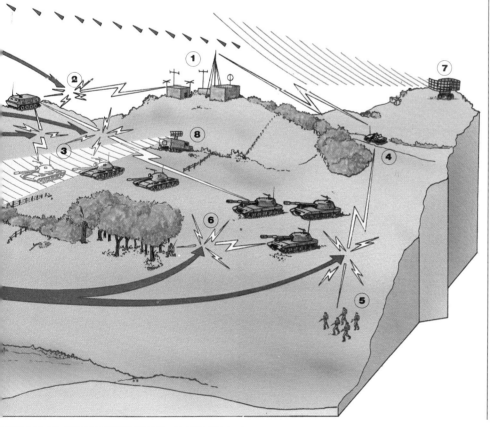

possible to calculate the number of available channels for radio communications. For example, HF (from 3 to 30 megahertz (MHz)) has 300 channels; VHF (from 112 to 135 MHz) has 2,300 channels; while UHF (225 to 400 MHz) carries 1,750 channels. The chart does not list the Very Low Frequency (VLF) band from 3 to 30 Kilohertz (KHz) or Low Frequency (LF) bands, both of which find military use, particularly for naval navigation and communications. This will be discussed later in more detail.

In communications/EW, a basic distinction is made between action which is directed at the transmission of the signal itself and that which is specifically directed to the information contained in the signal. In the context of the categories of EW, previously listed, for example, interfering with a signal communication transmission is ECM, while protecting the communications channel itself is classed as ECCM. Those functions that seek to "read" the enemy

message are called communications intelligence (COMINT) while the protective measures are referred to as Communications Security (COMSEC). Intelligence confined to locating or identifying the source of transmission is classed as electronic intelligence (ELINT).

Secret communications

COMINT and COMSEC involve the use of cryptology, the science of secret communications. Recent history is replete with many examples of the use of codes and ciphers and the damaging results of success, by one side or another, in reading enemy messages. Modern computer technology has extended the possibilities of secret communications as well as the means fo defeating them. Because a vast literature exists on the techniques of cryptology, the descriptions in this chapter will be confined to the general features of major systems.

One of the major employments of EW as suggested in the previous paragraphs is for the disruption of an enemy's command and control communications. This aspect of EW can be understood more easily when compared with modern ground weapons technology. While modern ground weapons systems incorporate electronic technology, these electronic systems operate, fundamentally, to improve the *functional efficiency* of the weapons system itself. In few cases is the function of the weapon wholly dependent on an electronic system for its operation. Modern electronics play an important role in target location, calculating ranges, aiming and re-targeting. In land warfare, for example, tanks, artillery and guns, as well as infantry mortars and rifles, can be used for their combat firepower without employing electronics.

On the other hand, *all* modern military forces have become highly dependent upon rapid, secure communications. The military

FREQUENCY BANDS AND DESIGNATIONS

One of the unseen battles takes place in the electromagnetic spectrum, which is becoming ever more crowded as an increasing number of people want to use some sort of transmitting device. The frequency of a transmission is measured by the number of oscillations per second, the unit being the "Herz". Thus, one Kiloherz (1KHz) is one thousand cycles per second, one Megaherz (1MHz) one million cycles, and so on. The lower end of the scale is the "audio" band which extends from about 20Hz to 20KHz, although most people's hearing is actually in the range 80Hz to 15KHz, despite what the "Hi-Fi" salesmen may say! The second characteristic of these transmissions is "wavelength", which is the distance between one wave and the same point on the next wave. As frequency rises the wavelength gets shorter and the radio path becomes more of a straight line. Radar bands have letter designations; the wartime system was revised in 1972 and is now as shown.

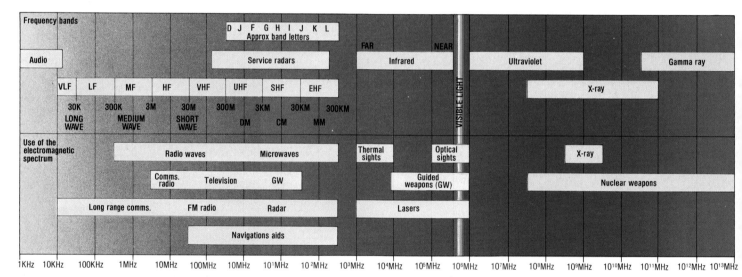

Frequency bands																								

Approx band letters: D J F G H I J K L
FAR — NEAR
Audio | Service radars | Infrared | Ultraviolet | Gamma ray
VISIBLE LIGHT
VLF | LF | MF | HF | VHF | UHF | SHF | EHF | X-ray
30K LONG WAVE | 300K MEDIUM WAVE | 3M SHORT WAVE | 30M | 300M DM | 3KM CM | 30KM MM | 300KM

Use of the electromagnetic spectrum:
Radio waves | Microwaves | Thermal sights | Optical sights | X-ray
Comms. radio | Television | GW | Guided weapons (GW) | Nuclear weapons
Long range comms. | FM radio | Radar | Lasers
Navigations aids

1KHz 10KHz 100KHz 1MHz 10MHz 100MHz 10MHz 10^1MHz 10^2MHz 10^3MHz 10^4MHz 10^5MHz 10^6MHz 10^7MHz 10^8MHz 10^9MHz 10^{10}MHz 10^{11}MHz 10^{12}MHz 10^{13}MHz

1 ▲

2 ▲

3 ▲

1 AN/FPS-49 (in the white radome) and AN/FPS-50 early warning radars of the US Ballistic Missile Early Warning System (BMEWS).

2 The huge radar arrays of the USAF's Pave Paws AN/FPS-115 radar are intended to give early warning of SLBM attack.

3 A poorly sited and camouflaged tactical control centre, with large and obvious tropospheric scatter antennas.

4 Another type of electronic sensor is the air defence target acquisition radar: this is Swedish Ericsson PS-70R Giraffe.

5 Another truck-mounted air surveillance radar is the West Germany Army's Mobile Pulse Doppler Radar (MPDR-45) by Siemens.

commander, at every level, must be in virtually continuous communication with his forces to send and receive information as well as to direct combat operations. Thus EW directed against weapons systems strikes at the enemy's combat arm; EW directed against communications strikes against the brain.

In EW as in other aspects of combat intelligence and operations, a distinction is made between *tactical* and *strategic* EW. At the strategic level, for example, EW is usually confined to monitoring enemy communications and to passive ELINT collection, which activities can be accomplished anywhere in one's own friendly area from around 62 to 620 miles (100 to 1,000km) away from contact with enemy forces. Such employment involves the use of quite large, complex, and, more or less, permanently fixed antennas and sites (see accompanying illustrations). Because of their location, these installations can be considered not too vulnerable to enemy attack. There is also a trend toward increased use of satellites, long-range electronic reconnaissance aircraft, RPVs and drones equipped with elaborate monitoring systems. Some typical systems are illustrated. Interception of enemy communications at the *strategic* level can provide intelligence information on enemy capabilities, operations and plans, while *tactical* reconnaissance and intelligence gathering systems provide data which can be put to immediate operational use.

Tactical and strategic EW

Tactical EW is conducted in or quite near to combat operations areas, 6 to 12 miles (about 10 to 20km) from points of contact with enemy forces, and is therefore directly related to immediate combat operations. While longer-range or strategic communications employ the lower or HF bands, they also use satellite communications and point-to-point microwave relay systems.

Because the command and control communications of all modern military forces have to operate in an EW environment, signal communications equipment today is designed with ECCM features which were practically unknown until the 1970s. In the NATO forces, for example, several types of systems all demonstrate common concern for operations in an intensive EW environment. The British Ptarmigan system is a mobile army command and control system, typically employed as shown in the accompanying diagram. Ptarmigan and the ambitious US Tri-Tac communications programme are designed to develop a virtually universal, multi-service family of equipment, compatible for use within and throughout the North Atlantic Alliance. The German Bundeswehr uses their Autoko system in a similar approach to modular tactical communications, as do the French with their Rita system.

4 ▲

5 ▲

PTARMIGAN COMMUNICATIONS SYSTEM

Command and control in 1 (British) Corps will be revolutionised in a few years time by the Ptarmigan communications system. This is a true area system with a grid of "trunk nodes" covering the corps area, each such node having at least three links to other nodes, ensuring that no node is critical to the system, giving considerable redundancy. Each HQ has links into at least two trunk nodes and they move within the grid, hooking up to the most appropriate nodes when they halt, according to the central signals plan. It is hoped this system will aid versatility.

✕ ✕ ✕	Corps
✕ ✕	Division
✕	Brigade
▼	Trunk node
◼	Headquarters Single channel radio access
◆	Brigade HQ Mobile radio subscriber

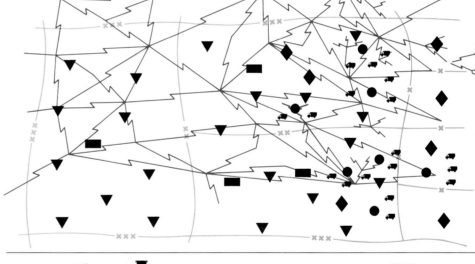

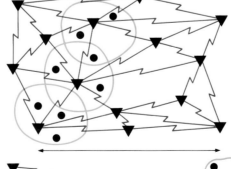

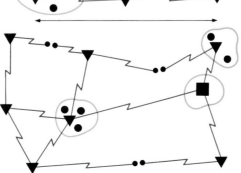

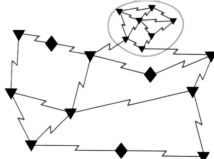

RITA COMMUNICATIONS SYSTEM

RITA (Reseau Integre de Transmissions Automatique) is a fully integrated and automatic tactical communications system, now in service with the French Army. The system provides direct dialling facilities; voice, telegraph and data circuits; net radio access; and all fully secure (ie, with on-line encryption!). Network control is exercised by the Centre de Commande du Reseau (CECORE) at the corps headquarters.

▼	Comms central
◼	Inter-comms links
◆	Brigade HQ
●	Microwave station shooting into Comms
●●	Relays

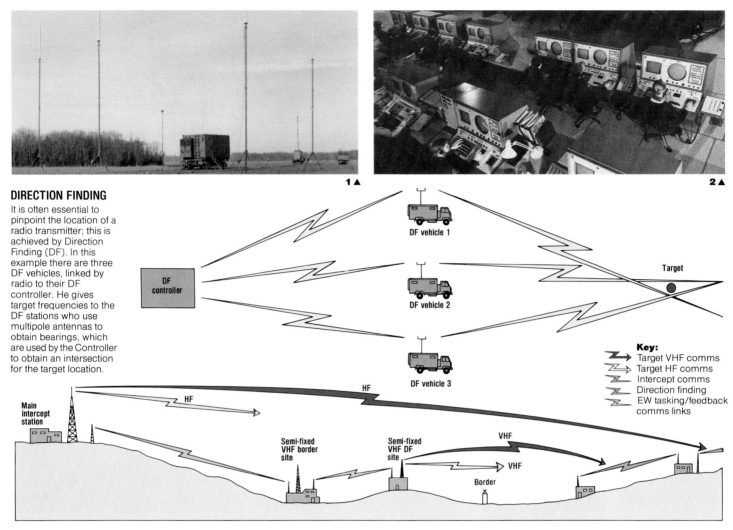

1 ▲

2 ▲

DIRECTION FINDING

It is often essential to pinpoint the location of a radio transmitter; this is achieved by Direction Finding (DF). In this example there are three DF vehicles, linked by radio to their DF controller. He gives target frequencies to the DF stations who use multipole antennas to obtain bearings, which are used by the Controller to obtain an intersection for the target location.

Key:
Target VHF comms
Target HF comms
Intercept comms
Direction finding
EW tasking/feedback comms links

INTERCEPT/DF DEPLOYMENT

Great resources are poured into DF and intercept activities; this diagram shows how such a system might be organised. LF, MF, HF transmissions can be intercepted from long ranges and monitoring stations can be sited well back from national borders. VHF and UHF, however, have virtually line-of-sight paths and an intercept station must be sited as close as possible to the transmitter, and also as high as possible. Typical of such sites is the Soviet EW station on the "Brocken" hill south-east of Goslar and just inside the East German border. From this 3,750ft (1,142m) site the Soviets monitor NATO VHF and UHF communications deep inside FRG.

These and similar communications systems are designed to provide reliable, secure communications for deployed forces. Advances in the design and use of space satellites must also be mentioned, since satellites used in communications and communications intelligence play an increasingly important role. NATO operates a satellite programme for Alliance communications, the US and UK operating compatible national systems. With portable or mobile units, such as those just mentioned, satellites can extend the ability to communicate virtually anywhere.

In recent years, satellites have assumed an increasingly important role in world communications. Satellites stationed in space permit instant linking of radio and television facilities without the need for extensive wire or point-to-point relay networks. Satellites provide precise navigational capabilities for ships and aircraft and can provide photographic imagery coverage for mapping as well as for geological exploration. These same capabilities can find similar employment in military and defence-related activities.

In the 1960s, NATO acquired a satellite capability through the US Defence Communication Satellite Programme. After further development, the NATO II programme was established, consisting of 12 earth terminals. The NATO III programme, currently under development, will provide for integration of satellite communications into the overall NATO Integrated Communicaton System (NICS).

Soviet/Warsaw Pact systems parallel generally those NATO systems outlined above in function, although they tend toward less complexity in design and manufacture and, in general, display greater uniformity than the diversity existing within NATO alliance equipment. Although Warsaw Pact forces are well supplied with signal equipment, their doctrine does not rely on electronic communications to the same degree as does NATO's, and "listening silence" is the tactical norm.

Soviet and Warsaw Pact forces also use satellite communications, although less is known about the extent of their use since Soviet civilian and military roles are performed by the same satellites. The Molynia series of Soviet satellites, begun in 1965, consisted of 33 satellites by 1975. In 1980, the Soviets launched a new class of multi-purpose, geostationary communications satellites called Volna, which now provide virtually world-wide coverage.

Satellites have proved their usefulness in many ways. For example, satellites can provide reliable, high speed signal transmission for all types of voice and data over distances of up to about 8,080 miles (13,000km). Satellite communications can also perform despite adverse atmospheric conditions and can be aimed with sufficient precision to reduce greatly the risk of interception. On the other hand, a jamming signal transmitted to a satellite can prevent signal transmissions. In 1975, the Soviets succeeded in blocking US satellite signals with a laser beam and recent experiments during US Skylab and Soviet Salyut missions have demonstrated that satellites are becoming vulnerable to physical destruction or damage from other space vehicles.

Communications, ECM and ECCM

The foregoing brief review of types of modern military communications systems is provided in order to introduce the reader to some practical, systematic developments in modern military command and control communications for the EW environment. It is clear that modern equipment must be able to transmit vital information despite enemy efforts to intercept or disrupt signal communications. Since the requirements are most immediate on or near the battlefield, tactical communications and corre-

1 Non-tactical display of French Thomson-CSF mobile monitoring and control centre, normally sited deep in a wood and heavily camouflaged to avoid detection.

2 An operational control centre in Denmark of the NATO Air Defence System Ground Environment (NADGE), the largest electronic defence system ever undertaken in peacetime.

3 Strategic missile surveillance in the West is achieved by BMEWS; this is the UK-based station in Yorkshire. Other stations are in Greenland and Alaska.

4 These SATCOM earth station antennas are very large by modern standards; truck-borne and even man-portable terminals are now in service with the US and British forces.

3 ▲

4 ▲

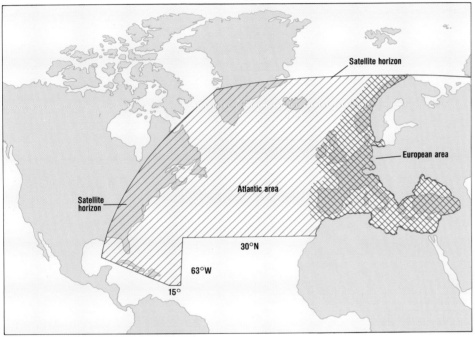

5 ▲

NATO SATELLITE COMMUNICATIONS

NATO's interest in Satcoms began in the early 1960s and the first was launched March 20, 1970. The NATO-II system comprised geostationary satellites some 21,750 miles (35,000km) above the Atlantic with 12 ground stations and others on ships. The NATO-III system shown here comprises three satellites giving the "footprint", ie, almost total coverage of the Alliance's territory. There are 21 static ground stations.

5 The NATO-IIIB communications satellite being prepared for launch, January 1977. Satellites provide cheap and effective communications, but how they could be attacked in war has been demonstrated by the Soviet Union.

---

sponding ECM and ECCM will be explored here in somewhat greater detail.

Military communications employ all signal modes, written messages, oral or voice communications, and graphic systems, using television or facsimile, to transmit photographic drawings or printed transmissions. Since all forms of transmission, wireless or wire signals, can be intercepted, military communicators employ various types of cryptology to deny information to unintended recipients. Cryptologic devices are designed with two different purposes. There are those which are to be used for *strategic* communications, such as between higher echelons of defence ministries, general staff and higher command levels—and intelligence traffic must be as advanced in technology and as secure as possible because such communications means are used to transmit information which is likely to remain sensitive for a very long period of time. However, messages from *tactical* units in combat do not require the same level of security, simply because their content has a much more limited time value. Information for artillery target data or the location of tank or infantry battalions may be of no use after a lapse of only a few hours. Thus tactical cryptosystems are designed more for portability, ruggedness and simplicity.

Cryptologic devices are frequently referred to as "first", "second", "third" or other generations of equipment. At present, six generations are identified:

First: Manual devices consisting of discs, slides, drums or wheels which re-arrange or substitute clear text for an enciphered text. The earliest such devices appeared around 450-475 BC.

Second: Mechanical devices or machines for ciphering appeared in the 19th century. By 1875, some of these devices could print text. These machines were elaborate clockwork-like devices.

Third: These devices developed along with telegraphic devices from about the middle of the 19th Century and some remain in use today.

Fourth: Developed on the eve of World War I, these machines were early electrified typewriters and used wired "codewheels" or rotors for the encipherment of clear text by substituting other letters or symbols.

Fifth: Introduced in the late 1930s, before World War II, this generation of device first employed electronic circuitry and "memory" storage.

Sixth: The "micro-electronic" device first appeared in the 1960s and developments continue at a rapid rate. The newest devices incorporate thousands of circuits on a single chip of only a few millimetres.

Military communicators designate cryptosystems as *on-line* or *off-line*. These distinctions are essentially procedural. An off-line mode simply indicates that the process of enciphering or deciphering a message is accomplished independently from the actual transmission or delivery. On-line operations indicate that the ciphering or deciphering element is connected to the means of transmission or reception and, as the clear text is entered at a sending station, it is received and deciphered in a single operation. Most modern military systems can operate in either mode and many incorporate a feature which can store the cipher text and transmit an entire message in a very short "burst" lasting perhaps no more than a few seconds but providing an added factor of security.

The encipherment of written messages is but one function of secure communications. Secure voice communication, by radio or telephone, is an important countermeasure to the possible interception of sensitive information. Within five years following the award of the telephone patent to American Alexander Graham Bell, in 1881, a patent was also given for a "speech scrambler" to be used with the telephone. The scrambling of speech is one of several methods of secure voice communications, another being speech encipherment. As elsewhere in cryptology, the degree of security depends on the use of the equipment; the degree of security needed, and the relative perishability of the information. Speech scrambling does not always provide the same degree of security as speech encipherment. This involves the conversion of speech into digital bits which are then enciphered, in similar fashion to an enciphered written message. Scrambling equipment, however, can be produced which is quite secure and which is less complex than the enciphered speech system. Newer devices use a combination of methods including the Vocoder, which synthesizes the voice into an artificial language and can provide an extremely high degree of security. All of these devices have some disadvantages in the form of speech distortion and some degree of loss in recognition and intelligibilty, as well as relative complexity of operation.

The communications (and basic countermeasures) outlined above apply generally to ground, naval and air forces. However, naval and air forces do encounter some communications problems which require a different approach. This is mainly because of the operational environments and distances involved. Submarines, for example, are able to receive routine messages without the need to expose themselves on the surface, but this involves the use of an antenna system or buoyed wire which can be detected by ECM infra-red sensors or radar. Low frequency (LF) and very low frequency (VLF) transmissions can help to overcome these deficiencies, as they can penetrate ocean depths to a considerable distance. Using these low frequencies, submarines are able to receive messages while travelling at normal speeds below the surface. Because of the considerable size of LF and VLF transmitters and antennas at present, the submarines are able only to receive signals and are unable to respond. The message using LF/VLF is also extremely slow and it takes around an hour to transmit a message consisting of only three letters.

Special naval and air approach

Until relatively recent times major problems of communications with an between operational aircraft basically arose from the need to keep size, weight and power requirements within the capacity of the aircraft. Today, improved aircraft capabilities and technological advances have eliminated many of the early problems and operational aircraft can now remain in constant touch with ground stations throughout the world as well as with each other. Generally, air operations are highly dependent upon rapid, secure voice communications. Because secure voice communications must operate in an ECM environment,

1▲

SECURE COMMUNICATIONS

Modern armed forces depend absolutely upon telecommunications for command, control and the passage of information/intelligence. As shown here, sea and air forces must have links both within their groups (1) (2), and back to their bases (3) (4), as well as to each other. The same applies to a ground force; for example, an armoured division (5), where there are many thousands of individual radio sets working on probably more than 200 radio nets, as well as links back to superior HQs (6). Against this, an enemy (7) deploys a sophisticated Electronic Warfare (EW) effort, which will comprise Electronic Support Measures (ESM) (intercept (8), direction-finding) and Electronic Counter-Measures (jamming (9), deception). The original force's reply to this is known as Electronic Counter-Counter Measures (ECCM). One of the prime ECCMs is to protect the content of the transmissions by encryption of the signals (10). This was first achieved by machines such as the Germany "Enigma", in which written messages were encoded "off-line" and then sent as jumbled figures and letters. Such mechanical devices are now obsolete, and highly sophisticated electronic "on-line"

devices have become commonplace, both for telegraph and voice links. The enemy thus has a dilemma: if he cannot learn anything by listening, is there any point in not just jamming? The answer lies in modern techniques of analysis in which the "signature" of individual sets and the characteristics of nets and links are used to build up a picture of the enemy order of battle and, electronically, of what is happening "on the other side of the hill".

(Source: Based on information from IAI Elta Electronics Industries Ltd.)

1 Infantry company commander using his VHF radio. Such a forward link, especially when using a hilltop site as here, would not be too difficult for an enemy to monitor.

2 US Army operator using a teleprinter over a GRC-142 radio link. Such a link will almost invariably have on-line electronic encryption which renders it virtually unbreakable, but developments in computer-aided crypt-analysis may catch up!

3 Bundesheer operator sitting at the console of the MPDR-30. Vast numbers of operators and technicians are now needed by all armies.

4 The GTE Systems SB-3614 portable automatic field telephone exchange, a 30-line switch-board. Two or three can be stacked to provide 60- or 90-lines. Such equipment is used in forward areas up to battalion level. Field telephones are more secure, but lack the flexibility of radios.

2▲

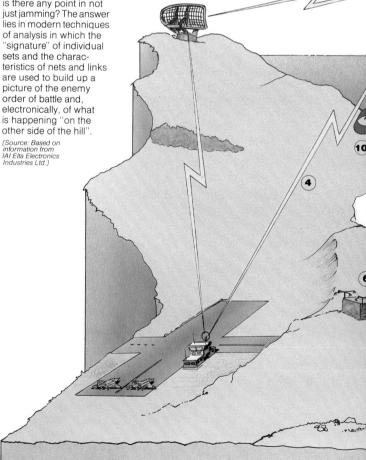

3 ▲

4 ▲

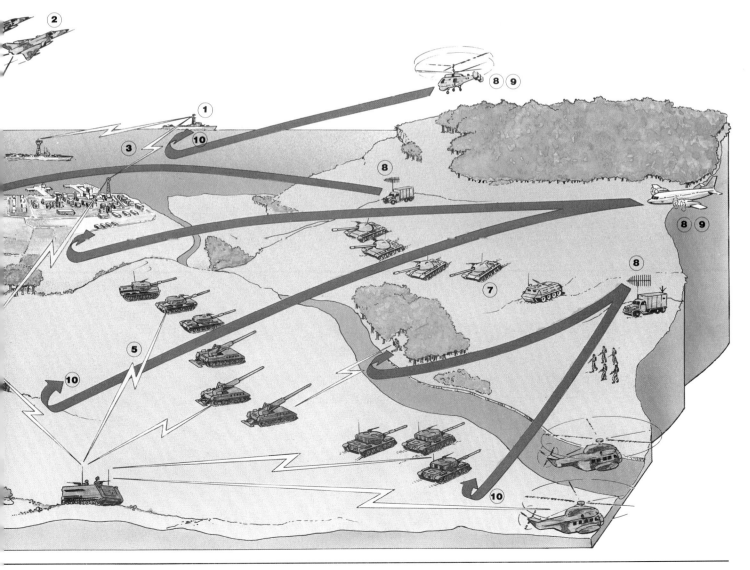

subject to interception and disruption, some distortion at the voice signal must be anticipated. Because the voice can be unrecognizable, *authentication* of the signal is of increased importance. The classic method of authentication is by means of an exchange of coded words or phrases. However, modern systems include many electronic means such as accompanying inaudible tones, digital codes, or electronic "gates" which reject false signals from attempted intrusions or from messages which do not possess the coded proper authentication.

Communications must be maintained

One can conclude that the basic ECM threats to signal communications are interception, jamming or intrusion (of a false signal). The protective measures (COMSEC) —such as secure or cryptosystems—must be distinguished from interference or "jamming", which is more complex. Some systems seek to "filter out" the jamming signals, while the newest techniques involve "frequency hopping". During World War II and for about 35 years thereafter, communicators changed frequencies manually to another pre-selected frequency when jamming or interference was encountered. Today, with modern computerized procedures, equipment has been designed which will detect the interfering signal and *automatically* change to a series of alternative frequencies to which the receiving station is synchronised. The accompanying sketch shows a type of jamming system and some representative equipment as well as some recent frequency-hopping equipment. The communications aspect of the electronic battlefield can be seen as a continuous conflict between the imperative need for commander to communicate with their units as well as to receive intelligence information. This must take place even when opposed by an adversary who is determined either to intercept the messages for intelligence purposes, or to disrupt operations by eliminating or interfering with these vital communications. Success and victory can go to the combatant who possesses the resources to communicate, while at the same time to deny communications to the other side.

In the more exotic realm of covert and clandestine operations, electronic warfare has provided some extremely interesting applications. Movie films and spy novels released since World War II have frequently depicted the shadowy world of espionage operations, with scenes of agents huddling over transmitters tapping out coded messages in Morse code. In the real world, however, the covert or clandestine signal has exchanged the Morse transmitter for more modern and ingenious devices.

Newspaper readers may have been surprised when American Congressional committee hearings during the 1950s publicised the existence of a small microphone-equipped radio transmitter disguised as an olive in a cocktail, but they were astonished when US Ambassador to the UN Henry Cabot Lodge displayed the Great Seal of the United States, embossed on a carved disc,

which had hung in the American Embassy in Moscow, in the Ambassador's office, and which contained an unusual device hidden in the eagle on the seal. A sensitive microphone was connected to a "resonant-cavity" transmitter which could be activated by a microwave signal from a distance and could then transmit anything being said in the Ambassador's office.

Modern miniaturised systems

It is obvious that the potential of disguised olives or ambassadorial seals may be somewhat limited. However, modern miniature electronic circuitry has been able to produce devices which are not only capable of providing for covert or clandestine communications, but which resemble quite ordinary items in everyday use. For example, when the Iranian Security Police in 1976 uncovered the espionage activities of Major General Ahmad Moghrabbi, then Chief of Iranian Planning and Logistics, their investigation revealed that after recruitment and training by the Soviet KGB, Moghrabbi had been provided with special electronic communication equipment. At the time of his apprehension and trial in 1977, the Iranian security forces discovered in Moghrabbi's possession a German-made UHER 4000 tape recorder which had been expertly modified so that 30 minutes of messages could be transmitted in a single "burst" of 30 seconds duration with a signal which, if intercepted, resembled normal static noises. This device was kept in Moghrabbi's residence where it could be activated remotely by his KGB masters from their passing automobile.

General Moghrabbi also had a Dutch-manufactured Philips tape recorder which had been converted to function also as a transmitter-receiver, and with which he could receive instructions. The Iranians also discovered a small, Japanese-made Sony radio which had three tiny lights; if one light illuminated, Moghrabbi's secretly transmitted message had been acknowledged, and he could erase his tape. A second light warned him against making contact with his KGB handler, while the third light alerted him to immediate serious danger so that he might escape. Unfortunately for Moghrabbi, the security services seized him before he could get away and, after a trial by Court Martial, he was executed in 1977.

Also in Iran, at about the same time in 1977, the security services apprehended Ali-Naghu Rabbanni, a senior civil servant who had worked for the KGB for 30 years. Rabbanni was caught while operating a very special device which resembled a small transistorized calculator but which, in reality, was capable of direct communication with Moscow, via satellite. The calculator received the coded KGB signals and instantly translated them into 5-digit groups which Rabbanni could decode at his convenience.

Another system designed for covert or clandestine communications use is a recent British device fitted in standard 7 × 5 military binoculars. While such specialized covert/clandestine devices have a role in

1 ▲

1 A control centre in a sophisticated EW system. It is essential for effective EW that control and coordination is exercised from a high level by dedicated Signals Intelligence (SIGINT).

2 US Army EW detachment; note steerable antenna at mast-head on left.

3 The old and faithful morse-key still has the ability to operate in an ECM environment.

2 ▲

3 ▲

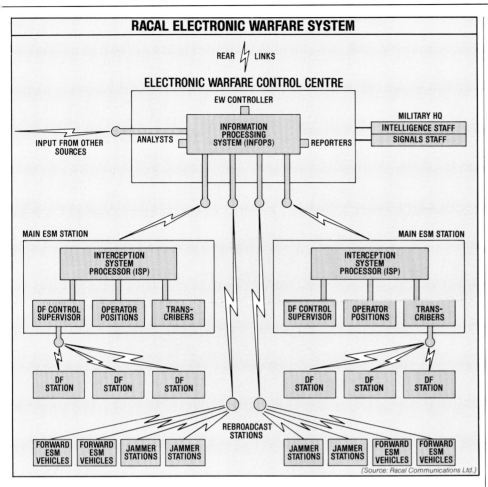

RACAL ELECTRONIC WARFARE SYSTEM

REAR ⚡ LINKS

ELECTRONIC WARFARE CONTROL CENTRE

EW CONTROLLER

INPUT FROM OTHER SOURCES

ANALYSTS

INFORMATION PROCESSING SYSTEM (INFOPS)

REPORTERS

MILITARY HQ
INTELLIGENCE STAFF
SIGNALS STAFF

MAIN ESM STATION

INTERCEPTION SYSTEM PROCESSOR (ISP)

DF CONTROL SUPERVISOR | OPERATOR POSITIONS | TRANS-CRIBERS

MAIN ESM STATION

INTERCEPTION SYSTEM PROCESSOR (ISP)

DF CONTROL SUPERVISOR | OPERATOR POSITIONS | TRANS-CRIBERS

DF STATION | DF STATION | DF STATION

DF STATION | DF STATION | DF STATION

REBROADCAST STATIONS

FORWARD ESM VEHICLES | FORWARD ESM VEHICLES | JAMMER STATIONS | JAMMER STATIONS | JAMMER STATIONS | JAMMER STATIONS | FORWARD ESM VEHICLES | FORWARD ESM VEHICLES

(Source: Racal Communications Ltd.)

ELECTRONIC WARFARE SYSTEM

A comprehensive EW system might well be organised as shown here. An EW Control Centre, served by an information processing system, is at the hub. From here the ESM (eg, direction-finding and intercept) and EW (eg, jamming) stations are controlled and coordinated. The main ESM stations would typically consist of mobile shelters housing operators' positions, transcriber positions, and supervisory elements. Forward ESM stations and jammers are mounted in trucks and are controlled from the EWCC by combat net radio links. Such systems make EW a battlefield in its own right.

4 A Soviet captain supervising the operators in a mobile radar station. The equipment and techniques used are outmoded by Western standards, but the sets may have been replaced.

---

electronic warfare, their role will probably continue to be confined to uses in which the need for concealment as well as security is paramount. It seems clear, however, that future devices are limited only by the ingenuity of their designs.

What, then, of the major element of electronic warfare which deals more directly with the weaponry of modern warfare? Electronics contribute significantly to the gathering of intelligence. In addition to signal intelligence (SIGINT), electronic intelligence and reconnaissance systems can: locate and identify energy targets for artillery and air attack; locate and identify enemy movements; give early warning of impending attack; locate and identify obstacles; store, analyze and retrieve data.

Various electronic devices are also used in land, naval and air combat, to aim, direct and fire weapons, and to aid navigation.

Locating enemy emissions

In a land battle, intelligence and reconnaissance assets are used to find, identify and locate enemy electronic emissions (ESM-ELINT). In a case, for example, involving two opposing Corps or Army forces, if ESM intercepts and identifies enemy signal communications, after coordination and analysis the commander will find himself with three choices of action.

First, he can continue to intercept and monitor, ie, to listen to the signals, with the possibility that the communications will reveal to him important intelligence concerning enemy operations. He can thus defer further action until the picture of the battlefield becomes clearer for him. This course of action entails the risk that, in a fast-moving situation, vital time may pass, during which the enemy may obtain a significant advantage.

A second option to the commander is to use his resources in an ECM mode, ie, to disrupt, prevent, or reduce the enemy's ability to communicate. This can be accomplished by "jamming" or disrupting enemy signals, or by transmitting deceptive signals of his own to confuse the other side. There are some inherent risks in this choice of action as it is possible that the enemy may make use of alternative means of communications, or even that the signals may be transmitted for deceptive purposes by the enemy and therefore such interference would be merely an ineffective and wasted effort. It is also possible that the friendly "jamming" could interfere with the commander's own tactical communications.

The third choice is, logically, to attack and destroy the enemy's signal emitters. This could prevent, or seriously disrupt enemy operations. However, looking back to the first choice, it could preclude gathering information from this source. In any case, it becomes apparent that *communications* is a key element in all modern military operations. As Lieutenant Colonel L. Titov, of the Soviet Army, pointed out in *Vovenny Vestnik* (1977): "Communications is the basic means to ensure troop control, and the loss of troop control in battle invariably leads to defeat."

In tactical operations under modern EW conditions it becomes imperative, therefore,

1▲

2▲

3▲

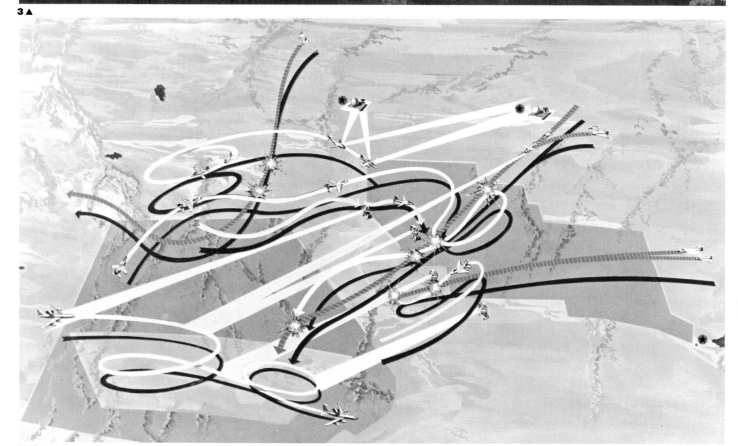

SURVIVABILITY OF AWACS

Schematic represen-
tation of a test to
demonstrate the
survivability of the E-3A
Airborne Warning and
Control System (AWACS).
A single E-3A was
confined in a 50x80
nautical mile box within
the Edwards AFB Range
area. Defending it were
two F-15s, four F-4Es, two
jamming aircraft, and an
F-105G tasked to attack
four hostile ground-based
jammers. Attackers were
USAF aircraft simulating
six MiG-23 and two
Yak-28. The E-3A was
able to initiate racks on
the hostiles at a great
distance, deployed the
defending fighters to
enable them to obtain
kills, and still maintained
its primary role of
radar surveillance. There
is no other aircraft
anywhere with these
capabilities.

COUNTERMEASURES SYSTEM DIAGRAM

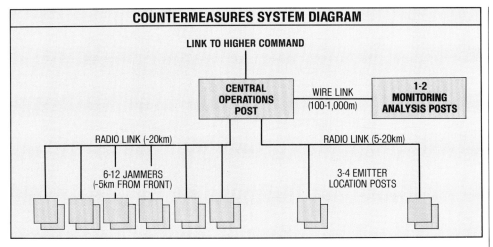

LINK TO HIGHER COMMAND

CENTRAL OPERATIONS POST

WIRE LINK (100-1,000m)

1-2 MONITORING ANALYSIS POSTS

RADIO LINK (-20km)

RADIO LINK (5-20km)

6-12 JAMMERS (-5km FROM FRONT)

3-4 EMITTER LOCATION POSTS

1 Beechcraft R-21D "special mission" aircraft of US Army, used in the Cefly Lancer programme. Antennas cover HF, VHF, and UHF bands, and could have a DF role.

2 The EF-111A is a high-power ECM jamming platform, and is nicknamed "Electric Fox". Serving with USAF, it has a vital role to play in suppressing Soviet air defence systems.

3 Grumman EA-6B Prowler is a much modified A-6 with a four-man crew and ALQ-99 EW system. Receivers are in the fin-cap pod, jammers are in underwing pods

4 An Israeli Army tactical jamming station mounted in an M113 armoured personnel carrier Jamming is a technique which needs to be used carefully and under strict control, as it can all too easily be counter-productive; under the right conditions it can be devastatingly effective.

5 Operators in the cabin of an EC-130, one of the many different types of aircraft converted to this specialized role, and probably the noisiest and least comfortable! The electronic suite is rather "rough-and-ready" by US standards.

4 ▲

5 ▲

to maintain continuous close coordination between intelligence, operations and EW elements. If the commander chooses to exploit enemy signals for intelligence purposes, he must re-evaluate this decision periodically: whether to continue to listen or to jam or attack the emitters. Modern commanders and their staffs usually develop a virtually automatic procedure for this. If they identify enemy communications which have major tactical value (such as an enemy artillery fire direction centre), but which have little potential to provide useful intelligence, they might be jammed automatically. Since the enemy may also be employing ECM, such as jamming, the location of enemy jammers could produce the automatic response to attack and destroy them. In every case, the commander may be limited in his response by the availability or capability of his equipment.

The foregoing discussion has highlighted some typical EW procedures in a tactical situations. While tactics, techniques and, in some cases, the problems may vary in air and maritime conflict, this same basic procedure will be involved. It must be kept in mind that, since time is the vital factor, EW hardware is increasingly developed for pre-programmed and automatic or computerised response which can be virtually immediate. In this respect, EW can be compared to the now popular small electronic chess-playing computers. When the human player makes a move, the computer instantaneously reviews possible countermoves and then selects, according to its programming, the best countermove. Human players can, and frequently do defeat the computer, because the programming is not perfect. As programming is improved, the computer becomes increasingly difficult to beat. In combat jamming, for example, is effective only for a relatively brief period until the enemy takes some evasive action or employs some countermeasure to include destruction of the jammer. In the latest types of communications equipment, built-in countermeasures against jamming are increasingly evident.

Airborne early warning

Airborne EW today must be able to detect enemy countermeasures employed for detection, such as radar, laser beams, and electronics signals used to guide missiles. It must also be able to protect the aircraft from immediate attack by enemy weapons systems. Protection can be provided by jamming and detection systems located on the individual aircraft itself, or by other aircraft dedicated to the EW role.

A typical aircraft system is the Rapport II, adopted by the Belgian Air Force for its Mirage III aircraft. The Rapport II is a modern, advanced system which detects, identifies and locates enemy radar and provides the pilot with an analysis of the threats facing him, in order of priority. The system can record or transmit back to a base specific data concerning enemy radars as well as programming on-board computers to jam the enemy signals. Thus, the Belgian pilot is given a warning of any SAM or AAA radar threat and instructed as to what action he should take. Against a major threat, automatic jamming is initiated. The aircraft is protected also by systems which can screen the aircraft by dispensing a material called "chaff". Chaff is a metallic material which can black radars, or deceive or cause misleading signals. "Decoys" can be employed which are "drone" devices that appear to an enemy radar like the aircraft itself, flying another course. Since many surface-to-air missiles are "heat seeking" missiles guided by infra-red (IR) sensors, decoys can lead the missiles away, or the aircraft can employ flare-type heat targets which will draw away the SAMs which the aircraft remains safely on course.

The primary mission of combat aircraft limits the EW equipment which can be carried on board, so special EW-dedicated aircraft are employed to precede or accompany missions in order to provide protection which is expanded or complementary to the system on individual combat aircraft.

With the increasing use of rotary-wing aircraft in a combat support role, it is not surprising to find an increased EW concern for these aircraft. Tactical helicopters operating in any combat role are exposed to a significant threat from enemy ground-based defence systems as well as from combat aircraft. Consequently, protective systems for helicopters must be developed parallel to those developed for high-performance aircraft. Since helicopters are particularly vulnerable to radar guided and IR homing weapons, their systems design includes special protective measures, some of which are illustrated. Helicopters do not merely employ active or passive systems for self-protection; they are increasingly used for an active EW role, particularly in reconnaissance and intelligence missions in the combat zone.

Today, prudent naval planners developing a new weapons system or ECM tend simultaneously to develop a counter to it. This is done on the assumption that an enemy will soon develop a new counter-technique. Since, historically, the element of surprise is fundamental to success in EW, the planners' purpose is to anticipate the threat rather than to react to it. The accompanying illustrations of some of the latest Soviet vessels clearly indicate the trend.

Earlier it was pointed out that electronic warfare, "for the most part", is not some means of combat using electrons as a weapon. The discussion up to this point has centred on the major contemporary employment of electromagnetic radiation for communications as well as navigation, target location, weapons guidance and related purposes. The possibility of using electronics technology as a weapon has recurred periodically (as witness Sir Robert Watson-Watts' "Death Ray Memorandum".) Today, electronic weapons are in the process of becoming a reality with the advances of laser technology and electromagnetic pulse, (EMP).

Laser (an acronym of Light Amplification by Stimulated Emission of Radiation), is a process of generating coherent light. The process uses a natural phenomenon in which molecules absorb electromagnetic frequencies. The energy is stored for a short

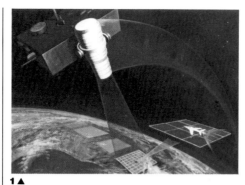

1 Technological wizardry is entering new spheres. This US DoD artist's impression shows a spaceborne laser system being used for surveilliance; now entirely feasible.

2 US Army YEH-60A has been converted to the EW role in a "Quick-Fix" programme to produce an airborne platform for intercepting and jamming hostile radio signals.

3 US Army soldier installing an AN/ALQ-44 infrared jammer on a UH-1H helicopter. This is a countermeasure device used against infrared homing missiles.

4 A US Air Force Boeing NKC-135 Airborne Laser Laboratory investigating the propagation of laser light "from an airborne vehicle to an airborne target", ie, as an air-to-air weapon!

2▲

ELECTRONIC COMMAND, CONTROL, COMMUNICATIONS AND COUNTER-MEASURES

The modern battlefield, with its overt and covert threats, its highly sophisticated weapons systems, and its multiplicity of specializations faces the commander with an increased management problem in efficiently utilising the resources at his disposal. This is leading, in most armies, towards an integrated command-and-control (or C²) system. Such integration will only work, however, if it is associated with a properly designed communications system, the so-called C³. This is the sort of concept the British Army is heading towards with its integrated Ptarmigan, Clansman, Wavell and Bates, giving a C³ system designed from the start to work as one. This diorama shows the sort of elements which may be expected on today's battlefield. Starting with the ground force HQ (1), this must clearly work to its subordinate armour (2) and artillery (3), and the latter must also work to their observation parties (4). The ground force HQ works back to its superior HQ (5). Tactical aircraft (6) must be able to communicate with the army units they are supporting (2), and back to their base (10). Within the air force

communications exist between airfields (9), air defence missile units (8), and the superior HQ (5). The early warning system (7) is also linked into the national HQ (5). The national trunk backbone system (11) links the civil capital (12), the naval forces (13) and reconnaissance (14), together with strategic air forces. Aircraft are shown using internal/external ECM systems to thwart attackers. The sheer complexity of such a

system and the volume of information to be transferred is increasingly leading towards data processing and digital communications. The problem is, of course, that while the C³ logic leads to this overall system the enemy is being provided at the same time with

an enormous EW target, and this is the dilemma which military planners in many countries are trying to reconcile. In most armies the two fastest growing corps are those responsible for communications and technical maintenance.
(Source: Based on information from IAI Elta Industries Ltd.)

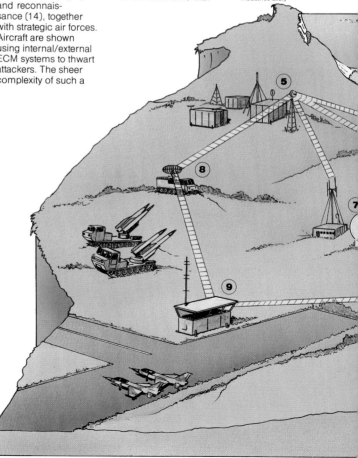

3 ▲

4 ▲

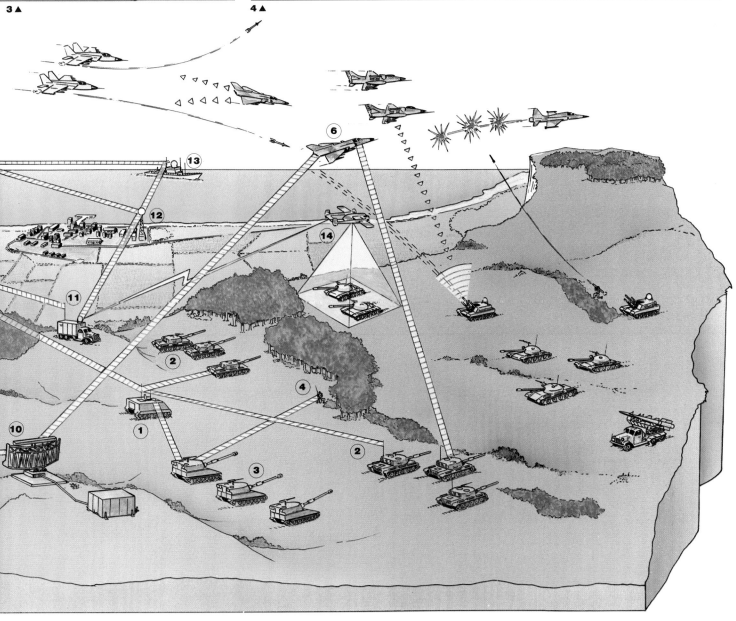

period and is then released in the form of light in an extremely narrow band of frequencies. Because of the major characteristics of a laser beam, it can be used for cutting or puncturing (as in surgery and transistor circuit manufacture or in photographic processing), to transmit communications, and to guide missiles to their targets. It can be recognized that these same characteristics can be used as potentially lethal weapons as well. In addition to their cutting and puncturing capabilities, the immense brilliance of the laser beam can have a blinding effect. For example, a tank commander or gunner, or the pilot of an aircraft, blinded by a laser beam, would be unable to function, and, under certain circumstances, could face immediate destruction. Since smoke and aerosols can be employed to obscure or diminish laser beam effectiveness, intelligence resources are used to determine enemy capabilities in advance.

Electromagnetic pulse (EMP) is another phenomenon. A simple natural example can be recognized by someone listening to a radio in an automobile driving past a powerful transmitter. If the radio is tuned to the same frequency, the emission can "blank out" reception, and if it is powerful enough it can actually "burn out" the receiver. Modern micro-wave ovens heat food by directing electromagnetic energy to a specific area in much the same way as medical diathermy machines can direct energy into the human body. Recent scientific literature indicates the possibility of developing large EMP generators which could be directed as weapons. At this time EMP weaponry is regarded as a scientific curiosity in a primitive stage of development. But the same was true of radar in the 1930s, yet within a few years quite advanced radar technologies were developed. Undoubtedly, EMP technology will continue to excite interest in scientific, technical and military circles.

Electro-optical systems

Of considerably greater current importance in intelligence gathering are electro-optical systems employing electronic night vision devices and infra-red or thermal-imaging devices. By using techniques developed for television, modern electronic image-enhancement equipment is able to transmit television pictures or photographic images under light conditions which are too poor for the human eye. The electronic equipment can use even the feeble illumination from stars, amplified by electronic circuits in a similar way to the amplification of music from a transcription, and display a scene in almost the same detail as if it were in sunlight. Low-light television (LLTV) is used in reconnaissance aircraft, RPVs and drones to detect enemy movements and equipment seeking to use darkness for concealment. LLTV is also used for security purposes for remote monitoring of large areas.

While LLTV and other image-enhancing techniques are relatively new, infra-red radiation has been employed for a longer time. Any object which emits radiation in

the infra-red spectrum is a source of IR. Natural sources, such as the sun or stars, are readily detected, as are some artificial sources such as flames, tungsten lamps or lasers. Fundamentally, any object which radiates heat can be an IR emitter—including humans, vehicles, or urban areas—and each emitter possesses particular patterns of emission, called the "IR signature".

IR was used in intelligence quite early as a means of detecting camouflaged objects. A camouflaged building, airfield or artillery battery, for example, could deceive the naked eye, but it was discovered that IR photographic equipment easily penetrated the camouflage because it could discriminate between natural vegetation and artificial or painted camouflage. It was later, discovered that sensitive IR photographs, taken at night, could detect tanks and other vehicles and objects because the heat given off by them would show on IR film.

Modern IR systems can detect objects, permit their identification by their IR signature electronically, and allow instantaneous observation or photography. Remote IR sensors (REMS) (described in the chapter on tactical intelligence in the land battle) can be employed that will detect nearby movement and automatically give an alarm while also activating LLTV equipment. Aircraft can use Forward looking IR (FLIR) techniques to reconnoitre the area in advance of the path of flight to detect IR emissions at a distance.

The early history of electronic warfare indicates that many of the lessons learned remain as valid today as when they first became apparent. However, the principal lesson has always been that any weakness in new electronic technology can be expected to be exploited quickly by some countermeasure.

The electronic battlefield has many dimensions. Intelligence is a major factor in electronic warfare not only because EW techniques provide an increasingly expanded means of intelligence acquisition, processing and dissemination, but also because intelligence concerning new techniques and countermeasures must be constantly updated in order to avoid possible surprise and defeat. Modern electronic technology can now provide virtually instantaneous communications throughout the world and into space. Modern transport can span great distances and deliver the means of great destructive capability in extremely short time. With the development of new electronic systems occurring at a rate heretofore unknown, research and development has moved from the more tranquil atmosphere of the laboratory onto the electronic battlefield.

Oliver Wendell Holmes was an American Supreme Court Justice who served with distinction during the Civil War (1860-1865) as an Infantry Officer. Holmes lived well into his nineties and died on the eve of World War II, before the advent of modern electronic warfare. However, one observation he made applies to the electronic battlefield of today: "The judgement of nature upon error is death. The rabbit, pursued by hounds, will take the wrong turn only one time."

1 Thermal imager with a x6 telescope made by Barr & Stroud. Thermal imaging has leapt ahead of image intensification and low-light TV as a military surveillance system.

2 ▲

3 ▲

2 A group of men and a vehicle as seen through the Barr & Stroud thermal imager, at a range of 400 metres. Apart from its military appications this device can be used by fire services to "see" through smoke.

3 US Army soldier using an earth-auger to make a hole for a Magnetic Intrusion Detector (MAGID) which can detect any metal object in its sensitivity radius. This is one of many such well-tried surveillance equipments.

4, 5 An air-delivered seismic intrusion detector (ADSID) is launched from a USAF helicopter over Laos (**4**). On landing it buries the body in the ground (**5**) leaving only a small antenna protruding.

6 The British Pilkington Glass Hawklite Night Observation Device uses image intensifying techniques. It was used so successfully during the 1982 Spring Falklands War that a repeat order has been placed by the British Army and Royal Marines.

4 ▲

6 ▲

5 ▲

Chapter six

Intelligence and the war in space

IN SEARCH OF the ultimate "high ground" from which to gather definitive information about enemy or unfriendly forces, military intelligence services around the world seek data from the advantageous platforms of orbiting satellites that only two superpowers have so far exploited to any measurable degree. Undeniably important for the prosecution of foreign policy and for the qualification of basic defence needs, surveillance from space takes on added significance when compared with more traditional forms of intelligence gathering.

Space reconnaissance establishes finite gates of credibility during international tension, effectively ensuring that a potential enemy's troop or ship movements cannot be kept secret, and that threats or hostile acts are not the spring-board for premature combat. It is only within the last twenty years that military forces have been able to enhance their peacetime value by the use of space satellites

But what all governments seek and only few can afford is a capability based on indigenous technologies rather than budgeted procurement programmes. Space surveillance and intelligence gathering requires a sophisticated infrastructure qualitatively superior to that possessed by most defence organisations around the world. It not only requires an existing space launch capability, and a strong supporting aerospace industry to provide the hardware, but also an adequate dissemination and communication structure to tap the new resource. Even with the resources of a major industrial base, the United States took nearly ten years to build up its initial, and very limited, space surveillance network involving satellites, launchers, aircraft, ground hardware and interpreters.

When President Eisenhower approved plans in 1954 for a US scientific satellite for the International Geophysical Year scheduled to commence in 1957, US Air Force plans gestating over the preceding decade coalesced around a basic research and development programme utilising an Agena rocket stage that would be launched on top of an Atlas ICBM, then the America's most powerful missile, although it had still to fly. Lockheed was signed up to provide the Agena, essentially a tank for propellants with a rocket engine at one end and provision for several alternative "payloads" at the other. This evolved under specification WS-117L and received additional money when the Soviet Union beat the United States into space by placing Sputnik 1 in orbit during October, 1957.

In response to this Soviet initiative, the Air Force realigned components of its surveillance programme and developed a three-phase operation based upon original objectives but incorporating a quick maturity through experimental development of several different roles. Called Discoverer, the first role was a purely research and development activity devised to get basic information on operating procedures and different technologies. Each Discoverer satellite was a bullet-shaped capsule built to survive re-entry and to be recovered by a specially equipped aircraft with a trapeze device aligned to snag the capsule's parachute line as it drifted down to earth. The satellite was an integral part of the Agena rocket stage, which weighed nearly 8,600lb (3,900kg) on top its Thor booster but only 1,720lb (780kg) after it had propelled itself to orbit and consumed most of its propellant. Launched south from the USAF Vandenberg Air Force Base, Discoverer shots would remain in a polar orbit until recovered over Hawaii, their 300lb (135kg) capsules returning with film of selected ground targets.

During the late 1950s development of radio-transmission systems for TV pictures made the quality and definition much worse than the film-return concept, although considerable effort was expended on a hybrid concept whereby electronic scanning of a film processed on the satellite provided a compromise with a much improved picture and no requirement for the capsule to return to earth. At this time the safe recovery of capsules from orbit was a major problem and many people in the intelligence community thought suggested solutions were far too exotic for repetitive operation. The first Discoverer satellite was launched in February, 1959 but it was not before Discoverer 13, in August, 1960, that the first capsule was successfully returned. It was, in fact, the first object ever recovered from orbit. By this time, however, Discoverer had done its primary job of pioneering techniques and procedures for the definitive, first-generation, area survey satellites.

Called Samos (an acronym of Satellite and Missile Observation System), the first was sent into space in January 1961, following a failure with the initial attempt more than three months earlier. This satellite weighed 4,000lb (1,860kg) and was placed in space by an Atlas-Agena. Samos employed

1 The key element in USAF Space Command's future planning is NASA's Shuttle, seen here returning from its second test flight to orbit. This vehicle will provide revolutionary new capabilities. Four will be on hand by the mid-1980s. **1 ▲**

Space-based sensors support land, sea and air elements, provide unique capabilities for more effective operations and generate new possibilities for halting aggression. The nation that wins the battle in space will control the conflict, contain the war and limit hostilities.

radio-transmission techniques and was therefore only appropriate for broad coverage. The cameras were built by Eastman Kodak and the scanners evolved at the CBS Laboratories. Close-look duties were to be the responsibility of a Discoverer derivative to be launched by the Atlas-Agena launchers into polar orbits from Vandenberg. But they were 18 months behind the Samos series and would not appear before March 1962. It was the area-survey satellites that were first in the field as semi-operational surveillance scanners.

There was a measurable relief among intelligence officials in the US armed forces when satellites became available for surveying Soviet and Eastern Bloc activity. In May 1960, Francis Gary Powers had been shot down by a Soviet surface-to-air missile during photo-reconnaissance activities over Soviet territory and the intention was clearly unambiguous: Russia would not tolerate spy flights by aircraft. It was a different matter when satellites were introduced. Loud noises were made through the United Nations but the country that had been first to overfly other countries in space was hardly in a good position when it came to indignant protests about US cameras in orbit. From 1960, the lines of constraint were clearly drawn: every country has the right to fly over any other country in space and national claim to the skies ends at the limit of earth's atmosphere.

Space — a theatre of war?

For the United States the justification and the need were inextricably locked together. In the months preceding the first Samos flight, John F. Kennedy and Richard M. Nixon had each fought for the Presidency along different paths but both affirmed the need for reconnaissance from space. Kennedy polarised the requirement when he said, "Only if the United States occupies a position of pre-eminence can we help decide whether this new ocean will be a sea of peace, or a terrifying theatre of war." To maintain effectively an equality of arms it was important to know with a high degree of confidence the actual forces deployed by a potential enemy, and satellites promised to provide that intelligence. US military sources reported major developments in Soviet ICBM technology and the CIA required detailed information on this activity which appeared to be coordinated at the Baykonur launch site. It was to obtain details of Soviet rocket work that Powers was sent across in the abortive U-2 mission.

Long range plans for US missile programmes would rely in part on the threat evaluated from good intelligence through pictures. But satellites would also play a part in plotting the number of missiles deployed by the Soviets in addition to providing information about launch operations. Finally, US missiles would not only be as accurate as the technology incorporated in their design but also as accurate as the navigation data employed by their guidance systems. It was known that the Soviets had gone to great lengths to publish erroneous maps displacing cities and towns by several tens of kilometres so as to confuse analysts

and targeting options during any future war. Satellites were to be used for updating and in some instances re-drawing the maps on which targeting data were based.

Results returned from the first Samos flight in early 1961 contributed to a definitive analysis of Soviet missile development and deployment that was to be used the following year to provide confidence for President Kennedy to take a strong line with Soviet initiatives at placing medium-range missiles on Cuba. Suspicion that earlier estimates of Soviet missile strength were considerably awry were confirmed when the first Samos flights revealed the limitations with existing SS-6 missiles and the small number actually deployed for operational use. By 1962 the United States was well on the way to a significant missile arsenal, with more than 400 land- and sea-based long range missiles. The Soviets had less than 80, an imbalance that provided muscle behind the blockade of the seas around Cuba and forced the withdrawal of the Russian missiles.

Yet even before this the classified nature of US Air Force satellite operations ran counter to the public and international image of American space activity. With a clear mandate from the United Nations to declare the launch of every satellite put into space, the USA invited accusation from the Soviet Union that military activities were threatening to undermine the peaceful co-existence of the two superpowers. For its part, the Soviet Union conducted all space activity through central organisations and failed to make the bold distinction between civilian and military activity. The establishment of NASA by President Eisenhower in late 1958 forced attention on Air Force space plans and polarised opinion around the directed nature of military activity. Accordingly, from November 1961, the US military satellites were given a number and while information was released on date and time of launch, with additional details on orbital parameters and so on, nothing was released about the satellite's design characteristics or purpose.

The Soviet Union similarly hid the precise nature of their satellite missions behind a blanket grouping under the Cosmos designation, the first in the series being sent into space during March 1962. Soviet reconnaissance operations got under way with the Vostok spacecraft designed to carry cosmonauts into orbit on flights lasting several days. Announced as Cosmos 4, the 9,920lb (4,500kg) spacecraft was sent up on April 26, 1962, and was the first in a long line of spy satellites based on the manned capsule design. From the outset, Soviet rockets have been larger and more powerful than their US equivalents, since the Russians preferred to build crude and heavy satellites rather than wait for technical refinements which would bring significant weight and volume reductions. This can, in some instances, lead to a lack of flexibility and inefficient operation of a major lifting capability.

One example of the limited capability accepted by the Soviets in their satellite reconnaissance programmes is in the method of data retrieval. The Cosmos spy satellites used cameras fitted inside the spherical re-entry capsule that on Vostok

1 ▲
1 Contrary to initial reports, Russia's SS-6 Sapwood ICBM employed 20 main and 12 vernier rocket motors in the first stage and not 2 or 4 very large motors. This enabled Russia to get a head start in missile and space-launcher technology, Sapwood becoming the first stage for more than 500 satellite launches in the 20 years beginning late 1957. Here, a manned Vostok capsule sits atop a second stage attached to the core stage and four boosters. It was additional stages attached to the SS-6 that put most military satellites in orbit.

2 Carrying the Midas-3 (Missile Defense Alarm System) satellite, an Agena A is moved to its Vandenberg AFB launch pad.

3 Launched July 12, 1961, Midas-3 would be put in space by an Atlas-Agena A, seen here being lifted into position.

4 Continuous testing provided development concurrent with operational flights. Here, on December 5, 1962, the last Atlas-F development flight gets away from its Cape Canaveral launch pad.

SPACE CAMERA SYSTEM
(1) Film supply.
(2) Camera lens.
(3) Mirror.
(4) Processor and dryer.
(5) Readout looper.
(6) Scanner.
(7) Film take-up and storage.
(8) Composite video to communications sub-system.

Some early spacecraft used film scanning techniques to get their pictures to Earth, much as Lunar Oribiter did in obtaining close-up pictures of the Moon. That 150lb (68.1kg) camera system included wide angle and telephoto lenses, an image compensation device to eliminate blurring, and a system for processing film automatically on board. The developed film was then scanned by a video system and images transmitted to Earth stations.

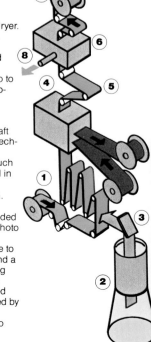

2 ▲

3 ▲

4 ▲

missions would carry a cosmonaut and his life support equipment. The complete capsule was returned to Earth at the end of the picture-taking session, necessitating a large number of separate spacecraft to cover global targets adequately throughout the year. The Vostok spy vehicles were usually kept in space less than one week, their film capacity being considerably greater than the operational life of the satellite. A high resolution derivative of the basic spy satellite appeared as Cosmos 22 in November 1963, by which time the USA had shifted to a new generation of area survey satellites and close look vehicles.

America had achieved great success with the first series of general observation satellites. From early 1962 a consistently reliable performance from the Samos type area survey satellites ensured adequate cover for photo-intelligence requirements. The new Kodak imaging system worked on the Bimat process and fed a reel of film through two optical systems with long and short focal length lenses, respectively. Held between the camera and a specially automated processor by a loop buffer, the film was wound on when ready to a gelatin surface coated with a combined developer and fixer. The surface carrying a negative image was then withdrawn and moved to pads where moisture was soaked away prior to drying by a small heater. The positive image was not used by this system but the negative was wound on a take-up reel ready for the CBS Line Scan Tube.

With this device a narrow beam of light was focused on to the film by a special lens which moved the spot across the film in a series of repeating scans, moving down the film until the complete image had been scanned. The modulated beam was picked up on the opposite side of the' film by a photo-multiplier tube which generated an electrical signal proportional to the intensity of the beam observed through the negative. Amplified in the communication system, the signals were sent to receiving stations on the ground where they were turned back into pictures, completing the line-scan transfer of the photographic image. This system formed the basis for area-survey work where long life was more important than the difference between a Bimat transmitted image and hard-copy photographs sent back by capsules. But capsules were an essential part of the close-look system and this back-up provided an ideal combination. Eastman Kodak developed the close-look cameras and General Electric built the recoverable capsules, pioneered in concept and design by the Discoverer series.

The first-generation close-look satellites followed the operating procedure of Discoverer by incorporating the rocket employed to slow the capsule for descent within the main body of the re-entry section itself. This was fired after the capsule separated from the Agena-B stage which had propelled it into orbit and left the stage to decay on its own due to friction with the tenuous outer layers of the Earth's atmosphere.

A new rocket stage formed the basis for a second-generation close-look vehicle when Agena-D was employed, beginning July 1963.

In the new procedure the re-startable Agena engine, provided for the first time, allowed the orbit to be changed before re-entry, which was now to be affected before capsule separation so that the stage and its payload section returned at the same time. The Atlas-Agena D series weighed about 4,410lb (2,000kg) and all were placed in polar orbits inclined between 90° and 100° to the equator, at an altitude of between 93 and 186 miles (150 and 300km). They carried out close inspection of specific regions and activities for three years.

The second generation area-survey satellites also appeared in 1963 when the Thor-Agena D was uprated with solid propellant strap-on rockets to improve lift capacity. The transition from an Agena B combination had been made during the life of the first generation series. The main difference between these lay in the use of ferret satellites flying piggy-back on the main spacecraft but separated in space to go about their own business, which was to pick up and record radio messages, electronic signals and radar transmissions over enemy or hostile territory and to dump that information over a friendly receiving station. Known as ferret subsatellites, because they were "launched" from a prime satellite already in space for photographic purposes, this series was supplemented by a family of much larger ferrets weighing between 2,204 and 4,410lb (1,000 and 2,000kg) and launched independently by rockets. The first subsatellite, weighing just a few tens of kilogrammes, rode into space on a second generation area-survey satellite during August 1963.

"Seeing through" camouflage

Throughout 1964 and 1965, Air Force operations with these paired systems became routine, almost a decade after the first major space defence studies had led to the initial Discoverer series. By this time, the Air Force was launching between 20 and 30 reconnaissance satellites into space each year and a new generation of area and close-look types evolved. These appeared in use during 1966 and first in service were the third-generation close-look satellite which employed the Titan 3B-Agena D, a combination capable of lifting the 6,613lb (3,000kg) satellites to an orbital height of between 87 and 248 miles (140 and 400km) above Earth. With added weight provision, the new satellites carried multi-spectral cameras built by the Itek Corporation, capable of looking at the ground in several wavelengths simultaneously, an asset of particular advantage where camouflage was used. For nearly a year the second-generation types were interleaved with their heavier successor but by mid-1967 only the Titan-launched model was in service, paired now with the third-generation area-survey satellites launched by stretched versions of the Thor-Agena D. This was the final variant of its type, a category replaced from 1972 by the Big Bird satellites of a completely different family.

From the mid-1960s, US Air Force plans included those for a major presence in space with astronauts working in a manned laboratory equipped with large telescopic

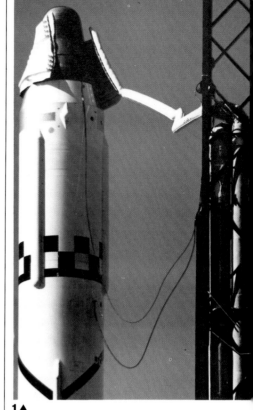

1 ▲

1 Protective shroud falls away from Discoverer 3 satellite seconds before Thor-Agena B launch.

2 Advanced, restartable, Agena D upper stage is seen with standard "unipac" shroud capable of encapsulating most payloads.

3 Agena rocket stages were standard carriers for early military satellites like Discoverer, Samos and Midas.

5 Two nuclear test detection satellites (Vela 5 and 6) are launched by Atlas-Agena D, July 1965.

2 ▲

3 ▲

EAST/WEST SATELLITES

The geographic location of the Soviet Union demands the use of several low orbit satellites for jobs that can be done for the NATO and US forces at stationary altitude. Here, the inclined orbit of Molniya communications satellite links remote Soviet spy ships while stationary orbit early-warning satellites keep watch for signs of a surprise attack. The Soviets were late to exploit stationary orbit, it having useful application for them only in early warning.

4 Conjectural drawing of the secret USAF Big Bird reconnaissance satellite which surveys the whole of the Communist world. Big Bird is thought to have "discovered" the Soviet SS-20 missiles.

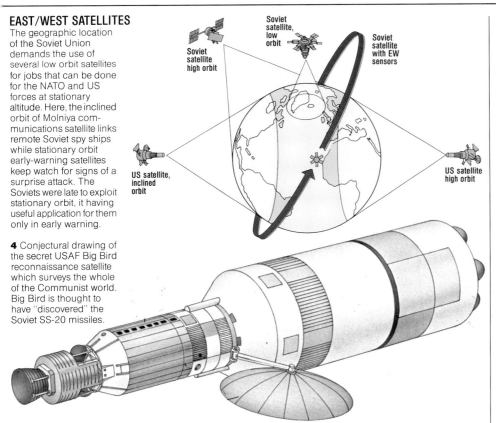

4 ▲

5 ▲

cameras and sophisticated sensors capable of imaging with a resolution as low as 5.9 inches (15cm) and in several parts of the spectrum to the near infrared. But by 1970 this so-called Manned Orbital Laboratory (MOL) had been cancelled and replaced in part by a large, unmanned, satellite weighing about 28,660lb (13,000kg) and built to fly into orbit on a specially developed Titan 3D. Officially known as Project 467, this satellite is better known as Big Bird; it incorporated all the more important objectives of the defunct MOL programme in a single design combining features of the two separate, area-survey and close-look, categories flown hitherto. Eastman Kodak developed and built a general survey camera and Perkin-Elmer put together a new high-resolution camera for specific analysis of small sections of the general, wide-angle views. The satellite itself was 49 feet (15m) long and could be fitted with side-looking radars. Transmissions from the area survey scanner were sent via a 20 foot (6m) diameter antenna unfurled from one end of the satellite, and up to six recoverable capsules with film packages could be returned to Earth on command.

Big Bird the mainstay

The first Big Bird was launched to sun-synchronous orbit, where the satellite views the same area at the same lighting conditions each day, during June, 1971. Precision was a vital part of getting value from the satellite and orbital adjustments were frequently made to maintain a true, sun-synchronous, orbit. Designed to operate continuously for several months, initial operations were limited to one or two months. Nevertheless, it was a significant improvement on the preceding third generation area survey satellites which remained operable for three weeks at most. Big Bird continued as the mainstay of survey work, much of the earlier haste in getting information about Soviet urban distribution and in building a file on military dispositions now gone. Having established a mass of intelligence about force levels and equipment, much of the work from the early to mid-1970s became a monitoring function. Two or three Big Birds were launched annually between 1972 and 1976 but after that only one a year was sent into orbit. The close-look satellites still kept up their work but on a less frequent series of missions.

Where once it had been common to have ten or more satellites of this type launched each year, by the end of the 1970s only one or two were sent into space annually. A run-down in this programme reduced the number of close-look satellites available and since 1977 the gap widened. One was launched in 1979 and another in 1981 but by this time only two or three remained in the inventory and those were retained for national emergencies.

Area survey satellites had gone out with the introduction of Big Bird and in 1976 a new vehicle called KH-11 began operations. Instead of scanning for transmission a photocopy processed on board, the KH-11 series worked by taking digital readings of the images viewed by the sensors, which have a multispectral scan like Big Bird. KH-11 weighs approximately 20,045lb (10,000kg) and is sent into sun-synchronous orbit by the same Titan 3D used for Big Bird. Much has been learned from NASA's Landsat earth resources programme where depth of intelligence often depends on interpretation rather than the direct, visual, observation of specific features. The multispectral resolution of the KH-11 sensors exceeds those of Landsat yet the NASA satellite itself is significantly more useful, even for military intelligence, than the last generation of area survey satellites.

Digitised "pictures" are never as good as hard-copy photographs but they provide a continuous source of information at an acceptable level and definition. The Big Bird satellites operate for six months and the KH-11 series are designed to work continuously for around two years. Their active propulsion systems nudge and jostle the orbit to maintain precise alignment with the rotating Earth and the shifting Sun, a combination that can play havoc with co-ordinated satellite tracks over designated observation points on the surface below. The cooperative liaison of Big Bird and KH-11 significantly reduced the number of satellites launched each year. By 1980 only two or three a year were being sent into

space and until at least the middle of the decade an average annual launch of just one reconnaissance satellite will be possible.

It is popularly assumed that space reconnaissance systems provide almost unlimited potential for a minute watch on happenings on earth, such that it is possible literally to read from space the headlines of a hand-held newspaper. Many claims have been made to that effect. In reality, however, there are certain limitations bound by the laws of physics.

Definition of resolution

Resolution is normally used as the single most important measure of a satellite's capability and is defined as the minimum distance separating two points of light with sufficient clarity to discriminate whether those points are dots or lines. The definition here is not as clinically defined as it is with an optical test, however, because the resolution varies under operational conditions according to atmospheric, environmental or induced phenomena, or at variance with operating techniques and system performance.

For example, atmospheric conditions might degrade the ability of the satellite's sensors (usually optical) to achieve optimum

performance. Heat, moisture content and haze effects can alter the performance. Induced environmental conditions include fog, artificial seeding of clouds to reshape the overcast and hide activities on land or sea, and large smoke dispensers which can with little or no skill on the part of the operator set up enduring palls of smoke to cloud surface features by trapping the aerosols under an inversion layer. For technical purposes, the optical capability of a reconnaissance satellite is evaluated as a goal toward which operational use will never actually approach. Moreover, because resolution depends to a large extent on the characteristics of the optical system, and more importantly the lens, chemistry and colour effects will shift with the life of the satellite; there is so much contamination in space that the influence of these factors soon reaches significant proportions.

Ground resolution is always expressed as the sum of the camera's altitude in kilometres divided by the focal length in millimetres and multiplied by the size of the image on the lens. Accordingly, the attitude and stability of the satellite bus (the major systems and the structural base supporting the "payload" or optical instruments) must always be greater than this theoretical value to prevent the limitations of the

ITEK PAN CAMERA

High resolution panoramic cameras work by rolling a strip of film across a rotating mirror which turns the image through 90° and provides stereo pairs by nodding back and forth. The illustration shows the Itek pan camera used in the civilian space programme and for which much defence work had been done. The satellite moves forward along its orbital track and views the surface at alternate angles, so providing a contour image of the scene below. The Soviets are not thought to use this technique.

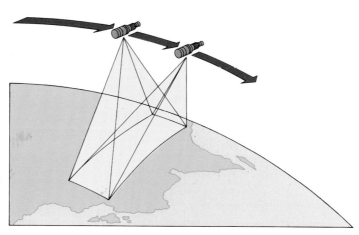

1 ▲

KH-11 reconsat backs up Big Bird, closely examining designated targets decided upon after appraisal of overall picture

Big Bird satellite surveys overall picture, designating positions of runways, oil storage tanks etc.

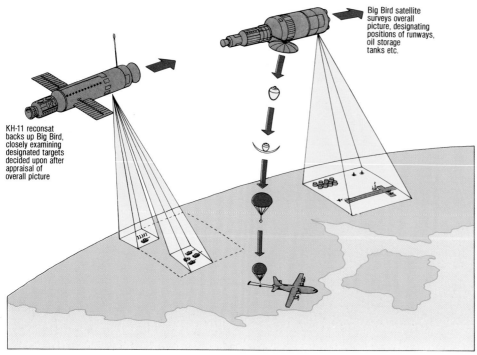

BIG BIRD

Big Bird reconsats like these shown here have replaced the area coverage satellites of the 1960s and early 1970s. With high resolution cameras, they provide broad views from which specific targets are selected for discriminatory analysis. Some pictures are returned to earth in recoverable capsules, as shown. Infra-red pictures can reveal the presence of heat-generating equipment and camouflage systems. Big Bird is backed up by the KH-11 digital reconsat which can take TV images of high clarity. Both will be replaced by new reconsats launched by Shuttle. Being retrievable, they will save money through re-use.

1 Converted C-130 flies into the descent path of a simulated space capsule, snagging the parachute risers with a trailing snare. Since the first successful recovery during descent of a Discoverer capsule in August 1960 many film canisters have been returned from space.

2 An alternative to air-recovery is seen here. "Sea-snatch" pararescue men attach a snare line to the floating capsule which rides up with the object as a recovery aircraft snags the wire. Note one-man raft.

3 Volga river seen by Landsat 1 typifies the information captured in a recce view. Note the low-lying, intensely cultivated, steppe to the east and high ground to the west broken by streams, also reservoir created by dam at Saratov.

satellite in space inhibiting the best achievable resolution. The derived resolution factor, therefore, relates to the number of lines per millimetre and is adjusted from the optical value by the type and quality of the film employed.

With the initial series of Samos satellites the optimum resolution achieved in operational conditions was a creditable 8.2 feet (2.5m) at no more than 124 miles (200km) distance; that is, the interpreter could, theoretically and with an optimum standard atmosphere during the best operating conditions, discriminate two spots 8.2 feet (2.5m) apart. By the early 1970s, line resolutions of better than 150 lines per mm were achieved from the same distance, producing a resolution of approximately 23.6 inches (60cm), and this class of technology was applied to the USAF Big Bird vehicles. Working toward the optimised, operationally limited, best resolution of a standard atmosphere it would be theoretically possible to produce a satellite system capable of 3.9 inches (10cm) resolution, and that is the absolute limit. By the early 1980s, a resolution of 5.9 inches (15cm) was possible from 248 miles (400km), forming the basis for successors to Big Bird. With this sort of resolution a skilled military analyst could determine the type and calibre of a piece of field artillery, or the size of engine nozzles of a fighter aircraft, or the size of a missile on a warship.

How a US reconsat operates

As related earlier, reconnaissance satellites now combine close-look and area-survey functions once applicable to respective types of operating mode but increasingly, as the TV and hard-copy photographs converged in performance and resolution (the latter always carrying a better performance factor), operating procedures changed. US reconnaissance missions begin in space because the large satellites employed for most of the work now track a series of opportunity targets whereas the Russian reconsats are kept waiting until needed, with only a nominal few kept in space for constant monitoring. A typical mapping operation works to a plan of target allocations, the coordinates of specific regions falling into a grid of orbital opportunities presented to the satellite on each successive pass around the Earth.

Many tasks require the monitoring role rather than a probing operation which, unlike the former, seeks to gather new information about some unknown or unclear activity; with so much long-term monitoring there are few sudden reconnaissance needs and most of the intelligence traffic is made up of component pictures blending to present a series of indicators such as might be presented by observation of a missile being slowly prepared for a test flight. Information of this kind is fed to other intelligence gathering operations so that telemetry or electronic ferrets can be activated. On any given pass, therefore, the satellite operators look ahead and obtain from a variety of sources information that helps them select a short list of objectives.

First, those areas which defence meteorology satellites show are clear of cloud or other obscuration are scanned for priorities and the finite capacity of the satellite is budgeted so as to obtain the most important information. For instance, a low priority target which is obscured 90 per cent of the time would take precedence over a medium priority target which is almost always clear. Special requests from the various users sometimes overwhelm the satellite's priority list and there is always a series of iterations in the selected short-list menu until final commands are uplinked to the satellite for several orbits ahead. The satellites are always programmed from the ground and almost never make real-time shifts, although the capability exists to do that in time of

2 ▲

3 ▲

threat or when a potentially unfriendly system tries to gain access to the communications line.

The satellites themselves carry jammers, code-switches (enabling them to change data format if interrogated through an unfamiliar sequence of commands) and random frequency-hopping channels. This latter provision is provided for several defence satellites in separate functional categories. Intelligence assessment takes the information requested from the shopping menu and translates it to an existing data bank of references. Specific tasks may be assigned when, for instance, a specific shadow-shaping is required. Here, if the configuration or shape of a distorted object presents a problem of interpretation, satellite orbits adjacent to the ground target are set up so that the cameras can view it under different lighting angles, thereby allowing a sun-shadow to "walk" around the object and present a three-dimensional view. This technique is being superseded by computer projections which literally make the object stand up and be counted!

The satellite's shopping list

A normal sequence of operations begins with the technicians providing an inventory of the satellite's condition and presenting on plot-boards the orbital parameters for several revolutions ahead. As a specific orbit approaches, the refined shopping list is updated and a countdown begins which passes a series of gates through which the satellite must be cleared before it can receive the targeting data, usually in the form of a timed sequence sent up to the satellite's on-board memory system so that the optical or scanning sensors can be stopped and started through a multitude of repetitious sequences until the programme is complete. Interpretation usually involves several analysts looking at different parts of the data spectrum.

Every so often a burst of telemetry relates the housekeeping condition of the on-board systems to engineers whose sole function is to keep the satellite operating. They must know of any extra-terrestrial activity like solar flares or unusual activity with the Earth's radiation belts and plot these on the situation board; interruptions in performance can be predicted if the engineers get a projection from physicists and meteorologists. Very often, satellite interpretation relies on ground information from discreet sources and this can be a two-way street: agents or informers operating under cover provide large volumes of information from which new targets are generated to monitor over several weeks or observe for a single orbital pass. These categorisations provide a secondary list which feeds into the main shopping list a set of priorities based on whether the target is likely to change structure, volume or position over an extended period. If it is, the object gets regular assignment.

Very often, satellites play leading roles in events and activities that frequently appear in media stories (such as the guessing games played by international media agencies over the use, and relative success, of

1 ▲

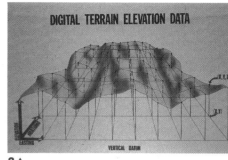

2 ▲

1 Dykes at Israel-Jordan end of the Dead Sea clearly seen in this Gemini photo.

2 Digital elevation scans provide from space detailed maps vital for terrain-following cruise missiles or manned intruders.

3 Landsat photo of Plesetsk where Soviet launch sites are located. Many high-inclination satellites fly from here.

4 TRW Vela satellites, first launched in 1963 to monitor nuclear test ban, have been replaced by EW satellite sensors.

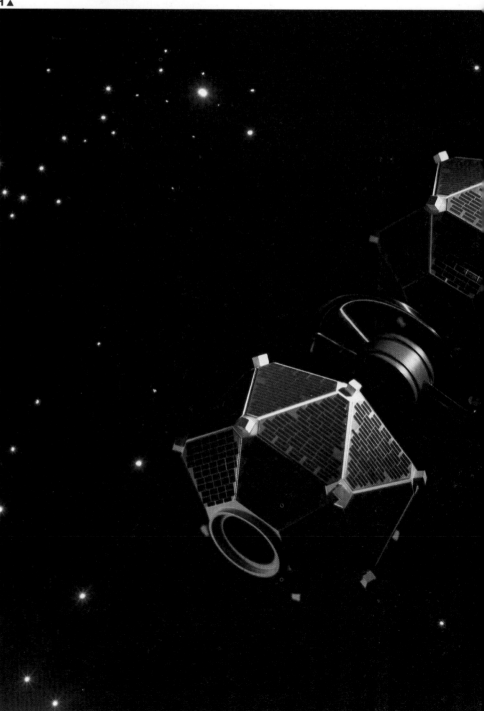

4 ▲

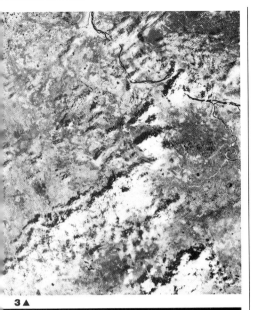

3 ▲

US and Soviet reconnaissance satellites during the 1982 Falklands conflict) but sometimes satellites play host to drama that never gets reported. One such event concerned the Middle East confrontation of 1973 when Arab army units pressed Israel back toward her borders. Fearing invasion and an all-too-plausible holocaust, Israel's Jericho surface-to-surface missiles were armed with nuclear warheads in a frantic three days of activity centred around Dimona in the Negev. These 20KT warheads could have been launched against targets in Cairo or Damascus, and a political decision had been made that if Israel's borders were violated the country would unleash a quick flurry to warn Arab forces that continuation of the war would result in their own destruction.

Activities observed by US reconnaissance satellites were confirmed in a spectacular and dramatic chase by an SR-71 photo-reconnaissance aircraft which departed from Florida and flew a non-stop return trip over Israel. Pursued by Israeli F-4 Phantoms, but too fast for its attackers, the SR-71 returned with film confirming the imminent availability of an operational nuclear capability that, if exploited, could have brought Soviet forces to the aid of Arab states. In Washington, the National Security Council met to consider their options and agreed to endorse a Presidential initiative using the hot-line satellite communication link to contact the Kremlin.

President Nixon outlined the situation and suggested he would not protest if Brezhnev dispatched Russian nuclear warheads to arm the Soviet Scud missiles sold to Egypt for use with conventional heads. In that event, the two Middle East powers could have responded to each other at a nuclear level without invoking the mandatory response from either superpower because each side would have had equal force limited to fewer than 20 active warheads. Washington's reading of the situation was that the nuclear conflict would not have spread to global proportions, it would not have provoked escalation and it would have been sealed as a contained counter-blow.

The seriousness of the situation so influenced the Soviets, however, that they moved decisively to back American initiatives in the UN at stopping the war. Fortunately, Israel's military success prevented the use of nuclear-tipped Jericho missiles, but the continued monitoring of Israeli activity was sustained for several months by Soviet reconsats, which began an extended monitoring role immediately the Nixon call reached Brezhnev.

In another episode, the deployment of major Soviet troops to the Sino-Soviet border introduced an important target for constant watch from space. Denied this sophisticated capability, Chinese intelligence sources made strenuous efforts to obtain advance information, and an agreement to exchange data at this level was one product of Nixon's 1972 trip to Peking. That provision was terminated by President Reagan shortly after coming to office, with an agreement, however, that the USA would pledge itself to warn China if the Soviets began major military activities likely to result in conflict.

More serious for the damage done to arms limitation agreements were the succession of SALT violations observed by US reconsats over an extended period. SALT-I carried with it a provision for monitoring by "national technical means" activities covered by the clauses and protocols of the agreement which, sometimes ambiguously, shaped the way both sides could prepare their respective deterrent forces. Of initial concern, very soon after the SALT-1 agreement had been signed in 1972, was the unexpected rapid deployment by the Soviet Union of a new generation of large ICBMs. This was not a violation of the agreement but rather a circumvention of its intent. Having been persuaded that the regulator on missile size should be the diameter of the silo, with the logic that missile diameter must be considerably less than that of its silo to allow the escape of exhaust products, the US was disturbed to find that the new missiles took full use of the silo's large diameter by adopting a so-called "cold-launch" method whereby the missile could be ejected by compressed gas before igniting its motor. This allowed a major growth in the applicable size of missile quite beyond the range presumed to be possible when the agreement had been signed.

Taking full advantage of a treaty shaped around the Soviets' own deployment plans, Russian SS-17, -18 and -19 series missiles were quickly brought in as replacements for the SS-11 Sego and SS-9 Scarp missiles in place when the treaty was negotiated. American reconnaissance satellites were worked hard between 1972 and 1975 as the new wave of Soviet ICBMs appeared in ever-increasing numbers. A Standing Consultative Commission, set up to monitor SALT abrogations, heard testimony about a series of new missile silos which were prohibited. The Soviets insisted the silos were underground control centres and four years later the US had to aquiesce.

Detection of Soviet ABMs

However, by using electronic ferret satellites, new anti-ballistic missile (ABM) radars were detected in contravention of the SALT 1 agreement. One was observed under rapid construction on the Kamchatka Penninsula, another at the Sary Shagan test area. The Soviets dragged out the interchange of messages in response to complaints from the Standing Consultative Commission and by the time a response was extracted the Kamchatka facility was in operation. The Soviets agreed not to build any more, but the single fully operational site remained. That is now a major target on US reconnaissance satellite shopping lists because it relates to possible operation with advanced ABM systems keyed to satellite operations.

The United States lodged numerous —contested—complaints with the Soviets as a result of intensive satellite observations. Hindsight has proven that the Soviets were quite deliberately testing the enthusiasm with which the US was monitoring activity associated with SALT-1, by the use of camouflage nets over new silos, hiding the facility from orbital sensors, which annoyed

US negotiators at the time. Soviet tests with silo re-loading operations, where the "dry-launch" method permits several missile rounds to be fired from each silo, went ahead with major efforts at hiding the activity and its results, and several false structures which were put up at the main missile sites were shown all too clearly to be artificial buildings to divert sensible interpretation. It has become accepted in US space intelligence circles that the Russians spend as much on cat-and-mouse tactics as they do on mature intelligence gathering!

For many years the space intelligence services have been starved of funds essential to developing the next generation of spies in space. They are a vital ingredient of foreign policy initiatives in addition to he obvious military advantage inherent in the concept. Systems being developed by the United States for the second half of the 1980s include a 31,970lb (14,500kg) radar imaging satellite with digital links to the ground. Developments in this field have significantly improved the resolution and could eventually permit unlimited access to the surface of the Earth, day or night, in fine weather or bad. No longer would the orbiting scanners find application only in good weather, a requirement that forced development of dedicated defence meteorological satellites built by RCA. Working to plot flight objectives over following orbits, photo-analysts generated weather predictions providing suitable observation slots for the reconnaissance satellites that needed clear skies to peer down at the surface.

Soviet Salyut space station

The Soviet Union evolved a new series of observation programmes linked with their manned programme, an activity which in several ways mimicked the published plans of the original US Air Force Manned Orbital Laboratory. The similarities between this programme and the Soviet Salyut space station is remarkable. Before telescopic camera work on Salyut, however, the Soviets developed a standard "workhorse" reconnaissance operation using manoeuvring versions of the Vostok derivative. By the end of the 1960s they regularly employed satellites of this type equipped with propulsion for switching orbital lanes and changing the geometry of their orbits to phase in with rapidly changing requirements. Still using the spherical re-entry capsule to carry the big camera, they attached other sensors on a periodic basis, and some versions carried a separate ejectable capsule which came back to earth before the main spacecraft.

These third-generation reconnaissance satellites first appeared in 1968 and weighed about 13,000lb (5,900kg) while the manoeuvring variant weighed 13,890lb (6,300kg) with the propulsion module attached. Their lifetime in space averaged 12 days, 50 per cent better than their predecessors, and by 1969 the Soviets were annually launching about 40 of these types to orbits variously inclined to the equator. The Russians frequently use satellites to gather photographic and electronic intelligence about published events, like US space shots, or brushfire wars that threaten to escalate and involve

the superpowers. Deprived by the geography of their expansive land mass from access to territories far removed from the Soviet Union, Soviet intelligence must rely on clandestine activities or satellites in space and the frequency with which the cameras are launched from their several rocket bases ensures flexible response by the Soviet leadership to changing political needs.

An example of this emerged during the 1973 Arab-Israeli war when the Soviets used satellite pictures to influence Egyptian allegiance. With an almost continuous watch on the evolving conflict from satellites synchronised in their orbital tracks with the battlefields on Earth, the Soviet Union committed seven satellites to the monitoring role so vital for an unbroken watch on the war. The investment here was large and expensive but it was commensurate with the demonstrated capacity for providing rapid response in time of emergency.

Because Soviet spy satellites are expected to play a larger part in the overall intelligence operation than their US counterparts, rapid transfer to ground stations of information processed on board the satellite is essential. To assist in this the Russians are developing a new generation of radar imaging sensors capable of transmitting through the vehicle's communication system a real-time relay of the processed picture. In this way, future applications will see the Russian reconnaissance programme evolve along two separate lines: the traditional area survey type with a rapid-response, real-time information transfer system; and the close-look types responsive to specific needs on a less time-critical schedule.

But there are several other forms of intelligence gathering from space that demand special attention. If the Soviet Union were involved in a conflict with the West, any major Soviet military thrust would necessarily involve the Russian Navy, and therefore ocean surveillance satellites occupy a very special position in the inventory of observation vehicles. Late in the 1960s, the first of this type was flown by the Russians in a move to track NATO ships and provide information about US naval movements. Here, the requirement was very different. Instead of monitoring the comparatively static disposition of forces and military installations, ocean surveillance called for timely observation of rapidly changing events with moving targets. Moreover, because the distances between targets would be so much greater than with land targets, total area coverage was to be greater than with the equivalent reconnaissance satellites. This introduced a need for higher altitude observation which necessarily reduced the potential resolution available to an optical imaging system. Radar was the only answer, providing information and, through interferometry, the positive location of specific ship targets.

On the American front satellites were developed through the US Naval Research Laboratory to fill this requirement, test flights beginning in 1971 and culminating in an operational mission by the end of the decade. Through programmes coded "White Cloud" and "Clipper Bow" active radar observation techniques were perfected. The

1 ▲

2 ▲

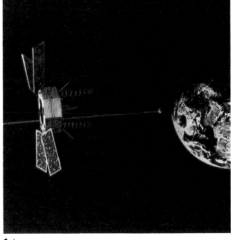

3 ▲

1 Cancelled in 1969, USAF Manned Orbiting Laboratory envisaged space station for surveillance and research combined.

2 Defence Meteorology Satellite Programme (DMSP) provides extensive global weather data for US and NATO forces.

3 TRW FLTSATCOM series provides US Navy with high-priority VHF from stationary orbit. The first of five was launched in 1981 and the series will operate until replaced by Leasat.

4 NTS-1 navigation satellite as part of Timation programme provided passive ranging combined with highly accurate clocks for global use.

5 Debris from the Soviet Union's nuclear powered ocean surveillance satellite Cosmos 954 fell across Canada in 1978. Another Cosmos satellite fell to earth in early 1983.

6 Seasat launched in 1978 proved the value of sea-state forecasts as prelude to a major ocean surveillance programme for the 1990s.

4 ▲

5 ▲

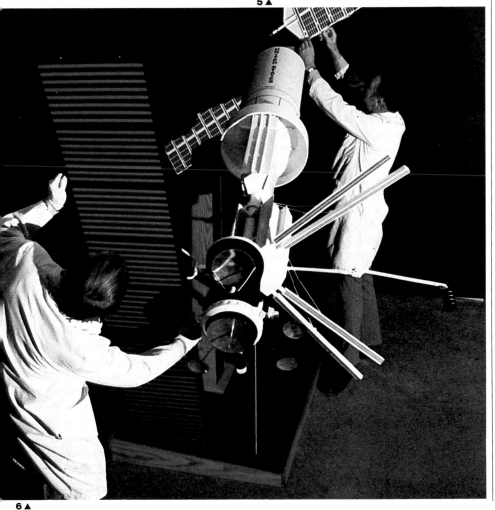

6 ▲

White Cloud programme anticipated the launch of three sets of three satellites, each set at a height of approximately 683 miles (1,100km) and displaced from its neighbouring set by about 120° of longitude. Each set would circle the Earth at an inclination to the equator of 65.3°. The total project would, therefore, maintain triple sets of spacecraft equally spaced at one-third intervals around the globe.

Within each set, the separate satellites flew in parallel orbits, each track no more than 31 miles (50km) from its neighbour. The satellites were to be displaced in a triangular pattern and, from their high position, "see" surface targets up to 1,990 miles (3,200km) away. Thus, three orbiting sets would monitor surface traffic in the Indian, Pacific and Atlantic zones respectively, utilising a total of nine satellites each weighing a few tens of kilogrammes only. The first subset was launched in 1976, the second in 1977 and the third in 1980.

The Soviets followed a different line of ocean surveillance, preferring to fly several separate satellites each year in low altitude trajectories designed to seek electronically quiet ships in the infra-red or sub-millimetre wavelengths from a powerful radar unit utilising a nuclear generator. Weighing approximately 9,920lb (4,500kg), 46 feet (14m) long, and 8.2 feet (2.5m) diameter, the satellite would go into an approximately circular path only 155 to 168 miles (250 to 270km) above Earth, inclined 65° to the equator. At the end of a four to eight week mission the main body of the satellite would release the primary instrument and sensory pod before firing itself up into a higher path 560 miles (900km) high. This ensured a safe orbit for the potentially dangerous nuclear fuel carried for electrical energy while the delicate instrumentation tumbled back down through the atmosphere from its lower path.

Cosmos 954 falls to earth

In September, 1977, however, a satellite of this type failed to work correctly and Cosmos 954 fell through the atmosphere with its nuclear generator intact. During the descent friction broke apart the satellite and its lethal cargo, spilling radioactive particles over Canada in January 1978. No permanent contamination of the surrounding area resulted from this incident, but it was a focal point of embarrassment for the Soviet Union, which immediately withdrew its nuclear ocean surveillance satellites until, three-and-a-half years later, a redesigned model appeared to replace solar-cell-powered surveillance satellites used in the interim. The solar-cell satellites were less efficient, flew considerably higher and therefore were unable to carry out certain tasks, and were at best a stopgap until the basic, high-powered design reappeared.

Like their US equivalents, Soviet ocean surveillance satellites were employed on electronic snooping to gather data and voice communications from ships on the sea below. But while the US originally included two separate series of ferrets, the Russians seem to have consistently employed specifically designed satellites launched separately on their own rockets. The US family of lone

SELECTED MILITARY SATELLITES

NAME	LENGTH ft (m)	DIAM ft (m)	WEIGHT lb (kg)	LAUNCH VEH	ORBIT miles (km)	PURPOSE
USSR						
Vostok-based recon satellite	16.4 (5)	6.56 (2)	8,820 (4,000)	A-2	105 x 186 (170 x 300)	Orbital reconnaissance. Satellites carry high resolution camera plus manoeuvre engine. Normal life time is 12 to 14 days. Numerous sub-varieties.
Ferret (large)	16.4 (5)	4.9 (1.5)	5.512 (2.500)	A-1	391 x 404 (630 x 650) x 81.2°	Detailed survey of operational characteristics of military radar and radio stations.
Ferret (small)	6.56 (2)	3.28 (1)	?	C-1	311 x 342 (500 x 550) x 74°	General survey of military radar and radio stations.
Nuclear-powered ocean surveillance satellite	45.9 (14)	6.56 (2)	?	F-1m	161.5 x 174 (260 x 280) x 65.1° (after separation) 590 (950) circular orbit	Locate shipping by use of radar. A pair of satellites are launched within a few days of one another. Uses nuclear reactor to power equipment. After completion of 60-70 day mission reactor unit is fired into higher orbit.
USA						
KH-11 also Project 1010	64 (19.5)?	6.56 (2)?	30,000 (13,605)?	Titan IIID	155 x 329 (250 x 530) x 96.95°	Orbital reconnaissance. Few details of equipment are known, but possibly both high resolution and search-and-find cameras as in Big Bird. May include five "real time" television transmissions of photos. Has on-board rocket engine and has demonstrated a lifetime in excess of one year.
Titan IIIB-Agena D reconnaissance satellite	26.2 (8)	5 (1.5)	6,615 (3,000)	Titan IIIB-Agena D	84 x 205 (135 x 330) x 96.4°	Orbital reconnaissance. Formerly used as high resolution satellite with film-return capsule. Now believed to be a search-and-find type which seeks out new targets for Big Bird and KH-11s. Has demonstrated a lifetime in excess of 50 days.
Big Bird also Project 467	50 (15.2)	10 (3.05)	30,000 (13,608)	Titan IIID	99 x 168 (160 x 270) x 97°	Orbital reconnaissance. Carries large high resolution camera, having resolution better than 1ft (0.3m). Film returned by six capsules. Also carries search-and-find camera equipment. Signals transmitted through 20ft (6.1m) diameter erectable antenna. Lifetime approximately 180 days. Has on-board engine to prevent orbital decay.
TACSAT 1	25 (7.6)	9 (2.7)	1,600 (726)	Titan IIIC	Geostationary	Tactical communications between US forces in the field using small transmitters.
FLTSATCOM	16 (4.9)	8 (2.4)	2,176 (987)	Atlas-Centaur	Geostationary	Communications between US Navy vessels.
NATO 2	5.25 (1.6)	4.5 (1.37)	285 (129)	Thrust-Augmented Delta	Geostationary	NATO Comsat, links US and NATO countries.
Defense Meteorological Satellite (Block 5D)	17 (5.18)	6 (1.8)	1,043 (473)	Thor-Burner 2	500 (804.5) x 98.7°	Provides weather information for US forces, available for civilian use.
DSCS 2	13 (3.96)	9 (2.74)	1,100 (499)	Titan IIIC	Geostationary	Real-time communications between the US air forces.
Vela *Data refer to Vela 11 and 12 throughout*	4.17 (1.27)	4.17 (1.27)	571 (259)	Titan IIIC	**Vela 11:** 69,106 x 69,696 (111,210 x 112,160) x 32.4°	Detection of nuclear detonations on Earth's surface, within the atmosphere and out to 100 million miles (161 million km); solar flares and other space radiation. Instruments: X-ray, gamma ray, neutron, optical electromagnetic pulse and energetic-particle detectors.
UK						
Skynet 2	6.83 (2.1)	6.25 (1.9)	517 (234.5)	Thor-Delta	Geostationary	United kingdom military Comsat, two channels

1 Midas 4 early-warning satellite launched Oct 21, 1961, by Atlas-Agena B also carried a piggy-back load of 350 million copper needles for Project West Ford radio communications experiment. Midas-4 detected Titan missile exhaust two minutes after launch, Oct 24, 1961.

2 USAF's Defense Support Program Satellite, the TRW Block 647, for providing early warning of ICBM launch. After initial USAF EW satellite tests were frustrated by sunlight and cloud reflection problems, great strides were made with the IMEWS (Integrated Missile Early Warning Satellite).

3 Earth watchers include meteorological Block 5D satellites, latest in a series that began operations in January 1965, following research in orbit starting three years before. New sensors profile area below clouds and monitor rain precipitation in addition to temperature. The data helps mission planning.

ferrets evolved through three generations between 1962 and 1971, in which year the last was sent into space. Since then, the expanding family of subsatellites, beginning in 1963 with flights riding piggy-back on area survey and close-look reconnaissance satellites have continued. From 1972, however, subsatellites for electronic snooping have ridden exclusively on the Big Bird family, two separate ferrets sometimes being released in orbit.

The role of the ferrets has never been more important than it became in the 1970s with the obvious expansion of Gorshkov's ocean Navy. Because the Soviets employ separate codes for each type of SLBM-equipped submarine, the United States' ferrets are the ideal and frequently the only means of identifying the specific Soviet boats, and type of warhead that they carry, and the nature of the operations (often intelligence-gathering and dissemination) upon which they are engaged, especially in coastal areas where NATO surface ships are denied access.

As soon as the Soviet submarines slip through the Greenland-Iceland-Faroes gap on their way into the Atlantic from the Baltic ports they are assigned a specific ferret which then seeks to obtain coded signals sent by the boats as they prepare to submerge to an assigned route in the North Atlantic. Each submarine sends a final code and this can be used to identify an otherwise anonymous message picked up several weeks later from an antennae on the surface several hundred, or thousand, miles away. Frequency and code-allocation can change according to how safe from detection the Soviets believe their boat to be but the satellite plays a vital role in bringing added benefit to the West's maritime surveillance operations, providing a fixed location for submarines that would otherwise go undetected.

US early warning satellites

With the planned demise of the dedicated ferrets launched by their own rockets, US attention turned to a family of satellites built to pick up and relay telemetry from the many Soviet rocket and ballistic missile tests carried out each year. This is the longest leg of intelligence gathering from space because it constructs a picture of weapons and delivery vehicles still several years away from operational duty, and reports on the generic development of rockets and missiles already in service. From geostationary orbit 22,370 miles (36,000km) above earth, ballistic missile

monitoring satellite of the 606lb (275kg) Rhyolite class look down on test sites far below. Built by TRW, they discriminate between confusing HF and VHF transmissions clustered around the main test sites and transmit the rocket's telemetry to data-receiving stations in the United States.

Four Rhyolites have been launched to date, with two serving as spares to the two prime satellites located over the Horn of Africa and the Indian Ocean respectively. They monitor the tests of solid propellant ICBMs from Plesetsk, SLBM flights from submarines in the White Sea, liquid propellant ICBMs from the big launch facility at Tyuratam, the anti-ballistic missile test area at Sary Shagan and the warhead re-entry zone in the Kamchatka penninsula.

Although intelligence gathering about future and pending development projects is a vital part of defence planning for opposing forces, more immediate concern surrounds the timely detection of potential attack from large ballistic land- and sea-based missiles. The conventional forms of radar detection derived from air-defence technology have been supplemented in recent years by satellites in geostationary orbit 22,370 miles (36,000km) above Earth. First American attempts in this direction, an obvious choice for potential military satellite developments

because of the superb position of geostationary orbit, evolved early in the history of space projects, but did not lead to a more advantageous position. In the Midas (Missile Defence Alarm System) project, at least eight satellites were to orbit the Earth with infra-red sensors at a height of 2,300 miles (3,700km) spaced to cover the Earth continuously and pick up the hot exhaust of an ascending rocket.

The idea sounded good but the technology was far behind the concept. Glare from the sun bouncing off cloud tops triggered the sensors and the correct spacing was difficult to achieve. In all, only nine satellites were launched between 1960 and 1963 before the whole idea was revamped into a geosychronous satellites with flights beginning in 1968, preceded in 1966 by three test flights of a TV-equipped satellite. The fully operational system did not appear until 1970 with Block 647 type satellites weighing 2,535lb (1,150kg) compared to 606lb (275kg) for the smaller generation they replaced. Also known as DSP (Defence Support Programme) satellites, the early warning vehicles were built by TRW and carried a Schmidt telescope capable of viewing comparatively large areas without the spherical aberration normally associated with other types of telescope; in that regard the Schmidt

is ideal for presenting a uniformally consistent image. The satellite itself comprises four solar cell panels on one (upper) end, with the telescope pointing directly down from the other end but offset by 7.5°. Because the satellite spins at approximately 6 revolutions per minute, the telescope prescribes a circle which improves the overall field viewed by the 2,000 infra-red sensor cells carried inside the satellite.

Ninety seconds' warning

Early warning satellites of this type are positioned to watch tests and firings from China and the far reaches of the Siberian missile fields, from the main missile launch silos in West Russia, and to warn of potential SLBM launches from the Altantic and Pacific oceans and sneak attacks from missiles coming in across the polar caps. It would take about 90 seconds to confirm a major Soviet missile attack, by which time the ground radars would see the ascending trajectories and plot a precise course, something the satellites cannot do because they measure azimuth only.

The Soviets have chosen to emphasize the capabilities of low-orbit early warning satellites, putting appropriate instruments and packages on satellites in the Molniya

(communications) and Electron (science) classes. Late in 1975, however, the first geostationary orbit slot for a Soviet early warning satellite was taken up by Cosmos 775. Situated over the Atlantic, this satellite looks for submarine-launched missiles, a capability denied to the lower satellites.

The integration of space and ground-based early warning systems is a vital component of the West's alert network, which needs access to both types of information to provide escape time for manned penetrating bombers, reaction time for silo-based ICBMs and dispatch of coded instructions to submarine and surface ships (from facilities that might not last long in the event of a nuclear attack). Accordingly, ground-based EW systems look toward space for discrimination between legitimate objects and possible warheads descending low and fast toward land targets. More than 5,000 objects orbit the earth, most of them pieces of debris from over 2,700 satellites and space probes launched since 1957. About 2,000 objects are clustered in geostationary orbit almost 22,370 miles (36,000km) above earth. The optical tracking of objects down to the size of a baseball is essential to adequate logging.

In low earth orbit the continuous movement of satellites and debris up and over the horizon is predicted by computers which look for a new piece of material, a satellite or a missile. Initially recorded by US satellites in space, the test launch of several hundred rockets and the firing into orbit of more than 100 Soviet satellites each year keep the operation in a state of continual change, with no two orbits carrying the same quantity or type of object inventory. Ground-based radars complement the response time from satellites, but no single level of alert is allowed to take precedence, confirmation being required from satellites and all ground-based systems.

False alarms: bombers scramble

However, the unfolding sequence of events made necessary by a valid alert is set in motion with sufficient time to retrace those steps should subsequent interrogation prove the alarm to be false. In this way, bombers can be (and have been over the last 25 years) scrambled before the confirmation of a false alarm brings them back to base. Because NATO's detection of hostile war-heads relies on the simultaneous alert of ground-based and space-based sensors, an indication of attack provided only by over-the-horizon (OTH) radars would not, of itself, invoke a strategic response. It would, however, call for bombers to be scrambled only because their bases would, in an actual attack, be unusually vulnerable. No other means of retaliation would be activated until the space-based sensors had been interrogated and assessed, and until other radars had confirmed the initial warning. Consequently, the scrambling of NATO bombers in the past can be viewed as a measure of both the sophisticated level achieved by alert systems and the high degree of verification essential to safety and built-in as a functional part of the system.

The reason that space-based surveillance and early warning systems are so important to NATO's overall defensive strategy is that the "no first use" policy means Western Europe or the USA will not strike without absolute confirmation of a Soviet attack, as affirmed by Eugene Rostow, Director of the US Arms Control and Disarmament Agency, in his address to the First Committee of the United Nations General Assembly on October 27, 1982:

"The Soviet Union has pledged great emphasis in its public statements on its pledge not to be the first to use nuclear weapons. The Soviet position is a cynical exploitation of one of the most troublesome moral issues of our age. The controversy about 'no first use' pledges nations (to) recommit them-selves to the principles of the (UN) charter. NATO has long followed a policy—one it has recently reiterated—that none of its weapons will ever be used 'except in response to attack'.

"We see no value in a pledge not to be the first to use nuclear weapons if a 'right', or at least the power to use conventional weapons in contravention of the UN Charter is claimed and reserved. The main effect of nuclear arms control agreements should not be

to make the world safe for conventional aggressive war.

"In any event, the Soviet 'no first use' pledge is unverifiable and unenforce-able. Its credibility is belied by the nature of Soviet military doctrine, and by the ominous Soviet buildup of massive land-based ballistic missiles, which present an obvious threat of first use."

Contrary to popular opinion from some circles, this ensures a high state of confidence that the system will not wrongly interpret warnings from several different sensors or radar installations and should be seen as a measure of how quickly airborne units can respond to alerts.

As will have by now become apparent, most military satellites are positioned in orbits below approximately 310 miles (500km). On the US side, only the four Rhyolite, nine White Cloud and several early warning satellites are positioned at greater heights than this. But outside the intelligence gathering family of military satellites other, vitally important classes play a fundamental role in defence operations and would, in wartime, provide a service unobtainable elsewhere. These include the several defence weather satellites in low orbit, the navigation satellites in intermediate and high orbit, and the defence communication satellites at geostationary altitude.

The weather satellites play a part in selecting reconnaissance objectives, sched-ules being arranged according to the cloud cover and precipitation levels, but the satellites are primarily intended for land, sea and air support at a conventional level. They occupy polar orbital slots at a height of approximately 510 miles (820km). Navigation satellites of the Transit class fly orbital paths variously inclined between 28° and 90°. The satellites were originally placed at an altitude of approximately 683 miles (1,100km) but advanced versions employed now are positioned in paths between 217 and 497 miles (350 and 800km). Nova satellites developed for the US Navy are placed in a circular path 683 miles (1,100km) high, while the complex and sophisticated Navstar Global Positioning System (GPS) satellites are in orbit 12,552 miles (20,200km) above Earth.

Integration with Navstar

The GPS network is designed for use by every major US combat unit on land, sea, or in the air. It has tremendous growth potential because of its broad design specification and can provide individual platoons with accurate position data from a back-pack readout station or give information to a Mach 2 bomber at tree-top height. Accuracy is measured in metres, and by the end of the 1980s many critical weapon systems will be integrated with Navstar. New generations of cruise missiles built to gather update information, ballistic missiles taking a position reading in space, and bombers flying silently to their targets on courses set by Navstar are but a few obvious applications of this important satellite system.

1 ▲

2 ▲

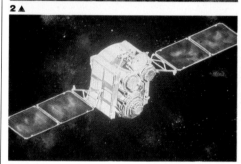

3 ▲

1 Developed from the Transit navigation satellite, this improved model carried a device to align it with earth's gravity field.

2 Developed from Transit, Nova pioneered the 26ft (7.9m) long astromast for gravity stabi-lization. Note solar arrays.

3 DSCS-3 communica-tions satellite is latest in a series employed by the United States for global service from a geostationary position.

4 Marisat Pacific and Atlantic Ocean satellites are used by commercial as well as US Navy operators.

5 Navstar Global Positioning System satellite seen here in USAF Arnold Engineering Development Center test chamber. Full set of 24 will be positioned 12,427 miles (20,000km) high, accurate to 33ft (10m).

6 Russia's Salyut space station, seen here withdrawn from forward shroud, conducts high-tech' and defence-orientated activity.

7 Salyut crews ride to their space station in the Soyuz, seen here during a launch by the developed version of Russia's first ICBM, the SS-6 Sapwood.

4 ▲

5▲

6▲

7▲

COMSATS

Military communication satellites are now required to carry more than voice messages between national command posts and field units or battle groups. From stationary orbit, US and NATO satellites provide command and control functions, keying in nuclear forces to the US President and SSBN commanders to the Pentagon. NATO comsats are increasingly used for ship communication and for relaying orders. The USAF and the USN operate dedicated satellites for respective services and considerable improvement in the existing system is planned for the 1980s and '90s. Soviet comsats, of which about 25 are launched each year, follow inclined orbits and are part of the intelligence network linking spy ships and aircraft to receivers.

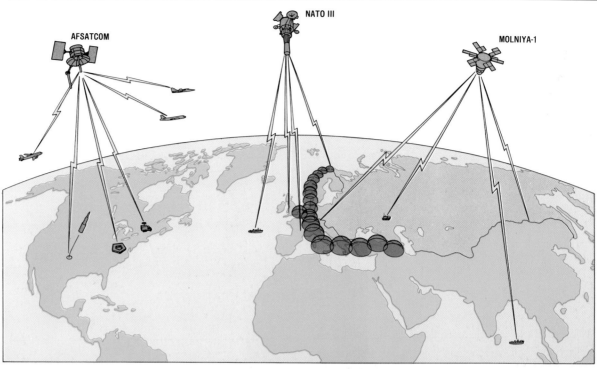

1 ▲

2 ▲

3 ▲

4 ▲

1 Pave Paws radar site at Beale AFB forms one link in a chain of phased-arrays warning of SLBM or air attack. Note the planar antenna and adjacent power house.

2 New Soviet Pushkino ABM radar provides 360° defence coverage in a structure 120ft (36.5m) high and 500ft (152m) wide. Note silo-launched interceptor missiles.

3 Cape Dyer DEW site here forms a vital link in the United States' integrated space and ground based alert and monitoring network enhanced by intersystem liaison.

4 Distant Early Warning (DEW) stations provide a chain covering CONUS approaches and monitor air space for possible intrusion by enemy bombers.

5 Personnel of the 7th Missile Warning Sqdn monitor screens displaying satellites at the Beale AFB Pave Paws site. Activity here monitors Soviet satellite traffic.

6 Individual cells on this phased-array radar display vulnerable elements posing priority target during conflict. Space-based sensors are vital backup.

5 ▲

6 ▲

Now, all military communication satellites reside in geostationary orbit 22,370 miles (36,000km) high, positioned to provide unbroken service between fixed and mobile ground, sea or air locations far below. The level of dependence on these satellites is measured by the reliance NATO places on them; 90 per cent of all intercontinental communication goes by satellite.

Clearly, satellites have become a prime instrument of keeping the peace, by ensuring precise and rapid conveyance of information about a potential enemy, and have matured into applied roles vital during any major conflict. Intelligence about a potential enemy has been the key which opened the door of strategic negotiations between the superpowers. Without violating the national territory of either side, each knows the other's true force strength. There is less ambiguity than at any other time in the history of conflict, ensuring a valid set of criteria for SALT or START (Strategic Arms Reduction Talks) negotiations with a reality hitherto denied to such talks.

The employment of "national technical means" for inspecting the military hardware of an opposing force prevents the surprise move that on so many occasions in the past has preceded a lightning attack. Pearl Harbor would not happen today, nor would the uncertainty about Nazi rearmament. Conflicting nations, denied the element of surprise, could be prevented from using force as an instrument of persuasion. Moreover, surprise development of "breakthroughs" in technical weaponry is less likely with continuous reconnaissance and intelligence gathering than it ever could be without satellites. But, if the deterrent should fail and war break out, the prosecution of global conflict is made so much more significant because of the space segment.

Space could tip the balance

In almost every supporting role, space would be the ingredient that could tip the battle in favour of one side. Alternatively, denied the eyes and ears to watch enemy force movements continually, the relay stations to communicate or the beacons by which to navigate, sophisticated weapons would be rendered impotent, ground and sea forces could be useless and air combat would fall back upon eyeball response. Clearly, denial of the space segment may prove a fundamental blow to battle management and, eventually, to the outcome of the conflict. This was clear from the beginning of the space age, and since the early 1960s both the United States and the Soviet Union have studied the possibility of destroying enemy satellites in space.

It is not as easy as it sounds. For one thing the distances are enormous; even comparatively low orbit satellites pose major problems for an intercepting satellite vehicle and distant spacecraft are inaccessible to all but the most exotic guidance technology. Nevertheless, US experiments in 1963 culminated in the interception over the Pacific of a previously orbited booster by a Thor-launched vehicle.

Several companies tried to link the con-

cept of intercepting incoming warheads with the need to disable satellites in space but here, too, the technology proved daunting and while US Congress was asked to fund the increasingly expensive campaign in Southeast Asia the sharp, exotic end of defence R&D found more near-term objectives. Nevertheless, through the Nike-Zeus anti-ballistic missile programme basic concepts were evaluated.

By the end of the 1960s, all US plans for a satellite interceptor had been shelved, just at the time the Soviet Union began flight tests with its own programme of anti-satellite development projects. The first successful demonstration of a killersat technique, where a satellite is first put into orbit before manoeuvring up to a target, unlike the "direct ascent" mode favoured in US studies, came in October 1968. Cosmos 248 was put into an approximately circular orbit about 323 miles (520km) above Earth, followed a day later by Cosmos 249, which went initially to a 84.5 × 158 mile (136 × 254km) path. On command, the interceptor portion of the chase vehicle separated from the main rocket stage and moved to a highly elliptical 319 × 1,353 mile (514 × 2,177km) orbit, Thus was Cosmos 249 placed in position to intercept Cosmos 248 from above with a high relative speed at close approach. Four hours after getting into this orbit, Cosmos 249 swept past its target and was detonated a safe distance away, the intention here being to prove all the activities required of a killersat but in such a sequence as to preserve the target intact for future fly-bys.

This was at a time when Soviet space engineers were making big efforts to perfect rendezvous and docking operations, flying test models of their Soyuz manned spacecraft to develop techniques later used on Salyut space station link-up flights and to serve the similar but diversely applied needs of killersats.

For two years the Soviets demonstrated interception tests following the format laid down by the first. Then, in March 1971, a second development programme practised a different technique: interception and inspection followed by return of the diagnostic satellite. It began with the launch of target vehicle Cosmos 400, put into an almost circular 621 mile (1,000km) orbit, an altitude about twice that flown by the earlier missions. The inspection satellite, Cosmos 404, moved into a path slightly below so that it gradually gained on the target. When the two were close Cosmos 404 demonstrated an electronic scanning process whereby it diagnosed the payload of the target satellite. It then moved to a lower orbit and fired a motor to return through the atmosphere.

This technique provided many optional possibilities that could be applied to potentially hostile satellites. With this method, Soviet satellites could diagnose the true purpose of foreign satellites or space vehicles from close up, transfer an electrostatic charge to disable its communication and power systems, or simply "show the flag" to another satellite in space with a cautionary threat of blowing it up at will. In a return to former techniques, a test in 1971 demonstrated an interception and kill capability on a target satellite 155 miles (250km) above earth, half the height of the initial series.

But so far all Soviet anti-satellite tests had been constrained by the need to get into a similar or higher path to the target, the latter made necessary so as to achieve high relative closing velocity without consideration to the full operating requirements of the technique, which included a need for surprise and "quick-fire" flights. Once the basic geometry of the technique had been proven, and a suitable operating mode demonstrated, these two facets could be incorporated in a fully operational mission profile. Surprise would be essential and the quick-fire requirement would validate the concept.

Continual monitoring of all objects placed in space would warn US and NATO watchers that a Soviet satellite interceptor was on a collision course, and appropriate defensive measures could be taken to save the integrity of the threatened satellite. So the next major step qualified the concept when, in June 1977, Cosmos 918 accelerated from its initial orbit below 124 miles (200km) to fly quickly past the target vehicle (Cosmos 909) orbiting between 621 and 1,242 miles (1,000 and 2,000km). It happened so quickly that within one revolution of the earth the

interceptor had dashed past the target and returned through the atmosphere. Four months later a low altitude demonstration of the same technique was carried out by Cosmos 959 and Cosmos 961, the interceptor showering the Pacific with debris as it burned up. Many reports emanated from Japan that flying saucers were in the vicinity but the reality was perhaps more threatening than alien encounters.

Talks on limiting killersats

During the early 1970s a hiatus in Soviet killersat tests had lulled the United States into believing that Russia had terminated the intensive development implicit in their initial activity. But, at the end of the decade, a flurry of accelerated spacecraft flight operations by the Soviets causing serious concern in the United States brought concerted efforts to agree a limitation on the operational deployment of killersats. Talks began during June 1978, but led to nothing, the Soviets refusing to abandon employment of a system they had apparently perfected to an operational level. Soviet negotiators even tried to get America's Space Shuttle cancelled as part of overall space demilitarisation initiatives, citing it as an advanced US anti-satellite weapon! Since 1976 only one calendar year has passed without some

form of Soviet killersat test. In response to this, US development of an equivalent capability has evolved along a completely different route.

Denied the long R&D experience resulting in an operational family of space-based interceptors used by Soviet forces, US technology developed for the ABM role has been successfully applied to anti-satellite operations. By marrying the modified rocket motor of a short range attack missile (SRAM) with the fourth stage of a Scout launcher, the sequential thrust of the two motors operating in tandem accelerates a small impact head out of earth's atmosphere and on course for a collision with some designated target in space. The ASAT (Anti-Satellite) device is carried beneath the fuselage of a converted F-15 Eagle fighter and is released close to the aircraft's operating ceiling (over 70,000ft, 21,000m). From the rarefied outer layers of the aerodynamic atmosphere, the ASAT is coupled to a guidance system relieved for precise target designation by an active, infrared, homing sensor in the nose of the impact head.

Separated from the two stages that propel it on course and to high speed, the 12-inch (30.5cm) long impact head incorporates tubular solid-propellant rockets around its 12.9 inch (33cm) diameter. These are used

ANTI-SAT SYSTEMS

This hypothetical montage shows various types of space and ground-based anti-satellite weapons and methods to destroy sensors vital to an enemy. Low orbit satellites are shown knocked out by missiles while high orbit navsats are destroyed by a combination of missile and directed-energy weapons. High and stationary orbit satellites are valid targets for laser or particle beam weapons. Soviet killersats capable of hitting only the low orbit satellites will, by the end of this decade, also target the high satellites. No comparable US or NATO system is planned or likely to be built in that time.

■ NATO

■ SOVIET

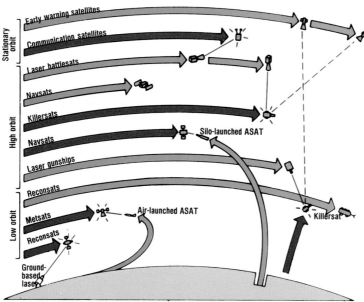

1 USAF F-15-launched anti-satellite device would use combination of stages from Boeing SRAM and terminal stage of Scout launcher to propel a Vought-developed impact head on collision course with Soviet satellite in low earth orbit. The System could be operational by 1986 and eliminate ocean surveillance satellites.

2 Anti-satellite (ASAT) Vought impact head here displays interior components, with sensor cluster at front surrounded by solid propellant rockets for directional control when fired in banks and final impact acceleration where all are fired simultaneously. Device has been developed from ABM impact head designed in 1970s.

3 Artist's view of Soviet ASAT discharging pellets in a single burst as the vehicle moves through its closest approach to a US defence satellite. Soviets regularly test operational procedures with ASAT vehicles, following extensive development programme that began in 1967. With rapid launch capability and pop-up orbital techniques, Soviets target prime US navigation satellites with this system, also threatening reconnaissance and ocean surveillance satellites. High altitude killersats are currently being developed through the facilities on board Salyut stations, and multi-barrel ASAT launchers in space pose a late 1980s threat.

1 ▲

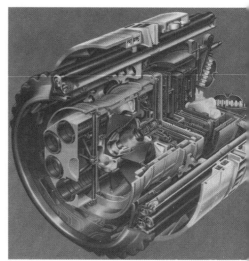

2 ▲

to fine-tune the trajectory and to fire collectively for a terminal acceleration designed to provide ram velocity at the satellite. It takes only one direct hit from even the comparatively small ASAT head to disable a satellite. As a satellite is prone to damage from any accelerated fragment, a collision would destroy its ability to function.

By the mid-1980s the US Air Force plans to have several units operating ASAT weapon systems with a capacity for knocking out comparatively low orbit satellites. Typical in this class of Soviet satellites are the ocean surveillance types which would prove vital in supporting missile attack from underwater submarines close to the US mainland, a particularly vulnerable area because the flight time of an SLBM would be measured in minutes rather than the half-hour or so taken by an intercontinental land-based missile.

The complete F-15-launched ASAT is approximately 17.7 feet (5.4m) long and weighs about 2,645lb (1,200kg). Yet, for all its effectiveness, the ASAT concept, like Russia's killersat programme, falls short of thehigh altitude kill capability mandatory for total protection of space systems support from opposing military operations. What is needed by both sides, and sought actively by the Soviets, is a means to knock out of action the geostationary satellites covering

communications and early warning, and the medium-orbit navsats increasingly employed for guiding existing conventional and nuclear weapon systems.

The Soviets have gone some way to that by flying adaptive modules capable of selectively switching roles. Coupled with their Salyut space station programme the Soviets have tested large, plug-in modules capable of providing high-altitude kill capacity. Cosmos 1267, launched in April 1981, was the first and has since been used for tests designed to accommodate advanced killersat technology. Cosmos 1267 weighed 15 tonnes and proved to be the progenitor of more complex systems built to coordinate with very large space stations the role of military space surveillance and attack for which the West has no equivalent system.

Shifts in role of space

If the 1960s were a time for conceptual experimentation, and the 1970s a period for consolidating the passive military foothold in space, the decade of the 1980s presents major shifts from monitoring and support roles to active participation in space conflict. The final shift will come perhaps when killersats are permanent residents in space, both as guardians of the satellites they protect and as potentially active participants

in rapid destruction of the space capability of an opposing force. In that regard, future wars may *begin* in space, even if they start on the earth below, because to leave active the several sets of space systems vital for prosecuting conflict on earth would be tantamount to giving advantage to the enemy.

The sequence of events that might be brought into play by a major conflict is speculative because it is dictated by the nature of the threat and the perspective from which the scenario is seen. With Soviet military doctrine based on the ability of a pre-emptive first-strike to decimate the enemy and prevent escalation to full war status, the recipe of events would be completely different for each side. Clearly, elimination of guidance and monitoring satellites is a prime consideration for the opening minutes of conflict. The Soviets rely heavily on their ocean satellites for guiding submarine-launched missiles and the USA will, by the end of the 1980s, have several major weapon systems integrated with navigation satellites.

The interplay between earth- and space-based systems is illustrated elsewhere in this chapter but should be considered a typical sequence only, since the object is to show the diverse accumulation of events and activities that would necessarily in-

fluence the air, sea and land operations below. As tactical and strategic weapon systems become increasingly integrated into the total defence equation, protection of the orbiting assets is vital to the war effort and is receiving at last the attention it deserves and needs to guarantee the effectiveness of tactical and strategic systems.

By 1990, major new developments will have taken place. The Soviets are known to have at hand a launch system far beyond the capability of the biggest rocket available in the West. In comparison with provision for sending to low earth orbit a mass of at least 150 tonnes, the maximum 30-tonne lifting capacity of the NASA/DoD Shuttle is significant only for its deficiency. But what, one might ask, do the Soviets want with such a behemoth? It cannot serve any functional purpose in war if only because the time to prepare it for launch would be so long that the site would be obliterated far short of the launcher's available launch time.

The primary function of such a system would be to place in space the hardware necessary for achieving unchallenged supremacy in the ability to dictate the pace of conflict. With a 150-tonne capability the Russians would be able to place in orbit a laser weapon aimed not only at military satellites but at ballistic missiles as well. For their part, US military advocates of directed-energy weapons point to the Shuttle as a capable means of lifting such a device.

The Soviets traditionally consume greater weight penalties in space-based systems, and by the end of the 1980s the USA would be well able to build a laser weapon sized to the limitations of the Shuttle. Only because the Soviets are philosophically committed to a major presence in space, and therefore to the fabrication of a large space station en route to that capacity, do they really need the mammoth lifting potential of a super-booster of the type described here and seen many times in US satellite reconnaissance photographs.

US advocates of space lasers

Laser weapons are not yet defined in hardware designs but the theoretical capacity to develop such a system has been around for several years. Ardent advocates of this device press constantly for major US funding in support of such a project but it seems very unlikely that US forces will have the benefit of a laser anti-satellite weapon in the 1980s. What is more likely is the development of a permanently manned orbiting complex, an assembly of Shuttle-launched modules equipped with sophisticated surveillance sensors—optical and radar—for diagnostic duties far beyond the reach of individual satellites. Only then would the provision of a directed-energy weapon system seem logical.

There is considerable speculation about the actual lines of space-orientated defence technology and the superficial satellite count belies the reality behind the apparent disregard given by US governments to space intelligence and battle management. For instance, in the mid-1960s, the United States was launching around 50 military satellites each year, the majority of these being comparatively short-lived reconnaissance satellites. During the 1970s that figure toppled quickly to an average of 15 to 25 and remained so for the remainder of the decade. By the early 1980s, less than 10 US military satellites were being launched each year. But the budget figures for military space expenditure tell a very different story of development and investment in space-based systems that will appear during the late years in this decade and introduce innovative concepts for the early 1990s.

US space budget increases

For more than ten years beginning in 1963, DoD space spending stayed around an annual budget of only $1,600 million, while the NASA budget plunged from a high of $5.5 billion in 1965 to around $3 billion in the early 1970s. But from 1977 DoD space money began a modest rise, reaching $3.8 billion by 1980, at which time the remorseless process of inflation had raised NASA's money to $4.7 billion while actually remaining static in real spending terms. A year later President Carter endorsed his self-confessed disillusionment at the failure of East-West detente by raising DoD space money by one-quarter, a process sustained by the Reagan administration which increased funds from $4.8 billion in 1981 to a staggering $8.5 billion by 1983. In the same two years, NASA's budget went from $4.9 billion to $6.1 billion, clearly reflecting the new mood of the White House. Thus, funds are in place, and development programmes have begun, for a major shift toward a leading military space expansion in US affairs. It will help pull back some of the slack vis-a-vis the enormous Soviet build-up in space capability, which knows no distinction between civilian and military segments since all projects are inter-leaved according to their lines of generic development.

A major US asset for the coming decade undoubtedly lies in the expanded capability of the manned, reusable, Shuttle to carry military payloads into space and to bring them back down to earth, or to go into orbit for one task and switch to a retrieval mission prior to re-entry, perhaps bringing back for diagnosis or modification a heavy piece of space hardware previously launched by Shuttle or some other launcher. Other launchers are available to the DoD for emergencies or for rapid response, a provision for which the Shuttle is not well suited.

A busy and expanding inventory of domestic and foreign space flights for commercial customers will keep the Shuttle tied to a comparatively inflexible launch schedule. NASA controls the Shuttle operating manifest and anticipates expanding from five flights in 1983 to eleven in 1984, fifteen in 1985, seventeen in 1986, twenty-two in 1987 and twenty-four in 1988. This traffic model is the maximum that can be funded with existing NASA budget constraints and it would take longer to implement a higher rate of mission build-up than could be accommodated in the time available between 1983 and 1988. Beyond that year, more funds would be required to build up to the 40 Shuttle flights per year that NASA

1 ▲
1 Supporting an imaging radar on a special pallet, NASA's second Shuttle flight demonstrates the expanded capability provided by the Shuttle. Although installed as a NASA science experiment, the radar could double as a space-based sensor package for monitoring activity on the surface of the earth, at sea or in the air. Comprehensive sensor package systems may be the most effective way to use the manned vehicle, in addition to its value as a satellite launcher. Maximum capability is 30 tonnes.

2 Teal Ruby is one element in the High Altitude Large Optics (HALO) programme developing a space-based mosaic IR array for detecting and tracking air activity over hostile or foreign airspace. The system will be Shuttle-launched.

3 Space-based laser ASAT system employing rotatable mirror assembly for target designation may be the only effective way of protecting US/NATO satellites from Soviet counter systems. DoD and NASA are already developing nuclear power concepts for ASAT.

would like to see by 1991, and even that would need funds made available by 1984.

Because of the need to build-in DoD flights that might develop faster than new Shuttle launch slots could be made available, the DoD will keep on hand several of the large Titan 34D launchers now available for sending payloads weighing more than 32,850lb (14,900kg) to polar orbit. The big Titans will also stand in should a catastrophic failure reduce further the already tight manifest for commercial and military payloads. So the Shuttle will fly reserved payloads needing the attention of astronauts in space or the fine articulating powers of the big manipulator arm, and leave for the unmanned launchers satellites sent routinely to duty in space. Moreover, the Shuttle will be employed to return to earth the new post-Big Bird reconnaissance satellites mentioned earlier, a project for which designed in the early 1970s.

Shuttle's military missions limited

Nevertheless, and in spite of popular belief to the contrary, military Shuttle missions will be few and far between for several years. From one military Shuttle flight in 1983 and one in 1984, the programme of DoD missions expands to four in 1985, seven in 1986 and eight or nine in 1987. Concurrent with this inventory, expendable launchers will continue to fly military missions from Cape Canaveral for all flights up to an approximate earth orbit inclination of 55°, and from the Vandenberg Air Force Base for polar and sun-synchronous missions. The first ostensibly military Shuttle flight was the fourth test mission carried out in June 1982 from the Kennedy Space Centre, but flights from Vandenberg will not begin before October 1985. The DoD is responsible for missions from this West Coast facility and has no need to change to the Shuttle before that date; until then all military Shuttle flights take place from the Cape.

This planned inventory of military and civilian flights depends on the timely availability of four space-qualified Shuttle orbiters; the second was delivered to NASA in July 1982, the third is due in late 1983 and the fourth by the end of 1984. A fifth orbiter will be built, and replacement vehicles as necessary to maintain a continuously operating fleet of five Shuttles, but the schedule for that is uncertain and it may not be sustained before the end of the decade. By that time several new and innovative technology developments will result in unique DoD space operations that are impossible at present.

Much is said about the "sharp" end of Shuttle-orientated defence technology but lasers in space are only one potential candidate for a heavy lift. Very large radar antennas erected in orbit and deployed outward from folded containers are an early application of the new and expanding launch capability. Air defence may come to rely primarily on space-based systems, where antennas several hundred metres across are a comparatively simple technology problem.

The passive monitoring of enemy air forces, down to a level where individual

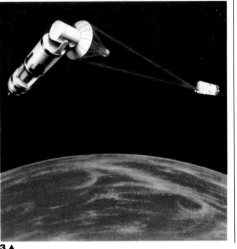

2▲   3▲

1▲

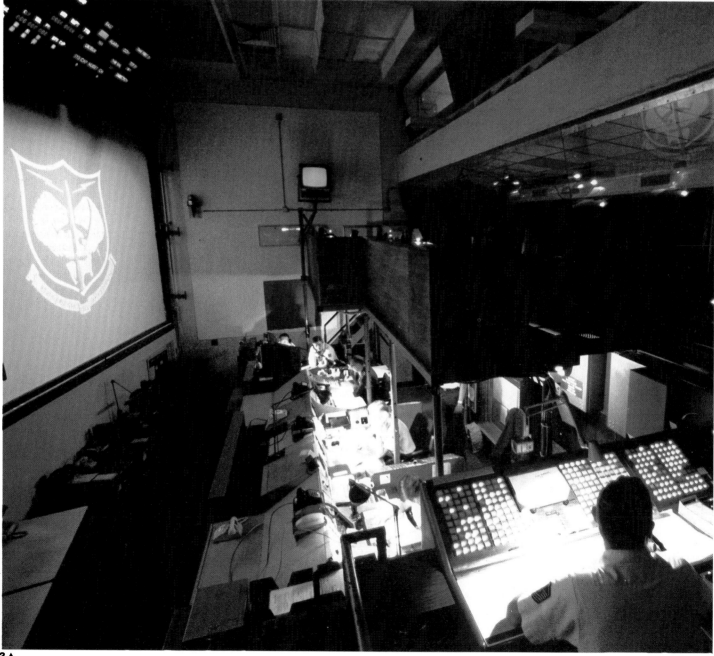

2▲

3 ▲

1 Exterior of GEODSS site at White Sands, one station dedicated to identifying passive objects in space that might be "ghosted" satellites capable of replacing active military satellites destroyed by ASAT.

2 Norad command post inside the Cheyenne Mountain complex, Colorado, where information is sent from global monitoring stations of optical and radar networks. Vital information on new Soviet satellites is generated here.

3 Ground based Electro-Optical Deep Space Surveillance (GEODSS) system at White Sands, N.M., comprises two telescopes for space object identification and a low light level TV camera at the back of each telescope.

4 Norad radar monitor surveys data screen. Tasks extend from passive monitoring of Soviet ASAT tests to active exercises aimed at perfecting techniques for discriminating from satellite breaking up on re-entry and warhead decoys.

4 ▲

aircraft can be satisfactorily discriminated with a high degree of reliability, is one space-applied role being developed by the US Air Force. Another embraces the monitoring of underwater vessels, nuclear submarines carrying Trident or Poseidon SLBMs. With very large reflectors deployed from Shuttle the continuous access to submarines denied today by the physics of available radio technologies would change to one in which laser frequencies would secure modulated signals carrying enormous quantities of data. In the early 1990s, large camera systems carried in the Shuttle's spacious cargo bay will probably become a routine exercise, ten-day missions every three months providing a phenomenal quantity of photographic and other data about changes in strategic and tactical force levels around the world.

Increasingly, space sensors will play a major role in monitoring the deployment and activation of forces from developing countries as more and more of the world's nations acquire nuclear weapons. What exists today as a force largely aligned with the cold-war mentality that survives as a legacy of post-World War II challenges will shift quickly in the coming decade to a surveillance organization geared to threats from small countries with power out of all proportion to their political and industrial might. It will be an essential part of global force monitoring, and the threat of wars between the superpowers triggered for self-determined ends by a Third World state in possession of a limited nuclear capability could become at least as serious as the two-power confrontation that exists today.

Satellites in the front line

But if war did break out on a colossal intercontinental scale, the satellites would be in the front line. Many would not survive the opening hours of attack and plans for that have been made already. Of the more than 2,000 satellites launched to date by major and minor countries around the world, the majority are dead or dying, purged of their electrical life by decaying solar cells or depleted propellant tanks no longer able to feed the thrusters that keep their antennas aligned with earth. Among these irregularly shaped satellites, and the more than 3,000 pieces of junk that represent the rubbish left over from satellite launches, hide apparently harmless shapes of metal and composites that are in fact ghost satellites waiting to switch on should the primary satellites be destroyed. Optical scanners employed by both sides to watch the satellites placed in space and photograph them as they pass overhead reveal the intent of objects in space only if some familiar or decipherable form is detected in the image. Skin-tracking (bouncing radio waves off the surface of a object) is not possible in geostationary orbit so only the highly refined optics of Ground-based Electro-Optical Deep Space Surveillance (GEODSS) cameras reveal unknown pieces of hardware that must be identified either as useless pieces of debris or potentially active satellites waiting in silence for the day they may be needed.

The United States has put great emphasis on the GEODSS programme because passive *and* active satellites may hide among the refuse of space flight. Steps have already been taken by the Soviets to guard against retrieval by systems like the Shuttle. Explosive charges are known to have been placed aboard certain defence satellites in the belief that, knowing this, the Americans would never risk destroying a Shuttle in a vain attempt to snatch a Soviet military satellite.

USAF's new Space Command

To coordinate effectively the accelerated activities of military space operations the US Air Force formed a new Space Command on September 1, 1982, with the prime purpose of integrating all military space interests into one plan, satisfying US needs in the field of space defence operations developing counter-technology to perceived threat from the Soviet Union, and operating the Consolidated Space Operations Center being build near Colorado Springs for control and management of space flight operations, including DoD Shuttle missions. Space Command is long overdue and the funds it will manage represent a small fraction of the overall defence budget, about 4 per cent even with the inflated 1983 DoD space fund. Yet the importance it has for the overall integration of American (and NATO) intelligence, surveillance and battle management is out of all proportion to the meagre resources it controls.

An attack upon any military satellite by a Soviet weapon system in space or on the ground would be regarded as an act of hostility, not war. But if war should break out through a concentrated, simultaneous assault on both earth-based and space-based segments of the West's defence structure, the sophisticated apparatus placed in space by the Shuttle would be on its own, the reusable transporter being too exposed on its launch pad at the Cape, and requiring too much time to prepare, to be a candidate for replacement flights. That task would fall to the ICBM vehicles in their underground silos, or, for small satellites, to Trident missiles under water. A percentage of the large US missile force acting primarily as a deterrent and secondly as a retaliatory strike force has been set aside for launching vital replacement satellites during a major nuclear war.

For the next several years those defence satellites will be passive in nature, or addressed to each other in an exclusively space-based theatre. But if the expanded development of lasers, and their advanced cousins the particle-beam weapons, are ever deployed in space their targets would be missiles ascending from under ground or under water and other defence equipment in the air. At that time the integration of earth- and space-based war scenarios will have truly formed a three-dimensional battle management equation with as profound an impact on warfare as the tank has had on land battles. Until that day and increasingly after it, sensors based in space will continue to provide an essential part of the intelligence gathering machine.

Chapter seven

Intelligence and the war in the air

TACTICAL AIR intelligence is one of the most important components of modern conflict and involves elements in the air and on the ground in an integrated role unique in potential value and usefulness. Yet it is one of the least funded activities in the air war; it assumes consummate importance when war breaks out but gains little notice or prestige in peacetime. Paradoxically, a large part of the tac-air intelligence machine can only operate at full potential during conflict if adequate and measured attention has been paid to its prosecution *before* the war breaks out. This is because, as will become apparent, the quality and depth of information obtained is largely dependent on the meticulous and time-consuming accumulation of data and intelligence over a very long period; rapid extraction of timely information is vital for the conduct of forces during a running war but it does little for the qualitative analysis essential to strategic and tactical information banks.

Tactical air intelligence can be divided into reconnaissance and information-gathering segments, the latter dependent to a very great degree on the former. Air intelligence works through six primary applications utilising common hardware and operating procedures:

(a) information gathered in peacetime which could affect the tactical air war during a sudden, pre-emptive, attack from an enemy;

(b) information and intelligence about enemy or "neutral" forces which might affect the global, or strategic, evolution of the air war;

(c) intelligence that proves politically valuable in balancing the size or disposition of forces in peacetime;

(d) sustained monitoring of tactical and strategic air elements as they evolve through optional technological paths with a view to shaping one's own defence technology;

(e) tactical support of ground and airborne attack units in the gestative stages of a sudden war;

(f) strategic force operations support to vector large land and air units in addressing the forward edge of the battle area.

In a generic tree of value and application, the first three provide simultaneous, and continuing, activity, the fourth addresses and supports those elements, and the fifth and sixth follow consecutively with some degree of overlap when war breaks out. The six primary components have expanded to their present number as a direct result of increasingly sophisticated requirements and a broadening technology base within which to secure the objectives. That means that the inventory of tasks and responsibilities placed upon tactical air intelligence units continually expands and can be expected to do so in the future as new elements and capabilities are added to the already impressive list of information-gathering elements. But it has not always been this way and the circuitous route taken by tactical air intelligence to its present posture provides valuable lessons for the future.

Early air reconnaissance

Early in World War I, when aeroplanes were an unknown component of the land battle, information gathering was the only visible role for these heavier-than-air winged machines, which allowed an extension of the role hitherto performed exclusively by the airship and the balloon. The aeroplane afforded the possibility of controlled and comparatively rapid access to the enemy battle lines from a position where it was considered within easy visual distance of artillery and infantry yet invulnerable to ground fire. This happy state of affairs prevailed for a few weeks at most until reconnaissance aircraft on both sides of the conflict were armed with guns that turned them into "scouts" equipped primarily for clearing the skies of opposing forces.

But from 1916 the dedicated reconnaissance aircraft was in a niche of its own and, although lightly armed with defensive armament, was to become a specialised design concept with unique needs. At first the air reconnaissance role was essentially a tactical activity, one of support for traditional forms of intelligence gathering on the ground. With no experience in air-reconnaissance, observers frequently made stupendous misinterpretations, mistaking cloud shadows for swarms of infantry or tar patches for tarpaulin covers! But by the end of 1914 both sides on the Western Front came to accept the aircraft as the prime method of obtaining intelligence about the enemy, visual sightings being aided by photography, which was also used

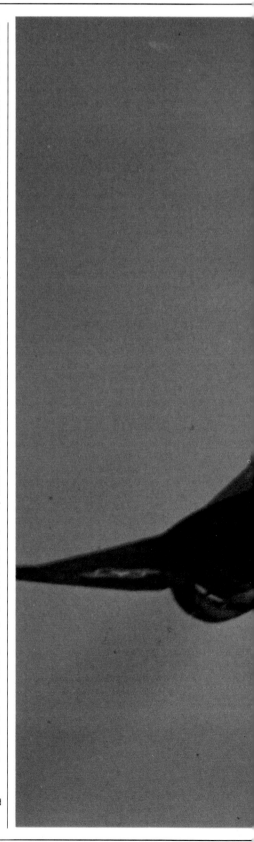

1 The basic role of air intelligence is epitomised by the SR-71 Blackbird, highest flying of all the large reconnaissance aircraft operated by the US Air Force. With optional sensor pods and equipment, it has intercontinental range.

Air intelligence is not an end in itself. Information is useless without interpretation. It is not the job of air reconnaissance to acquire as much data as possible but selectively to acquire pertinent information, and survive long enough to deliver it for assessment.

1 ▲

for mapping. New tasks evolved too, including artillery ranging, which made direct air-to-ground communication vital. Messages dropped in cans, flags waved from the rear cockpit, sighting lamps flashing coded signals and pyrotechnic charges let off from the air were all tried with various degrees of success before the wireless transmitters and receivers were introduced early in 1915.

Soon, infantry were working with the air reconnaissance units to signal their progress to stipulated positions. On the ground it was becoming frequently impossible for infantry to know where they were, all visible landmarks being quickly obliterated. Only the aerial platforms could provide the information essential to the senior officers and commanding generals. As the great battles of the 1914-1918 war progressed, aerial armadas were sent up at critical periods of the attack to shield the swarms of reconnaissance aircraft going about their essential duty.

Temporary decline

After the end of hostilities in Europe and the reduction of armed forces and equipment, air intelligence went into serious decline, virtually disappearing from the inventory of military tasks retained by the leading powers. In the firm belief that reconnaissance during World War I had been exclusively tactical in value, air intelligence became a matter for army co-operation rather than independent support. Not until 1935 did Britain's Royal Air Force appreciate the long-term value of gathering this type of information, when a threatened breakout of hostilities in the Italo-Abyssinian conflict prompted the RAF to photograph areas of Eritrea, Abyssinia and Sicily. The possible escalation of this conflict to other areas of the Mediterranean, with all the damage that that could do to effective Middle East communication, led Britain to reassert its photographic reconnaissance capability, but only with side-looking cameras shooting oblique views. All major powers were surprisingly reluctant to violate national air space, but the shifting balance of threats in central Europe made them recognise the imperatives. The expanding need for adequate intelligence about German and Italian military developments prompted a reappraisal of the organisational infrastructure. Almost too late, Britain recognised the need for extensive surveillance and intelligence-gathering activity, not only for tactical objectives but for the longer-term benefits of strategic analysis and interpretation.

But even as the open acquisition of photographic-reconnaissance information was ignored, other activity aimed at more directly assessing the air threat had been addressed and met: through a series of radar (the American term, radio detection and ranging) installations looking out across the North Sea and the English Channel, Britain's air defence would benefit from advance warning of approaching enemy aircraft. It was a unique asset, and one which provided the second dimension to tactical air intelligence: added to the capa-

1 ▲

2 ▲

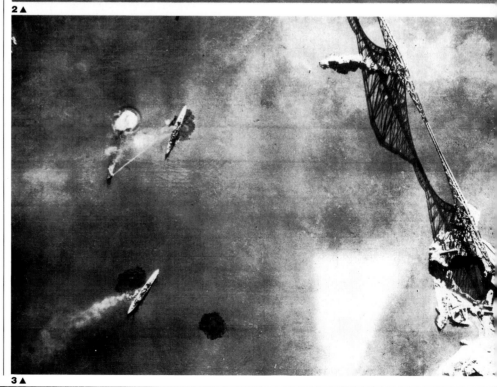

3 ▲

4 ▲

1 Balloons had been used for overlooking enemy positions before WW1 but the first serious application came in the 1914-18 war when both sides used aerial "spies."

2 Even peacetime demands continuous activity by a wide range of recce aircraft, such as this C-45 on mapping duties.

3 Taken by a German long focal length aerial camera, this WWII picture of the bridge across the Firth of Forth under attack by bombers shows the difficulty of hitting such a slender target.

4 Most cameras used by small, high-speed aircraft were fixed, but large cameras in bombers and converted transport aircraft were hand held and manually controlled, as shown here, providing greater flexibility and expanding the opportunities for useful reconnaissance.

5 RAF recce photo after a November 1940 attack on the Italian fleet at Taranto shows two damaged Trento class cruisers in the inner harbour. Large quantities of oil can be seen, in addition to other warships.

5 ▲

bility of using aerial cameras to judge and monitor the progress of the land battle, other regions of the electromagnetic spectrum would be utilised for coordinated air interception.

In a very real sense, the technical developments that shifted air intelligence from a remote probing function to an active defence screen for British air space promoted the evolution of reciprocal advancement by German scientists that exposed the need for greater emphasis on photographic reconnaissance. As indicated earlier, reluctance to support an active tactical air reconnaissance programme left Britain and the major Allied combatants ignorant of potentially important projects under way in Germany. The need for an active tactical, intelligence gathering operation became suddenly and rudely apparent when Hitler's forces attacked Poland.

A significant part of the air intelligence operation was gathering information about known installations and searching for derivatives of predictable lines of development, but much of the air intelligence battle during World War II involved the active search for new and unexpected weapon systems or facilities indicative of new scientific and technical developments, such as the aerial photography of Germany's rocket research facility at Peenemunde from May 1942.

Learning the lessons

After the war major efforts were made to retain photographic reconnaissance units in the strength which they had attained through six years of conflict, and also to heed the lessons learned about both the importance of aerial intelligence-gathering, and the techniques and equipment developed by all major combatants. The importance attached to a continuous, strategic, surveillance and mapping operation did persist, but in the general demobilisation that followed little could be done to maintain full services. Yet for all that, with hard-won lessons learned to a degree, both US and British air arms retained the nucleus of a strategic and tactical net. The new weapons made that imperative. With an expanding force of nuclear bombers the need to know with precision the location of towns and cities across land masses totally unfamiliar to American mappers generated new tasks as urgent as any routine reconnaissance exercise in wartime.

To deter progress in the land battle, Russian maps were found to have built-in errors, placing towns, cities and physical obstacles several kilometres from their actual location. In the reorganisation of 1947 that brought in a Department of Defense and an independent US Air Force, Strategic Air Command was created and with it responsibility for the long range nuclear deterrent. An essential ingredient of viable threat projection was to have an integrated war plan with pre-assigned targets for the free-fall nuclear weapons. The known irregularity of Soviet maps forced emergence of a new task, met at first by reconnaissance versions of the wartime B-17 Flying Fortress and B-29 Superfortress

bombers converted into RB models which were equipped with banks of cameras and ample film for continuous exercises.

By the mid-1950s, US Air Force reconnaissance units had completed the initial survey of Russian towns and cities, correcting all the many errors and displacements on previously published maps. This, in turn, spurred acceptability of strategic missile applications, because targets had now been pinpointed to a greater accuracy than that provided by rockets of the day. Through the experiences of World War II, intelligence and surveillance had promoted applications inappropriate without the new, sophisticated, techniques of reconnaissance.

Gradually, surveillance became more important than reconnaissance and along with a wealth of information about Russian and Chinese urban and industrial development came recognition of weapons programmes unidentified through the usual espionage channels. This caused an overreaction about the level of preparation achieved by Soviet and Chinese forces but spurred efforts to consolidate knowledge at a spatial level by watching the temporal changes over several months.

It also invoked development of electronic intelligence gathering from the air. SIGINT (Signal Intelligence) became the second primary component of tactical air intelligence and, stimulated by a need to monitor enemy missile developments by listening-in to the radio commands and (later) the telemetry, this form of ferreting created a need for high-flying aircraft beyond the ceiling of fighters and ground-to-air missiles. It was to generate the technology for mapping SAM sites when they emerged as a primary tool for air defence.

Additional tasks given to these aircraft included COMINT (communications intelligence), but this diverts from the support role for tactical battle operations. Discovering the frequencies employed by military units, and resolving the information from their equipment, became the responsibility of EWSM (electronic warfare support measures) and formed the continuation of a role pioneered by the World War II German Signal Intelligence Unit.

With the introduction of mechanical sweep in the 1950s the rapid surveillance of potential frequencies in a given area was made both simpler and more reliable. Today, electronic turning allows coverage of several GHz bands each milli-second and the added advantage of "signature comparison" permits almost instant access to an identity for observed radio emissions; by referencing a bank of known enemy equipment the system can generate a readout telling the crew not only the frequency and the likely band of channel-hopping sequences, but also the type of software involved. This greatly assists tactical field operations in addition to probing SAM radars and radar-guided anti-aircraft artillery.

During the 1950s the then-revolutionary RB-36 Peacemaker was the definitive strategic reconnaissance tool, but in 1959 it was replaced by an inventory of tactical aircraft that today form the nucleus of the air intelligence machine, peripherally feeding strategic, satellite and naval intelligence that in turn supplies the Central and Defence Intelligence Agencies with the information necessary to counter pre-emptive strike and rapidly deploy ground, air and naval units to the affected sector.

An important intermediary was the RB-57 version of Britain's Canberra bomber. The RAF Photographic Reconnaissance Canberra replaced the Mosquito in this role from 1953 and, equipped with up to 11 cameras of up to 35.9 inches (91.4cm) focal length lens, 20 were still in service in early 1983, but were due to be retired that year.

The American version of the Canberra was modified with a high-aspect ratio wing and it carried out a reconnaissance function from 1956. Employed as high altitude aircraft, RB-57s flew more than 1,000 sorties a year over Vietnam during the second half of the 1960s, providing the high altitude surveys with which the tactical units, with RF-101 and RF-4 aircraft, could perform their tasks in support of air or ground strikes.

The first truly effective tactical reconnaissance tool was the Lockheed U-2 which appeared operationally in 1955 with a range of over 2,175 miles (3,500km), later increased to more than 3,730 miles (6,000km). It bridged the gap between tactical and strategic intelligence gathering but forged a link that has remained the cornerstone of competent battle preparation, establishing the set of tasks and responsibilities outlined at the beginning of this chapter. Capable of flying at heights well in excess of 72,000ft (21,945m), the U-2 was employed on over-flights of Soviet territory, gathering information about Russian missile development on tasks employing airfields as far apart as Peshawar in Pakistan and Bodo in Norway. Other aircraft, like the Martin P4M Mercator and the EB-47 Stratojet, were employed for SIGINT tasks along foreign borders or high above unfriendly terrtory.

SR-71 in Mid-East conflict

The strategic reconnaissance successor to the U-2, and in some respects to the RB-36 also, appeared in 1965 but was not unveiled to the public for several years. Called Blackbird, the SR-71 has a Mach 3 capability, a ceiling in excess of 82,000ft (25,000m), a range of more than 3,420 miles (5,500km) and a reconnaissance role allowing it to photograph about 100,000 square miles (259,000sq km) in one hour from maximum altitude. About 30 SR-71 aircraft were built and nine were still operational in 1983.

These aircraft were effective in supporting a major political initiative midway through the 1973 Arab-Israeli conflict when, acting on information that Israel was preparing to arm its Jericho missiles with nuclear warheads, USAF's 9th Strategic Reconnaissance Wing sent an SR-71 from Beale AFB to overfly the territory. Equipped with infra-red scanners, optical cameras and electronic listening equipment, the aircraft was refuelled off Spain for a high-altitude pass over the Negev Desert. As the Blackbird performed a run over the area where Israeli nuclear weapons were being

moved, a US Navy Hawkeye COMINT aircraft orbiting over the eastern Mediterranean picked up two Israeli F-4 fighters climbing fast to intercept the SR-71, which they were unable to catch because the Blackbird, after being warned, accelerated to high altitude above the Phantom's ceiling. When the SR-71 reached Gibraltar it was refuelled again and headed back to Beale.

The intelligence it brought before a hastily convened meeting of the National Security Council was sufficiently impressive to leave then-President Nixon little alternative but to use the Washington-Moscow "hot-line" and advise then-Soviet leader Brezhnev to move nuclear warheads down to the Soviet-built Scud missiles ringing Cairo and the Aswan Dam. With both sides similarly equipped, possessing a finite quantity of nuclear warheads, involvement of the superpowers would be avoided and unnecessary confrontation averted. On October 13, 1973, a Soviet freighter left the Nikolaev Naval Base at Odessa and put to sea with nuclear warheads on board. By the time the ship reached Egypt, Israel had consolidated its forces and turned the Egyptian army units into reverse. This removed the need for Israel to use its last-ditch weapons, cooling a potentially disastrous confrontation involving nuclear strikes on major Middle East cities.

In other areas, the SR-71 has been usefully employed monitoring the movement of Soviet SIGINT and COMINT units on the eastern edge of Russia's border. But there are tasks that the Blackbird cannot perform and the need for a loitering capability to watch the tests of new Russian missiles is frequently so profound that it generates its own political inertia.

An example of just how vital air intelligence can be occurred when the revolution in Iran denied to US intelligence assessors large radar listening posts on the border with the Soviet Union. Deployed to listen to and collect telemetry from the Soviet missile tests at Baykonur, the radars were the only means by which Western intelligence experts could obtain electronic information about the performance of these important rockets.

Similar listening posts in Turkey were prevented by undulating terrain from "seeing" the missiles during the first few minutes of flight, an important part of the ascent where much about the operational capabilities of the vehicle could be learned. Accordingly, a high-altitude flight high above the Afghanistan border was the only option remaining and diplomatic moves begun by then-President Carter were aimed at re-establishing convivial relations with Pakistan, from where the overflights would have to originate. Hitherto, relations with Pakistan had been clouded by political changes within the country but the agreement to resume the flow of technical (including nuclear) assistance brought a reciprocal agreement to use Peshawar once more for electronic surveillance of the southern border with Russia.

It was not only for the observation of missile tests that reconnaissance of the entire region was considered important. With oil resources controlling the barometer

1 ▲
1 With increased capability over earlier versions, the E-2C carries an advanced radar processing system for early warning duty.

2, 3 Developed initially as a replacement for the U-2 spy-plane, the SR-71 has unique capabilities. Here its unusual aerodynamic shape is displayed. Note fin-mounted snake (Vietnam) emblem on lower photo.

4 U-2 of the 349th Strategic Reconnaissance Squadron takes off from RAF Wethersfield, England on a routine mission. NATO is ever-vigilant of surprise attack from across the East European border.

5 Early, unpainted U-2 aircraft provided useful information about border activities and helped build a file on Soviet global activity

2 ▲

3 ▲

4 ▲

5 ▲

of western economic health, the Soviet Union knows that any significant threat in the Gulf could topple the free-market money system. Therefore, probably more than in Europe, the need for tactical air intelligence over the Gulf is paramount, especially since the area is as potentially hostile and alien to Western forces as the snow fields of western Russia were to Hitler's army.

Tactical air intelligence depends, as we have seen, on adequate knowledge to make the right assessments of need; during World War II the RAF was unable to provide information leading to a correct interpretation of Peenemunde in less than one year after the site was first photographed, and the intelligence experts in Britain were unaware for a full seven years that German rocket research was going on along the Baltic shore.

The important lessons learned during the 1939-45 war led directly to the political shaping of Middle and South Asia policy. Unfortunately, Afghanistan air space was brought within the Soviet umbrella when Russian forces occupied the country in December 1979, but the need for adequate reconnaissance remains. It is the tactical level that now provides the more important channels of defence intelligence in support of air operations, and this was developed in depth by the United States in the early 1950s.

Eisenhower's influence

Very little formal debate has been generated about the decision by President Eisenhower to place high priority on the acquisition of tactical air intelligence, and aerial cameras to build comprehensive information banks on almost all potential war zones. With first-hand experience of the value obtained from photographs of the battlefield, Eisenhower was a staunch advocate of tactical intelligence gathering. But more than that, in the immediate post-war environment much was researched about the lessons from World War II, during which studies have shown that 80 per cent of all useful military intelligence came from aerial reconnaissance photographs. Recognising the inadequacy of existing airborne intelligence equipment, the President was directly responsible for ordering CIA chief Allen Dulles to place a contract with Lockheed for construction of the U-2.

This aircraft had been designed by Kelly Johnson's 23-man team at the Lockheed "Skunk works" and was to be developed as Project Aquatone into a high altitude spyplane capable of flying as far as a B-52 with cameras and electronic sensors. A special Mylar-based film developed by Eastman Kodak greatly increased the number of images the cassettes could take and, with special lenses designed by Harvard astronomer Dr James Baker, the system could resolve detail down to a resolution of 60 line pairs per millimetre, compared with 12 to 15 lines per mm for Word War II reconnaissance cameras. When used with a special panoramic strip camera called the Hycon-B it enabled a single aircraft to make sweeping coverage of a large area with unprecedented detail. The camera weighed only 450lb

1▲

2▲

3▼

4▼

1, 2 These Itek images of downtown Los Angeles were taken with an Itek KA-102 pod-mounted camera system on an aircraft, and reveal the depth of field and clarity of the buildings in 6x enlargement (**1**) and 24x enlargement (**2**). The picture was taken from a slant range of 45 miles (73km). Shadows, scale height of known buildings and elevations reveal important information about the type and size of new or modified work. In (**2**), specific activities can be deduced from vehicles in or around the buildings.

3 Early pictures of the nascent Soviet rocket facilities were taken by U-2 spy planes operating from Peshawar in Pakistan. Here, the main SS-6 launch pad and blast trench can be seen clearly.

4 Francis Gary Powers was shot down in 1960 during a recce flight over Soviet territory. His U-2 was one of several in use at the time for clandestine missions to obtain details of missile and air defence activity. Such flights led to a reassessment of America's strategic weapons policy.

(204kg) which made it suitable for the U-2.

Each U-2 was able to carry 11,954ft (3,650m) of film and covered a swath 745 miles (1,200km) wide with a central strip 150 miles (240km) across, in stereo. The unique capabilities of the U-2 would have provided full coverage of the continental United States in just 12 flights.

The first flight across Soviet airspace was successfully carried out on July 4, 1956; less than four years later, on May 1, 1960, the Soviets succeeded in shooting down the first spyplane, with Francis Gary Powers at the controls. What the U-2s had discovered proved that the bomber gap was a myth, and directly resulted in cancellation of the B-70 Valkyrie, a US supersonic bomber project, when President Kennedy came to power in 1961. But those early flights also proved that considerable efforts were under way in the Soviet Union to develop strategic missiles, and it was that that spurred the Kennedy administration to order 1,000 Minuteman ICBMs.

But the tactical air intelligence role emerged with clarity only two years after Powers had been shot down over the USSR,

when a U-2 photographed SAM sites under construction in Cuba. On August 29, 1962, the first film landed on the desk of Art Lundahl, head of a small photo-intelligence unit in Washington. Requests made by Kennedy for clarification brought hot denial from Soviet leader Kruschev that larger missiles were planned which could threaten the continental USA. Further intelligence analysis was carried out, including U-2 "sheep-dipping" flights, where missions running parallel to the coast were punctuated with sudden, snap diversions inland and out again. They failed to provide new evidence until the US Intelligence Board authorised a U-2 mission directly over San Cristobal where the SAM sites had been built.

The CIA-owned U-2, flown by Air Force officer Maj Richard Heyser, and specially equipped with ECM, took 928 pictures in a six-minute overflight on October 14, 1962. These provided Lundahl with evidence that the Russians were massing equipment and facilities for nuclear armed SS-4 ballistic missiles. What happened after that became a matter of history as Kennedy blockaded Cuba and forced Kruschev to withdraw his

missiles in return for a withdrawal of American Thor and Jupiter rockets from Europe.

How photo-recce is used

The importance of photographic reconnaissance has increased since 1962, with most of the strategic mapping and surveillance duties now carried out from space. Reconnaissance aircraft directly applicable to the air and land battle are diminutive versions of their larger forerunners. Today, fighters and interceptors have given the tactical air reconnaissance role a new pace, with versions equipped to procure intelligence information and pass it rapidly to the analysts on the ground. Despite significant and sophisticated monitoring devices, SIGINT, COMINT and radar surveillance, the photograph is still perhaps the most important piece of information a unit commander can receive.

Today, PR camera shutter speeds vary between 1/1,000 sec and 1/3,000 sec with frame rates (the speed at which the shots are taken) varying according to image motion

5 U-2 picture of Soviet air base reveals important features including buidlings, aircraft numbers and type, etc.

6 Activity at Soviet submarine base is revealed here showing number and types of boats, stores, equipment and personnel.

7 F-14 Tomcat equipped with tactical air reconnaissance pod system (TARPS) designed for low to medium altitude clear-air-mass operations with cameras and IR.

5 ▲   **6** ▲   **7** ▼

compensation needs. Image-motion compensation (IMC) calculations are derived from inputs about the aircraft's speed and altitude, the v/h (velocity/height) ratio being the determining factor. To avoid blurring, the film must be pulled across the frame at the same rate that the image traverses the aperture. Silicon photo-detector cells compensate for varying shutter speeds and film speeds, with rotating shutters providing a fast frame cycle. Working with better effect than a reciprocating shutter, the variable-width slit drum shutter provides a smoother and faster sequence of marginally overlapping shots. Most NATO film is specifically prepared for the job at hand and ASA speeds go up to approximately 3,000, although the speeds are different from those of commercial film.

Panoramic coverage is especially useful for broad-scale intelligence of wide areas with high definition and resolution. One approach to this type of camera is seen in the successful Vinten 900 system, which is essentially an optical bar camera producing 180° images from horizon to horizon on 2.75in (70mm) film continuously wound

round an optical bar. With a format of 2.2 × 9.4in (5.7 × 23.9cm), the image covers 41° along the track in a single frame. The IMC mechanism corrects the apparent speed of the aircraft past the image so that at 180° (extreme horizon) to 90° (nadir) the motion speeds up to maximum compensation and reduces again to zero between 90° and 0° (opposite horizon). The normal mode of operation would be to employ two cameras for stereo overlap, one being separated by 84° from the other, with both connected to the aircraft's guidance and navigation system for v/h ratio assessment. The 2.9in (75mm) focal length lens is automatically adjusted by two detector cells with the aperture linked to an open-loop servo.

From an aircraft travelling at Mach 0.9 at a height of 200ft (61m), 1,000ft (305m) of film would produce stereo cover for 39 miles (63km), or for 55 miles (89km) if the two cameras are operated in series. By increasing the operating height precisely 98ft (30m), the same coverage could be obtained with 748ft (228m) of film.

The development of modern lenses allows the option of some extremely long focal

lengths, but stability becomes a compromising problem with the low-flying aircraft usually employed as platforms. Above about 39in (100cm) focal length the image is blurred by the minor changes in roll and pitch associated with all small, low-flying aircraft. Only aircraft like the U-2 can safely utilise lenses up to 72in (183cm) focal length, most low altitude reconnaissance types being limited to 36in (91cm) or less. These lenses, however, are installed with their cameras along the longitudinal axis of the aircraft, the image turned through 90° by a mirror looking directly down at the ground. With this arrangement the mirror itself can be turned through 360°, providing oblique, panoramic or rolling shots at high or low altitude. Environmental control is important here because sensitivity to changes in temperature or atmospheric density can alter significantly the performance of the equipment and the quality of the recorded image.

Much debate has centred around the pod and integrated camera installations for tactical air reconnaissance. Advocates of the pod extol its flexibility, which allows unserviceable sensors to be uncoupled from otherwise operational aircraft, in turn maximising the integrated systems. Opponents of the pod system prefer modularised packages with less equipment and fewer installations.

With increasing numbers of lightweight fighters coming on to the market, and expanding requirements around the world, aircraft have to fill several roles including light attack, interception and photo-reconnaissance. The pod can be retained when aircraft inventories change and this has been demonstrated to good effect already where air forces switch from one aircraft type to another. The pod provides a flexible adaptation without major change to the aircraft's geometry. A typical subsonic recce-pod weighs only 77lb (35kg) and presents a diameter of only 14in (36cm) along a length of 44in (112cm), much less than a standard store for ground attack or a jettisonable fuel tank. Aircraft like the Northrop F-5, General Dynamics F-16 and Northrop F-20 Tigershark (development of F-5) present a considerable market for such devices.

Infra-red linescan units are becoming increasingly popular because they provide more information than a conventional black and white image. With ability to discriminate not only colour but surface conditions, the IR scanner is a valuable asset in tactical reconnaissance. The significant developments achieved with space-based multi-spectral cameras have spurred research on similar systems for air reconnaissance and most pods are capable of carrying such equipment. As one example of the sophistication and variability offered by modern reconnaissance aircraft, analysis of the RF-5E's sophisticated sensor packages displays current state of the art in its most diminutive form, exploiting the chief competitor to future reconnaissance applications, the pallet.

Northrop's classic recce plane

By combining all the better features of integral and pod systems, the palletised RF-5E is a classic example of future export choices. With space extremely limited, Northrop has put the extreme forward nose section on rails, allowing it to slide forward and expose 25.8sq ft (2.4m²) volume for one of up to three optional pallets installed in a V-shaped insert. One pallet is for low-to-medium altitude day and night use, one is for low or high altitude panoramic medium-range standoff use, and the third is for long-range oblique photography. V-shaped windows in the nose afford 190° scans with a separate retractable door for infra-red linescanners.

The first pallet comprises a KS-87B forward oblique camera in the nose with 5in (12.7cm) film and variable focal length lenses of 5.9in (15.2cm) or 11.9in (30.4cm). The pallet proper carries a KA-95B medium altitude panoramic camera with an 11.9in (30.4cm) lens, vertical scans of 40°, 90°, 140° and 190°, oblique scans of 90° left or right centred on 40°, a resolution of 43 line pairs/mm and an altitude of 2,495 to 20,010ft (760 to 6,100m). The second camera is a panoramic KA-56E using the same film but

with a 2.9in (7.6cm) focal length, a vertical scan of 180°, a resolution of 18 line pairs/mm and an operating altitude of 98 to 5,000ft (30m to 1,525m). The third camera is an RS-710 IR linescanner running on to 2.7in (70mm) film with a vertical scan of 120°, a resolution of 0.5°C in the far infra-red and an operating altitude from 200 to 3,000ft (61 to 915m). An optional fourth station provides for re-location of the forward KS-87B for vertical mapping.

The second pallet retains the KS-87B in its forward mounting and carries a panoramic KA-93B using 5in (12.7cm) film and with a focal length of 24in (61cm), a vertical scan of 45°, 70°, 95° and 145°, an oblique scan of 45° left or right centred on 40°, a standoff range of up to 17.2 miles (27.8km) and a 41 line pair/mm resolution at altitudes between about 10,000 and 50,000ft (3,050 and 15,240m). The third camera is the KA-56E also provided on the first optional pallet and with identical characteristics.

The third pallet omits the forward KS-87B and puts a long range KS-147A on stations 2, 3 and 4, with a 65.9in (167.6cm) focal length, oblique coverage of 10-30° below the horizon, 3.9° in a single frame, 11° in a multiple frame and a standoff range of up to 58 miles (93km) for a line pair resolution of 50/mm with 56 per cent overlap. The long range oblique photography (LOROP) pallet requires a different door arrangement, the V-shape replaced by two separate windows with a central flat section. Reference points are located on each side of the cockpit to help the pilot aim his aircraft.

The selected pallet is connected to the RF-5E's LN-33 inertial navigation system for height and ground speed inputs which afford semi-automatic operation for the single-seat aircraft. The APN-22 altimeter computes angular velocity and the cameras are switched on from the control column. Information is impressed on the film according to instructions from the cockpit, with a light-emitting diode (LED) matrix printing latitude, longitude, time, altitude, pitch, true heading, and attitude angles on each frame. A cathode ray tube (CRT) in the cockpit is linked to a silicon-vidicon TV camera positioned in the starboard gun bay depressed 50° and with a 50° field of view (fov). The camera has a 10:1 zoom lens and penetrates haze with near-IR wavelengths.

The RF-5E retains underwing and wing-tip external stores positions and has Side-winder missiles for self-defence, although the APO-159 radar is necessarily deleted from the nose position it usually occupies. The RF-5E, appropriately named Tigereye, has (in 1983) been flown by 19 countries and Northrop estimates that the total market may exceed 150 aircraft.

The reconnaissance Phantom

Typical of integrated reconnaissance versions equipped to carry tactical intelligence cameras and sensors inside the airframe, the McDonnell Douglas RF-4C Phantom has been the mainstay of US tactical reconnaissance forces in Europe since the type replaced the RF-10C. With a radius of action around 1,120 miles (1,800km), the aircraft is devoid of all armament and carries an

1 ▲

2 ▲

1 With a photographic/IR reconnaissance pod in the ventral position, a Tornado provides survivable access to rear stores and supply lines, information vital to NATO's capability.

2 Displaying its camera ports and view windows, the RF-5E presents a low-cost, subsonic reconnaissance platform with optional equipment and standard kits for various camera loads.

3 Cameras are revealed in a British Vinten recce pod on a light plane. It is suitable for small air forces for counter-insurgency (COIN) work where cost-effective, very slow speed applications are sought.

4 The RF-5E provides one of the world's most versatile recce aircraft and is seen here with the characteristic sloping nose cut-out for a camera window. With integral and podded stores capability the RF-5E is attractive as a low cost tactical air reconnaissance platform.

5 The extreme forward nose section of this RF-5E is on rails to provide easy access to palletised equipment carried inside. The V-shaped window area affords 190° scans while a separate door covers the IR linescanners. Three optional pallets are marketed for the RF-5E, incorporating oblique or panoramic views on four positions.

3 ▲

4 ▲

5 ▲

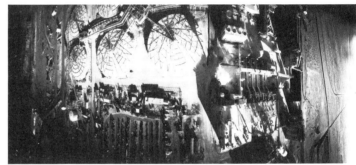

7 ▲

6, 7 A photo recce aircraft using one forward and one lateral coverage camera. The forward-looking camera is mounted in the nose and set for a scan of 40°. The cross-track camera, a Zeiss KA-106A, uses three lenses and one film to give a 182.7° panorama and a down-track coverage of 48.5°. At an aircraft height of 300ft (91m), this gives the coverage shown in the picture (**7**). Such cameras can be used by day, with normal film, or by night using panchromatic or IR film. Film speed varies from 0.56 to 5 frames per sec and a Forward Motion Compensation (FMC) ensures the entire film format is free from blur resulting from the movement of the aircraft during exposure. Various lens systems can be used but in this camera there are three lenses with fixed prisms in front of two lateral lenses. Cross-track coverage is six times the height of the aircraft above the ground. Because photo-recce aircraft must fly low to avoid attacking fighters, or simply avoid detection, the technical advantages of high to medium altitude flight are necessarily compromised. Moreover, with bad weather the norm in Europe, ideal conditions almost never apply.

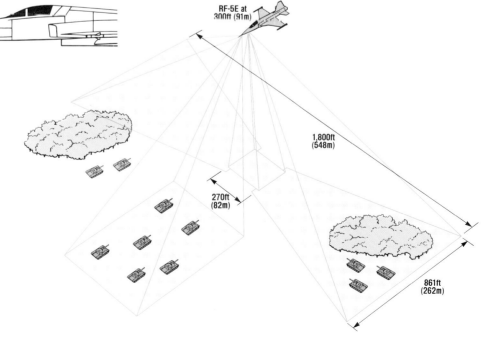

1 ▲

2 ▲

3 ▲

4 ▲

5 ▲

1 Seen here beneath an F-111F, the IR Pave Tack pod provides a TV image and recorded video of ground or air targets.

2 Operated exclusively by the Luftwaffe, this RF-4E, adapted from an F-4E airframe, provides reconnaissance capability in central Europe.

3 A derivative of the F-18A, the RF-1-8A is seen here with a FLIR pod attached. Later developments could give the aircraft synthetic-aperture radar for night and bad weather use.

4 This RC-135V parked on the ramp at Offut AFB, Nebraska, carries an elongated nose radome and side-looking radar in fuselage panels.

5 Sitting inside a USAF NKC-135, operators monitor electronic signals during ELINT activity. This aircraft is deployed for ECM/ECCM duty and doubles in a variety of research roles.

6 USAF RF-4Cs were specially developed as unarmed sensor pod carrier aircraft deployed in large numbers globally.

6 ▲

(84cm) extension on the nose housing a small APQ-99 forward looking radar with mapping, terrain-following and terrain-avoidance capability. Cameras just behind the radar comprise optional configurations for low altitude day, low altitude night or high altitude day operations.

Usually, a forward oblique camera, a 180° pan camera and various arrangements of window sections are grouped along the under-strake which carries an APQ-102 side looking aircraft radar (SLAR) providing high-definition images of the side-track. IR line-scan images are obtained from an AAS-118 unit behind the SLAR, and comprehensive electronics include the ALR-17 ELRAC working with the cameras to provide automatic target identification and allocation of radars on photo maps. A large centreline pod is optional, and carries the AIL ALQ-61 ELINT (electronic intelligence) receiver and recorder. With crystal video receivers providing rough bearing information of hostile threats, an APR-26 missile launch warning unit and Westinghouse nose and repeater jammers, the RF-4C is not as vulnerable as its unarmed condition suggests.

A series of highly classified ELINT and ECM packages provides high confidence in survivability over the target and through hostile airspace while a powerful high-frequency, single-sideband radio gives immediate contact with base. Optional camera packages have ejection tubes for processed film which can be dropped from the air over forward command posts, leaving the aircraft to head for home. Other doors facilitate the upward ejection from the rear fuselage of flash cartridges for target illumination.

USAF's Pave Tack

An impressive addition to the RF-4C's inventory of equipment is the Pave Tack pod, originally developed for day or night weapons delivery through precise target identification. European-based RF-4Cs share their limited number of pods with the F-111Fs of US 3rd Air Force based in Britain.

The Ford Aeroneutronic AN/AVQ-26 Pave Tack is carried in a pod on the fuselage centreline and contains an IR detection unit providing a TV cockpit image with a laser designator. The pod is 163in (414cm) long, is 20in (50.8cm) in diameter and weighs 1,276lb (579kg). A hand controller allows the navigator to control the IR pointing angle and radar, to operate the laser designator and to change the field of view (fov). Two separate screens allow separate display of IR and radar acquisition images, the latter usually being run on the primary screen to obtain the target area before shifting to the IR image close in. Slant range computations are displayed on the screen, as are fov settings and the tracking mode. Cassettes rapidly plugged in or unplugged are available for immediate post-flight analysis.

A major advantage with this system is that it has a memory track which allows it to hold on the target automatically, a particularly useful asset for reconnaissance pilots but one not so well liked by weapons operators, because in this mode the laser target indicator cannot be presented on the screen. Pave Tack can provide day or night damage assessment and present moving television displays of surface targets with a high resolution, permitting positive identification of vehicles, personnel, stores and equipment down to a few inches across.

Europe's recce Jaguar

But if the RF-4C is the mainstay for reconnaissance with the United States Air Forces Europe (USAFE), the Sepecat Jaguar GR 1 is the RAF's medium range equivalent. During the mid 1970s, the RAF developed plans to use the Jaguar as a low-level tactical air reconnaissance platform and the pod mode was an immediate choice for this aircraft. Built by British Aerospace, the pod contained the standard infra-red linescan (IRLS) and optical camera combination linked to the NAVWASS digital computer for latitude, longitude, height, speed and attitude information. As with the Phantom pod, detailed reference information is printed on the film.

The IRLS is fitted to the rear of the pod, forward attachment points accommodating two rotatable camera drums in tandem. The forward drum carries two cross-track F95 Mk 10 cameras with 1.5in (3.8cm) lenses at F2.8 and a forward looking oblique F95 Mk 7 camera with 6in (15.2cm) F28 lenses. The rear drum has optional equipment. In the medium altitude mode, it carries one F126 camera with a 6in (15.2cm) F5.6 lens while, for the low altitude tasks, two Vinten F95 Mk 10 cameras with 3in (7.6cm) F2 lenses are installed.

Integrated with the aircraft's electronics and control systems, the under-fuselage pod allows the pilot to programme the targets and control all operations from the HUD (head-up display). The course navigation would switch to a close-in mode for more precise identification of the target two minutes before acquisition. With a ground target acquisition marker displayed on the HUD and a count-down display to the precise target previously placed in the aircraft's computer, the Jaguar pilot simply has to switch on the cameras to rotate them to pre-set positions and fly the aircraft across the target, or to one side, as preferred. The computer is then transferred to the next mission objective, displaying the appropriate information on the HUD.

This semi-automated mode frees the pilot to fly the aircraft and monitor other information relevant to his survival. In that respect NATO reconnaissance crews consider their survivability ceiling to be no higher than 245ft (about 75m), a vertical wedge of sky perilously close to the ground but one which affords little or no opportunities for an attacking aircraft or SAM. Staying at that altitude all the way through hostile airspace would, in wartime, pose unique but not insurmountable problems.

Remotely piloted vehicles

Nevertheless, while many people consider that the application of tactical air reconnaissance tasks to the land battle is permanent, debate is rife on the type of system which should be sent to get the information. In that regard, in parallel to the arguments over

pod, pallet or integral sensors and cameras is one challenging the assumption that manned aircraft are an inevitable choice. In at least one major application, combat-proven RPVs (Remotely Piloted Vehicles) have been seen to work to good effect.

Israel has long had an interest in RPVs for real-time electro-optical information, tactical air assessment and threat identification. Using a high-wing design with a nose mounted engine, the Mastiff 1 entered service with the Israeli Army during 1979. The Mk 2 design, developed by Tadiran/ Israel Electronics Industries Ltd., is a second generation RPV with a twin-boom tail, high-wing, pusher engine configuration capable of lifting a sensor package of up to 55lb (25kg). The vehicle has an endurance of more than four hours, can fly at over 9,840ft (3,000m), weighs less than 220lb (100kg) at launch and is catapulted into the air along an inclined ramp on the back of a standard army truck. Retrieved by a tail hook and arrester wire arrangement, the RPV carries a zoom lens TV system and the vehicle can accept gyrostabilised laser designators for target illumination to a secondary weapons system. A small portable control station near the launch truck controls the Tadiran during flight.

Development and highly successful flight trials with the Mastiff 2 prompted official support for design and construction of the later Israel Aircraft Industries Scout RPV surveillance platform. Larger than Mastiff, Scout adopts the same configuration and basic design layout but has a length of 12.1ft (3.7m), a span of 11.8ft (3.6m), weighs 260lb (118kg) at takeoff and carries a 90lb (41kg) payload. Scout has a twin-cylinder 18hp engine driving a pusher airscrew, and consists of an aluminium, square-section fuselage supporting glassfibre wings, booms and tailplane. The RPV has a maximum speed of 92mph (147km/h), a ceiling of just over 10,000ft (3,050m), can remain airborne for more than 4½ hours and operate up to 62 miles (100km) from "base". The base comprises a truck-mounted, air conditioned ground control station with provision for a pilot to command by remote control the altitude, speed and bearing via control knobs, feeding instructions through a roof mounted command-uplink antenna and receiving via a downlink antenna.

If communication with the Scout is lost, the RPV senses this, rises to a pre-set height and, if no further contact is established after four minutes, turns back to base. A secondary, navigator's, position in the ground control station allows the operator to command specific positioning information, using a 1:125 scale map for sensor targeting. Cameras and other equipment on the Scout are controlled by the third member of the control station staff, the observer. A 14in (35.5cm) CRT display shows the TV image from Scout, which is video-recorded for analysis, control of the zoom facility being effected through a potentiometer while a mini-stick controls the image line of sight. Using a light pen, and a linked computer in the same facility, the observer can direct artillery from the ground using the image for software identification with appropriate coordinates. Each Scout unit

1 ▲

2 ▲

1 Photo film from a recce Jaguar is processed and examined, standard NATO references being used for subject identification.

2 Exposed film is removed from a recce Jaguar and taken to an interpretation facility while a fresh pack is loaded in the pod.

3 Equipped with a multi-purpose recce pod and fuel tanks, an RAF Jaguar can fly low and fast to gather intelligence behind enemy lines, using oblique and pan cameras, plus IR sensors.

4 Displaying its stabilised TV camera, the Israel Aircraft Industries Scout mini-RPV provides real-time reconnaissance and aerial surveillance, as well as ELINT when necessary.

5 The Scout has a pusher engine driving a single propeller. It spans 11.8ft (3.6m) and is 12.1ft (3.7m) long. Wheels are jettisoned.

6 The Scout is launched from an inclined ramp for flights lasting up to 4½ hrs at 10,000ft (3,048m) and a speed of 63 mph (102km/hr).

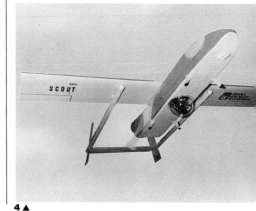

4 ▲

3 ▲

OPERATION OF SCOUT RPV

The Scout RPV is controlled by a Ground Control Station (GCS) from which commands are sent up to a normal maximum operating distance of 62 miles (100km). The normal 1,312 x 656ft (400 x 200m) viewing area can be reduced to a 164 x 131ft (50 x 40m) by the zoom lens, providing high-resolution TV of selected areas of interest.

Up to 62 miles (100km)

5°

15°

9,840ft (3,000m)

2,637ft (804m)

1.9 miles (3.2km)

1,312ft (400m)

164 x 131ft (50 x 40m)

656ft (200m)

4.3 miles (7km)

4.3 miles (7km)

5 ▲

6 ▲

comprises five RPVs, a ground control station, launcher, retrieval net and 12 personnel. The RPV is transported in a plastic box broken down into its three component sections.

The Scout is built primarily for use in the air reconnaissance role but can also operate as an effective ECM vehicle, artillery spotter, target designator or damage assessment and surveillance vehicle. The TV camera is the heart of the Scout's success, and comprises a 30lb (13.6kg) module stabilised in pitch and yaw, with slew motion through 360° and from 5° above horizontal to −15° beyond vertical.

Scout would normally operate at 9,840ft (3,000m) and provide at that altitude surveillance over a 19 square mile (50sq km) area with a 130 × 164ft (40 × 50m) fov at maximum zoom. With a 625-line format at 50 frames/sec, the Scout can view an area 1,310 × 655ft (400 × 200m) centred 10,500ft (3,200m) ahead of the vehicle. Panoramic cameras can be carried in addition to the TV cameras, and laser designators and thermal IR imaging can be attached as alternatives.

Increasingly, reconnaissance duties in the Israeli sphere of interest have been relegated to the unmanned RPV, the Mastiff 2 and the Scout being particularly useful in the loiter/surveillance role. They are *not* replacements for the low-flying manned aircraft moving deep inside enemy airspace, but the kind of activity to which they have been applied in the Middle East epitomises the changing base on which technology will benefit military activity. During the 1982 operations against PLO sites in Lebanon, and especially in the area around Beirut, Scout came into its own in a unique series of applications that, not for the first time, provides lessons from the Middle East to shake doctrinal philosophy in other theatres.

Establishing what has been referred to as an almost exclusively real-time electronic battlefield, the role of the Scout was to provide electro-optical and digital data links between Syrian positions and Israeli battle commanders on the ground. Continuously observing Syrian fighters on their airfields and activities around SAM sites, the RPVs were able to provide live TV coverage for target assignment and threat identification in a way never before demonstrated in war.

With an astonishing level of success, Israeli attacks on air defence sites were almost unopposed as drones directed by information processed through the Scouts were sent in to provoke illumination by SAM acquisition radars that in turn presented identifiable targets for Wolf surface-to-surface missiles.

Scouts used for ECM

When the radars were neutralised, and confirmed so by the RPVs, ground strikes were made from the air with Blue-72 cluster munitions digging out the hardware, which was either surface-to-air missiles or anti-air artillery. Operating as electronic ECM, Scouts flew circuitous routes to avoid known Israeli jamming operations actively in progress and to position themselves for their own countermeasures work. A third, highly effective role was active artillery spotting and fire adjustment while simultaneously gathering reconnaissance information. Using FAC (forward air controller) units at the forward edge of the battle area, Scouts also served as target designators for airborne

AIRBORNE SURVEILLANCE DRONE SYSTEM

The low-level environment is becoming very hazardous for photo-recce aircraft and increasing emphasis is being placed on drones for such missions. One of the most effective of these vehicles is the AN/USD-502 drone, developed from the AN/USD-501, which is in service with the British, Canadian, French, German and Italian armies. The 502 is launched from a standard 4-tonne military truck (1). Launch is achieved by means of a strap-on rocket-booster which is jettisoned once the 240lb (108kg) turbo-jet has taken over. After launch the drone follows a pre-rogrammed flight-path (2), with the sensors being switched on at a pre-determined point (3). The drone carries a Zeiss camera and an infra-red line-scan sensor, with the latter having a real-time data transmission link (4) back to the base site (7). This gives a substantial advantage over the AN/USD-501 which had only cameras, and thus nothing was known of its mission until the photographs had been developed. Having completed its task the AN/USD-502 returns to base (5) where a parachute opens and lowers it gently to earth (6).

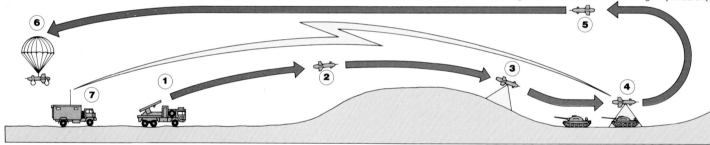

attacks on prime military targets, and as damage assessment monitors afterwards.

The effectiveness of the Scout was enhanced by its place within a unique, integrated, electronic battle operation involving E-2C Hawkeye EW aircraft modified to plot simultaneously 155 separate airborne targets, and the modified Boeing 707 saturating the air with electronic jamming signals. In the Lebanese war almost all Syrian communication was stopped, sending their aircraft and ground units into confusion, a situation actively exploited by the Israelis through careful monitoring via the Scout RPVs. The single most incredible fact from the Lebanese operation was the safe return from all missions of every Scout deployed on active reconnaissance and surveillance.

Israel, of course, is not alone in possessing RPVs, although their use in the larger air forces of Europe and the USA has not followed actively the trend originated during the Vietnam War, when they came into their own. But the lessons from the Lebanese war are now being reworked into planned evaluation of several candidate RPV design concepts. The shift from manned airborne reconnaissance tasking to deployment of these diminutive carriers has begun.

Mini-RPVs in Europe

In several respects, RPVs provide solutions to enduring problems on the NATO central front where large numbers of Warsaw Pact forces could rapidly saturate defensive positions in the West. With low life-cycle costs, the absence of expensively trained flight crew and low vulnerability to size and suppressed radar signature, the robot can be maintained in a high state of readiness, present larger numbers on the battle front due to low cost and provide rapid turnaround.

At the lower end of the option is the mini-RPV, usually a small helicopter capable of hedge-hopping and target acquisition. One example of this class of mini-RPV is the Canadair CL-227 "helicopter" shaped like a peanut and only 5.47ft (1.67m) high, with an altitude ceiling of 984ft (300m) and a top speed of 80mph (130km/hr). With its thermal imaging and laser designators, the heli-robot can provide vital links to give the infantryman eyes above the horizon, over the nearby forest or around farmyard buildings—and to give him the means to designate targets and dispatch his weapons around the corner.

But up a notch from the localised battle, large offensive operations and adequate, in-depth, consolidation of a defensive front still require the manned aircraft able to get in low and fast for a multi-sensor scan with cameras, thermal imaging, IR, and SLAR packages.

In Europe, considerable reduction in tactical air reconnaissance capability stretches the tasks assigned to existing USAFE and RAF units. As of early 1983 less than 40 USAFE tactical reconnaissance aircraft (RF-4C and RF-4E) were on strength, operating from Zweibrucken in Germany and from Alconbury in the UK. The RAF operates 20 Jaguar GR.1 from three reconnaissance units, but considerable increase in capability will emerge with the use of Tornado aircraft in the low-altitude reconnaissance role, employing the IR linescan pack or a pallet of cameras in the bomb bay.

Changes to the operating role of the

1 Grumman E-2C Hawkeye early-warning aircraft provides detection to a range of 230 miles (370km) from its APS-125 radar, simultaneously tracking 250 targets and controlling 30 interceptions. Israel used these in the Lebanon.

2 With 3-lens recce camera and IRLS, the Canadair/Dornier CL-289 airborne surveillance drone is fired from a zero-length launcher by a BAe rocket and sustained by a Dornier turbojet for real-time read-out. Recovery is by parachute.

3 Dornier's 6.5ft (2m) Mini-Drone has a sensor package with stabilised TV camera and optional laser illuminator. The drone is recoverable, can operate at heights up to 9,842ft (3,000m) for a maximum of 3 hours. Max speed is 155mph (250km/h).

4 Yet another variation for battlefield RPVs, this Dornier model hovers like a helicopter but has limited range and high vulnerability. For local, point-to-point recce, they are increasingly becoming a necessary part of intelligence work.

1 ▲

3 ▲

4 ▲

Luftwaffe's 75 reconnaissance RF-4Es have enabled them to carry stores and ordnance, where previously they were exclusively involved in unarmed tactical air intelligence. But improvements by the MBB company to the sensor package attached to these aircraft puts them more in line with 3rd and 17th US Air Force units, enhances survivability through chaff dispensing and uprates the cameras and linescan IR equipment. Belgium uses 18 Mirage 5 aircraft in the reconnaissance role and Denmark has a similar number of RF-35 Drakens. French reconnaissance duties now carried out by the 45 ageing Mirage IIIR/RDs will be significantly enhanced by 30 new Mirage F-1CRs.

The USAF method

Despite the age of many aircraft employed for reconnaissance duty, and the constant fight to preserve adequate numbers in the inventory, many lessons have been learned from Vietnam and Middle East conflicts in the 1960s and 1970s. These lessons are still applicable in today's enhanced electronic warfare environment, and training for typical battle operations in a war in central Europe establishes today's tactical air intelligence philosophies.

Most missions in peacetime must shape their flight patterns around commercial traffic, civilian considerations and flight restrictions set up by the country concerned. In Europe, simulated battle conditions are easier because the altitude concessions are greater than they are, for instance, in the United States where flying is prohibited below 50ft (152m), except during Red Flag exercises. At that altitude the crew would be dead—victims of a barrage of enemy anti-air fire.

To provide good environmental experience of the European theatre, US Air Force crews are rotated back through the continental United States (CONUS) approximately every two years, taking with them knowledge about flying conditions in Europe and consolidating the value of Reforger exercise units they would comprise in the event that a war did break out. Plans are to reinforce the tactical reconnaissance units within 24 to 28 hours of war, starting to rotate through the sortie-gates crew/aircraft cycles that maximise operating time and minimise fatigue and stress.

High rate of recce sorties

Training is a key element in any armed force and USAFE reconnaissance squadrons average 14 sorties per day—all year round. About 25 per cent of these are directly in support of NATO exercises or for information requested by ground units for some localised operational evaluation. Surge rates during wartime would significantly exceed the peacetime sortie levels and are expected to top 60 a day, a figure that was actually achieved during a training exercise, when 18 aircraft flew missions to peacetime regulations on man-hours in the air.

During training, which is considered by USAFE reconnaissance units to be a continuous, unending activity, a typical one-hour sortie requires three to four hours of

1 ▲

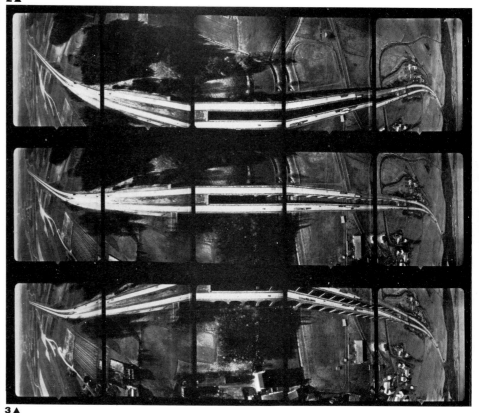

2 ▲

1 An early example of US Air Force's recce drone research, from the 1970s, Cope had a 30-hour endurance at high altitude.

2 Northrop's MOM-74C Chuka II aerial target is seen in new guise as a recce RPV, converted by the addition of a camera-equipped nose.

3 Taken by a Zeiss KRB 6/24 camera, this panoramic view was shot by an RF-4E at 593mph (955km/hr) and a height of 492ft (150m). Note effect of lighting angles on surface features.

4 Danish AF Draken with Red Baron recce pod under port wing.

5 Mirage IIIRS reconnaissance aircraft of the Swiss Air Force. Note nose optical window.

6 Linescan IR view of dock area showing ships, buildings and circular storage tanks. Such real-time surveillance can permit detection through camouflage.

7 IR thermal image from a BAeD Linescan unit showing aircraft in various states of readiness, some being fuelled and some with engines running.

3 ▲

4 ▲

5 ▲

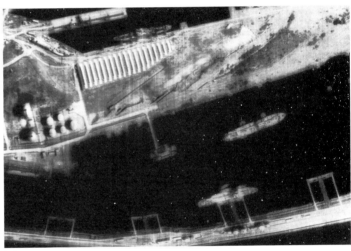

6 ▲

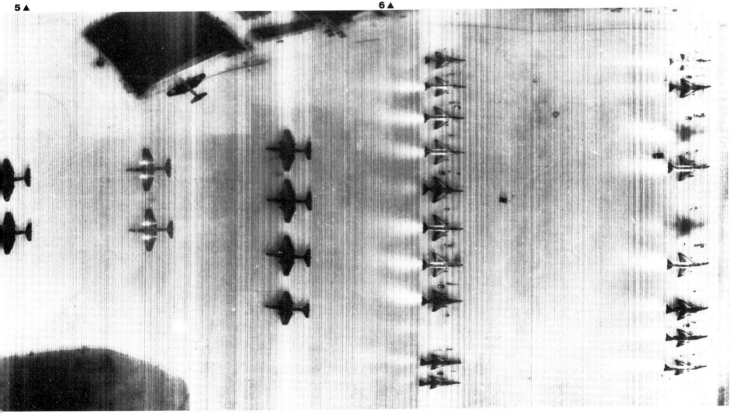

7 ▲

pre-flight preparation; in war that would be compressed to one hour at most. Familiarity with the terrority in western Europe is important also, and crews use Ordnance Survey-type maps of the entire region and, where possible, plasticised relief maps of target areas. With a vertical exaggeration of 10, such maps allow pilots to "see" terrain features without the expense of specific computerised simulator software. Training operations are set up by a mission controller, whose job it is to assess the weather conditions relevant to a shopping list of separate targets.

The purpose of these flights is to provide experience in low-level navigation, formation flying a various altitudes and target identification. In war the prime function of tactical air intelligence is to give the army commanders information for target development, provide details on where the enemy lines of communication are being laid down, where the air and ground traffic is and where it is coming from, and to provide information about where it is likely to develop in the next several hours.

The primary function toward which all these factors converge is intelligence on where the main thrust is developing—the neck of the hour-glass through which the previous elements converge. The military commanders must then receive information from deeper zones inside enemy airspace. They must know which enemy airfields are being used for the most effective strikes against NATO targets, where the most threatening elements are massing and how the enemy plans to exploit the battlefront through conditions along the FEBA.

Further intelligence provides Air Force units with munitions allocation decisions. What types of bombs or cluster canisters are needed? Which are prime and secondary strike targets to inhibit the enemy's movement? Where will the second echelon of targets evolve? How will that leave munitions stocks for knocking out re-formed positions?

The integrated network of decision-making factors essential to winning the war is based on good intelligence derived from broad-scale information and accurate, speedy, assessment.

To improve chances of survival the aircraft will traverse the friendly airspace in packs, breaking down to single-ship level only as they penetrate hostile airspace. Top-cover might be an advantage en route to the FEBA for clearing away enemy aircraft limping back east, or roving hunters looking for targets in the air. Between the airfield and the FEBA the outgoing reconnaissance aircraft are clustered to help flight controllers handle the traffic. They must be routed through complicated and circuitous channels bypassing friendly SAM radars, streams of outbound strike aircraft and known waves of attacking fighters, all the while being simultaneously positioned to avoid enemy forward acquisition radars behind the FEBA.

Once threaded through the complex and rapidly changing traffic patterns, each aircraft is on its own. Before it crosses out of friendly territory, however, local problems pose challenges to its pilot as he searches

2 ▲

1 Prior to a recce mission, USAF flight crew conduct a briefing on targets and routes to be flown.

2 Selected cameras matched to the sortie are here being fitted to the aircraft, an RF-4C.

4 Rapid analysis carried out on the processed film is a priority above detailed appraisal of the images, coming later.

3 When the film is returned from the recce sortie, rapid processing is conducted in an automatic developing room where rollers move film at preset rates.

5 New recce pictures are compared with maps of the photographed area, and features from earlier shots to determine level of new activity, such information being rushed to the field.

1 ▲

4 ▲

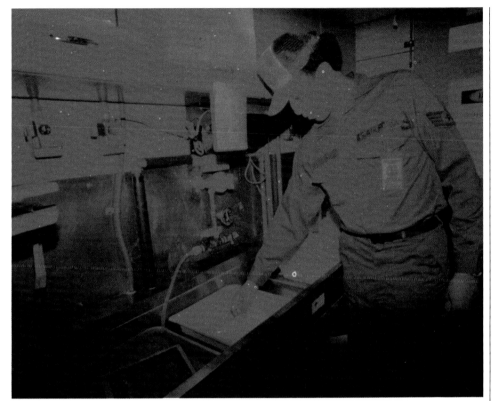

3 ▲

5 ▲

visually for crippled aircraft too low for good ground control radar plots and swarms of low-flying military helicopters. Across the FEBA the aircraft will remain below 245ft (75m) and fly very fast to its turn points and targets. Complex flight patterns will increasingly call for computer-controlled guidance and navigation systems. Already, USAFE reconnaissance Phantoms employ computer control tapes made up on the ground pre-flight with plug-in cassettes ensuring continuous HUD information to thread them through the threat zones.

In war, LORAN navigation updates would be almost non-existent, given the electro-magnetic environment likely to prevent good signal identification, although INS (inertial navigation system) updates would be pos-sible at selected points.

The dash to the target area would not use top-cover, for several reasons. The high-flyer would not survive long in the hostile air environment, the low-flying reconnaissance aircraft would be pin-pointed by visual tracking of the top-cover, and aircraft com-mitted to protective flights would be diverted from some other, more important, objective.

The use of Pave Tack pods for stand-off target evaluation is an advantage, although its place on the fuselage centreline pickup point means long range fuel tanks cannot be carried. Many reconnaissance pilots feel the Pave Tack to be an asset, in that it improves survivability in a region where the high value of the photo-target would almost always carry high defensive value to the enemy.

NATO flight crews feel they are trained adequately to evade the look-down/shoot-down fighters scrambled on air attack or interceptor missions. It is felt that the very low- and very fast-flying aircraft would defeat enemy SAMs which could not get the reconnaissance aircraft before the missile hit the ground. However, survivability car-ries with it the raison d'etre of the whole mission plan, unlike other aircraft which can accomplish a large part of their objective even if they fail to return. Information gathering implicitly requires the information to be returned for assessment into useful intelligence, and that means the reconnais-sance crew must get back to base to be effective.

Film processing

When the aircraft lands, NATO rules demand release of a field intelligence report of the processed film within 45 minutes of engine-stop. While the pilot goes to a de-briefing and delivers a ground-crew systems report, allowing technicians to receive ver-bal information about the condition of the aircraft, the back-seat occupant travels to the processing facility. USAFE reconnais-sance units accept film at a semi-hardened facility on the base, providing a filtered, chemical-biological isolated environment with underground fuel, water, power generators and with showers, bathrooms and food stocks for protracted survival. The facility houses several mobile vans with collapsible walls. These vans, or shelters, perform specific functions in the photo-analysis chain.

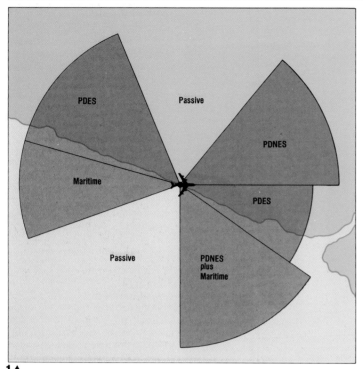

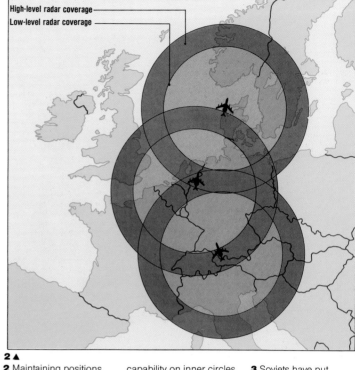

1 ▲

1 AWACS operating principle is shown by this E-3A watching a coastal area. The radar rotates at 6rpm; surveyed is an area divided into as many as 24 sub-sectors, each with a separate surveillance mode. One combination shows Pulse Doppler Non-Elevation Scan (PDNES) giving position and range, Pulse Doppler Elevation Scan (PDES) providing height as well, and Maritime which carries out optimised ship detection.

2 ▲

2 Maintaining positions well behind the border, AWACS watches for Warsaw Pact aerial activitity. E-3A coverage shown displays low-level capability on inner circles and high-level to outer circles. Full USAF inventory of 34 E-3A Sentry is due for completion by 1985.

3 Soviets have put additional effort into the AWACS concept and a Tu-114 Moss displays aft fuselage radome. Note refuelling probe.

3 ▼

When film arrives it is tagged with information about the camera system, the sortie number, the aircraft number, the names of the aircrew, and times of departure, arrival and engine shut-down. Normally, film from two targets will be processed simultaneously, maximising the capabilities of the unit but compromising the interpretation tasks set against the 45-minute deadline. When film is fed to the automatic processing shelter it moves through the Kodak tanks at 20ft/min (6m/min). From there it goes to the WS-428A photographic interpretation facility, three shelters (vans) where the information is obtained. Emphasis throughout the reconnaissance operation is to use as little film as possible, both to conserve stocks of uncontaminated film and to ease the load of the interpreters who must release their report within the mandatory time.

British, Dutch and Belgian reconnaissance film is in a different size format to that used by the German and USAFE units, but the facilities can cater for all kinds of NATO aircraft from other bases which arrive with film.

In the interpretation facility the intelligence technician sits down with the back-seat crew member and puts together a standard NATO reconnaissance exploitation report. This means that any NATO crew member can bring any film and compile any report, standardised throughout the network. The interpretation shelter provides a film roller to which a computer is linked for memory identification of components within the image vital to the unit requesting this information. The computer memory is also loaded with the format of the report, and the interpreter works to a shopping list of 17 standard NATO target categories (bridge, road, tank, etc.) through which he processes certain analytical interpretations according to the initial reconnaissance request from the army field commander.

Binary code signals located between the film frames are read by the computer as the film goes through, and the matrix lets the storage assembly know all the relevant information so that it can move the film to the specific target. This speeds up the process of search and identification and gives the interpreter more valuable minutes to look for unusual activity or objects. A light pen working through the computer system allows the interpreter to obtain an almost instantaneous readout on the precise coordinates of a specific feature and that is simultaneously referred to a map of the area allowing the report to contain location-specific references to the unusual object.

In summary, the aircraft's navigation system has impressed between the frames information that the computer needs to move the imaging reference instantly to specific coordinates requested by the interpreter. Thus, from the aircraft in the air through to the processed negative in the interpretation shelter, references are maintained on precisely where the picture area is located geographically. When the report has been typed into the computer it is moved to the communications shelter, the second of three photographic interpretation

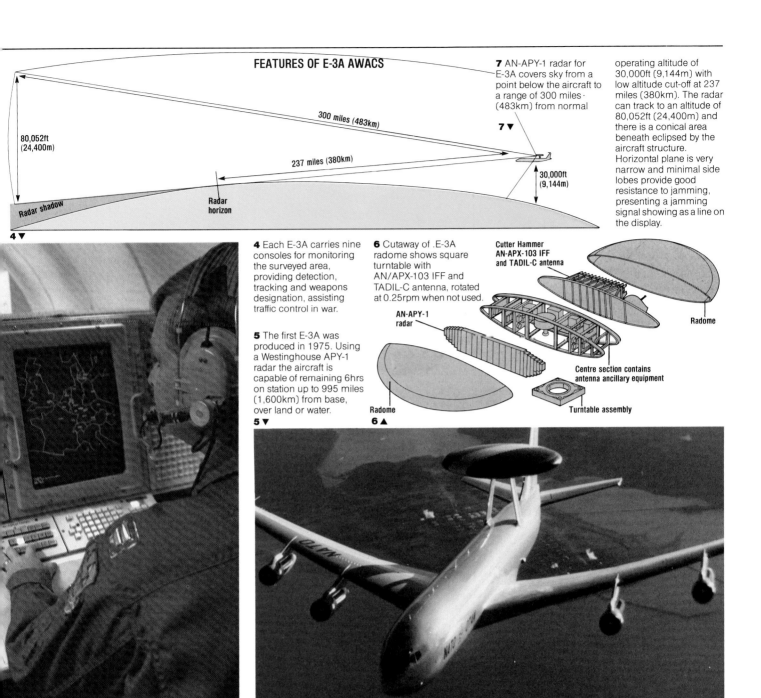

FEATURES OF E-3A AWACS

7 AN-APY-1 radar for E-3A covers sky from a point below the aircraft to a range of 300 miles · (483km) from normal operating altitude of 30,000ft (9,144m) with low altitude cut-off at 237 miles (380km). The radar can track to an altitude of 80,052ft (24,400m) and there is a conical area beneath eclipsed by the aircraft structure. Horizontal plane is very narrow and minimal side lobes provide good resistance to jamming, presenting a jamming signal showing as a line on the display.

300 miles (483km)

80,052ft (24,400m)

237 miles (380km)

30,000ft (9,144m)

Radar shadow

Radar horizon

4 Each E-3A carries nine consoles for monitoring the surveyed area, providing detection, tracking and weapons designation, assisting traffic control in war.

5 The first E-3A was produced in 1975. Using a Westinghouse APY-1 radar the aircraft is capable of remaining 6hrs on station up to 995 miles (1,600km) from base, over land or water.

6 Cutaway of .E-3A radome shows square turntable with AN/APX-103 IFF and TADIL-C antenna, rotated at 0.25rpm when not used.

Cutter Hammer AN-APX-103 IFF and TADIL-C antenna

AN-APY-1 radar

Radome

Radome

Centre section contains antenna ancillary equipment

Turntable assembly

---

facility (PIF) vans, from where it is quickly checked and then transmitted to the appropriate field unit by microwave or landline. If prints are required the print shop processes the number requested and sends them on. In the American system, a strength of 23 USAF and 12 US Army personnel mans each photographic interpretation facility. During wartime, photographs are sent back to the USA for processing by the Defence Intelligence Agency, where a more concentrated analysis of the information is made.

The prime objective in tactical air intelligence is to provide, as rapidly as possible, information vital to the prosecution of the battle and to the need to stop and reverse the westward surge of enemy forces—not to provide in-depth and largely academic analysis which can be left to the DIA.

An important element in the air reconnaissance war is tactical electronic surveillance for passive identification of ground control interception (GCI) sites on the other side of the FEBA, for acquisition of enemy weapons radars, HF networks, microwave transmit-

ters and other communications equipment. That job goes on in peacetime so that information is continually available on the distribution and dispersal of forces on the other side of the border, minimising significantly the possibility of a surprise attack.

TR-1 looking into Eastern Europe

Roles like that require deep electronic penetration of Warsaw Pact territory from extremely high altitude, literally looking over the Iron Curtain without physically entering East European airspace. That mission, close to the border but on the NATO side of the wire, will be carried out by the Lockheed TR-1 tactical reconnaissance aircraft derived from the U-2R flown by USAF's Strategic Air Command.

Operating from RAF Alconbury in the UK, TR-1 aircraft provide a capability for photographic reconnaissance, electronic surveillance, high altitude TV and communication relay, and border patrol. Thirty-five TR-1s have been ordered by the USAF and the first

was delivered in September 1981. Alconbury receiving its first early in 1083. The TR-1 is equipped with an astro-inertial navigation system, phased array radar, UHF relay, data link systems and TEW. Effectively able from its operating altitude of 65,615ft (20,000m) to "see" 310 miles (500km), the TR-1 carries optional sensor packages to provide information on pre-attack enemy force buildup, make a continuing assessment of NATO/Warsaw Pact forces, and present rapid reaction time for the reconnaissance task.

With synthetic aperture radar and other items of equipment weighing up to 3,748lb (1,700kg), the TR-1 can provide area coverage of regions far into Eastern Europe. Providing all-weather, day or night, battlefield surveillance, the TR-1 would in time of war patrol about 150 miles (240km) behind the FEBA for stand-off observation up to 200 miles (320km) across enemy lines. The aircraft has a wing span of 103ft (31.4m), a length of 63ft (19.2m) and a takeoff weight of 29,980lb (13,600kg). It has a maximum speed

1 ▲

2 ▲

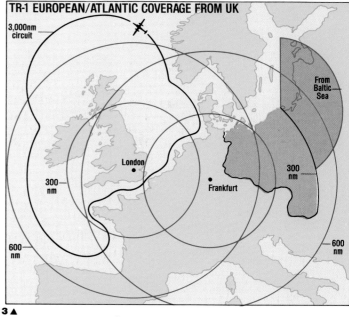

TR-1 EUROPEAN/ATLANTIC COVERAGE FROM UK

3 ▲

1 Extending and broadening the role of AWACS, Lockheed's TR-1 provides essential monitoring of distant targets and maintains surveillance on aerial activity. Note the high aspect ratio wing which provides sustained flights of up to 12hrs on patrol and altitude of up to 90,000ft (29,432m). Note unusual landing gear.

2 TR-1 provides multi-pod capability with sensors tailored to mission needs including imaging or radar. Aircraft has ground surveillance radius of 316 miles (507km).

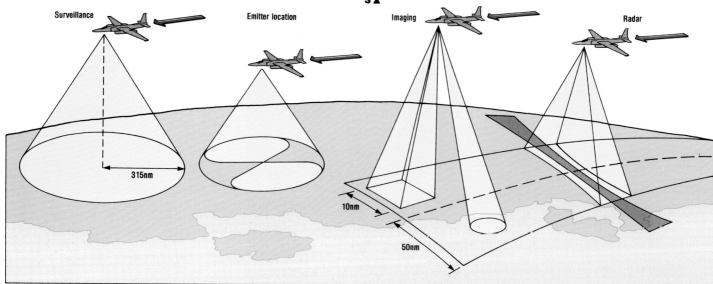

4 ▲

3 TR-1 can lift payload in excess of 3,000lb (1,360kg) along a patrol route shown here originating at one of two sites in Europe, the UK base at Alconbury, where the aircraft became operational with USAFE's 9th Strategic Reconnaissance Wing. From Germany, the TR-1 can survey deep behind Warsaw Pact borders using synthetic aperture radar (SAR).

4 Separate capability functions include (l to r) basic surveillance, emitter location, radar scans and imaging, with appropriate windows shown. In surveillance mode, TR-1 can cover 263,014 sq. miles/hr (681,170sq km/hr) from altitude of 65,000ft (19,812m). The US Air Force will receive 35 TR-1s, and the aircraft is also on offer to friendly governments for $20M (less sensors).

5 How TR-1 could have been used by the British to provide surveillance protection of the Falklands Isles. Surveillance from above Port Stanley would cover large areas of Argentina and its Atlantic coast, TR-1 flying a loop. Providing real-time multi-mission capability, it could be used in other trouble-spots transmitting information to distant bases by satellite, or by a UHF link through local HQ.

6 ▲

of 435mph (700km/hr) at 70,000ft (21,355m), a ceiling in excess of 88,580ft (27,000m) and range of nearly 3,045 miles (4,900km). The aircraft can remain airborne for 12 hours.

TR-1 will not replace the tactical air reconnaissance mission deep within hostile airspace, and there is a rapidly approaching need for the Phantoms to be replaced by a more capable system for the air battle of the late 1980s. That need could be met by the RF-16B, a modified Fighting Falcon fighter retaining wingtip missiles for defence but with the gun replaced by a GPS (Global Positioning System) navigation satellite receiver. Effectively reduced to operating with a combination of eyeballs and INS, the RF-4 needs a better means of navigating through an increasingly complex, circuitous and crowded wartime sky. The aircraft itself cannot be made to do the job anticipated for the RF-16B and, although no firm commitment has yet been made to adopt this variant, USAFE is enthusiastic for an aircraft of its type.

Soviet air recce

Today, Soviet forces put great faith in the ability to strike quickly and with impunity in the initial stages of a blitzkrieg war aimed at neutralising significant elements in the forward echelons. To do this they presume to make strident efforts to secure air space above and beyond the FEBA but for sustained assault with heavy armour and air strikes at rear stations and deployed positions they must have tactical air intelligence, albeit in a very different form from that required by NATO. The single big advantage in having a defensive policy, like that of NATO, is that it allows for the hardening of command posts and facilities that would otherwise be vulnerable to attack.

NATO communication lines, support facilities, fall-back dumps and stores are all in pre-designated locations; it is NATO country the enemy would be required to fight on, whereas Warsaw Pact forces would necessarily have to deploy and re-deploy until a measured consolidation of the main front permits hardened emplacement of mobile land units in the second echelon or rear areas of the battle. The single major drawback, however, is that Warsaw Pact forces know to within a few hundred metres where almost all the NATO equipment is located and where the main bases are positioned. The need for NATO tactical air intelligence information is predicated by the rapidly moving disposition of men and equipment on the other side. No such in-depth search is necessary for Warsaw Pact elements. Nevertheless, information vital to the forward progress of the FEBA, and to second-level battle management, will be sought and obtained through use of several hundred reconnaissance aircraft operating with Warsaw Pact forces.

Great emphasis has been put on providing battle and field commanders with adequate intelligence about the moving front and the changing disposition of enemy ground and air forces. The largest number of any one reconnaissance type gives the Yak-28 Brewer D a numerical advantage over all others, with 200 deployed among air and

7 ▲

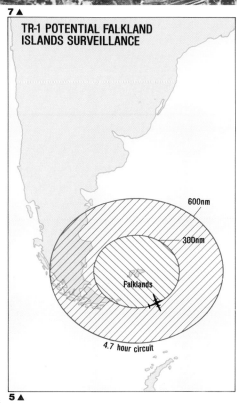

TR-1 POTENTIAL FALKLAND ISLANDS SURVEILLANCE

600nm

300nm

Falklands

4.7 hour circuit

5 ▲

6 This air-to-air recce view of the Soviet Backfire bomber epitomises the integrated nature of surveillance and intelligence-gathering, enabling expert analysts to study the wing glove detail and lower fin extension.

7 U-2 recce view of Diriamba, Nicaragua, proved Soviet involvement in C America in 1982.

8 The first published photograph of the Soviet Blackjack bomber typifies the quality available from long-range air-recce pictures. It has been electronically processed and enhanced through a system not unlike that used to improve pictures sent from missions to the planets. Note the Tupolev airliners close by, providing scale.

8 ▲

ground attack units. The aircraft carries multiple sensor packages of cameras, IR and other instruments for ECM and ELINT operations. Next in numerical strength are the 150 MiG-25 Foxbat B/D models specifically operating high-altitude/high-speed roles on missions where they have been tracked at Mach 3.2. Carrying cameras for panoramic, wide area coverage, these Foxbat versions are regularly seen on training and operational duties over the Middle East. Not the easiest of targets to acquire, they are nevertheless vulnerable to interception but carry out a major role in putting together intelligence information covering large areas on the ground.

Some 130 MiG-21 Fishbed H models are still in use with the Soviet air units and 160 Sukhoi Su-17 Fitters are in service but mainly for use as reconnaissance tools for Warsaw Pact units in Eastern Europe.

Collectively, the Pact countries field an additional 211 reconnaissance types, mostly MiG-17, -21 and -23 although Poland still operates five Il-28R types in addition. It is interesting to note that the main reconnaissance task set for the Soviet Air Force has been accomplished by space-based cameras carrying out a similar mapping operation to that requested by the German Army in the late 1930s. Soviet battle orders follow similar lines of conflict management where pre-determined strikes sever vital enemy lines. Such maps are essential for this task.

Considerable attention has been paid by Soviet scientists to developing optical equipment for use on aircraft and satellites. The tactical air intelligence role shows every sign of using both areas of operation just as it does, increasingly, in the West. With a significant resource in East Germany, the

indigenous optical skills of scientists and technicians were applied to reconnaissance requirements and the equipment dictated by the need from just after World War II. There is every indication that Russian optical equipment is at least as good as that in the West and several new aircraft seem increasingly to have dual roles, one of which is invariably reconnaissance. For example, Sukhoi Su-25 Frogfoot ground attack fighters operating in Afghanistan have been seen with sensor pods of a new and unique type.

Although Frogfoot is primarily an attack aircraft it has been used on search-and-exploit missions, looking for targets of opportunity. This real-time tactical intelligence activity, where detection and identification is made in the air prior to an immediate strike, may well prove to be the pattern of emerging operations for the European theatre where other Russian air-

1▲

2▲

3▲

craft have been seen to fly similar profiles on exercise.

Lessons from the Falklands

In the end, sustained commitment to a progressive tactical air intelligence network in peacetime is the only way to have the information available for a rapid response to pre-emptive strikes and to have the procedures and equipment to start active reconnaissance and surveillance of what would inevitably be a fast moving battle-front from the start.

That lesson was learned the hard way when inadequate preservation of a long-range tactical air reconnaissance capability nearly cost Britain the Falklands War in 1982. Because there were no means of surveying South Georgia, a hastily converted Victor tanker was flown in to take pictures of the coastal area to see if any Argentinian ships remained in the vicinity. Fog prevented the Victor from getting pictures, but Royal Navy ships generated radar images which ensured that there were in fact no ships there.

Later, when Vulcan bombers hit the airfield at Port Stanley and Harriers bombed the runway, incorrect damage assessment was generated by relying exclusively on reports from the attacking aircraft. As heavy losses had been suffered already, no aircraft were sent to carry out a post-attack reconnaissance, and British forces were stunned to find aircraft operating from the airfield a few days later. More strikes were planned but with cloud preventing satellite observation the damage went unassessed, and again was erroneously interpreted. Following that experience the Royal Air Force is concerned to acquire a tactical reconnaissance capability for the Tornado.

The Falklands conflict was won by British forces because of their professional conduct, their extremely high standard of training, their well utilised equipment and remarkable operational flexibility. It would probably not have made very much difference to the eventual outcome of the conflict if adequate intelligence were possible and correct assessments had been made.

But in almost every other theatre anywhere else, it would have proved the conclusive factor. That has been seen to good effect in Europe during the 1940s and in the Middle East in the 1970s and '80s. Coupled with the human factor, and with the continual preparedness for full operational activity, the tactical air reconnaissance role is assured its niche as one of the more important elements in the intelligence gathering machine.

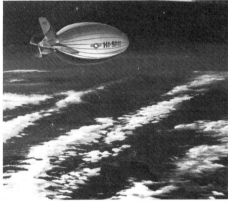

5 ▲

6 ▲

4 ▲

1 Most common of all Soviet recce types is the Yak-28 Brewster D, although most are probably converted attack aircraft. Emphasis is put on the EW/ECM role and the type carries no armament.

2, 3 High-altitude, high-speed, recce missions are flown by MiG-25R, more than 150 having been deployed in this role. Capable of Mach 3, they are comparatively vulnerable but useful on area survey missions.

4 Recce work does not require highly sophisticated EW platforms. Had Britain deployed even the old Shackleton during the Falklands war, ground and air operations would have been enhanced.

5, 6, 7 Future surveillance tests will need specialized aircraft. New technology helps revitalise old concepts for surveillance and reconnaissance and even the airship (**5**) could get a new lease of life maintaining a watch on hostile forces over inaccessible terrain or swamp. Defence must not be driven exclusively by the imperatives of strategic confrontation. Solar powered concept (**6**) carries solar cells on vertical surfaces for power during day and optimised aero profile at night, when wing tips are lowered and aircraft is battery powered. Lockheed methane-powered concept (**7**) would cruise at Mach 5, 98,427ft (30,000m) high as a replacement for the SR-71 strategic reconnaissance aircraft.

7 ▲

Chapter eight

Intelligence and the war on land

DURING THE operations of the UK Task Force in the Falklands campaign in 1982, tactical intelligence played a major role in the ultimate success achieved by the British commander. As pointed out by Major General Edward Fursdon, Defence Correspondent of *The Daily Telegraph,* "The unqualified success of the many small SAS intelligence-gathering patrols deployed in the Falklands campaign could probably well count as one of the major factors which led to victory." General Fursdon observes: "They operated both in the offensive mode—to provoke the Argentines to give away information—and in the passive one of reporting from close proximity observation . . . . One very important lesson of the outcome is to appreciate the sheer quantity of detailed intelligence such highly-trained well-positioned teams can generate. But, ... the viewpoint of any one small SAS patrol is inevitably narrow and only part of the whole picture. This highlights for perhaps the first time something relevant in the South Atlantic as much as in NATO Europe. This is the modern need for sufficient qualified staff dedicated to co-ordination, processing, and interpreting quickly enough the volume of tactically detailed and updated battlefield intelligence provided by both the SAS patrols and wider intelligence sources. It is important to integrate and disseminate this to the right people in time."

In his commentary, General Fursdon indicates, "Of course, a practical balance must always be struck between the updated topicality and immediate relevance of battlefield intelligence and the staff effort devoted to dealing with it. A judgment must similarly be made as to its application to plans in train, and to those whose execution is actively imminent . . . . Sadly, military history is studded with examples of failures to get this balance right and of last-minute disregard of intelligence resulting in a heavy price in terms of lives lost. The problem is eternal, but inescapable; and we neglect it at our peril."

Around 500 BC, the classic Chinese military theorist, Sun Tzu, commented, "To remain in ignorance of the enemy's condition is the height of inhumanity . . . . What enables the good general to strike and conquer and achieve things beyond the reach of ordinary men is foreknowledge . . . . What is called "foreknowledge" cannot be elicited from spirits, nor from gods, nor by analogy with past events, nor from calculations. It must be obtained from men who know the enemy situation."

On October 6, 1973, a coordinated attack by Egyptian and Syrian military forces struck a marginally prepared Israeli Army in a series of violent and destructive battles which continued until the UN-mandated ceasefire took effect on October 24. The turning point in the "Yom Kippur" War occurred late in the conflict when Israeli Forces, initially on the defensive, were able to cross the Suez Canal and isolate the Egyptian Third Army. This achievement occurred as a direct result of critical intelligence obtained through sound reconnaissance. An Israeli armoured reconnaissance unit was patrolling the Grafit area in a westerly direction on October 9 and, when no enemy forces were encountered, continued moving to the Bitter Lake where it turned to the north, still observing no enemy. At dusk, the patrol commander decided to turn around at Kishuf and return to Bitter Lake where he reported to his headquarters that there was an open "seam" between the Egyptian Second and Third Armies. This knowledge enabled the Israeli force to accomplish their daring canal crossing, and assume the offensive in an attack that was to assure a successful conclusion to the campaign.

The early defeats and heavy losses suffered by Israel in 1973 and their subsequent successes emphasise the concluding remarks quoted from General Fursdon's commentary in 1982. It is interesting to note that the earliest recorded history of organized military combat occurred in the same general area of the "Yom Kippur" War when, during 1479 BC, the Egyptian Pharoah, Thutmose III, was confronted by a revolt led by the King of Kadesh, allied with the neighbouring kings of Syria and Palestine. Thutmose advanced through Gaza with the Egyptian Army between mid-April and early May. His reconnaissance discovered a concealed route of advance through a pass near Mount Carmel, and he was able to surprise his enemy, then occupying the fortified city of Megiddo (Armageddon), and to defeat him decisively.

These few examples, from the most ancient to the most modern, give evidence of the fundamental needs of the commander of tactical military forces in the land battle. As the Duke of Wellington reminisced that he had "spent half of my military career wondering what was on the other side of the hill", so must every modern-day commander

1 The Fulda Gap on the Inner German Border, with East German soldiers observing a NATO photographer observing them. This type of mutual surveillance takes place every day and every night on all East-West frontiers.

1 ▲

The Duke of Wellington (1769-1851) once said
that he had spent half his military career wondering
"what was on the other side of the hill".
The problem for today's land force commander is
quite unchanged.

have knowledge of the three basics of tactical intelligence: *strength, capability and disposition of enemy forces.*

The first chapter of this book deals with the question "What is Intelligence?" in the broader and more general aspects. In this chapter will be explored the specifics of intelligence in the sharp point of ground combat—the place that veteran infantry soldiers describe thus: "When you are here, there is nothing in front of you but the enemy."

Middle East lessons

Adequate tactical intelligence permits the commander to equalize enemy advantages; to offset superior numbers of forces and weapons, or unfavourable terrain. Inadequate intelligence usually presages defeat. This is particularly clear in the campaigns in the Middle East when, after their stunning victory in the Six Day War in 1967, Israel was brought near to defeat in 1973, achieving success only after exploiting tactical intelligence. Since the forces, equipment and leadership were essentially the same, one must seek to find relevant points of difference.

Intelligence obviously is a major item. After 1973, Israeli Major General Chaim Herzog pointed out, "One field in which the Egyptians had made great advances was that of military intelligence. After the Six Day War, the Soviet Union had reorganized the Egyptian intelligence system and provided it with modern, sophisticated equipment for all forms of electronic warfare. Radio interception, electronic surveillance and locating equipment were all introduced and attained a satisfactory standard of operation. And in addition to dispatching agents to operate inside Israel, the Arabs also benefited from Soviet surveillance over Israel by means of electronic intelligence ships and satellites."

Since so many different terms are encountered in discussions of intelligence, such as "strategic", "combat", "tactical", "communications" and "counterintelligence", the terms can be confusing when accompanied by technical jargon. As "combat" or "tactical" intelligence for the ground forces are terms used more or less interchangeably, "tactical" intelligence will be used here as the more inclusive and descriptive term.

In this sense, tactical intelligence is distinguished from strategic intelligence mainly by reason of its intended use. Thus, the many components of strategic intelligence are produced by nations in peacetime as well as during time of war. Strategic intelligence is used principally by policy- and decision-makers at higher national levels. Strategic intelligence is concerned mainly with data relating to political and economic activities, about armed forces and defence capabilities as well as industrial, scientific and technological matters. The main thrust of strategic intelligence is usually directed toward determining the "intentions" of actual or potential adversaries, while the main effort in tactical intelligence is supposed to be concentrated upon the military capabilities of hostile, or

potentially hostile forces, and is therefore normally produced in wartime or immediately prior to an outbreak of hostilities.

It is generally accepted that the most significant differences between strategic and tactical intelligence are the *purpose, utilization* and *level* at which it will be used. The precise line of demarcation between these two categories of intelligence, however, may become blurred or indistinct and, as a practical matter, circumstances often occur when the categories appear to overlap completely. Good examples of this latter case are seen in the very detailed combination of strategic *and* tactical intelligence used by General Eisenhower's planners for the Allied invasion of Normandy in 1944 during World War II, and by the British Task Force Commander in wresting back the Falklands Islands from Argentinian military control in spring 1982.

The basic and underlying premise for all tactical intelligence is that every military organization, friendly or enemy, and without regard to size, level or location, has a mission responsive to the command of some higher headquarters. The higher headquarters then has responsibility to provide subordinate commands not only with the mission and direction, but with the resources needed to accomplish the mission. Military organizations of battalion size and at higher levels today thus have staff elements dedicated to tactical intelligence.

Visualizing the battlefield

The intelligence requirements of a commander in the land battle are generated by his mission and by the level of command which are developed by his need to *visualize* or *see* the battlefield and are modified by his own perceptions. Thus, at the company level, the captain and his troops must actually fight the enemy in a designated area which is prescribed by the limits of visual observation and the direct fire of their weapons. Control and direction of this battle is accomplished by the lieutenant colonels and colonels who command the battalions and brigades, while the generals who command the divisions and corps (and higher echelons) concentrate the forces under their command to achieve the proper combination of resources at the point or points of actual combat.

So where is the information which makes up the intelligence product obtained? What are the sources? Put most simply, all sources can be grouped into three distinct categories:

1. The *electro-magnetic* spectrum.
2. *Imagery* from overhead platforms.
3. *Human-source intelligence* (to include direct visual observation).

The accompanying chart displays the intelligence assets, categorized by source, available to commanders at each level of command.

Electro-magnetic intelligence is obtained by detecting and using information collected from the electronic emissions of the enemy— signal intelligence (SIGINT) or communications intelligence (COMINT). This source can be exploited by cryptanalysis, or "code-breaking", signal and communications

1 ▲
1 Despite the marvels of technology the land intelligence battle still depends largely on special advance forces using their eyes and ears in daring reconnaissance. Who knows how often it happens for real?

2 Document found on the body of Vietnamese in Laos, 1954. Land intelligence still gains great value from such traditional sources as interrogation of prisoners-of-war and papers, badges and equipment taken from enemy dead. Ironically, the penultimate sentence on the document reads: "Note: To be destroyed after reading."

3 A computer-generated tactical display, but will it lead to rows of people staring at screens unable to see the enemy at the door?

4 For 20 years the helicopter has seemed the answer to the battlefield commander's need to "see over the hill", but the low-level environment is now extremely hostile.

5 US troops questioning a prisoner in Vietnam. Human Intelligence (HUMINT) can be very productive and prisoners, if treated in the right way, often give far more information than they intend.

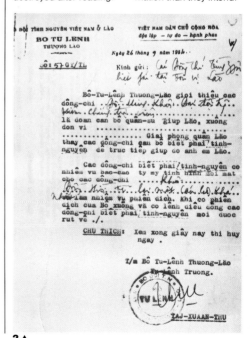

2 ▲

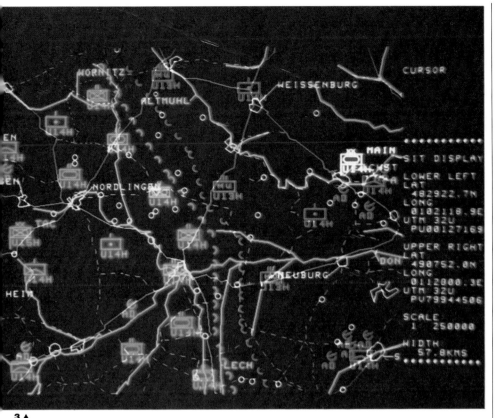

3 ▲

4 ▲

5 ▲

analysis, location or direction finding of the emitter itself, or analysis of patterns of emission (traffic analysis). Electronic or electro-magnetic intelligence (ELINT) can also provide information about enemy physical activity by using mobile or portable ground surveillance radar (GSR) and remote sensors (REMS).

Imagery intelligence is obtained from radar, including the newer types of side-looking radar (SLAR), infra-red, radiation (IR) detection and photographic sensors carried by overhead platforms (aircraft or spacecraft).

Human intelligence (HUMINT) includes all other types of collection, such as reports from reconnaissance elements, information from captured prisoners (interrogation of prisoners of war—IPW), documents and equipment.

As we can begin to see that the needs of commanders for tactical intelligence vary by level and scope of command, it is also clear that the reason for this lies in the fact that the battle itself varies from the direct fire battle fought at battalion level and lower to the more complex battle involving larger forces and an expansion of the factors of *time* and *space* as they impact upon operations. It is wise to keep in mind the distinction between the land battle, in the classic sense, and other military experiences in recent times such as in Malaya, Algeria and Vietnam. This is not to imply that these experiences are totally irrelevant or that they did not involve danger or violence, but rather that they are more peripheral to this exposition. As John Keegan put it succinctly in his study, *The Face of Battle,* "For there is a fundamental difference between the sort of sporadic, small-scale fighting which is the small change of soldiering and the sort we characterize as a battle. A battle must obey the dramatic unities of time, place and action. And although battles in modern wars have tended to obey the first two of these unities less and less exactly, becoming increasingly protracted and geographically extensive as the numbers and areas available to commanders have grown, the action of battle—which is directed towards securing a decision by and through those means on the battlefield and within a fairly strict time limit—has remained a constant."

Time, place and action

The land battle is, in fact, the sum total of battles fought at the various echelons of command all "obeying the dramatic unities of time, place and action". Since differences in intelligence requirements and the perceptions of the commanders are dictated by the battle role of the command, it is helpful to examine the aspects of the land battle in more detail before proceeding to the means by which modern commanders are able to obtain and employ tactical intelligence.

Just as there is a distinction between strategic and tactical intelligence, there is a further distinction between *information* and *intelligence*. Intelligence is data which has been processed; that is, it has been confirmed or validated, integrated with other relevant data, compared or analyzed and interpreted as to significance. Information for combat or tactical use on the other hand is raw data, not delayed by any processing, which can tell a commander immediately where the enemy is and what he is doing.

Tactical *information* thus can give a commander knowledge which will allow him to bring immediate fire on targets or take immediate defensive action against attack. Tactical *intelligence* on the other hand can be used to plan and conduct future operations.

Because tactical commanders must think in terms of time and space and conduct operations in designated areas, they must, therefore, visualize their battlefield in terms of areas. Of primary interest to the commander is the area in which he must exert his influence immediately. At the same time there is another area which demands his attention or interest, because enemy forces in this area can affect his future operations. Quite simply, it is these *areas of influence* and *areas of interest* that prescribe the information and intelligence requirements of a commander.

The accompanying diagrams depict the areas of influence and areas of interest of echelons from battalion to echelons above corps. The charts display both time and space factors and are drawn from the perspective of the commander looking forward in the direction of an enemy beyond the *forward line of his own troops* (FLOT). (This, incidentally, is not necessarily the *forward edge of the battle area* (FEBA), and is becoming increasingly significant in an age of nuclear and "neutron" weapons.)

Comparing the tables and diagrams here with the information shown in Chart 1 on page 152 helps to build a complete picture of the battlefield from the viewpoint of the commander and his staff intelligence officer at echelons from battalion to corps and above.

Dispersion of forces

The time and distance factors in battle are among the "constants" to which earlier reference was made. However, while time and distance, as determinants, have remained constant, the actualities of either factor have changed greatly over the years and are determined by escalation in the war-making potential of contending forces or advances in weaponry and technology. In ancient times, foot soldiers armed with individual hand weapons were normally dispersed about one man in every five to fifteen metres for combat. In an hour of combat, the ancient warrior could, theoretically, account for perhaps fifteen or twenty of the enemy. After the introduction of gunpowder during the 15th Century, dispersion and lethality of combat began to increase. During the October 1973 War in the Middle East about 100,000 men occupied an area of almost 1,550 square miles (about 4,000 square kilometres) — about 43,750 yards, 40,000 metres per man — with a front of 35 miles (57km) and a depth of about 44 miles (70km). The accompanying charts illustrate not only the evolutionary aspects of battle, but portray graphically the comparative magnitude of the tactical problem faced by modern commanders.

AREAS OF INTEREST			AREAS OF INFLUENCE		
LEVEL OF COMMAND	TIME BEYOND FLOT*	DISTANCE BEYOND FLOT* miles (km)	LEVEL OF COMMAND	TIME BEYOND FLOT*	DISTANCE BEYOND FLOT* miles (km)
BN	0-12 hrs	9 (15)	BN	0-3 hrs	3 (5)
BDE	0-24 hrs	43 (70)	BDE	0-12 hrs	9 (15)
DIV	0-72 hrs	93 (150)	DIV	0-24 hrs	43 (70)
CORPS	0-96 hrs	186 (300)	CORPS	0-72 hrs	93 (150)
EAC	96+ hrs	621+ (1,000+)	EAC	72+ hrs	93+ (150+)
*FLOT: Forward Line of Own Troops					

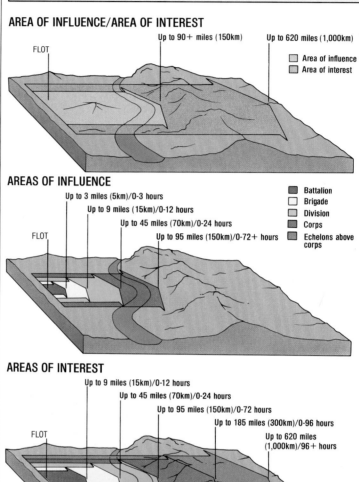

AREA OF INFLUENCE/AREA OF INTEREST

Up to 90+ miles (150km)
Up to 620 miles (1,000km)
FLOT

☐ Area of influence
☐ Area of interest

AREAS OF INFLUENCE

Up to 3 miles (5km)/0-3 hours
Up to 9 miles (15km)/0-12 hours
Up to 45 miles (70km)/0-24 hours
FLOT
Up to 95 miles (150km)/0-72+ hours

■ Battalion
☐ Brigade
■ Division
■ Corps
■ Echelons above corps

AREAS OF INTEREST

Up to 9 miles (15km)/0-12 hours
Up to 45 miles (70km)/0-24 hours
Up to 95 miles (150km)/0-72 hours
Up to 185 miles (300km)/0-96 hours
FLOT
Up to 620 miles (1,000km)/96+ hours

Military commanders divide the area beyond the *Forward Line of Own Troops* (FLOT) into two areas. The first is the *Area of Influence* in which they are able to acquire and attack targets; the second (and larger) is the *Area of Interest,* which is that occupied by enemy forces capable of affecting the commander's future operations. These definitions are used, among other things, to specify the design parameters for weapons, surveillance and target acquisition systems. The overall picture at Army Group level is shown (top) and is broken down into command levels for *Areas of Influence* (centre) and *Areas of Interest* (below). Whether these ranges are achieved in practice is, however, another matter altogether. In particular, the ability of a corps commander to "see" out to 600+ miles (1,000km) is open to question. The areas shown here are those defined for the United States Army; whether the Soviets use the same criteria is not certain, especially as their use of echelons means that follow-on formations are held back from the FLOT until they are committed to battle.

INCREASE OF WEAPON LETHALITY AND DISPERSION OVER HISTORY

This chart shows the main weapons that have been developed over recorded history and their lethality assessed in terms of their estimated killing capability per hour. Up to the middle of the 19th Century the increase in lethality was marginal, and in personal weapons the only apparent improvement was in the distance between the firer and his victim. At the end of the 19th Century, however, the first major fruit of the technological revolution was the machine-gun which gave a 3-man crew the killing power previously that of a battalion. From then on new types of weapon conferred a new lethal capability an order of magnitude greater than that of their predecessors. The left-hand scale depicts the dispersion of men in the combat area expressed in terms of men per square metre. This, too, remained fairly even up to the mid-1800s, but then increased rapidly. The problem now is to correlate the need, unchanged over centuries, to concentrate for shock action with the great dispersion required to counter the effects of nuclear weapons. It is also possible to see from this chart how the range at which a man is able to inflict damage has increased from 2 to 13,000km.

From "The Evolution of Weapons and Warfare" copyright ©, by T.N. Dupuy, used with permission of the publisher, The Bobbs-Merrill Company, Inc.

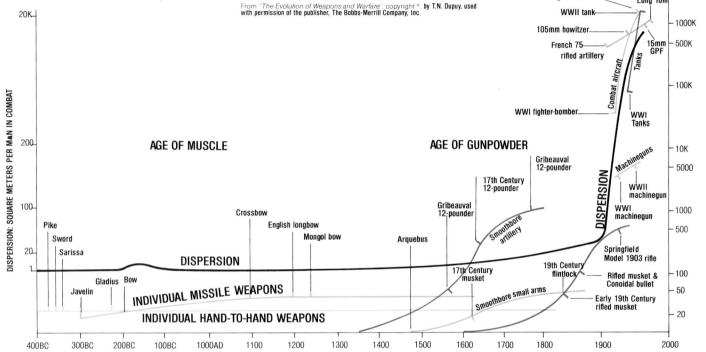

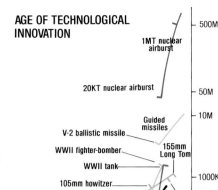

LEAD TIME REQUIRED FOR COMBAT INFORMATION

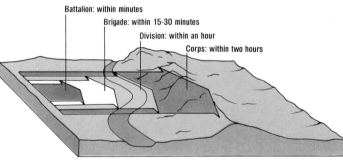

Battalion: within minutes
Brigade: within 15-30 minutes
Division: within an hour
Corps: within two hours

Having acquired a piece of information the real problem is only just starting, because the acquisition effort is totally wasted is the information is not given to someone able to react to it and in time to do it. This diagram shows the lead times necessary for each command level; whether it is achieved is a function of communications and staff work.

3 ▲

1 A frequent activity is the intelligence briefing. Unfortunately the recipient is totally in the hands of the analysts and can be easily misled by a glib manner and good "stage management."

2 A US Army foot recce patrol on exercise. Commanders and strategists need the grand picture, while infantry such as these often need only to know what is on the other side of the hedge.

3 General Giap (standing) briefs the Viet Minh Politburo on plans to defeat the French at Dein Bien Phu. A brilliant general, Giap had a good intelligence service, and also knew how to use its product to advantage.

2 ▲

1 ▲

OPERATION OF GROUND SURVEILLANCE RADAR

A characteristic of modern warfare is the high manoeuvrability of ground forces. Reliable information is therefore required against sudden major attacks as well as from small infiltration groups. One of the answers to this, and clearly derived from its experiences, is the Israeli EL/M-21 ground surveillance radar. This has four operating modes: general search (360°), sector search (up to 360°), zoom (5°, 10°, 20°) and identification (stationary). In the latter spectrum analysis of the doppler signal is compared with library data. There is an 80 per cent probability of detecting a man at 12.4 miles (20km) and a truck at 43 miles (70km).

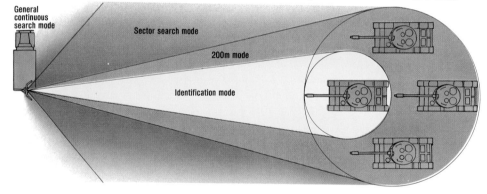

1 French officers monitoring radar displays. As such technological advances are brought to the assistance of intelligence and command staffs their ability to handle masses of data inputs is improving; the use of systems in tactical decision-making, however, is still in the conceptual stage.

2 Tactical communications systems will be a high priority target for both sides, and communications intelligence (COMINT) staffs will devote much effort to locating radio sites such as this tropospheric scatter station.

3 The essential intelligence tasks remain the same whatever the evironment, although recce will obviously be more difficult in the Artic.

4 Tactical success in anti-terrorist operations depends absolutely upon good intelligence, which, as these soldiers in Northern Ireland well know, means getting out on the ground.

5 US Army soldiers with a ground surveillance radar, just one of the many assets now available within forward units for information-gathering. Indeed, so many devices are now being issued that it is a problem to find the soldiers to man them.

CHART 1: INTELLIGENCE ASSET AVAILABILITY					
INTELLIGENCE SYSTEM	**GENERALS**		**COLONELS**		**CAPTAINS**
	CORPS	**DIVISION**	**BRIGADE**	**BATTALION**	**COMPANIES**
National Strategic System	●				
USAF/USN Systems	●	●			
Tactical System					
ELECTROMAGNETIC					
Sigint — Comint	●	●	●		
Sigint — Elint	●	●	●		
Remote Sensors (REMS)		●	●	●	●
Ground Surveillance Radar (GSR)		●	●	●	●
Weapons Locating Radar		●	●		
IMAGERY					
Photo	●	●			
Infrared (IR)	●	●			
Side-looking aircraft radar (SLAR)	●	●			
HUMINT					
Reconnaissance Units	●	●		●	
Troops				●	●
Interrogation of POWs (IPW)	●	●	●		

* This chart illustrates the echelons at which these assets are normally assigned, attached, or in direct support.

2 ▲

3 ▲

4 ▲

5 ▲

In earlier times, the commander could view the battlefield and combatant forces from some convenient vantage point, but as warfare became more complex and as combat leaders began to control more men, more widely dispersed than could be viewed at one time, specialized staff functions began to evolve. By the time of Julius Caesar, the staff intelligence function began to be institutionalized as each Roman legion consisting of about 5,000 men had 10 individuals, called *speculators,* assigned specifically to full-time intelligence tasks. Toward the end of the nineteenth century in Europe, there existed, fundamentally, two types of staff systems: the Prussian (adopted by British and Russian forces as well), consisting of five sections, which assigned a primary role to operations, and the French system consisting of four equal, coordinating staff members. By the end of World War I, the Americans had adopted the French system, but setting out the functional duties as they were applied in the German system.

Today, all military staffs have an intelligence element. At the battalion and brigade levels, the intelligence staff elements are concerned mainly with tactical information and intelligence obtained from higher or adjacent headquarters as well as from organic units. At the higher echelons, however, the intelligence staffs are larger, more specialized, and are involved in virtually all phases of the intelligence process such as collection, integration, collation, analysis, interpretation and dissemination to users.

In examining how tactical intelligence needs are satisfied the author has taken it as read that intelligence requirements and staff element responsibilities in all contemporary military forces have more basic similarities than differences. The two major military aggregations in the world today are the forces of the North Atlantic Treaty Organization (NATO) and the forces of the Warsaw Pact. While many other nations, including neutral and non-aligned nations, possess military structures of varying capabilities, upon close examination it will frequently be found that these forces, often equipped from one or the other (in some cases both) of the major alliances, resemble those of one or other major powers, in some degree, in the way in which tactical intelligence is used. This may be particularly noticeable in military actions in the Middle East during the past decade in which forces employing Soviet/Warsaw Pact equipment, tactics and techniques, have been in conflict with Israeli Defence Forces equipped mainly with US and NATO weaponry as well as some items of indigenous design and manufacture.

Doctrinal and organizational differences

Differences in military doctrine as well as organization exist among all forces and significant differences will be noted in the discussion which follows. Initially, some structural distinctions in combat forces should be recognized. In the US Army, as well as those of other major NATO nations, the Corps is the principal combat force in a theatre of operations. Corps structure is flexible and its organization during operations is predicated on the nature of the enemy threat, the mission, the particular characteristics of the area of intended operations and the availability of forces. A US Army Corps is normally structured with two combat divisions, a separate brigade, an armoured cavalry regiment and diverse support elements such as artillery, engineer, signal and intelligence units. Corps in other armies of NATO are similar in that they are flexibly structured, although they frequently have more divisions since divisions in, for example, the British, German and French armies, are somewhat smaller than those of the US Army. the division is the fundamental combat organization of any modern army and in most armies is a permanent, structured combined arms organization.

In the Soviet/Warsaw Pact organizations different terms, such as Front and Army, are employed. The Front is flexibly structured with from three to six Armies and attached elements, while a typical Army might be composed of four to five divisions together with assigned as well as attached support elements.

Every modern battlefield commander has some organic intelligence assets available to him and thus receives tactical information and intelligence from these assets as well as from other organizations. To describe and discuss the acquisition and exploitation of tactical intelligence, the natural order displayed in Chart 1 will be used.

Electromagnetic systems

The chart shows that Signal Intelligence (SIGINT) assets, further subdivided into Communications Intelligence (COMINT) and Electronic Intelligence (ELINT), are available to Corps, Division and Brigade Commanders. Remote Sensors (REMS) and Ground Surveillance Radar (GSR) are provided at Division, Battalion and Company level, while weapons-locating radar are at Division and Brigade levels. In a general sense, with proper allowances being made for differences in doctrine and terminology, the availability of assets may apply to combat force commanders of any major modern military power.

COMINT and SIGINT are both used to produce combat information as well as intelligence which can be extensively used by tactical commanders. COMINT information is obtained by monitoring enemy radio and telephone systems, and ELINT by intercepting enemy non-communication electronic signals such as radar. Analysis of each signal can provide intelligence about the emitter and the particular enemy force identified with the emitter. When this information is integrated with other intelligence, it can be used to provide the commander not only with accurate targetting data but an be used as a basis for determining the enemy's intentions.

COMINT elements of a command can intercept enemy communications and obtain information from voice or code transmissions in clear (unenciphered) messages, possibly decipher other messages or analyze the volume or direction of communications traffic. ELINT elements can locate emitters and relate them to particular items of equipment which are assigned to certain enemy headquarters or units. Today's ELINT units employ a technique known as Advanced Identification Techniques of Radio Frequency Devices, or "Electronic Fingerprinting". "Electronic Fingerprinting" operates on the same concept as is used in fingerprint identification of individuals; that is, as every individual has a unique fingerprint, each electronic emitter emits a signal with unique, identifiable characteristics. The appearance of a particular emitter in a new area may be used to identify its unit and may indicate possible enemy intentions.

At Corps or equivalent echelons, SIGINT is received not only from adjacent and subordinate levels, but from higher levels, including national level agencies and from exchange with other nations. All intelligence information is *fused* at Corps level to provide commanders with vital data and intelligence.

Soviet reconnaissance

The Soviet/Warsaw Pact concept of reconnaissance and intelligence (razvodka) is quite broad and more inclusive that that of NATO and other forces. A Front Commander, for example, will direct the use of high altitude, high performance aircraft such as the MiG-25 (Foxbat). Each Frontal Tactical Air Army has a Foxbat unit as well as an Air Reconnaissance Regiment equipped with MiG-21 (Fishbed) and Su-7, Su-17 and Su-22 (Fitter) and an increasing number of MiG-23 and MiG-27 (Flogger). While helicopters such as Mi-24 (Hind) can serve with fixed-wing aircraft for SIGINT collection, the Warsaw Pact forces have not stressed this use. The Soviets include all aspects of offensive electronic warfare under the term *Radioelectronic Combat* (REC) and place major emphasis on their function. Specialized Soviet intelligence units perform the same basic functions as comparable NATO units in collecting and analyzing data.

At the Soviet Army level both a Signal Interception Battalion and a Radioelectronic Combat Battalion are organic. With between 400 and 500 officers and men, these units are organized and equipped for signal monitoring and intelligence tasks and have an impressive array of equipment for interception and location purposes alone.

SIGINT assets employed at Division and lower echelons in all armies have, fundamentally, the same mission as Corps and higher echelons but direct their operations more in their own commander's area of influence and provide combat information of an immediate or urgent nature to the Division, Brigade and Battalion commander in order for him to engage the enemy by all available means. At the same time, this information is provided to Corps and echelons above Corps where it can be fused with other information to provide overall intelligence.

The concept of using some unmanned device to provide an early warning of possible enemy involvement and prevent surprise has existed for a long time. According to legen, the cackling of geese on the Capitolene hill in Ancient Rome provided

1 ▲

1 A reconnaissance version of the BMP in Polish Army colours crossing a river under cover from smoke. Warsaw Pact (ie, Soviet) tactical doctrine places great emphasis on ground recce deep into enemy territory. In close country this may be feasible, but in open country such as the north German Plain, it will be very hazardous.

2 A Soviet Army recce patrol, comprising an M-72 motor-cycle combination and a BRDM-2 scout car. Divisional recce elements such as this will move

up 31 miles (50km) in front of the main body in an advance and may well be supported by sub-units of tank or motor-rifle regiments, together with engineers.

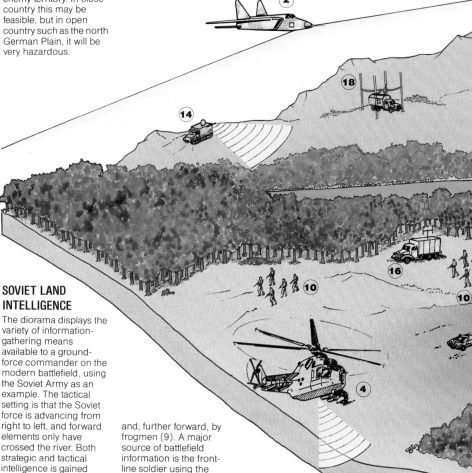

SOVIET LAND INTELLIGENCE

The diorama displays the variety of information-gathering means available to a ground-force commander on the modern battlefield, using the Soviet Army as an example. The tactical setting is that the Soviet force is advancing from right to left, and forward elements only have crossed the river. Both strategic and tactical intelligence is gained from satellite surveillance (1) and high altitude aircraft recce (2). These are complemented by fixed-wing aircraft (3) and helicopters (4). On the ground itself deep recce is carried out by foot patrols (5), scout cars (6) and, in a reversion to former methods, motor-cycles (7). A particularly important task is the recce of river-crossing sites, here being carried out by BMP units (8)

and, further forward, by frogmen (9). A major source of battlefield information is the front-line soldier using the "Mark 1 Eyeball"—both infantry (10) and the artillery in their observation posts (11). An invaluable source of information is prisoners-of-war (represented by a downed airman) (12). The location of artillery and mortars can be achieved acoustically using a sound-ranging base (13) or electronically using radar (14). Fixed-wing aircraft, helicopters and drones are located using air

defence radars (15), aided by visual observation. Because of its line-of-sight properties VHF radio intercept must be done from a position well forward (16), but HF intercept can be done from much further back (17). HF radio direction-finding (18) requires several stations, but only one is shown here. A new trend is to

use helicopters for radio intercept, especially of VHF and UHF links (19). Finally, high altitude aircraft are also used for electronic intercept (20), the Tu-126 having especially comprehensive electronic support measures (ESM).

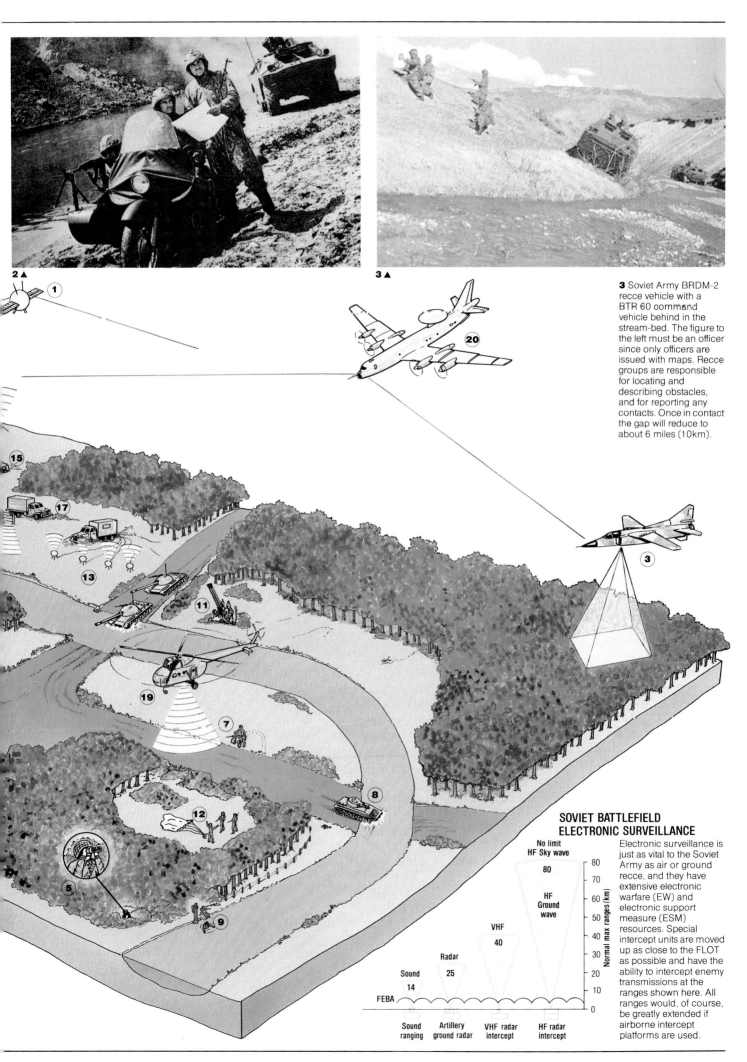

2▲

3▲

3 Soviet Army BRDM-2 recce vehicle with a BTR 60 command vehicle behind in the stream-bed. The figure to the left must be an officer since only officers are issued with maps. Recce groups are responsible for locating and describing obstacles, and for reporting any contacts. Once in contact the gap will reduce to about 6 miles (10km).

SOVIET BATTLEFIELD ELECTRONIC SURVEILLANCE

Electronic surveillance is just as vital to the Soviet Army as air or ground recce, and they have extensive electronic warfare (EW) and electronic support measure (ESM) resources. Special intercept units are moved up as close to the FLOT as possible and have the ability to intercept enemy transmissions at the ranges shown here. All ranges would, of course, be greatly extended if airborne intercept platforms are used.

No limit
HF Sky wave

80

HF
Ground
wave

VHF
40

Radar
25

Sound
14

FEBA

Normal max ranges (km)

80
70
60
50
40
30
20
10
0

Sound
ranging

Artillery
ground radar

VHF radar
intercept

HF radar
intercept

1 ▲

SOVIET/WARSAW PACT ELECTRONIC INTERCEPTION AND LOCATION SYSTEMS								
DESIGNATION	**MISSION**	**FREQUENCY RANGE**	**MODES**	**ANTENNA**	**RECEIVER SENSITIVITY**	**POWER**	**REQUIRED TIME**	**GAIN**
SR-53-V (System A)	HF intercept	3-30MHz	AM, voice CW, MCW	Rhombic	−105dBm	15kW	3h	15dBm
SR-52-V (System B)	VHF/UHF intercept	30-300MHz	FM, voice	LP	−110dBm	15kW	2h	10dBm
SR-51-V (System B-1)	VHF/UHF intercept	30-300MHz	FM, voice	Whip	−110dBm	5kW	15min	1dBm
SR-50-M (System C)	VHF/UHF intercept	30-450MHz	FM, voice	Whip	−110dBm	Battery	2min	1dBm
SR-54-V (System D)	relay intercept	30-300MHz	Voice, TTY	Dish or LP	−110dBm	10kW	1h	40 or 15dBm
SR-20-V (System 1)	HF/DF	3-25MHz	AM	Adcock	−90dBm	15kW	5h	10dBm
SR-19-V (System 2)	VHF/DF	30-300MHz	FM, voice	Loop or Adcock	−90dBm	10kW	2h	0 or 10dBm
SR-25-V (System 3)	VHF/DF	30-300MHz	FM, voice	Loop	−90dBm	5kW	10min	0dBm
SB-20-V (System I)	Artillery and surveillance radar	50MHz-11GHz	—	Dish	−110dBm	15kW	1h	40dBm
SM-21-V (System II)	Surveillance radar, intercept and DF	50MHz-10GHz	—	Dish	−110dBm	10kW	30min	40dBm

From *Weapons and Tactics of The Soviet Army*. David C. Isby (Jane's Publishing Co.)

1, 2 In the Vietnam War techniques of air-dropping acoustic, seismic and combined sensors to detect passing humans and vehicles reached an advanced stage in the Igloo White programme. Here an F-111 drops a parachute-retarded detector (**1**), while another version had petal-type airbrakes (**2**).

3, 4 Another device extensively used in Vietnam was the Air Delivered Seismic Detection Sensor (ADSID). This was either released from a wing station (**3**) or by a somewhat more primitive method from the door of a transport aircraft (**4**). Note the ADSID camouflage.

5 The AQUOBUOY acoustical sensor, seen here hanging from the branches of a tree near Nakhon Phanom airbase in Thailand. In the close country of Southeast Asia this would be very difficult to spot.

2 ▲

3 ▲

4 ▲

5 ▲

military defence against a surprise enemy attack. During the static trench warfare of 1914-1918, soldiers on both sides of the front were emplaced in trenches behind barbed wire. Empty food tins, sometimes filled with stones, were hung along the wires so that the noise caused by their movement would give advance warning of enemy action.

Modern electronic technology during the past 30 to 40 years has produced numerous intrusion detection devices used in commercial banks, stores, warehouses and similar locations by which it is possible for surreptitious entry to be monitored at a distance. The first major military deployment of REMS was by US forces in 1967 in Vietnam in the so-called "McNamara Line". A variety of sensors were used to provide indications of infiltration by enemy forces and supply transport from North Vietnam. The early use of sensors gave hints for future development, but like all pioneering techniques did not prove an unqualified success. REMs were and are still viewed by many as fundamentally useful for defensive purposes, to cover gaps in ground coverage where ground troops cannot be employed, or for longer-range intelligence collection purposes.

A factor which modern commanders will have to consider is that REMs can be employed in an offensive mode as well. A single example can illustrate this point. During 1969-1970, US Marines located in Vietnam employed REMS as a reconnaissance tool, and in the An Hoa basin the sensor-equipped troops of the reconnaissance battalion of the First Marine Division successfully ambushed a North Vietnamese Army unit, virtually eliminating the unit without casualties of their own. Seismic REMs detected enemy movement and alerted the intelligence section, which confirmed the presence and location of troops by using night observation devices and radar. An airborne OV-10A then directed A-6A aircraft into the zone using TPQ-10 radar for precise target location. After the A-6A attack, flares were dropped so that F-4 aircraft could complete the ambush.

REMs in Europe

In 1972, a US field demonstration under the codename of *Mystic Mission* introduced modern sensor technology into the European environment. Today, NATO force commanders have a wide variety of REMs at their disposal. Modern REMS are categorized according to the means of detection they employ and the method of emplacement which is used. The four means of detection are: *Seismic, Acoustic, Magnetic* and *Electromagnetic.*

Seismic detection is based upon detecting vibrations carried through the ground, caused by anything from rainfall to earthquakes. Present-day sensors can detect an individual moving at distances up to 100 feet (30m) and vehicles up to about 1,000 feet (300m) and skilled operators can distinguish between types of vehicles or numbers of individuals.

Acoustic sensors operate in much the same fashion as sensitive microphones and their range is about the same as the human

ear. Normally, acoustic sensors are activated after an indication from a seismic sensor. Magnetic sensors operate by detecting the movement of some ferrous metal up to about 13 feet (4m) for personnel or about 82 feet (25m) for vehicles. Technicians use magnetic sensors for confirmation of seismic data. Electromagnetic sensors are intrusion detectors which detect movement through their electro-magnetic field and, since any movement will activate them, indications must be confirmed by other types of devices.

Sensors can be *emplaced* by hand (by long range patrols, manoeuvre units or special REMS teams). REMS can also be emplaced by air delivery from aircraft, or from special artillery rounds.

Soviet/Warsaw Pact forces have not emphasized REMS, but they are believed to have acquired sensors and sensor technology from US devices obtained in Vietnam, and it is logical to assume that REMS would be employed by the Warsaw Pact in future operations.

Other forms of surveillance

Ground Surveillance Radar (GSR) can be employed to detect and locate moving targets under conditions when other means of surveillance are difficult or impossible. Deployed from division to company level, GRS assets are able to provide combat information as well as target locations, but can also provide security by early warning of enemy movement. Because of limitations of terrain or equipment, intelligence from GSR must usually be confirmed by other sources. NATO forces, employing for example, the Radar Set AN/PPS-5A, can detect moving vehicles to a distance of about 11,000 yards (10,000m) and moving personnel to just over 6,500 yards (about 6,000m). This transportable device can be manpacked into position, can distinguish between tracked or wheeled vehicles and is accurate to within 22 feet (20m).

A comparable Soviet/Warsaw Pact unit, the GS-12, is able to detect moving vehicles to about 13,125 yards (12,000m) and moving personnel to around 3,828 yards (3,500m). The GS-12 is normally mounted in a light truck but can be transported in three-manpack loads. The GS-11 and GS-13 in Soviet/Warsaw Pact forces have varying capabilities, as do the NATO AN/PPS-4A and AN/PPS-15. However, all GSR units require communications in order to be effective and also place additional security demands on the elements they are supporting.

From the primitive use of aerial photography, or more often, aerial sketches from captive balloons used by both sides during the American Civil War (1860-1865), aerial photography, or more properly photo-imagery interpretation, is today a highly sophisticated source of combat information and tactical intelligence. While the more exotic forms of imagery intelligence, such as from satellites or specially designed aircraft, excite considerable interest, the tactical commander is more concerned with "real time", immediate information, or intelligence on activities in his own area of influence or interest. The modern commander makes use of information which can be provided by air force tactical reconnaissance, but frequently from aircraft under his own control. A single aircraft can combine photos, infra-red and radar imagery capabilities.

There are five basic types of conventional photo-imagery used in tactical intelligence. *Vertical* furnishes coverage of a subject from directly overhead. Because the scale of vertical photographs is essentially constant, it is most useful where accurate scale is important. *Oblique* photography gives a view of an area from an angle which resembles the normal "eye-view". An interpreter can also use oblique views when clouds might prevent overhead photography. *Panoramic* photo-imagery is useful because, as the name implies, it can be obtained by the use of special "panoramic" cameras, which can cover a wide area in one pass over a target area. *Stereo* photography allows a photo-imagery interpreter to obtain a three-dimensional view of a subject. In tactical intelligence, stereo views permit analysis of terrain, as well as identification of individual items of equipment. *Infra-red* imagery permits detection of thermal, or heat, waves emanating from the terrain and objects. Present-day IR sensors can distinguish minute differences between objects and are able to reveal attempts at camouflage. The latest IR equipped aircraft can not only photograph objects on the ground, but can also allow the operator to view the target area while simultaneously transmitting the imagery to a ground-based terminal for immediate use. A major advantage of IR imagery is that it is entirely passive and gives no indication of use to an enemy. *Side-looking Airborne Radar* (SLAR) can be directed to the right or left (or both) sides of an aerial platform and observe fixed or moving targets without the radar having to overfly the target itself. The most recent SLAR aircraft can also transmit imagery to the ground. In recent years, as development of Remotely Piloted Vehicles (RPVs) or "drones" has progressed, it has become possible for small, unmanned aerial platforms to perform imagery collection missions without risking costly manned aircraft. (A fuller explanation, with illustrations, of aerial reconnaissance methods and RPV use is given in the chapters on electronic warfare and intelligence in the air battle.)

Human observation

In addition to the normal reports made by combat troops, reconnaissance units are employed by all modern armies. There are doctrinal differences between reconnaissance employment in the Soviet/Warsaw Pact forces and in NATO and most Western forces. The Soviet Army places its primary emphasis on ground-based reconnaissance units. These units, unlike those of their NATO counterparts, are used fundamentally for reconnaissance and do not have a primary screening and security mission. This difference is reflected in tactics as well as equipment. NATO units tend to be armed and capable of fighting on their own, while Soviet elements are designed for speed, mobility and concealment.

1 ▲

2 ▲

3 ▲

1, 2, 3 The low-level airspace over the enemy forward areas is now so hostile to aircraft that remotely piloted vehicles (RPVs) and drones are being developed in the place of manned recce vehicles. This problem has become especially acute because some modern weapons such as Multiple-launched Rocket System (MLRS) have ranges which exceed the current target acquisition means. Lockheed is developing a mini-RPV system for the US Army. The RPV is launched from a truck-mounted pneumatic catapult (**1**) and is controlled in flight from a cooond truck (**2**). On return the RPV is flown into a vertical ribbon barrier (**3**). Payload comprises a TV camera, target tracker and a laser ranger/designator, all being stabilised to alleviate the effects of manoeuvres. There is a real-time down-link.

4 The Canadian CL-227 represents a slightly different approach. This, too, is an RPV but vertical take-off and landing is possible.

5 The US Army's OV-1D Mohawk, of which some 200 remain in service. The long pod contains an APS-94 sideways-looking airborne radar (SLAR).

6 An OV-1OD Bronco showing its steerable chin turret fitted with AAS-37 Forward-Looking Infra-Red (FLIR) and laser target marker.

7 Teledyne-Ryan drones and RPVs are used for photo-recce, SIGINT/FI INT recce, active and passive ECM, laser designation and SLAR/FLIR.

8 In contrast to all this very costly and sophisticated gadgetry there is still a vital place for the man on the ground, using his eyes.

6 ▲

4 ▲

7 ▲

5 ▲

8 ▲

Modern military forces are provided with a number of types of units organized and trained for reconnaissance work. NATO forces, for example, at corps level, have an armoured cavalry regiment, employed in the traditional cavalry role of reconnaissance and security. Equipped with fast-moving light tanks, armoured personnel carriers and other armoured vehicles (both tracked and wheeled), as well as light scout vehicles, these elements are the conventional, organic reconnaissance forces of the commander. When equipped with aircraft, both fixed-wing and helicopters, commanders control a significant air-ground reconnaissance capability. Some NATO forces also use motorcycles in reconnaissance units. Similar units, normally of battalion size, are organic to combat divisions with a similar mission.

Soviet emphasis on HUMINT

From a comparison of the organic reconnaissance elements available to NATO commanders with those in Soviet/Warsaw Pact armies it can be easily concluded that the Soviet/Warsaw Pact concept of reconnaissance is relatively straightforward with less emphasis on radar and sensors and more on direct visual observation. The Warsaw Pact places somewhat greater reliance upon troop reconnaissance, or patrol activity of individual units. Soviet units continue to rely on the aged PT-76 amphibious tank in reconnaissance units, although this is being replaced by the newer, tracked BMP-R armoured vehicle. Soviet forces also use the BRDM-2 and BTR-50 or -60 light armoured carrier with the UAZ-469 or older GAZ-69 as a light scout vehicle, and motorcycles as well.

In NATO forces, special long-range elements are generally to be found as corps assets, while long-range reconnaissance companies are in the divisional reconnaissance battalion of Soviet combat divisions. Some distinction should also be recognized between the special forces of various nations. While US Army Special Forces and the British Special Air Service (SAS) Regiment can, and do, perform reconnaissance missions, this is frequently secondary to their other assignments, and these highly-trained troops are normally assigned at high level (above corps). US Army Ranger battalions are also trained for reconnaissance work but, again, have other missions. While most armies, particularly NATO forces, have a long-range reconnaissance patrol (LRRP) capability, assets usually belong to the corps commander while, as indicated, Soviet/Warsaw Pact forces have these units available at a lower level, consonant with their doctrine. These units are also to be distinguished from Soviet/Warsaw Pact special forces which are trained and equipped to impersonate NATO troops for raids and sabotage in NATO rear areas. Although such units can perform reconnaissance tasks as well, this is not their primary mission.

From the foregoing review of major items available for modern tactical intelligence, it should be clear that modern commanders have a formidable array of assets with which to "see" the battlefield. The increase

SOVIET GROUND FORCES RECONNAISSANCE CAPABILITY

UNIT	EQUIPMENT	GROUPING	DEPLOYMENT	RANGE (FROM FEBA)
MOTORISED RECCE				
Div recce bn	7 x PT-76/BMP 19 x BRDM/BRDM-2 4 x BRDM rkh (NBC recce) Up to about 30 motor-cycle combinations.	Recce groups are normally of reinforced platoon strength divided into 2-3 patrols of 1-3 vehicles each. A regt recce coy might form 1-3 such groups and a div recce bn about 5-10.	Each group will deploy on a frontage of up to 1.8 miles (3km). Within the group vehs will move by bounds of up to 0.9 miles (1.5km) at top speed, halting under cover to observe. Leading vehs will be covered by fire from others of the group at the halt. Detached patrols may operate up to 6.2 miles (10km) from the main body of the recce group. A recce group is given a target or direction of advance.	Up to 31 miles (50km) (normally closer to main body after contact).
Regt recce coy (one per regt)	3 x PT-76 5 x BRDM/BRDM-2 3 x BRDM rkh 9 x motorcycle combinations. One manpack ground surveillance radar.			Up to 9.3 miles (15km) (normally closer to main body after contact).
Tank and motor rifle troops	Tanks APCs Mortars.	*Recce detachments* may consist of a tank or motor rifle company or bn. They may be accompanied by arty. *Recce groups* as above, based on tank or motor rifle platoons. (Also known as independent recce patrols—ORDs).	A recce detachment is normally tasked with fighting recce and given a recce sector. Recce detachments are currently seldom formed. Deployment as for Div. recce bn and Regt. recce coy.	Up to 18.6 miles (30km) Up to 12.4 miles (20km)
		Combat recce patrols of section (tank) or platoon strength.	Formed for local recce and route security by leading tank and motor rifle bns.	Up to 6.2 miles (10km)
LONG RANGE RECCE				
Long range recce coy (div recce bn)	5 x UAZ-69 jeeps 5 x HF manpack radios.	The coy forms 5 groups, each of 6 men including a radio operator.	The coy operates in an area of some 18½ x 18½ miles (30 x 30km). Each group operates in an area of some 9½-15 sq miles (25-40sq km). They may be delivered by helicopter or infiltrate on foot, on skis or in their jeeps.	Up to 62 miles (100km), but more likely about 25 to 50 miles (40-80km)
ELECTRONIC RECCE				
Radio and radar intercept coy (div recce bn)	3 x VHF radio intercept/DF posts 3 x radar intercept/DB posts.	Radio and radar intercept/DF posts are normally co-located.	The 3 posts are deployed on a frontage of 6-12 miles (10-20km) some 1.2-2.4 miles (2-4km) behind the FEBA. They will set up on high ground clear of obstructions.	Radio and Radar: 15.5 to 24.8 miles (25-40km) (dependant on siting)
Arty radars	2 x ground surveillance radars (PORK TROUGH)		Ground surveillance radars: 1.2-1.8 miles (2-3km) behind the FEBA on high ground facing the enemy. Sets up in 5 mins.	Detects movement to range of 18.6 miles (30km) (approx)
	1 x mortar locating radar (SMALL YAWN)			Locates mortars to range of 7 miles (12km) (approx)
ARTILLERY RECCE				
Div arty obsn bty: a. Radar pl. b. Sound ranging pl.	Serial 6 above. 5 trucks.	One sound ranging base of four microphones.	Base line 2½-3 miles (4-5km) can be set up in 30 mins.	Mortars: 2½-3 miles (4-5km) 105mm guns: 7-9 miles (12-15km) 155mm guns: 12-15 miles (20-25km)
c. Flash spotting pl.		Four observer teams.		Line of sight
ENGINEER RECCE				
Div engr bn recce pl	3 x BRDM 1 x K-61/PTS Diving eqpt.	May operate independently or as part of combined arms patrols.		As for motorised recce

1 Modern armies can only fight as cohesive bodies through the use of telecommunications to link the many elements together. This Soviet regimental command post receives its orders from division and issues its own orders to battalions by radio; without radio it is simply a useless, disconnected collection of men.

2 From FEBA to division HQ, signals go by HF or VHF radio. From division rearward radio relay (microwave) is used, as shown here. These systems use frequencies in the UHF band; the beam is very narrow making interception very difficult, although airborne stations are now being used to listen to these vital circuits.

1▲

3▲

2▲

4▲

5▲

6▲

3 A Soviet Army radio exercise in East Germany. Such exercises not only give practice for the direct participants, but also the hostile EW operators sitting many miles away across the border, who are eager to monitor radio procedures, callsign systems, operators' idiosyncracies, and tactical plans and drills.

4 A West German infantry platoon commander (left) with his radio operator (right). Useful SIGINT can be gained, even from low-level links.

5 US Special Forces on exercise in South Korea. Isolated SF parties are especially dependent on communications, and very vulnerable.

6 Canadian Army infantry in M113 APCs. A modern infantry battalion has about 90 such vehicles all dependent upon radio for command and control.

There are many variants of the M113, and one, the M577A2, is specially equipped with communications gear and used as a command post vehicle in lethality and corresponding increase in dispersion encountered on the present-day battlefield magnify the area and concerns of the commander, but it is the significant increase in mobility of the modern military force which improves both the capability and the threat faced on the battlefield. As recently as World War II, a marching infantry unit took five hours to advance 18½ miles (about 30km), while mechanized units could move the same distance in two hours. Today's airmobile units can cover the same distance in 15 minutes. Obviously, the commander, and his intelligence units, must always be ahead in tactical intelligence to avoid costly failure.

With the vast increase in the quantity of combat information and tactical intelligence, it becomes apparent that the management and administration of the intelligence process must receive special attention in order not to malfunction, lose some vital piece of data, or simply become inundated. With the adoption of modern Automatic Data Processing Systems (ADPS) employing modern computer technology, the ever-present problem of recording, storing, sorting, transmitting, retrieving and displaying intelligence is minimised. Today's intelligence officer can reduce the large amount of time spent by intelligence specialists in procedural actions, and give full-time attention to analysis of intelligence and providing the commander with vital intelligence on a "real-time" basis.

As indicated by General Fursdon, a military commander's need for tactical intelligence — where is the enemy, what is his strength, what is he doing? — will always remain a problem. "The problem is eternal, but inescapable; and we neglect it at our peril".

Tactical intelligence in operation

There have been a number of published estimates of what might occur in some major military confrontation in Central Europe between NATO forces and the Warsaw Pact. Scenarios prepared by Major General Sir John Hackett in *The Third World War, August 1985* (published in 1978) and a sequel, *The Third World War — The Untold Story* (published in 1982) show Soviet and other Warsaw Pact forces, after a build-up in Eastern Europe, launching attacks against the West making use of the traditional Fulda Gap and Hof Corridor across the north German plain. Another scenario, suggested recently in *Silent Night* by Cyril Joly (published in 1982), envisioned a somewhat different scenario in which the Warsaw Pact, without a lengthy build-up, attacked Western Europe more covertly, making extensive use of saboteurs, diversionary units and clandestine operations. These methods, according to Joly's scenario, allowed for a successful surprise invasion without resort to nuclear weapons or even extensive conventional combat.

Of course, it is possible to imagine yet a further scenario which combines main elements of both Hackett's and Joly's. All would pose tremendous problems for the NATO intelligence machine. Since a top priority for any intelligence officer is to ensure that

1▲

2▲

3 ▲

1 After a period when they were out of fashion, wheeled armoured cars, such as this Panhard ERC-90 Lynx, are becoming more popular for long-range and flexible recce patrol use.

2 These Israeli soldiers are using an infra-red laser communicator, which provides line-of-sight voice or data communications between two locations, as well as being a binocular!

3 A Norwegian Army ski patrol carrying out reconnaissance in the snow. Much combat intelligence is still gained from such traditional methods, and always will be.

4 A corporal of British Parachute Regiment using a Lasergage LP7 hand-held laser rangefinder. Among the prime roles of such special forces are covert reconnaissance and observation.

4 ▲

his commander is not surprised, the basic implications of this major principle of warfare must be examined first.

In a major doctrinal treatise, *Scientific — Technical Progress and the Revolution in Military Affairs*, the Soviet High Command states:

> "Surprise is achieved by:
> Confusing the enemy of one's intention.
> Keeping secret the overall purpose of the forthcoming actions and preparations for them.
> Rapid and concealed concentration and deployment of forces in the area under attack.
> The unexpected use of weapons, and particularly nuclear weapons.
> The use of tactical procedures and new weapons unknown to the enemy."

In another major doctrinal work, *Soviet Military Strategy*, it is pointed out, "Concealed mobilization is possible even under present-day conditions, but it will be realized (in ways) somewhat differently than previously . . . however . . . widespread mobilization measures, even though concealed, cannot go unnoticed."

The Soviet Military leadership say, in *Basic Principles of Operational Art and Tactics*, that mass mobilization has become unnecessary because, "With the mass introduction of nuclear missiles into the armed forces of imperialist States, Soviet military science arrived at the conclusion that war can be begun by available groups of troops, and not by previously mobilized armed forces, and the beginning of a war can have a decisive effect upon the outcome."

Applying the principles of surprise as outlined above to a basic scenario, the situation can be examined with respect to the defensive intelligence process.

The realities of tactical intelligence can be summarized as a repetitive cycle of *collection, processing, dissemination* and *use.* Fundamental to the process is overall *direction.* This necessitates the establishment of *requirements:* What must the commander know? In what order of priority is the intelligence to be provided? The intelligence officer must then look to available sources to collect the information which must then be *recorded, evaluated* as to accuracy and reliability and then *interpreted* as to meaning. When this is accomplished, the intelligence must be *disseminated* to those who need it. If all or most of the intelligence gathering systems are fully functional in an active situation, the volume can become quite high and great care must be exercised to ensure that the critical evaluation, interpretation and dissemination activities do not become inundated and unable to operate properly. This, of course, is dependent upon proper direction.

Intelligence is an art rather than a science (although modern science contributes a great deal to its work). Thus, while the intelligence officer must be an "artist", not everyone can be a Michelangelo or Rembrandt. With information and intelligence originating from many sources and (in the case of alliances) from many nations, responding to a vast list of requirements,

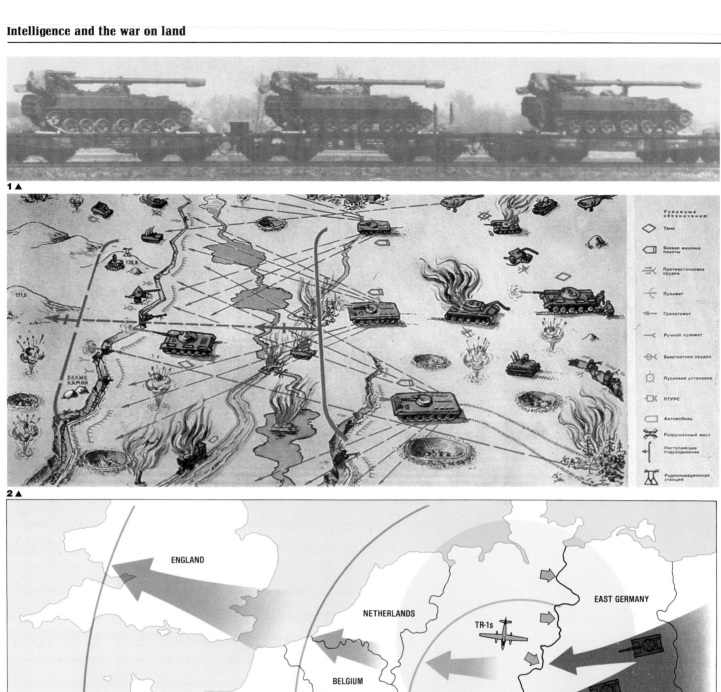

1 ▲

2 ▲

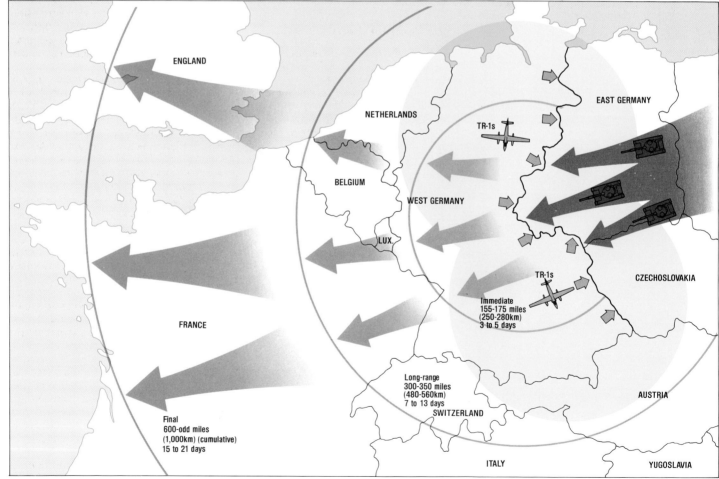

POTENTIAL WARSAW PACT THRUST ACROSS CENTRAL EUROPE

Intelligence staffs have three main tasks. First, discover the potential enemy's order of battle, his strategy and tactics, and his equipment. Then assess his capabili-

ties. These are relatively simple compared with the third: assess his intentions, which can either change overnight or be changed covertly over a long period.

This map shows what might happen to Western Europe if NATO intelligence staffs fail in their third task. Each red arrow represents an Army across a front 25

to 50 miles (40-80km) wide; 52,000 men, 1,000 tanks, 2,000 APCs and over a thousand guns. Their build-up and thrust is being monitored progres-

sively by TR-1 and other reconnaissance aircraft, and ground units. The further the advance, the more is known about the attackers. Cold comfort . . .

Key
Each arrow represents one Warsaw Pact Army.

3 ▲

1 New items of enemy equipment must be quickly identified and analysed. These are the brand new 152mm SP guns of the Soviet Army on rail-flats in East Germany; who took the picture?

2 Tactics, too, must be analysed and counterplans prepared; this is from a Soviet manual on platoon tactics.

3 Revealed at last is the object of a 10-year Western intelligence operation: the Soviet T-80.

4 Following analysis of NATO anti-tank tactics, the Soviets are rethinking their tank drills.

5 Pictures such as this can be used to deduce tank, and tank/infantry tactics and drills.

4 ▲

5 ▲

some means of discrimination must be applied so that commanders and staffs all receive the intelligence they need, and are not inundated with irrelevant data. This difficult task is undertaken by the establishment of fusion centres at appropriate levels of command. These centres receive data and information as well as processed intelligence, sort it out and then distribute it to the appropriate users in accordance with prior established requirements, which are thereafter changed as needed. Modern computers can lighten the administrative burden on intelligence specialists, enabling them to concentrate on substantive work. Considerable use is made of modern communications systems to accomplish this work; however, modern forces must cope with situations in which communications may be disrupted, jammed or interrupted and they must then rely on couriers — airborne, ground vehicles or even on foot. Various alternative light, sound and visual signals can be used as well.

The accompanying diagram illustrates Warsaw Pact conceptual front operations in an offensive mode. First echelon attacking formations are concentrated in an area approximately 62 miles (100km) deep and 125 to 155 miles (200 to 250km) wide. According to published Warsaw Pact doctrine, immediate objectives of 155 miles to 175 miles (250 to 280km) are sought to be achieved within 3 to 5 days after initiation.

Forecasting a massive attack

Seen from the viewpoint of the NATO intelligence officer, it must be recognized that *assembling* the numbers of troops displayed in the diagram and *moving* them into their attack position requires many actions which have a high probability of providing some advance indication; human sources, active or passive sensors including advanced technology equipment, could deliver an instant glimpse some 50 to 250km beyond the East German border.

While Warsaw Pact forces, doctrinally, do not place extensive reliance upon electronic communications as do NATO forces, it is nevertheless virtually inevitable that in an attack, moving out of their own area, the offensive forces would resort to electronic communications at some time in order to control movement and maintain effective command. Warsaw Pact forces, as indicated in the chapter on intelligence in the electronic battlefield, have an impressive jamming capability. However, Pact forces employ mainly "barrage" jamming techniques which tend to interfere also with the barrage jammers' own communications. While both sides could employ a wide variety of alternative communications this, in turn, could cause delay and slow down operations. Certainly, the ambitious objectives shown in the diagram would become difficult to achieve. Electromagnetic Pulse (EMP) generated by a high-altitude nuclear explosion could also neutralize unprotected communications using modern, solid-state circuitry — with similar results.

The historical "rule of thumb" used by ground tactical intelligence officers is that 10 to 20 per cent of the enemy's situation can be learned in each day of contact. Thus, when even one or two days of contact are added to the store of basic intelligence existing the tactical intelligence officer has a good overall view. However, the major problem which can be anticipated is that of analysis. With all of the modern techniques now available the biggest obstacle to effective tactical intelligence now has shifted from collection to the interpretation and assessment factors of intelligence analysis.

For example, it is not a difficult task to count the numbers of various items of military equipment. It is quite another matter, however, to determine the capabilities of many items, or to determine the enemy's assessment of his equipment capability, and, most difficult, to answer the question, "given the enemy's assessment of his equipment, what does he intend to do with it?" As Ray Cline has commented in the introduction to this book: you cannot photograph what a man is thinking.

The analyst must be concerned to have all of the information needed as soon as possible but equally concerned to avoid being inundated with trivial or irrelevant matter. Thus, while Lieutenant Colonel A, commanding an infantry battalion, may be vitally interested in the fact that 20 enemy soldiers are observed in a position 1km to his front, this is of distinctly lesser concern to Colonel B, the Corps intelligence officer. The most effective use of tactical intelligence will occur in those cases where careful planning and realistic training, and proper fusion of intelligence at appropriate levels have all occurred in advanced of the need.

With a variety of systems supplying intelligence information, the intelligence staff can provide NATO commanders with timely information which could enable them to react to a variety of situations in a timely way. The scenario depicted in the diagram, together with existing tactical intelligence resources, illustrates a situation in which NATO commanders and their intelligence staffs could expect to meet a threatening contingency with confidence. However, it must always be kept in mind that tactical or strategic surprise, if or whenever it occurs, can be complex and responsibilities can be diffused due to bureaucratic functions. Surprise can occur through gaps in vital intelligence or because the intelligence, being ambiguous, is not interpreted accurately, or even because some vital element of data has been transmitted incorrectly or has been overlooked. Even where all elements of intelligence may coincide properly, the danger is always present that the human factor can defer a needed decision until it is too late because the analyst is not sufficiently convincing or because introduction of some novel factor into the picture by the enemy has misled the decisionmaker.

There is no simple answer to this problem. Intelligence now plays a greater role in determining the outcome of military conflict and failures of command or inadequate intelligence will exact a heavy penalty. Conversely, proper investments in effective intelligence can guard against — or mitigate — such occurrences.

Chapter nine

Intelligence and the war at sea

THE INTELLIGENCE battle at sea concentrated for centuries on the movement of surface ships, with the knowledge of enemy maritime activities being derived from visual sightings at sea, supplemented occasionally by espionage. Even when such sightings had been made there were great problems in passing the information to the fleet. Whatever the means used on land, speed afloat was always reduced to that of a sailing ship. The invention of wireless telegraphy was quickly seized upon by various navies for its ability to pass intelligence on enemy movements. Thus, in World War I the movement of fleets and of individual ships was controlled and coordinated by ratio at a time when armies depended almost totally on land-line telegraphy/telephony and the physical delivery of messages. For the navies the use of radio for passing commands and information spurred the practice of interception of enemy radio communications, followed by the widespread use of encryption systems as a countermeasure. In both world wars one of the most critical victories was the capture of the enemy's naval cipher.

In World War I two new elements crept into the naval picture. The first was aircraft —both fixed wing and lighter-than-air— which extended the eyes and ears of the naval intelligence staffs as well as giving some promise of offensive capability. The second was the submarine which developed from a somewhat eccentric toy in 1914 to a major strategic weapon in 1917.

In the inter-war years the funds allocated to research in virtually all maritime nations was meagre, but despite conflicting claims for the money the ability to search for surface and underwater vessels was pursued. In the former a major breakthrough came with the invention of radar, which at last enabled a naval commander to see through bad visibility and to detect ships and aircraft when the "Mark I Eyeball" could not do so. The breakthrough was known in the UK as "ASDIC" (derived from the name of the Allied Submarine Detection Investigation Committee) and elsewhere as "sonar" (from Sound Navigation and Ranging). Both radar and sonar depend upon the same basic technique: the transmission of an electromagnetic pulse and the detection, by a very sensitive receiver, of the minute amount of energy reflected back by a target. The unique characteristics of the media in which they operate—air and water— account for the major difference, radar being in the radio frequency band, while sonar operates in the audio frequency range.

At the end of World War II the position with radar was that any suitably equipped ship could find another ship in any weather out to a range which depended upon certain well understood parameters. The ability to detect enemy radar transmissions was shared by all navies, but there was little possibility of misleading the enemy totally. Thus, there is no maritime equivalent of an aircraft's ability to "fly under the radar", and while an enemy surface radar can be confused or duped it cannot be defeated altogether.

Throughout World War II aircraft were used to locate, identify and track enemy ships, using visual means first, but subsequently extending their range by the use of airborne radar. A major breakthrough has come recently with the use of surveillance devices mounted in space satellites, which with a combination of photographic and radar sensors can locate any surface vessel at any time, limited only, so far as is known, by exceptionally severe terrestrial weather. With real-time down-links naval commanders of the more advanced navies will know precisely where their opponents are at any time. It is, indeed, not inconceivable that such systems could also identify the type of ship, if not the individual class as well (ie, cruiser, destroyer), judging by the shape and size of the return signal.

Man's limited knowledge of the sea

Man is essentially a land animal and over the centuries has come to terms with this environment. Many centuries of sea-faring have for long given the impression that man was also starting to understand the oceans, but it is only now being realised that man's knowledge of the sea is, both literally and metaphorically, confined to the surface, and that the sea is actually a three-dimensional world about which comparatively little is known. Indeed, man probably knows more about the topography, climate, environment and the resources of the Moon than about the oceans.

It is worth reiterating that the Earth's surface is predominantly oceanic, the ratio of land to sea being 1:2.43 or 29.2:70.8 per cent. Unlike the land, the oceans form a continuous belt around the Earth with a total volume of some 1.3×10^{27} cu yd (1 billion cu km). This is a most important factor in the intelligence battle at sea, because the oceans are still largely unex-

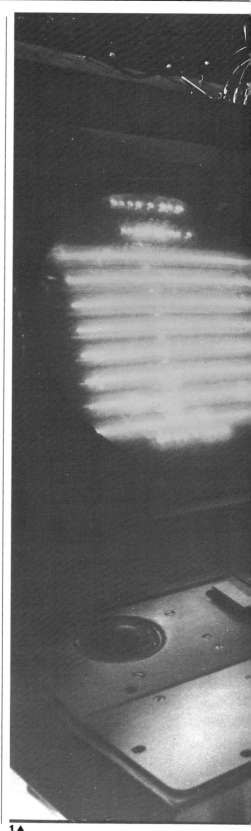

1 Exemplifying the electronics orientation of the naval intelligence battle, these Royal Navy crewmen search their sonars for threats to the fleet.

1 ▲

Although man's knowledge of the sea is limited largely to its
surface, the intelligence battle concerning what
goes on beneath, on and above the three-dimensional oceans
is vital to freedom of movement of the world's navies
and strategic supplies.

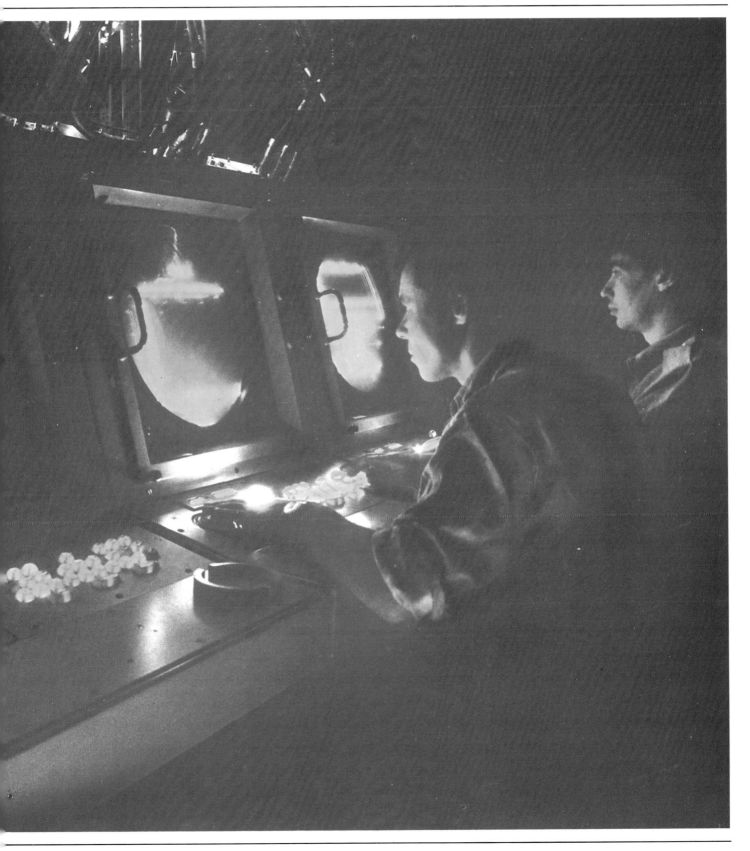

plored and many aspects of their properties and behaviour are even now only imperfectly understood.

One of the major reasons for the intensity of the maritime intelligence battle in peace is that if the predictions for a short war are correct (and military strategists must always plan for such a "worst-case" situation) then the strength and dispositions of the opposing naval forces at the opening of the conflict will be crucial. It follows from this that an aggressor will seek to obtain an advantage over the victim in the opening phases of such a conflict by sending as many ships as possible—both surface and sub-surface—to sea prior to the outbreak of hostilities. This would involve a change in the pattern of deployments, and both sides are thus constantly seeking to identify the "normal" pattern of deployments for any potential enemy, and then watching for, and analysing, any deviations.

In the submarine sphere, for example, NATO has established over a long period that the usual Soviet deployment pattern is for some 13 FBMSs to be at sea at any one time; therefore any increase beyond the normal reliefs becomes a matter for concern. Similarly, in the Falklands War of Spring 1982 the first serious indication to the British naval planners that the Argentinians might be about to invade was when their fleet veered away from its usual exercise area and headed for the disputed islands. Unfortunately for the British it was then too late, as they had no warships anywhere in the area which could take effective action.

No major naval battles since 1945

There have been many advances in naval tactics, weapons and systems, and in command, control and intelligence methods since the last major fleet actions in 1944-45. There have, of course, been numerous instances of the use of naval forces, eg, in Korea, Suez (1956), the Vietnam War and in the various Middle East conflicts, but these were all either very one-sided affairs (in naval terms), or involved simple ship-to-ship engagements. When, therefore, the British Royal Navy task force set off for the Falkland Islands in May 1982 all naval eyes focused on the conflict to see what promised to be the first-ever fleet engagement between the new and untried generation of ships and equipment. In the event a major surface action never took place although the naval war was intense and crucial to the outcome of the campaign; most intense of all, in fact, was the intelligence war which was fought with unremitting zeal by both sides.

The Royal Navy was constantly endeavouring to ascertain the whereabouts and operational status of the five Argentinian vessels, any of which might have been able to change the course of the war. These were the aircraft carrier 25 de Mayo, the cruiser General Belgrano and three submarines— one ex-US Guppy type, the Sante Fe and two German Type 209s, the Salta and the San Luis. The Santa Fe was disabled early on during the retaking of South Georgia and the General Belgrano was sunk south of the Falklands shortly afterwards.

This particular action in sinking the elderly cruiser was a classic intelligence dilemma. Once the ship was spotted by a British submarine the problem was to try to assess her captain's intentions. He could have simply been carrying out a foray to satisfy the Argentinian Navy's desire to make a gesture, following which she would have turned for home. On the other hand she could have been preparing to turn north and run in towards the British task force, possibly in conjunction with an air strike, intending to cause damage to the two aircraft carriers which were absolutely vital to the British operation. In the event the British War Cabinet appears to have taken the view that the military consequences of inaction would have been far more severe than the political repercussions of sinking her, and they issued their instructions accordingly.

That left the 25 de Mayo, the Salta and the San Luis. The carrier appears to have spent most of the war in harbour undergoing repairs, and she was too large a ship to have sailed undetected. The two Type 209 submarines, however, were quite another matter, and the British task force devoted considerable efforts and resources to seeking them out. Various anti-submarine actions took place, but whether the targets were either of the two Argentinian submarines is not known.

On the other side the Argentinian Navy was absolutely crippled by its inability to locate the British nuclear hunter-killer submarines (SSNs). Their problems started with a considerable intelligence coup by the British, who declined to confirm or deny newspaper and TV reports that HMS Superb (S109) was in the South Atlantic, and as a result the Argentinian Navy had little option but to assume that she was there. It later transpired that Superb was thousands of miles away and had never been anywhere near the Falklands, and the Argentinian admirals must have felt very foolish.

Following proof positive of the presence of British SSNs (on the sinking of the Belgrano), the Argentinian fleet remained within the 12 mile limit dictated by Britain because their very limited ASW capability was quite unable to cope with the threat. This meant that the Argentinian admirals were blinded by their lack of intelligence in this sphere just as the British fleet was by its lack of AEW aircraft, as a result of which so much damage was done by Argentinian aircraft strikes.

Maritime trade vital to West

Strategically the world's oceans are every bit as important now as they have ever been, carrying vast quantities of international commerce. Taking oil alone as an example 1,563 million tonnes were moved by sea in the year 1978 of which 1,271 million tonnes were destined for NATO countries, Japan and Australasia. Many other energy source materials (eg, bulk natural gas) are moved by sea as are virtually all raw materials. A glance at a map shows, however, that it is the West that is dependent upon the sea. For the Soviet Union trade or travel by sea is a bonus; neither is critical to national survival.

CHARACTERISTICS OF THE OCEANS

ITEM	MAGNITUDE	
	IMPERIAL	METRIC
Earth's total surface area	197×10^6sq m	510×10^6km²
Land surface area	57.5×10^6sq m	149×10^6km²
Ocean surface area	139.4×10^6sq m	361×10^6km²
Ocean volume		$1,370 \times 10^6$km³
Ocean average depth	12,450ft	3,795m
Pacific average depth	13,215ft	4,028m
Atlantic average depth	10,932ft	3,332m
Indian average depth	12,785ft	3,897m
Ocean mean temperature	39.02°F	3.90°C
Seawater mean density		1.03gm/cm³

DIMENSIONS OF SOME PACIFIC TRENCHES

TRENCH	DEPTH	APPROX WIDTH	APPROX LENGTH
Aleutian	26,575ft (8,100m)	43.5 miles (70km)	1,429 miles (2,300km)
Kurile	34,587ft (10,542m)	74.6 miles (120km)	1,367 miles (2,200km)
Japan	32,185ft (9,810m)	62.1 miles (100km)	559 miles (900km)
Mariana	36,200ft (11,034m)	43.5 miles (70km)	1,584 miles (2,550km)
Tonga	35,702ft (10,882m)	34.2 miles (55km)	870 miles (1,400km)
Peru-Chile	26,427ft (8,055m)	43.5 miles (70km)	3,666 miles (5,900km)

THE MAJOR CONSTITUENTS OF SEA-WATER

SUBSTANCE	CHEMICAL SYMBOL	% BY WEIGHT OF THE TOTAL MAJOR CONSTITUENTS
Sodium	Na	30.62
Magnesium	Mg	3.68
Calcium	Ca	1.18
Potassium	K	1.10
Strontium	Sr	0.02
Chloride	Cl	55.07
Sulphate	SO_4	7.72
Bicarbonate	HCO_3	0.40
Bromide	Br	0.19
Borate	H_2BO_3	0.01
Fluoride	F	0.01

CONVERSION FACTORS

1 fathom = 6ft = 1.82m	1 nautical mile = 6,080ft = 1,853km
1 metre = 3.28ft = 0.55 fathom	1km = 0.62 miles = 0.539 nautical miles
1 knot = 1 nautical mph = 1.15mph=1.853 km/hour	

1 The Argentine cruiser General Belgrano in harbour shortly before her ill-fated foray towards the Falklands. It would appear that her ASW sensors never even detected the British SSN before the torpedoes struck.

4 "Chaff" can be used to reduce radar performance and confuse guided weapons, as the British did in the Falklands. Here it is seen being used in the Straits of Dover during a recent exercise.

2 The British frigate HMS Antelope sinking in San Carlos Water on May 24, 1982. The bravery of the Argentine pilots was a complete surprise.

3 Two British sailors on HMS Invincible maintain contact with the protecting screen of escorting destroyers and frigates.

5 If the British forces had had a Nimrod AEW Mark 3 available in the Falklands War, there would not have been so many ship losses.

1 ▲

2 ▲

3 ▲

4 ▲

5 ▲

This maritime trade could not simply cease in time of war. Many so-called strategic commodities are stockpiled in most countries (eg, oil, coal, sugar, cereals) but these would last for only a very limited period, and a continuation of maritime resupply would be essential. Further, in periods of crisis and war military movements by sea on a large scale would be absolutely essential, especially across the north Atlantic. The British naval deployment to the Falklands Islands reminded the world of the importance of such movement by sea, but that was all achieved without any significant inteference from the Argentinian Navy on the route down. It is inconceivable that the Soviet Navy would allow NATO navies such a free run across the north Atlantic in any future conflict.

If NATO admirals are going to have a major task in fighting to keep the sea lanes open it should not be thought that the Soviet Navy will have everything its own way. Indeed, the Soviet Navy suffers from some very severe maritime problems, primarily because its fleet bases are all constricted in their access to the open ocean. The Northern

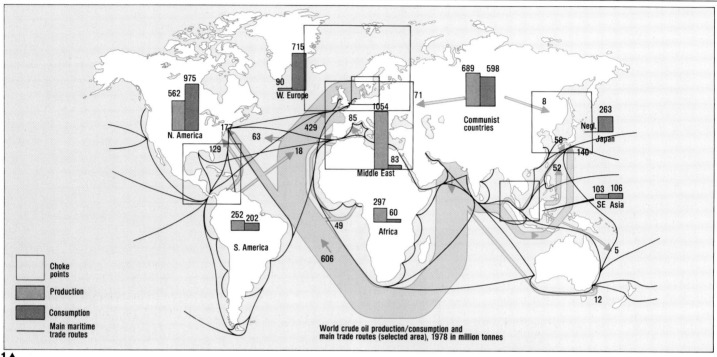

Choke points

Production

Consumption

Main maritime trade routes

World crude oil production/consumption and main trade routes (selected area), 1978 in million tonnes

1 ▲

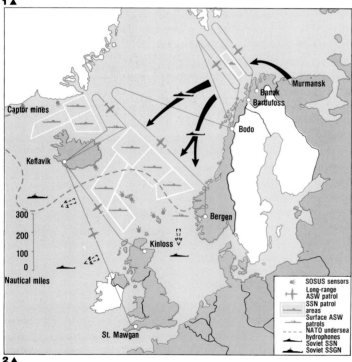

SOSUS sensors
Long-range ASW patrol
SSN patrol areas
Surface ASW patrols
NATO undersea hydrophones
Soviet SSN
Soviet SSGN

2 ▲

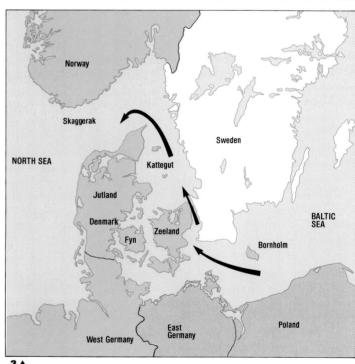

3 ▲

INTELLIGENCE AND THE STRATEGIC SIGNIFICANCE OF THE WORLD'S OCEANS

1 The top map shows world shipping routes, oil shipping routes and oil consumption. The world's oceans will always carry the lion's share of the West's international trade since it is only ships that have the bulk capacity to move the commodities at an economic rate. Further, the movement of military manpower, stores and fuel in major quantities still requires sea movement, especially the crucial US reinforcements to Europe in the early days of any future conflict. Unfortunately this dependence upon the sea really applies only to the West, because the USSR operates on interior lines and does not depend upon the sea for the strategic materials vital to its surivival.

2 One of the great naval intelligence battles is fought everyday in the Greenland/Iceland/UK (GIUK) gap. Any Soviet Navy ship requiring to leave the northern Russian ports must transit this gap, and NATO's concern is that the Soviets will try to build up their naval strengths in the open oceans as a prelude to major military action in Europe. This map, taken from a Soviet source, shows how they see the problem. The map also shows the value of Iceland to NATO and why the USSR would so dearly love to prise the Icelanders away from the Alliance.

3 The Soviet Navy has a considerable fleet in the Baltic, with its HQ at Leningrad. Operations in the Baltic itself would be of considerable value, but the Baltic Fleet would be bottled up until and unless the USSR was able to obtain control of the sound between the Danish island of Zeeland and the Swedish coast, and of the Skaggerak. The importance of Sweden in the Baltic is clear, and recent Soviet submarine operations inside Swedish territorial waters suggest that they have plans to use them in war.

4 More naval "choke points" are to be found in the Caribbean. For a century the Americans have been able to consider themselves in control of the waters surrounding CONUS, but Soviet penetration, especially in Cuba, has changed all

Fleet must move round Norway's North Cape and then transit through the heavily protected Greenland-Iceland-United Kingdom (GIUK) gap before reaching the Atlantic, whilst the Baltic and Black Sea Fleets must pass through the Kattegat and Bosphorus, and even then will find themselves in the relatively restricted waters of the North Sea and the Mediterranean.

These problems are fundamentally similar to those which faced the German Navy in the two World Wars, but the Soviet Navy does have another option resulting from its possession of a Pacific Fleet, based on Vladivostok. Even this, however, is not at all ideally placed and egress from the Sea of Okhotsk into the Pacific, or from the Sea of Japan into the China Sea, will not be easy.

Admiral Gorshkov, the commander-in-chief of the Soviet Navy, wrote in the 1976 edition of the *Soviet Military Encyclopedia* that a third priority had been added to the Navy's previous two missions of strategic and counterforce tasks. This third priority, that of the interdiction of enemy sea communications, means that the Soviet Navy has now been formally tasked with getting

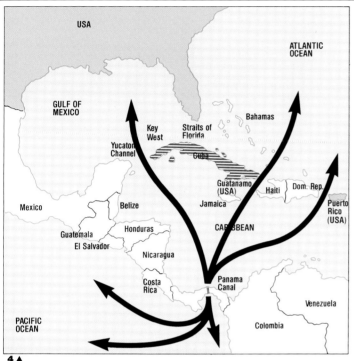

4 ▲

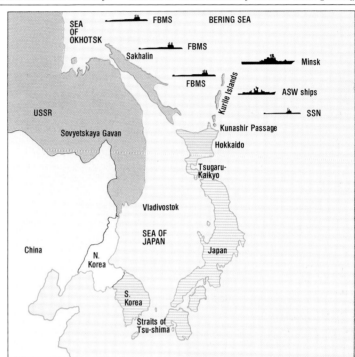

6 ▲

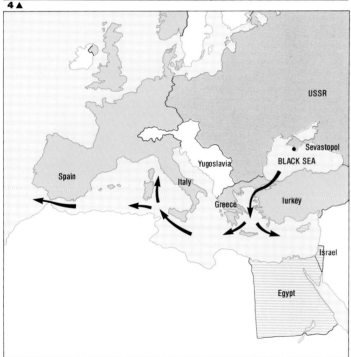

5 ▲

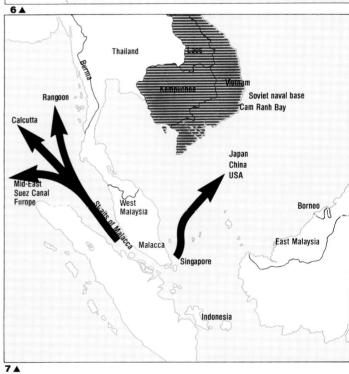

7 ▲

that. Some 65 per cent of all US oil imports go through either the Florida Straits or the Yucatan Channel, both of which are dominated by Cuba. Also, the routes to and from the Panama Canal lie through either the Yucatan Channel or through the Paso de los Vientos between Haiti and Cuba. The reverse side of the coin is that in a war Cuba

would be totally isolated from its sponsor and were it to fight it would have to be with what was available at the time; there could be no reinforcement.

6 The Soviet Pacific Fleet is based on Vladivostok (the HQ), Sovyetskaya Gavan and Petropavolvsk, but none of these has direct access to the open ocean. The

Kurile Islands stretch in an arc between the Kamchatka Peninsula and Hokkaido and all these islands have been firmly in Japanese hands since 1945. The major exit to the Pacific is the Kunashir Passage, between Kunashir Island and Hokkaido. Petropavlovsk does have direct access to the Pacific and is south of the ice limits, but it is

totally cut-off from the rest of the Soviet Union.

5 The Mediterranean poses severe problems for the Soviet Black Sea Fleet with choke points in the Bosphorus, the Aegean Islands, the Straits of Kithera and Karpathos in the Aegean, and then the Sicilian Channel and the Straits of Gibraltar. Following the collapse of

Soviet influence in Egypt the Suez Canal will be impassable in war without the use of considerable force.

7 Another choke point, frequently forgotten in the West, is the Straits of Malacca, which lie between the Malayan Peninsula and the Indonesian island of Sumatra. Virtually all

Japanese oil imports go through this passage and there is a strong feeling in naval circles that the Japanese should assume responsibility for keeping it open in time of war.

out into the open ocean and fighting a traditional maritime war.

In all this the naval intelligence problem for the two sides will be that of ensuring that they know where the other fleet is, its numbers, capabilities, condition and deployment, and what it may be planning to do next. This is a question which is little different for the NATO and Warsaw Pact admirals today from that which faced Drake and Medina-Sidonia in 1588, Nelson and Villeneuve in 1805, and Togo and Rozhdestvenski in 1904.

Naval intelligence is gathered from a variety of sources, some covert, but most overt and obvious. Espionage plays its part although it is scarcely surprising that the details are not known. It is, however, public knowledge that the USSR has for many years made especial efforts against anti-submarine warfare research and development establishments in a desperate effort to catch up with the Western navies in this field.

Every warship of every navy has, as one of its primary functions, the task of gathering intelligence by watching other navies' exercises, monitoring radio or radar transmissions, or simply observing oceanographic conditions. Such tasks not only help to train the ships' own crews but also serve to build up an overall picture of the capabilities of potential enemies.

Soviet spy trawlers

Some nations use specialist intelligence gathering ships, usually converted merchantmen. For many years these were small ships, mostly ex-trawlers, which have especially good sea-keeping qualities for their size. The USSR has built up the world's largest fleet of such vessels, which are normally referred to by their US Navy designation of AGI (Auxiliary Vessel, Miscellaneous type, Intelligence). These Soviet ships are a familiar sight on the world's oceans, particularly when a Western naval exercise is taking place.

The Soviet Navy originally utilised converted trawlers, a typical example being the *Okean* class of 720 tons displacement and with a crew of 32. Ever-increasing amounts of electronic gear and the requirement for more on-board specialists has led to an inexorable growth in the size and complement to the point where the latest ships—the *Balzam* class—are purpose-built intelligence gatherers of 4,000 tons displacement, and with a crew of 180. There is no doubt that the patient, plodding activities of these ships has not only helped to build up a detailed picture of the NATO naval strengths, tactics and deployment patterns, but has also saved years of research and experiment for the Soviet Navy in areas such as refuelling at sea, and the operation of aircraft carriers.

The Soviet Navy's AGIs are not on arbitrary routes, steaming around the oceans to see what they can pick up in the way of electronic intelligence. Rather, they are obviously following carefully planned missions, tasked by a central agency. That there are so many ships, and that they carry on with tasks long after a Western navy

1▲

2▲

1 The US Coastguard oceangoing tender USS *Conifer* keeping a Soviet trawler under observation off the coast of Virginia.

2 Converted trawlers no longer suffice and specially built AGIs are used; this is the Soviet Primorye class *Zakarpatye.*

3 Soviet oceanographic research ship *Khariton Lapter* monitors a Poseidon SLBM test firing off FLorida, July 31, 1970.

4 A Soviet AGI following USS *Franklin D. Roosevelt* in the Mediterranean. The Soviet Navy has saved years of research by its close observation of Western carrier operations.

5 Soviet navy AGIs cover every ocean in the world; this ship, the *Gidrofon*, is in the Gulf of Tonkin watching US Navy ships. In 1982 a Poseidon launch was delayed by Soviet spying.

3▲

4▲

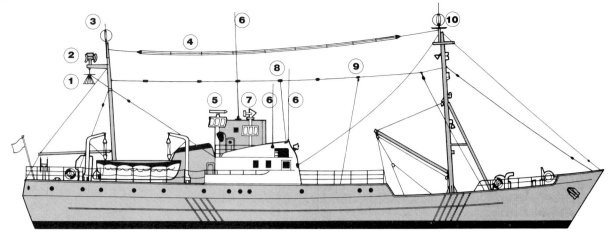

Communications fit on Okean "trawler"
(1) Disc cone omni-directional receiver antenna.
(2) Radar receiver.
(3) Direction-finding loop.
(4) Folded dipole for HF reception.
(5) Don 2 navigation radar.
(6) Vertical rod antennas.
(7) Radar receiver.
(8) Coaxial feeder to wire dipole antenna.
(9) Wire antenna apron for dipoles, end feds, etc.
(10) Direction-finding loop with Earthplane.

SOVIET SPY TRAWLERS

The Soviet Okean class trawlers were built in East German shipyards from 1959 to the mid-1960s. Of over 100 built, more than 20 have been converted to AGIs, and these are typical of the many small intelligence gathering ships which patrol the oceans under the Soviet flag. The particular version illustrated here exists in two ships only—the *Linza* and *Zond*—with the additional accommodation forward of the bridge.

AGIs such as these are used either to follow NATO fleets on the high seas, or to stay on a particular patrol line for a special purpose. One such AGI position is off the coast of Northern Ireland where the ship can monitor British Army and Royal Ulster Constabulary radio nets, as well as check on SSBNs entering and leaving the Clyde.

There are doubtless many sensors on these ships which are hidden, either in the superstructure or on the ship's bottom. The visible sensors have been marked on the drawing. There are direction-finding loops on the top of each mast. There is a large structure on top of the bridge, presumably containing extra working space for the monitoring specialists and for their equipment. Yet further working space is provided by the extension of the upper deck forward of the bridge. Displacement of Okean class AGIs is 720 tons; range is 7,500 miles (1,207km) at 11 knots.

Over the years these AGIs must have provided the USSR with vast amounts of information, some of it of great value, but much of it probably useless. Nevertheless, there can be no doubt that the AGIs have been able to monitor NATO exercises closely and to watch procedures on aircraft carriers and during underway replenishment which have subsequently been put to good use in the Soviet Navy.

The more modern AGIs, such as the *Primorye* class, are much larger, specially designed ships, and are doubtless much more comfortable for their crews than these rugged little ex-trawlers.

There is no such thing as a "standard" fit for these AGIs, and the same ship will appear with quite different antennas and sensors from one patrol to another. The fit depends, of course, on the mission.

5 ▲

SATELLITE SYSTEMS WITH MARITIME INTELLIGENCE FUNCTIONS																	
YEAR LAUNCHED	PHOTO-RECONNAISSANCE SATELLITES			ELECTRONIC SURVEILLANCE SATELLITES		EARLY WARNING SATELLITES		OCEAN SURVEILLANCE SATELLITES		NAVIGATION SATELLITES		COMMUNICATIONS SATELLITES			METEORO-LOGICAL SATELLITES		GEODETIC SATELLITES	
	USA	USSR	PRC	USA	USSR	USA	USSR	USA	USSR	USA	USSR	USA	USSR	NATO	USA	USSR	USA	USSR
1976	4	34	1	1	11	1	1	4	2	1	8	11	29	1	3	3	1	1
1977	3	33			8	2	3	4	3	1	8	4	16	1	2	3		1
1978	2	35	1	1	6	2	2	1			4	8	6	42	1	4		1
1979	2	35		1	5	2	2		3		6	3	27		2	4		
1980	2	35		1	6		5	4	4	2	6	3	36		2	2		
1981	2	37			4	2	5		8	1	5	2	39		2	2		

(Source: SIPRI Yearbook 1982, pp 304-305.)

1 ▲

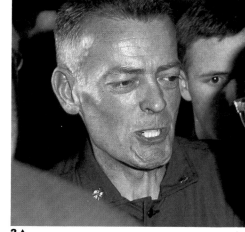

2 ▲

3 ▲

1 USS *Pueblo* (AGER-2), a US Navy electronic intelligence gathering vessel and direct equivalent of a Soviet AGI, achieved some notoriety when she was seized by the North Koreans on January 23, 1968. Many threats were made by the USA but no reprisals were taken.

2 The captain of the *Pueblo* and his crew were held captive in North Korea until December 22, 1968, when they were released under the terms of a complex deal arranged through the Mixed Armistice Commission at Panmunjom.

3 Oceanographic research ship, USS *Hayes*.

4 USS *Vanguard,* a missile tracking ship.

5 *Kosmonaut Vladimir Komarov* of Soviet Navy.

6 USS *Vandenberg,* US Navy missile range instrumentation ship, setting out to support a Trident 1 launch.

7 USS *Observation Island* fitted with a USAF Cobra Judy phased array radar for missile data collection.

8 Soviet Navy's space associated ship the *Kosmonaut Yuri Gargarin*.

9 A submarine communications system in which a radio beam uplink modulates the laser down-link. The radio signal also contains direction and signal strength commands.

10,11 Two different satcom antennas aboard US Navy ships. Such antennas have reduced dramatically in size and complexity in the past ten years.

12 A different type of satellite communication search antenna aboard USS *Schofield*. Ships fitted with this system have two antennas.

4 ▲

7 ▲

5 ▲

6 ▲

8 ▲

9 ▲

10 ▲

11 ▲

12 ▲

would have been forced through lack of resources to discontinue, are signs of the Soviet craving for ever more information on the West as well as of the virtually limitless resources of manpower available to the Soviet armed forces. The AGIs follow well-known patrol lines, sometimes sitting on the same station for months at a time, or they follow NATO ships on every conceivable mission. Their interests seem to be all-embracing, from missile launches to mine-sweeping, and from aircraft carriers flying-off their aircraft to the most humdrum of naval tasks.

A large part of the intelligence "take" must be recorded and taken home for analysis. Nevertheless, some "hot" items are sent home by faster means. There has for many years been a noticeable pattern of flights by Bear-D aircraft over AGIs, and it could well be that there are ship-to-aircraft links over which information can be passed. Such information is now, however, more likely to be passed over a satellite link. Quite a number of AGIs now have large rectangular housings on the bridge and one possible use of this is to cover a satellite communications antenna.

The US Navy also operated AGIs for many years and one of these — the USS *Pueblo* — achieved some notoriety when, on 23 January, 1968, she was seized by North Korean gunboats on the pretext that she had infringed that country's territorial waters. The crew were held captive for precisely 11 months and were released on 22 December, 1968.

Few other navies admit to possessing this type of specialised intelligence gatherer, but they undoubtedly do exist.

Satellite surveillance

In ocean surveillance the USSR appears at first sight to have a lead over the USA, but the fact is that satellites offer the Soviets the only practicable way of overcoming their chronic lack of overseas bases. *Cosmos 198* (December 1967) was the first test mission for a system which became operational in 1974. Two of these satellites were launched within a few days of each other, each carrying a powerful radar for locating ships in any weather and a radio-isotope thermal generator for the provision of power. These "nuclear-powered" satellites are supposed to split into two elements when they have completed their task, with the power element being boosted into a high orbit for safety, while the electronic elements are allowed to burn themselves up on re-entry. This has gone wrong twice, however, first in 1978 when *Cosmos 954* returned to earth complete with its nuclear package and crashed in northern Canada, and on a second occasion in January 1983 when control of *Cosmos 1402* was lost.

Following the *Cosmos 954* disaster the Soviet ocean surveillance programme underwent a reorientation; no satellites were launched in 1978, but two non-nuclear types were launched in April 1979, which were described at the time by US Secretary of Defense Harold Brown as being capable of targeting US Navy ships at sea. Also, since 1976 an advanced reconnaissance

satellite has been under development, which is believed to be based on a modified *Soyuz* spacecraft; the first was *Cosmos 758*. Initially there were about two launched per year, each having a lifetime of some 30 days.

The most advanced reconnaissance satellite is a modification of the *Salyut* space station, which gives the USSR a capability at least equal to that of the USA's KH-11 (*Key Hole*). With automatic un-manned resupply by *Progress* spacecraft or a manned shuttle they could conduct missions for well over a year in duration.

In contrast to the USA, the USSR was slow to fly weather satellites but since 1967 the *Meteor* series has been operational. Soviet navigation satellites use exactly the same procedures and frequency bands as the US Transits, and about five a year are launched.

One of the interesting aspects of the Soviet space programme is that they launch surveillance satellites to cover specific crises, and they can position them exactly where they need them to give the best coverage. The most recent example was one launched in May 1982 to cover the South Atlantic in general and the Falklands Islands in detail. Contrary to Press speculation at the time, this was most unlikely to have been used to provide information to the Argentinians (although a small amount of information may have been passed), but is far more likely to have been used to satisfy the Soviets' insatiable appetite for as much information as possible on any foreign military activity in order to improve their own forces. They would thus have been able to observe all the Argentinian missile attacks against the Royal Navy's ships, and the Royal Navy's defensive and offensive operations, and analyse the lessons for the benefit of the Soviet Navy.

The USA tends to launch far fewer satellites than the USSR, but its "birds" tend to be individually far more capable, and more flexible in their application. "Big Bird", for example, is launched at a rate of about two a year, with flight duration of 90-180 days. A CIA satellite, KH-11 is similar in size to Big Bird but uses a much higher orbit. Both have an application in the ocean surveillance role and in particular in monitoring SLBM launches.

The US Navy's Transit system is designed to provide position fixes for FBMSs, accurate to 0.1nm (160m). Its successor, soon to enter service, is the Navstar Global Positioning System which is accurate to 33ft (10m) if the full 24-satellite network is deployed, but it appears that budgetary restrictions will limit it to 18 with a decrease in accuracy to 53ft (16m). As an indication of the increasing threat to satellites it was announced in 1979 that Navstar will be fitted with devices to detect whether it is being illuminated by laser energy or has been touched by another satellite.

Satellites have up till now been used to gather information by various sensors and then pass it either physically or electronically to a land-based centre for interpretation analysis and dissemination. The need for up-to-the-minute information at

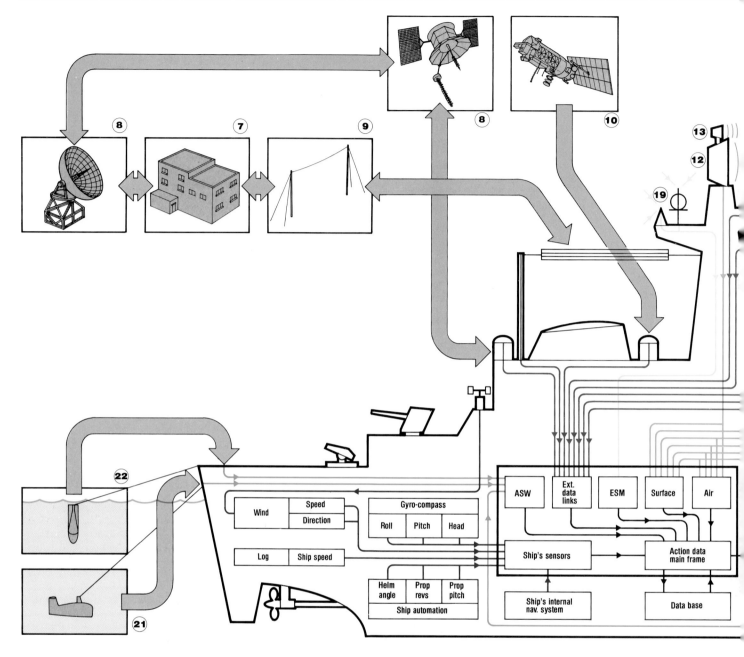

A SURFACE WARSHIP'S INTELLIGENCE SYSTEMS

Modern warships are designed to operate as part of a task group, deployed according to the commander's assessment of the threat. Here a ship is operating as part of such a group and the inputs which enable the captain to build up an overall intelligence picture are shown. The aircraft carrier (1) is passing information to all ships in the group, which, in turn, pass their "take" back to the flagship. Most task groups will have at least one submarine in company (2), although it is not easy to communicate to surface ships, and is being done here by a radio buoy (3) transmitting a message on a cassette recorder.

Further information is passed from any friendly aircraft in range: AEW (4), ASW (5), or recce (6). Data is also passed from the home base (7) by satellite (8) or high frequency radio (9). Further inputs come from sensor-equipped satellites (10). The ship's own sensors start with the helicopter (11) with an on-board data processing capability. Airspace surveillance is conducted by a large radar (12)

sea is now so urgent, however, that systems are being developed whereby satellites will pass their information in real-time by digital down-links direct to ships at sea. Indeed, the day is fast approaching where a task force commander could have satellites under his control as an integral part of his sensor and information gathering systems. Thus, AEW aircraft might become irrelevant if they can be replaced by equally reliable, but even more capable, surveillance and early-warning satellites.

Task group intelligence

No modern surface warship can exist in an operational environment on its own, except in the most unusual circumstances.

It will, therefore, almost always be the case that surface warships will combine together in a task group and not only will they act together in a tactical sense, but they will also cooperate totally in a full exchange of information and intelligence. Once achieved only by lengthy signals this interchange is now achieved by data links, which link the ships' automatic data processing systems together.

The commander is thus not only able to utilise sensors spread over a large area of ocean, but also has access to a database which, in a well trained naval force, should provide a capability greater than the sum of the individual components. Nor will the task groups act in isolation since they will have links back to their home base and to other task groups over which they will obtain

intelligence and information gathered by strategic means, eg, from ELINT operations.

The sensors now available to each ship are becoming increasingly numerous and individually more capable. Radars not only have very considerable ranges, but are also now able to provide three-dimensional pictures, while their associated computers are able automatically to allocate designations to tracks. Indeed, radar echoes, when associated with the pattern of electronic emissions (as identified by the ship's ESM suite) can well lead to the identification of a target by type, if not by individual ship.

Electronic countermeasure (ECM) and electronic counter-countermeasure (ECCM) outfits are now very elaborate and possess great capabilities. The antennae on modern

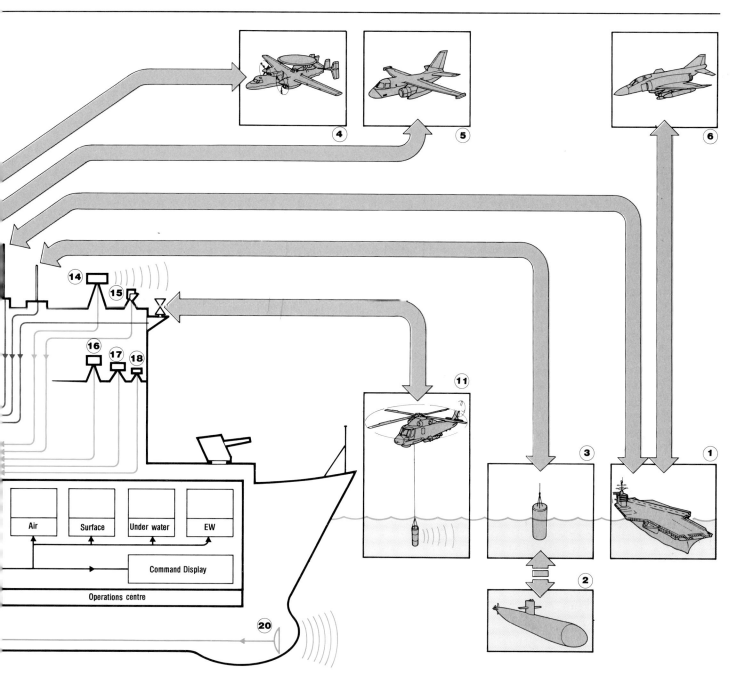

usually a mounted at the highest point of the ship's structure and incorporating IFF (13). Surface surveillance is conducted by radar (14), visually (15), and by infrared (16), image intensifier (17) and thermal imaging optronic devices (18). A whole range of devices conduct Electronic Support Measures (ESM) (19) which involves monitoring the electromagnetic spectrum, classifying enemy transmissions and taking the appropriate countermeasures. The ship's ASW sensors include bow-mounted sonar (20) and a variable-depth sonar (21). The temperature gradient is analysed by an expendable bathythermograph (22). All these inputs are integrated, processed, compared with the data-base, and then displayed in the operations centre. Operators can also select which information they want displayed on their screens, even that on another operator's screen. All this amounts to a major management problem, especially when fire control systems are added in as well.

Soviet Navy warships are far more numerous than those on an equivalent Western ship and they seem to have every frequency band and every mode of transmission covered. Their electronic warfare operations rooms must be very complex, and the management of all these inputs must require a very high degree of automation. (This is not to imply, of course, that warships of the more sophisticated Western navies are not equally capable in the EW sphere.)

Infra-red, image-intensification and thermal-imaging techniques are all now being used by various navies to augment direct observation. One of the major developments at sea, however, is the addition of a helicopter to a ship's outfit, to the extent that it is now virtually standard on all but the smallest ships (say, below 1,000 tons).

Where no aircraft carrier is available the helicopter gives an invaluable over-the-horizon capability for surveillance as well as providing a long-range anti-submarine capability.

The drive to learn more about the oceans is spurred by their rapidly increasing strategic importance, which has three main elements. The first is the traditional one of a trading highway, particularly for the West. Secondly, and growing rapidly in importance, are the economic resources of the sea: once confined to fishing, these are now expanding to include oil, minerals and, possibly, power. Thirdly, there is the military importance of the sea. In the past only a relatively small number of countries, such as the United Kingdom, have been strategically dependent upon the sea. Thus, for

example, in both world wars Germany could have defeated the UK at sea by starving her of food, fuel and munitions. Conversely, however, while the German Navy was defeated at sea in both wars this was no more than a setback for the Germans—for them the land battle was the critical one. So, too, Russia has for centuries been strategically undefeatable at sea; she has also lacked in the past the ability to menace anyone else at sea, either.

Today, however, the sea is militarily important as never before, due in the main to the existence of the fleet ballistic missile submarine (FBMS): both superpowers have sufficient nuclear weapons at sea in these boats to destroy each other. Further, since submarine detection is still a very imprecise science the FBMS is currently the ultimate deterrent, since it provides a survivable counter-value weapon system. Additional urgency is lent to the anti-submarine battle by the possibility that submarine-launched ballistic missiles (SLBMs) may be fitted with manoeuvrable re-entry vehicles (MaRVs). Because MaRVs have on-board facilities to guide them down onto a target with a precision measured in tens of metres, thus overcoming the inaccuracy inherent in current SLBMs, they appear to offer to the SSBN the possibility of a counter-force first-strike role.

If the oceans of the world are a vast area and imperfectly understood, and if they are of vital strategic importance, then it would naturally follow that great resources would be devoted to research and deep-ocean intelligence gathering. Surprisingly, this is not the case, although the USSR is allocating much greater resources to the problem than Western nations are. The Soviets deploy 56 oceanographic research ships (24 of which are "civilian" crewed), 130 surveying ships (35 crewed by civilians) and an unknown number of deep-diving craft (two are known to be associated with the sole India-class submarine). Against this, US naval resources include 14 oceanographic research ships (AGOR), 9 surveying ships (AGS) and 7 deep submergence vehicles, although other in-service ships are used in research activities from time to time. Some aircraft are also allotted, and there are a further 4 oceanographic and 3 hydrographic survey ships in the National Oceanic and Atmospheric Administration. The third strongest navy—the Royal Navy—has a meagre 4 ocean-going, 4 coastal and 5 inshore survey ships. The comment on this in *Jane's Fighting Ships* 1982-83 is worth repeating in full:

"In 1974 the Minister of State for Defence set up the Hydrographic Studies Group which reported on 27 March 1975. Among the recommendations made by this group was an increase of the Royal Navy's Hydrographic Service by 4 coastal survey ships between 1978-79. By this year (1982) the only change in this service has been a reduction of 2 inshore survey craft and the promise of an additional coastal survey ship in the future. With unstable areas in the southern North Sea/Channel area, the planned introduction of the Trident submarines and increasing offshore exploration, the UK is now seriously deficient in its hydrographic surveying capabilities."

Acoustical detection

The presence of a submarine in the ocean can be detected by a variety of means, although there is frequently a considerable gulf between an awareness that there is something somewhere and knowing exactly what the something is and precisely where it is. The main method of detection is acoustical. In the active method—sonar—an underwater sound pulse is transmitted and a receiver detects the reflected signal; in the passive method a listening device (hydrophone) simply attempts to hear and identify

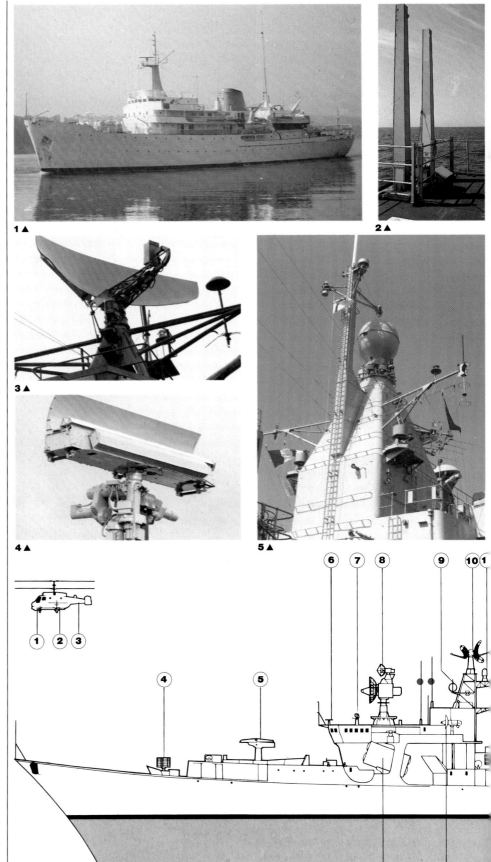

1 ▲   2 ▲

3 ▲

4 ▲   5 ▲

ELECTRONICS AND WEAPONS FIT OF A SOVIET KARA CLASS CRUISER

The electronics fit on a warship is a complex affair and must accommodate: surveillance radars, weapons control radars, navigation radars, sonar (both bow and variable-depth), electronic support measures (ESM) suite, electronic countermeasures (ECM) suite, and communications links. The art of fitting all these electronic devices into a hull which is both small and made of metal involves many compromises, and inevitably results in less than ideal positions and less than optimum performances. Shown here is a Soviet Navy Kara class ASW cruiser, but the general principles—and the problems—apply to all warships of all navies. *VDS* is the prime ASW detector and is streamed from the stern. *Headlight Group B* is the fire-control system for the

1 British oceanographic research ship HMS *Hecla*, part of a small fleet of such ships.

2 Twin Tilt radio antennas on the deck of USS *Hewitt*.

3 Plessey AWS-4 radar, gives general coverage of the surface.

4 Plessey Dolphin missile detection radar.

5 A plethora of radio and radar antennas on a French M-20 frigate.

6 US Navy SPS-39 planar array radar antenna

aboard the missile destroyer USS *Lawrence*.

7 A direction-finding (DF) antenna, used to find the bearing of hostile radio transmissions.

8 The enormous dome at the foot of the stern of USS *Spruance* houses the sonar transducer.

9 Sonar dome for a US Navy nuclear attack sub.

10 IFF antennas for a USN Aegis cruiser.

11 French air and surface surveillance radars.

10 ▲

6 ▲

8 ▲

11 ▲

7 ▲

9 ▲

Key:
(1) Radar.
(2) Dunking sonar.
(3) MAD.
(4) Anti-submarine rocket launcher.
(5) SA-N-3 launcher.
(6) Don-2 radar.
(7) Don Kay radar.

(8) Headlight Group B fire control system.
(9) Cross loop HF/DF.
(10) Head Net C radars.
(11) Bell ECM.
(12) High Pole IFF.
(13) Top Sail radar.
(14) Side Globe ESM antenna.

(15) Bass Tilt radar.
(16) Variable depth sonar (VDS).
(17) Torpedo tubes.
(18) Close-in weapon system.
(19) Pop Group fire control system.
(20) SA-N-4 launcher.

(21) Twin 76mm gun.
(22) Owl Screech fire control radar.
(23) SS-N-14 launcher.
(24) Hull-mounted sonar

● HF whip aerials
● Wire antennae (communications)

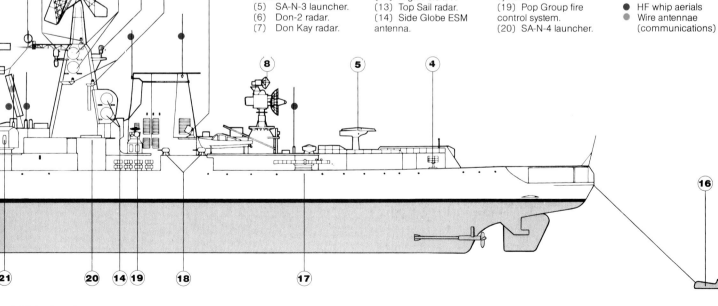

SA-N-3 missile batteries.
BassTilt is the fire-control radar for the Close-In Weapons Systems (CIWS).
Pop Group is the fire-control system for SA-N-4 air defence missile system.
Side Globe is an ESM

antenna; all modern Soviet warships have at least four; some have eight.
Top Sail is a long-range air surveillance and target designation radar, with an IFF antenna above the main array.

Head Net C is a back-to-back combination of two Head Net As set at a 30 degree angle to give a "V" beam for height-finding.
Owl Screech is a fire-control radar for the waist-mounted twin

76mm guns.
Don Kay is a conventional navigation radar.
Hull-mounted sonar is normally in the bow.
Kamov Hormone A is an integral part of the ship's sensor

and weapons systems. It has a chin-mounted radar, a dunking sonar and a Magnetic Anomaly Detector (MAD). A more specialised version, Hormone B has a larger

chin radome and retractable ventral radome. It is used to acquire targets for long-range anti-ship missiles.
Ships work in groups to make best use of their combined sensors.

1 The aim of intelligence is to detect and analyse military threats so that they can be countered effectively, and a new threat may demand new intelligence measures or a change in emphasis in old ones. Such processes are currently taking place because of the threat to land targets from weapons such as the USA's submarine-launched cruise missile. The SLCM is launched from a normal torpedo tube and about 33ft (10m) ahead of the sub a lanyard pulls taut and fires the boost motor. The missile then heads for the surface at an angle of 50 degrees and as it breaks the surface four tail fins spring open and lock into place, following which the wings deploy. The cruise engine starts up and the missile does a zero-G pushover to minimise the apogee to avoid detection by hostile radar, following which it descends to a very low altitude and heads towards the land. The land-attack version has TAINS guidance (TERCOM-Aided Inertial Navigation System). TERCOM (Terrain Comparison) matches the ground beneath the missile with on-board data fed in by the launch vessel before firing. It is used when crossing over the coast to provide a first position update and thereafter when passing over selected small matrix areas of terrain to update the inertial system which remains in command throughout. Everything about the mission profile of this missile is a challenge to intelligence systems.

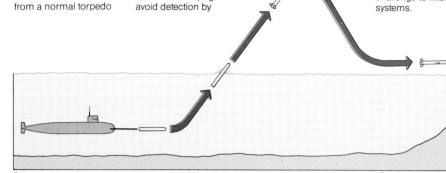

1 ▲

3 ▲

4 ▲

6 ▲

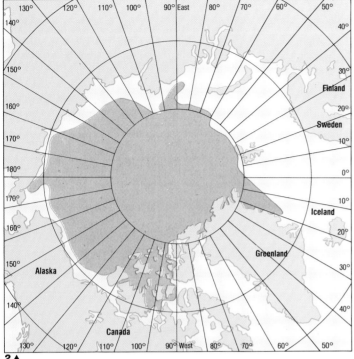

2 ▲

2 Mean ice conditions in the Northern Hemisphere, September 1 to 15. Nuclear powered submarines of the United States, Britain and the Soviet Union have publicly demonstrated the ability to move under this ice cap. During a conflict, doubtless FBMSs of both sides would seek to use its shelter for at least part of the time, although they would have to emerge into the open sea to launch their missiles. Methods of avoiding detection are as important as those to detect submarines. The oceans of the world, now designated "inner space", are so vast and unexplored that the battle for the control of this difficult and alien environment is only just beginning.

the passage of a foreign body through the ocean. Other, more esoteric methods are now being developed to try to overcome the increasing problems of ASW and the growing urgency of the threat.

In the past ASW has been a tactical operation, since the only threat was to friendly surface vessels. The range of the only weapon available to the submarine in World War II—the torpedo—was at the most some 11,000 yards (10km) and this determined the range at which detection was necessary. Today, however, three major changes have occurred. In the first the range of torpedoes has greatly increased; the Mark 48 torpedo, for example, used in the USN's current attack and fleet ballistic missile submarines, has a range of 30 miles (48km). Secondly, some submarines are now fitted with submarine-launched cruise missiles (SLCMs). One type of SLCM—the Soviet Navy's SS-N-7—has an anti-ship role with a range of some 62 miles (100km). Now, however, the US Navy is introducing into service the BGM-109 Tomahawk cruise missile with a range of 700 miles (1,126km). This is a land-attack missile, which is capable of carrying a nuclear warhead and is the latest manifestation of the capability which began with the Polaris—that of a submarine-based threat to the US and Soviet homelands.

Thus, whereas the ASW sphere of intelligence interest 40 years ago was a circle of some 20 miles (32km) around a surface task-group or convoy, the area now to be covered is the entire ocean. Further, because SLBMs are no longer range-limited, the launch vehicles (SSBNs) need not deploy outside their own country's immediate maritime zone, and at least some of the Soviet Navy's Delta-class SSBNs patrol within the limits of the Barents Sea in the west and of the Sea of Okhotsk in the east.

5 ▲

3 The Hotel II class SSBN moved the intelligence battle at sea into a totally new area, because this was the first submarine able to fire its missiles while submerged. The three fin-mounted missiles had a range of 994 miles (1,600km).

4 Another surfaced Hotel II. Deployed off the Western and Eastern seaboards of the USA, these boats threatened SAC bomber bases, not least because of the missiles' 6 to 10 minutes flight time. Hotel IIs now have a theatre role.

5 Soviet Echo II is armed with eight SS-N-3 cruise missiles and poses a significant threat to NATO task groups. The many holes and recesses cause a considerable noise underwater; thus detection is fairly simple.

6 After the unsophisticated Soviet ballistic missile submarines, the US SSBNs such as this Lafayette-class boat swung the balance firmly back in the US favour.

7 US Navy Trident I (C-4) SLBM is now operational and its range is such that the area of ocean to be searched by Soviet ASW forces has been enlarged by a factor of 100.

8 Both US and Soviet ASW forces must take into account in their intelligence operations the "third-nation" factor. This is a French MSBS M-20 SLBM.

9 USS *James Madison* displays her Poseidon missiles. The attempt to find a reliable means of tracking such boats seems as far away as ever —fortunately.

7 ▲

8 ▲

9 ▲

East/West ASW needs

The maritime problems facing NATO and Warsaw Pact navies are quite dissimilar because geography serves the two sides in different ways. Thus, the West needs ASW capability for two major tasks: to protect surface ships (task groups or convoys), or to detect FBMSs. To achieve these two disparate aims both passive detection devices (eg, seabed acoustic surveillance devices such as SOSUS) and the active detection/attack devices such as SSNs can be utilised for both missions. The Soviet Navy, however, does not have such a geographical ally and their submarines must pass through NATO-dominated choke points to reach their patrol areas and then transit great distances to reach their operational areas, usually having to cross at least one further SOSUS-type array in the process. The surface picture is, of course, the reverse, since it is the NATO maritime forces and commercial traffic which is most vulnerable at the surface choke points. As with the wartime German Navy, however, the USSR cannot be defeated by a naval victory, even if every Soviet naval ship is sunk.

A study of the great ASW problem cannot be undertaken without an understanding of the peculiar nature of the ocean.

Undersea speed of sound

The ocean is virtually opaque to most forms of radiant energy, but fortunately an exception to this is acoustic energy which can travel great distances under water. The exact speed of sound in water depends upon the precise combination of temperature, pressure and salinity, but an average speed is about 4,757ft per second (1,450 metres per second), some four times faster than the speed of sound in air—1,148ft per second (350 metres per second). Sound can be transmitted under water and a sensitive receiver will detect any return echoes, reflected in the main by solid objects. Unfortunately the science of sonar is by no means a simple one and the detection of an echo is just the start in a laborious process of trying to decide just where the reflecting body is and just what it might be. There are many factors which may affect this.

The oceans are a most complex environment with a dynamic nature equivalent in some ways to "weather" in the atmosphere, and whose nature is difficult to predict or characterise. The problems are due to man's only relatively recent interest in oceanography, to the sheer size of the oceans, to the paucity of resources so far allocated to research, and finally to the difficulty of getting there, and of on-site examination.

Indeed, only a few of the oceans' phenomena, such as surface wave activity, ice, tidal effects and local weather, can be observed by the human eye.

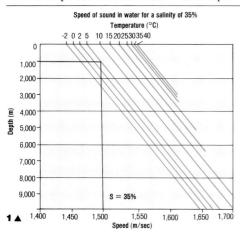

1 ▲

1 Salinity varies from 32 to 37 parts per thousand, but can fall to 23ppt in fjords. Diagram shows speed of sound in sea for a salinity level of 35%; eg, at 3,228ft (948m) and at 5°C, sound velocity is 4,904ft/sec (1,494m/sec).

2 ▲

Source: General Oceanography, by G. Dietrich and K. Kalle (Wiley-Interscience , New York)

2 Salinity levels vary: diagram shows the correction factors. If salinity level is actually 30%, speed of sound is 4,904ft/sec minus 26ft/sec (1,494 minus 7.9m/sec) giving a speed of 4,878ft/sec (1,486m/sec).

3 ▲

3. The different acoustic characteristics of the world's oceans are shown. Such variations might affect ASW aircraft on protracted patrol. Note how close to the surface is minimum sound depth in the Weddell.

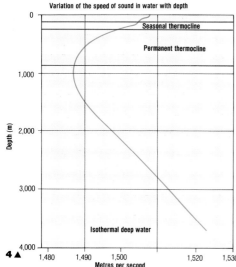

4 ▲

4 For acoustic detection of submarines to be effective precise knowledge of the speed of sound is essential. This graph shows a typical pattern in a temperate area. The layer of minimum velocity is the "deep sound channel".

6 ▲

7 ▲

6 Frogmen on exercises with the US Navy's Deep Submergence Rescue Vehicle (DSRV-1).

7 A PAP-104 mine hunting and destruction vehicle in service with the French Navy.

8 An American submersible rescue vehicle (DSRV-2) mounted on the after deck of the RN submarine HMS *Repulse*.

8 ▲

5 The vertical temperature distribution at a series of stations along a meridian in the Atlantic Ocean. Solar radiation heats the surface and it can be seen that the depth of this layer varies widely. Below this surface layer the temperature falls with depth in layers sometimes as small as 2-4 inches (5-10cm) until it reaches the thermocline, where it falls rapidly with depth until it stabilises and decreases evenly to the bottom.

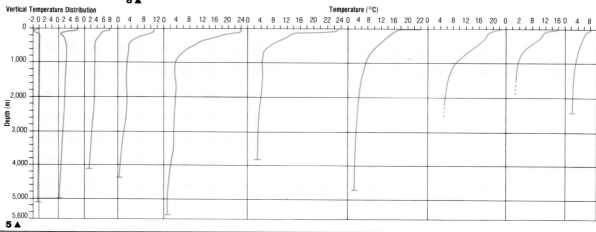

5 ▲

The major difference from fresh water is that the oceans contain many dissolved chemicals, including, of course, the characteristic salt (sodium chloride). The second well-known characteristic is that of depth and the corresponding increase in pressure. There are, however, many other factors such as variation in salinity (haloclines); variations in temperature (thermocline); sub-surface currents, counter-currents and waves; the effects of the topography and nature of the ocean bottom; and the exis-

tence of macro- and micro-organisms. All these in turn have effects on the optical and acoustic properties of the environment.

One of the major factors in ASW is the temperature structure of the sea. Solar radiation heats the surface layer of the ocean, the depth of this layer varying from tens of metres near the Equator to more than 100 metres in the high latitudes, and the temperature then falls with depth in layers as small as 2 to 4 inches (5 to 10cm) to a layer where it falls fairly sharply with depth (the

thermocline) and then decreases at a more gradual and even rate to the bottom. The depth at which the permanent thermocline is found varies from 984 to 1,312ft (300 to 400m) in equatorial areas to 1,640 to 3,280ft (500 to 1,000m) in sub-tropical areas. There is also a seasonal thermocline above the permanent thermocline and even, in some areas, a diurnal thermocline known more descriptively as the "afternoon effect".

The thermocline separates waters of slightly different densities, and a variety of

11 ▲

11 A US Navy Swimmer Delivery Vehicle underway at a depth of 35ft (10.6m). The vehicle is manned by men from an underwater demolition team and is engaged in a daylight recovery operation with the submarine USS *Grayback,* which can carry out clandestine operations. Note similarity to WW2 human torpedo.

12 Knowledge of sound velocity is essential to an ASW tactician and this Expendable Sound Velocimeter (XSV) is used to measure such velocities to an accuracy of ±0.82ft/sec (0.25m/sec) down to a depth of 6,560ft (2,000m). Data is read direct into onboard computer.

Grayback.
to WW2 human torpedo.

9 (A) Sound waves from a vessel above the thermocline gain in velocity as a function of depth until the thermocline reverses the trend, leading to sound "shadows".
(B) In the deep sound channel sound signals travel for great distances with little loss.
(C) At certain angles sound waves are refracted

in the depth of minimum velocity and return to the surface some distance away; in technical terms this is called convergence zone propagation.
(D) At certain angles sound waves bounce off the ocean floor and return to the surface, but within the convergence zone. Technically this is known as bottom bounce.

10 ASW aircraft, ASW ships and submarines all have an urgent need to know the temperature gradient of the ocean in which they are operating. This is done by an expendable bathy-thermograph which falls at a controlled rate, transmitting its readings up a wire (see graph). The only difference lies in the method of

launch. An aircraft XBT drops under rotochute control and a buoy then lowers the XBT, passing the readings back to the aircraft by radio. A surface ship needs only to drop the XBT over the side. However, for submarine operations a special float is necessary to ensure the wire does not foul the propeller.

12 ▲

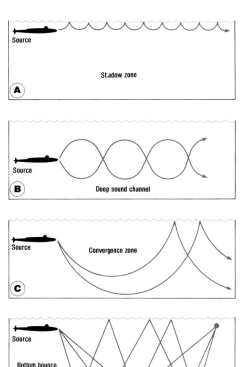

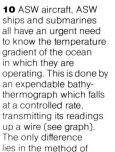
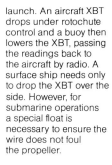
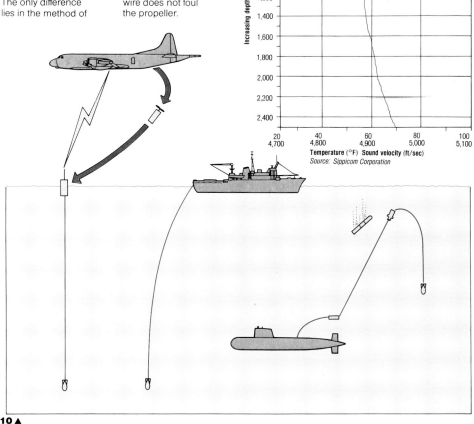

9 ▲

10 ▲

organic and inorganic particulates tend to concentrate in it since they lack sufficient energy to fall further into deeper water. Inorganic substances include the material deposited either deliberately or naturally from the land, products of erosion of both land and the ocean bed, and general debris. Organic objects in the thermocline are mainly planktonic organisms which attract fish and shrimps in large numbers.

The thermocline has a major influence on ASW as it affects the velocity of sound, and in the permanent thermocline the velocity reaches a minimum. This layer of minimum velocity, known as the deep sound channel, has a variety of effects, one of which is that a sound signal can travel in it for over 620 miles (1,000km) and still have 1 per cent of the energy it had 6.2 miles (10km) from the source.

The significant effect of this "layering" and of continuous variations of velocity with depth is that the paths of sound waves in the ocean are never straight lines, but are arcs of circles in accordance with Snell's Law.* Further, sound waves are scattered by the barriers of the oceanic medium at the surface and the bottom and this, combined with the circular arc trajectories, causes convergence of the sound paths leaving large volumes of the oceans which are just not penetrated by sound from a given source. This phenomenon, known as the "convergence zone" is quite independent of the power intensity of the sound wave. A submarine in this zone will not be detected even when it is very close to the sonar transmitter, and a number of warships were lost in World War II because of this effect.

If the acoustic transmitter is depressed below the horizontal and the depth of the water column is sufficient—more than 2,000 fathoms (3,650m)—the propagation path will bottom-out in the deep sound duct at the depth of minimum sound velocity and be refracted, returning to the surface some distance away. This convergence zone phenomenon occurs at about 38 nautical miles (70km) in tropical waters and about 22 nautical miles (40km) in northern waters and the Mediterranean. The width of these zones is about 5 to 10 per cent of the range. Increases in sound intensity of some 15 to 20dB in the convergence zone are common.

The transmission profile and the length of the convergence zone are also influenced by the depth of the water column and of the acoustic source and receiver. In shallower waters the type of bottom and its topography can affect the quality of the signal, with a smooth rocky bottom giving good reflection but mud, slime or sand causing considerable attenuation.

Ambient noise

The ocean itself is inherently noisy due to the abundance of marine life, seismic disturbances from underwater volcanoes and

* Snell's Law was discovered in relation to rays of light, but is equally applicable to sound waves in water. The consequence of Snell's Law is that where a sound wave passes from one layer to another of a different density the path of the wave is bent towards the normal when it enters a layer of greater density, or away from it if the density is lower. Thus, where the density alters gradually the sound wave will be bent (refracted) similarly.

SURVEY AND RESEARCH SHIPS OF THE WORLD'S NAVIES			
COUNTRY	**NO. OF SHIPS**	**COUNTRY**	**NO. OF SHIPS**
Argentina	4	**Malaysia**	1
Australia	4	**Mexico**	4
Belgium	2	**Netherlands**	3
Brazil	14	**Nigeria**	1
Bulgaria	3	**Pakistan**	2
Canada	4	**Peru**	4
Chile	1	**Philippines**	4
China (PRC)	27	**Poland**	3
Colombia	5	**Portugal**	4(1)
Cuba	13	**South Africa**	2
Denmark	9	**Spain**	6
Ecuador	2	**Sweden**	6
France	9(5)	**Taiwan**	4
Germany (DDR)	4	**Thailand**	6
Greece	3(1)	**Turkey**	5
India	5	**USSR**	127
Indonesia	4	**UK**	12
Iran	4	**USA**	14
Italy	4	**Venezuela**	3
Japan	7(1)	**Yugoslavia**	1
S. Korea	6		

(Source: *Jane's Fighting Ships 1982-83*)

3 ▲

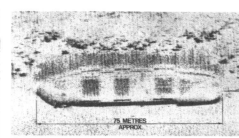
1 ▲

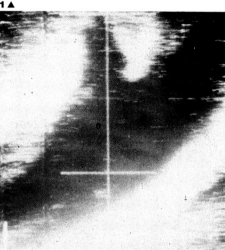
2 ▲

1 Underwater scanning methods are becoming increasingly sophisticated and effecitve; this is a sunken ammunition barge on the seabed, as shown by a Plessey Marine Speedscan record.

3 USS *Pigeon,* one of two ships of a class which can be used for submarine work (see below). They have catamaran hulls with a 34ft/10.4m well between, heavy-lift gear and multiple anchors.

2 A sonar "picture" of a sunken submarine. Clarity such as this may soon enable positive identifications to be made from sonar, even of individual named vessels, a development almost impossible to have foreseen even a few years ago.

5 An American H-bomb which fell into the sea after an aerial collision was found, photographed at 2,500ft (762m) as shown here, and then safely recovered.

4 The US Navy's Deep Submergence Rescue Vehicle (DSRV) is typical of a new type of vessel in many of the world's navies; the Soviet Navy has similar types used in association with the India class rescue submarine. In the US Navy a mission can be mounted from a surface vessel, e.g., Pigeon class, or from another submarine. Apart from its rescue role, however, the DSRV has an obvious intelligence application as it could be used in association with an SSBN/SSN for covert missions. The DSRV can be moved by truck or in an aircraft to the nearest port to the operational area and then meet up with the mother submarine. The DSRV is 49ft (15m) long and can accommodate up to 24 survivors from a submarine accident. It is constructed of formed fibreglass reinforced plastic with titanium and aluminium framings.

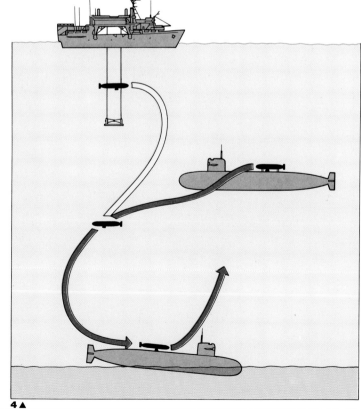
4 ▲

5▲

6▲

7▲

6 Specially developed photographic equipment is used by this underwater team whose role is described as "to disrupt and confuse the enemy". Such operations might include ASW activities.

7 A cable-controlled underwater vehicle designated CURV-111 in use on the seabed at the US Navy's Undersea Center at San Diego. This centre has also experimented with dolphins in an ASW role.

8 A stern view of the famous *Glomar Explorer* which was used to recover a sunken Soviet submarine in an operation involving Howard Hughes and the CIA. The specially built ship is now awaiting disposal.

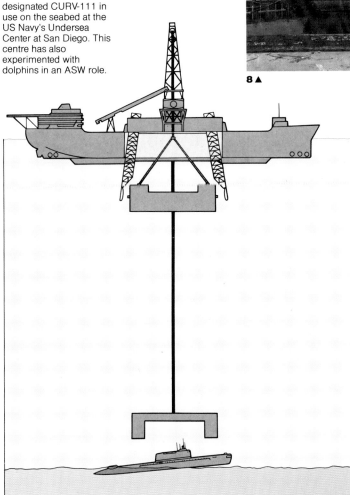

8▲

9▲

9 One of the most imaginative intelligence operations of recent times was the recovery of at least part of a sunken Soviet Golf class submarine in a combined USN/CIA operation "Project Jennifer". The submarine sank accidentally in the Pacific and the Soviet Navy presumably wrote it off since it lay at a depth of some 16,000ft (4,687m). The US Navy thought differently; they knew from their ASW detection systems the 10 mile square in which it had gone down and the USS *Mizar* was quickly able to pinpoint the wreck. Using the principle that any problem can be solved if enough money is thrown at it the Americans proceeded to build a 63,300-ton ship—the *Glomar Explorer*—for just this one mission. The diagram shows the enormous claw which was lowered from the centre of the vessel and brought the bow section up.

crashing of waves. In addition, there is a growing amount of man-made noise from merchant ship activities and "third nation" naval vessels, as well as increasing use of seismic exploration methods and offshore drilling on the ocean floor. The problem for the ASW operator is to recognise and screen out all these noise sources, whereas the submarine commander seeks to utilise them for his benefit.

Deep scattering layer

The deep scattering layer is usually composed of a thick layer and three sub-layers consisting of microscopic photo-plankton and zooplankton which reflect and scatter sound waves. The composition of the layer, its thickness and the depths at which it occurs all vary from area to area, and also by the time of day. Sound waves projected at or near the vertical will generally penetrate the layer, but if projected at or near the horizontal to the layer they will be scattered and diffracted. The effects of the deep scattering layer can be overcome by optimising the relationship of frequency, pulse length and power output, but often the ASW operator will have little choice but to resort to passive methods.

Average salinity

The average saline concentration in the open ocean is 34.5 parts per thousand (ppt), varying normally from 32 to 37 ppt. These variations are the consequence of a number of competing processes: concentration effects such as evaporation and ice-flow formation, and dilution effects such as rainfall, river run-off and melting ice. Sound velocity is affected by changes in salinity— 4.3 feet per second (1.31m per second) per 1 ppt change. Salinity is one of the least significant factors affecting sound propagation in water, but operationally salinity is important in areas of current mixing where sharp salinity gradients, coupled with sharp temperature gradients can produce a marked refraction of sound energy. They can also produce severe underwater turbulence, and are thought to have been at least partially responsible for the loss of the USS *Thresher*.*

Bathymetric effects

The bottom of the ocean can have two effects which seriously affect ASW. If the bottom topography is irregular and rocky there will be echoes from these surfaces and a submarine hugging the bottom in such circumstances may well escape detection due to the complexity of echoes returned to the detector. This effect is known as "reverberation".

Where the ocean bottom irregularities are sufficiently marked a submarine can shelter in the shadows of "hills". This is a

* The *USS Thresher* (SSN-593) underwent an overhaul in 1962/63 and in April 1963 went to sea on post-overhaul trials. She was about 220 miles (354km) east of Cape Cod when she was driven down to a depth where catastrophic hull failure occurred. In August 1963 the bathyscaphe *Trieste* found the wreck at a depth of 8,500ft (2,590m) and was able to photograph compressed elements of the ill-fated submarine, including her sail.

1 As water is a complex medium it is first necessary to establish existing conditions. Satellites monitor weather (1), seastate (2), oceanographic data (3) and thermal variations (4), while one of the functions of seabed surveillance systems (5) is to identify all unwanted noise sources, eg, fish. Another satellite (6) relates solar activity to natural variations in the earth's magnetic field. Merchant vessels (7) are eliminated either by voluntary reporting (8) or by satellite tracking of their radar emissions (9). The first step in tracking SSBNs is by satellite photography (10) as they leave port and by electronic monitoring by satellite (11) and land-based stations (12). ASW aircraft (13) use a combination of detectors including MAD, sono-buoys (14) thermal measurements (15) and forward-looking infrared

(16). Rapidly Deployed Surveillance System (17) is air-delivered. Surface ships (18) depend mainly on sonar, while ship-based helicopters (19) use both sonar and MAD. Attack submarines (20) depend upon sonar, both hull-mounted and towed. The critical passive devices are the USA's Sound Surveillance System (SOSUS) (5), and large coils (21) have been laid on the sea-bed to monitor variations in the electric field of the ocean. Finally traces of a submarine's passage can be detected

at considerable distances by Over-The-Horizon (Backscatter) radar (22), aircraft-counted FLIR (16) and satellite. All these sensors produce

such a vast volume of raw data that it must be fed into a computer for analysis (23). The Americans, for example, use a computer called

Illiac-4 for real-time collation and analysis of array-gathered information; this uses 64 normal computers in parallel, with a one-billion bit memory.

The purpose of all this in war is clear, but the ASW battle in peace is equally vital to establish deployment norms and to monitor changes.

particular case which illustrates that the more that is known about the ocean bed from oceanographic survey the more successfully will submarines be able to make use of the effect.

For the submariner a knowledge of the topography of the ocean bed is, of course, more than just being able to take advantage of it to hide from the enemy's sonar. For him a knowledge of the continental shelf is vital for survival as he must climb over the slope and the shelf proper on his return from a deep ocean patrol. Ballistic missile submarines either patrol the open ocean or under the ice cap and are unlikely to need detailed bathymetric information of such areas, but the attack submarines need this information, as well as for the bottom topography in operational areas such as the 1,000 fathom (1,820m) choke points.

Surface effects

The main effect of surface currents is upon sonobuoys as these will be dispersed from the impact point, thus affecting the accuracy of fixes on a target. Further, under

certain conditions sonobuoys moving with a current will give the impression that a stationary target is, in effect, moving in the reverse direction to that of the current.

Surface waves have a variety of effects, the principal one being that really severe conditions may eventually prevent the launching or recovery of helicopters, variable depth sonar (VDS) and towed arrays. Similarly, waves can degrade the performance of air-dropped sonobuoys, with a 75 per cent transmission loss in 10ft (3.04m) waves and a total loss in 15ft (4.57m) waves. In addition, high sea states cause a mixing of water on either side of the thermocline, giving a relatively thick layer of isothermal water which increases the noise problem for sonar systems. Finally, breaking waves add to the ambient noise levels, again adding to the sonar problem.

Weather also has its effects. Thunder, rain on the sea surface and associated wave activity all add to the ambient noise level over a very considerable area, decreasing the signal: noise ratio at receivers, and thus reducing target discrimination.

Above the surface is an atmospheric duct

which can be as much as 500 to 600ft (152 to 183m) thick, which can affect the electro-magnetic performance of ASW aircraft. If both transmitter and receiver are within the duct communications links are unlikely to be affected; indeed, range and detection will be enhanced. If, however, the ASW aircraft is above the duct not only will its radar fail to detect targets on the surface (periscope, sail, schnorkel) but its receivers will also fail to pick up signals from sonobuoys.

Detecting a submarine

A submarine moving in the ocean has a number of characteristics and causes certain effects, some or all of which may be utilised to detect its presence. Naval intelligence staffs, together with their research and development counterparts, are striving all the time to refine existing methods and to discover new ones in order to make the detection and localisation of an enemy submarine faster, more accurate and less prone to the vagaries of transitory and often capricious oceanic conditions.

2 US Navy divers checking the progress of lowering a submerged antenna array mounted on a barge, off Andros Island in the Bahamas. Note huge vertically oriented dish antennas.

3 The operator at the control station of the EDO Corporation Variable Depth Sonar System. His left hand is on the Action Entry Panel and his right is on the track ball for target designation. EDO also produce the world's fastest-towed sonar array.

4 Communications to FBMS are critical and much effort is being devoted to try to improve the system. This is the test site at Clam Lake, Wisconsin, for the US Navy's much-troubled Extremely Low Frequency (ELF) system.

5 Variable Depth Sonar (VDS) is deployed on a swinging arm from the stern of a ship. By varying its depth maximum advantage can be taken of oceanic conditions in searching for subs.

2 ▲ **3 ▼** **4 ▲** **5 ▼**

The operational profiles of submarines can be divided into three main patterns which relate directly to their type and role: FBMS, SSN, and SSK. Virtually all submarines start their patrols by leaving harbour on the surface, an event obviously open to detection by both direct visual means and by satellite observation. These submarines must then pass over the relative shallows of the continental shelf, where they are not too difficult to detect, before reaching the open ocean. Further, some nations' submarines, particularly those of the Soviet Union, must transit through choke points—sealanes which are restricted either laterally or in depth—where detection by the "other side" is particularly easy. Once in the deeper ocean the three main types split.

An FBMS, once clear of the continental shelf, tends to move fairly rapidly and deep to its patrol area, but taking special care to avoid being picked up by a trailing SSN. Once in its patrol area the FBMS cruises at about 3 knots (5.56km/hr), varying its depth in accordance with prevailing oceanic conditions to hide itself from detection. The greatest vulnerabilities of the FBMS, how-

ever, are its need to be in communications with its National Command Authority (NCA), and the requirement periodically to update its Ships Inertial Navigation System (SINS).

The principle means of communicating with a totally submerged submarine is by Very Low Frequency (3 to 30 KHz) radio, but external antennas are essential for reception. On patrol at its operating depth a US FBMS deploys a plastic buoy in which is embedded a crossed-loop antenna; but when moving at speed a wire antenna some 1,673ft (510m) long must be streamed (according to SIPRI Yearbook 1979, p397). Other communications systems necessitate coming up to some 9.84ft (3m) below the surface, but Extra Low Frequency (300Hz to 3KHz) transmissions can be received down to depths of 328ft (100m). In addition, to update its SINS, which is even more relevant to missile warhead terminal accuracy than to current submarine positions, an FBMS needs to expose a whip antenna above the surface for a minimum of 7 minutes and a maximum of 13 minutes. Not surprisingly major efforts are being made to develop new systems of communications and navigation

which will overcome such dangerous ventures to the proximity of the surface.

SSNs are faster and much more agile than FBMS and operate routinely at much greater depths. They, too, may have a need to communicate with, or receive communications from their base. This was exemplified during the Falklands War when HMS *Conqueror* had to signal a sighting report of the Argentine cruiser *General Belgrano* and then await receipt of authority to carry out an attack. Any radio transmission by a submarine is, of course, immediately detectable by enemy electronic surveillance, which will seek to analyse the content of the signal as well as to pinpoint the site of the transmitter. One way of overcoming this is a device such as the American AN/BRT-1 radio transmitting buoy, which contains a cassette recorder and transmitter, and which can broadcast a message up to 4 minutes in duration to a ship or an aircraft. A preset time delay of 5 to 60 minutes enables the submarine to be a considerable distance away before transmission starts, and at 30 knots and with a 60 minute delay a submerged SSN could be anywhere in an area of 3,749 square miles (9,597km²).

The greatest problem for SSNs is that they must routinely come up to the surface to obtain air to run their diesel engines to recharge their batteries, and also to expel diesel exhaust. This can be achieved by exposing only the head of the schnorkel tube, but even this is a relatively easy target for modern radars and infra-red sensors. Further, the exhaust fumes from the schnorkel are detectable by "sniffers" mounted on most ASW aircraft. Thus, SSKs are faced with the paradox that submerged they are the quietest of all submarines and the most difficult to detect, but they are inherently vulnerable by this inescapable requirement to approach the surface at regular intervals.

A submerged submarine has several properties which make it susceptible to detection. The first is that the submarine itself makes noise, partly from its machinery and partly by its motion through the ocean. Machinery noise comes from unbalanced rotating parts such as turbine blades, gears and pumps, and the cavitation noise of fluid flowing around the closed-loop internal system under pressure.

The US Navy has gone to great lengths to try to reduce the internal noise of their nuclear submarines, and this probably typifies the efforts of other similarly-placed navies. USS *Tullibee* (SSN-597), launched in 1960, featured turbo-electric drive which dispensed with the need for steam-turbines

and noisy gear trains. USS *Narwhal* (SSN-671) followed seven years later with the S5G natural circulation reactor which was said at the time to promise "increased reactor plant reliability, simplicity and noise reduction due to the elimination of the need for large reactor coolant pumps and associated electrical and control equipment", according to Admiral Rickover (as quoted in *Jane's Fighting Ships* 1982-83, p602). *Narwhal*, however, still had steam turbines and it was not until 1973 that the USS *Glenard P Lipscomb* (SSN-685) appeared, combining a free circulation S5Wa reactor with turbine-electric drive. *Narwhal* and *Lipscomb* are still in active service, but remain one-off experiments, and it must be presumed that other, more satisfactory means of silencing machinery and fluid circulation noises have been utilised in later classes.

As far as is known nuclear submarines of other navies all have pressurised-water-cooled nuclear reactors, with their associated pumps, and steam turbines, and it would thus appear that the line of development culminating in the USS *Lipscomb* has come to an end, at least for the time being. One additional factor in overcoming this type of noise is that some submarines are being coated with anechoic tiles to defeat active sonar, but which could also well have the effect of screening internal noise as well.

Most submarines now have only one propeller, although older Soviet SSNs, and

all their FBMSs, have two. Propeller noise is due mainly to tip-vortex cavitation, in which air bubbles at the blade tips collapse with a characteristic hissing sound. Such propeller noise is radiated mainly in a horizontal plane and is greatest in line with the blades (ie, abeam of the submarine). This noise increases with the rate of revolution of the blades and is thus most pronounced during acceleration, high speed runs and abrupt changes of direction. At lower speeds this propeller noise is modulated at the natural frequency of the propeller blades to produce an idiosyncratic "beat" which can be utilised for identification of individual submarines. The Soviet practice of using two propellers produces an additional intermodulating beat which again aids identification.

The third factor is hydrodynamic noise which is a consequence of the flow of seawater over the hull of the submarine. This arises from protrusions and orifices in the outer hull, and Soviet submarines have for long been much noisier than their Western counterparts due to the continued use of free-flood holes. The Soviets, like other navies, have a long-standing programme to reduce hydrodynamic noise, aided by such research vehicles as the *Lima*-class submarine. Measures to reduce such noise include retractable domes, bollards, etc, and remotely activated doors over periscopes and antennas on top of the fin. There is a further component in the noise problem in that long-wire towed

1 This submarine captain's nightmare came true when his Whiskey class conventional boat ran aground during a clandestine reconnaissance of a Swedish naval base. Diesel-engined submarines are particularly suitable for such a role and it is strongly suspected that this was not the first spy trip in Swedish waters. It was embarrassing for the USSR, but then the Swedish authorities detected nuclear radiation from the bow section and the incident took on an even more sinister twist, with the suspicion of nuclear mine-laying.

2 The latest version of the French-designed Atlantique ASW aircraft has proved a success with several NATO navies.

3 The P-3 Orion has been the mainstay of USN's landbased ASW effort fo some years and also serves other navies.

4 The Lockheed P-2 Neptune gave years of valuable service; this Kawasaki-built version is still in production.

5 Sonobuoy dropped from a USN Orion. Note fixed magnetic anomaly detector boom behind the tail empennage.

6 Sonobuoy about to hit the surface. When its task is finished it will automatically sink itself to prevent recovery.

7 The sonobuoy launch tubes on the underbelly of an S-3A Viking antisubmarine aircraft of the US Navy.

8 A Soviet Navy Ilyushin-38 (May) ASW aircraft spotted by the US Navy. Deployment of such aircraft is more difficult for Soviets.

9, 10 S-3A Vikings on patrol. Note that in lower picture the retractable MAD probe has been deployed.

1 ▲

3 ▲

2 ▲

4 ▲

antennas may themselves vibrate at their natural frequency.

A submerged submarine moving through the water also leaves a wake, which is detectable by active sonar. In addition to this, however, the turbulence, conical in shape, eventually reaches the surface at some distance astern of the boat where it causes minute variations in the wave pattern. Both the USA and the USSR are experimenting with Over-the-Horizon-Backscatter (OTH-B) radar in an effort to detect this phenomenon at considerable ranges. Depending upon the depth of the submarine and the prevailing oceanic conditions it may also be possible that the wake turbulence will force colder water to rise and mix with the warmer surface water, thus causing a temperature differential detectable by satellite or aircraft-mounted infra-red sensors.

When a submarine is moving at a shallow depth there is a tiny but nevertheless perceptible rise in the surface of the water above the hull. This rise is potentially detectable by satellites such as the USA's SEASAT launched in 1978, which has a radio altimeter with a vertical resolution of 3.9in (10cm). The USSR is known to be particularly interested in this technique.

Submarines are also detectable by the electrical and magnetic fields they create. According to a Soviet author, V. Nikyaylin ("Physics and ASW Defence", *Krasnaya Zvezda*, March 10, 1962) there are electrochemical processes on the hull of a sub-marine which generate varying electrical potentials, and an electrical current flows between these using seawater as the conductor. The rate of change of the resulting electrical and electromagnetic fields is detectable by various extremely sensitive detectors, one approach being to place very large electric coils on the seabed.

A submarine hull is a large, mainly ferrous body, and when on the move it is passing through the lines of force of the Earth's natural magnetic field. This obviously creates a magnetic anomaly which is detectable, especially by an airborne detector: magnetic anomaly detector (MAD). MAD detector units are mounted in extensions behind the tail in fixed-wing aircraft, and in an aerodynamic body ("bird") which is towed on a cable behind a helicopter. All advanced ASW aircraft are fitted with such a device, including the US P-3 Orion and S-3 Viking, British Nimrod, French Atlantique and the Soviet Il-38 (May). MAD techniques are not suitable for large area searches, but are invaluable in the precise locating of underwater targets detected by other means.

Active sonar

Active sonar devices transmit acoustic pulses in the audio frequency band; pulse length is variable (roughly from 12.5 to 700 milliseconds) as is frequency (roughly 5 to 2 KiloHerz). These variations are necessary to enable adjustments to be made to suit the prevailing oceanic conditions. Active sonars are deployed in submarines, surface vessels and helicopters, and are also used in sonobuoys, thus giving an active capability to ASW aircraft. One characteristic of all underwater-mounted hydrophones is *self-noise* which is generated by the relative movement between the hydrophone and the water surrounding it. A further complication is that transmission power is limited by the cavitation effect, in which gaseous bubbles appear on the emitting surface. However, the greatest complications for sonar are the complex variations in the prevailing conditions of the ocean, and to maximise a platform's performance it is frequently necessary to carry various different sonar sets optimised for different regimes.

Passive detection

The principal passive acoustic detector is the hydrophone, which is basically a very sensitive listening device capable of picking up noise in the oceans. Obviously, in its design the hydrophone is optimised for submarine noises. Such passive devices are deployed as static arrays on the ocean bed or on buoys, on the hulls of submarines, on surface ships (although their effectiveness is limited at speed), and in sonobuoys.

Wide ocean passive detectors are typified by the US SOund SUrveillance System (SOSUS), which consists of arrays of hydrophones deployed on the beds of the Pacific

5 ▲

6 ▲

7 ▲

8 ▲

9 ▲

10 ▲

and Atlantic Oceans. SOSUS was intended originally to detect Soviet FBMSs in the days of the shorter range SLBMs. Now that the Soviet Navy's Delta and Typhoon class FBMSs can strike at continental United States (CONUS) from the Barents Sea and the Sea of Okhotsk SOSUS must be of reduced value unless its detectors have been improved to give extremely long-range performance. SOSUS is certainly known to have reasonable sensitivity and was reported some years ago to be able to detect some of the noisier Soviet submarines at ranges of "several hundred kilometres". Arrays such as SOSUS, however, can do little more than establish the presence of a submarine at very long ranges together with its approximate direction. It is suggested by at least one authoritative source (*SIPRI Yearbook*, 1979, p433) that SOSUS can locate a submarine to within a 15km (9.32 mile) radius circle, thus considerably easing the problem for the follow-up platform, eg, an ASW aircraft, which actually has to pinpoint the target.

The case of the long-range passive contact is an interesting one; take, for example, the case of a submarine moving at 25 knots (43.3km per hour) at a distance of 100 miles (161km) from such a detector. Since the speed of sound in water is approximately 4,757ft per second (1,450 metres per second) the sound will take 111 seconds to reach the detector, in which time the target will have travelled a further 0.89 miles (1.43km).

The next advance is the SURveillance Towed Array Sensor System (SURTASS) in which surface ships will tow sensor arrays along designated patrol lines, the resulting intelligence "take" being passed in real time via satellite links to two shore-based data processing centres. In his Fiscal Year 1983 statement to Congress, Caspar Weinberger, the US Secretary of Defense, said:

"Mobile surveillance systems complement our fixed systems by providing the necessary flexibility to respond to changes in Soviet submarine deployment patterns and by extending coverage in remote areas not presently monitored by fixed systems. They would also serve as an emergency backup in the event some of our fixed systems were incapacitated. The Congress has appropriated funds in FY 1984 for the first twelve TAGOS SURTASS ships. We are requesting funds in FY 1984 to construct an additional ship, an AGOS, incorporating advanced design features."

TAGOS is a civilian-manned, unarmed, specialised sonar ship, operated by Military Sealift Command. The significance of the AGOS to be funded in FY 84 is that it will be manned by servicemen of the US Navy. Both SOSUS and SURTASS are vulnerable in a crisis or in war, as implied in Weinberger's statement. The position of the SOSUS arrays must be fairly well known by now to the Soviet Navy, as must the lines of the cable links and the location of the processing centres. The SURTASS ships, unarmed and slow moving, are also easy to track and to destroy, and again the position of the proces-

sing centres will be known. It can be assumed, therefore, that the two systems will be early targets in a war, but at the very least they should be able to give an accurate picture of Soviet submarine deployments up to the moment of their destruction.

The vulnerability of SURTASS is due, at least in part, to the fact that, to enable it to operate at long ranges, it must use low frequencies, which necessitates a "wide-aperture" array of considerable length. This, in turn, means that it can only be towed at very slow speeds.

To overcome the wartime vulnerabilities of SOSUS and SURTASS, the USA has developed the Rapidly Deployed Surveillance System (RDSS). This is basically a very large sonobuoy the size of a Mark 46 torpedo, which can be delivered by any platform (ship, submarine or aircraft) capable of delivering such a torpedo. RDSS automatically anchors itself to the ocean bed, and comprises a series of hydrophones connected to a buoy floating on the surface. This buoy contains a "burst" transmitter which passes data to aircraft such as the P-3 Orion, or possibly to satellites, either at predetermined intervals or on demand.

Towed arrays are also utilised by surface warships and submarines, which can be either active or passive. For a surface ship the major advantages of a towed array are its separation from ship-produced noise and its capability of operating at reasonable speed without losing the ability to detect submarines.

Processing intelligence

The amount of real-time information on ocean conditions and on acoustic and other detections from all these means is simply enormous. This has led to some unique and extremely powerful computers, and in several fields advances in computer technology have been the result of pressure in the ASW field.

Another significant advance has been the dramatic reduction in the size of computers, which has led to the ability to process information on board ASW aircraft, eg Orion, Nimrod. Most ASW helicopters, however, still have to act simply as relays back to processors on board their parent ship.

The effectiveness of the submarine threat was well illustrated in the Falklands War, when at least three SSNs were sent to the South Atlantic. One, HMS *Conqueror,* was able to approach the *General Belgrano* totally undetected, launch two torpedoes and then make off unscathed. Following this the very threat of SSNs was sufficient to keep the entire Argentinian surface fleet within twelve miles of the coast. On the other side the two Argentinian Type 209 diesel-engined submarines posed a threat which kept the Royal Navy's anti-submarine forces extremely busy for most of the campaign.

This is one of the greatest of modern intelligence battles, and one which is becoming more important, more complex and more expensive as the years go by. Both superpowers and their respective alliances are struggling to achieve a breakthrough, but neither has achieved it so far.

1 ▲
1 Hughes 500 light ASW helicopter. A search radar is fitted in the nose and the object on the pylon is the "bird" for the Magnetic Anomaly Detector (MAD).

2 Crews on a practice "scramble" with their Kamov Ka-25 (Hormone) anti-submarine helicopters of the Soviet Navy aboard the carrier *Minsk,* which carries 18-21 ASW helicopters.

3 A Sikorski SH-3A ASW helicopter lowers its dunking sonar. This gives such aircraft a unique listening capability and is a serious threat to submarines.

4 Mine warfare is an increasing threat in the naval battle and here an RH-53 minesweeping helicopter is transferring equipment to a conventional minesweeper.

5 The crew of HMS *Conqueror* display the Jolly Roger to show that they have done it for real; *Conqueror* sank the Argentine cruiser *Belgrano* in the Falklands war of April 1982.

6 A USN sonobuoy which is dropped by aircraft and descends under control of a rotochute. It then acts as a sonar, passing its information to the aircraft by radio link.

6 ▲

2 ▲

3 ▲

4 ▲

5 ▲

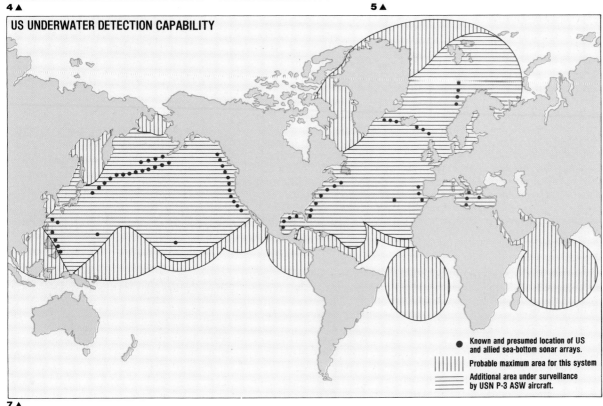

US UNDERWATER DETECTION CAPABILITY

● Known and presumed location of US and allied sea-bottom sonar arrays.

||||| Probable maximum area for this system

Additional area under surveillance by USN P-3 ASW aircraft.

7 ▲

7 The US and its allies have a wide coverage of the world's oceans to detect Soviet submarine activity. Shown here is just the US capability. The fleet of P-3 Orion ASW aircraft are deployed world-wide and are supplemented by aircraft operating from carriers on deployment. In addition there are a number of sea-bed sonar arrays, eg, along both US coastlines, from the Aleutians to Japan, and across the GIUK gap. The survivability of these arrays in war is open to question as it must be presumed that the Soviet Navy has a reasonable knowledge of where they are. Nevertheless, if they do nothing more than show changes in the normal pattern of Soviet deployments they will have fulfilled a valuable task. The USN is striving all the time to increase its submarine detection ability.

Chapter ten

The importance of coping with intelligence

WHETHER BY espionage or by sophisticated mechanical means of surveillance, we see in the previous chapters an enormous amount of information dumped down every day on the desks of intelligence analysts and the top officials of government. The vast daily flow of information and processed intelligence must be synthesized for presentation in the few minutes each day during which an intelligence chief or other adviser "briefs" the chief of state.

What assurance is there in any nation, great or small, that national decisions will be based on complete, accurate and timely information? None whatsoever.

Britain's intelligence services were seriously damaged in the post-World War II era by betrayals that had their roots in the excessive class consciousness of British society. On the one hand some, at least, of the traitors were people genuinely resentful of the injustices their own class had imposed on the poor. On the other hand, the treachery was protected, uknowingly, by people from the same upper classes who refused to believe that people such as themselves could be traitors. Although administrative corrective measures have been taken it remains to be seen whether the underlying social conditions have changed enough to prevent a recurrence.

The French Government and, perforce, the French intelligence services have been riven by the same ideologial conflicts that have divided French society into hostile camps ever since the French Revolution. West Germany has built an intelligence service on the wreckage of deeply flawed World War II intelligence agencies. Whether General Gehlen's reforms have been effective is yet to be proved. We have seen that a highly efficient, seemingly unbeatable Israeli system failed, in 1973, when an almost imperceptible change began to take place from a brilliant, imaginative staff to run-of-the-mill bureaucracy.

But none of the world's intelligence services is more deeply flawed than those of the two chief antagonists on the world stage today—the Soviet Union and the United States. Yet the life of each person on Earth depends in some degree on the efficiency of one or more of the national intelligence systems to guide national leaderships away from the catastrophe of nuclear war.

The citizens of a democratic society can cope with the technical, political and emotional limitations of their country's intelligence and security system if they choose to do so. The citizens of a totalitarian society are at the mercy of those limitations. It is all the more important, therefore, that the citizens of the free societies make every effort to understand the mistakes of the past and to refashion intelligence services that will perform effectively—without at the same time becoming a threat in themselves to democratic institutions.

What are the strengths and weaknesses of the Soviet KGB and its extensions in the other Communist countries? How can these be countered and exploited? What is it about the US Central Intelligence Agency that has made it, as West German journalist Carl Schopen has described it, "notorious" to such an extent that prominent Americans are now urging that it be reorganized, renamed or simply done away with, and an entirely new start be made?

From an attempt to answer these questions and from review of the strengths and weaknesses of the other major intelligence agencies we may be able to sort out the ideas necessary to put together a new, more effective intelligence system in the democratic nations, while protecting individual liberties from renegade intelligence and counter-intelligence bureaucracy.

Recent experience in almost every country tells us that it is a mistake to exclude intelligence from continuous parliamentary supervision and from close coverage by the press. Had there been independent supervision in the form of a Parliamentary committee or a Royal Commission in the 1950s it is difficult to see how traitors could have been so influential for so long a time in Britain's MI5 and MI6. The British Official Secrets Act blocked effective press reporting and commentary. The result was that, while Britain's intelligence and security agencies, except perhaps for GCHQ—the electronic surveillance agency—were virtually naked to the country's worst enemies, the British public were blissfully unaware that anything was wrong. Once the storm broke, journalists such as Chapman Pincher were able to put much of the story on the record and thereby provoke a public demand for substantial reform. Even today, there is no independent supervisory agency and the Official Secrets Act continues to protect not only the country's legitimate secrets but, quite possibly, any miscreant in high office who might need it to cover up his misdeeds.

1 Indicating how deeply KGB penetrated British intelligence, Tom Driberg (2nd from right), who worked for both KGB and MI5, is seen with fellow Labour politicians (l to r) Wilson, Bevin, Morrison and Castle.

Intelligence agencies are supposed to devote their efforts to external issues. All of them are, however, large bureaucratic institutions and many spend much time and effort in trying to resolve self-generated internal problems. Such domestic difficulties are exacerbated by the secrecy in which they are cloaked.

(Incidentally, Chapman Pincher said in a BBC radio interview on April 20, 1982, that he believed that Britain's Secret Service was "clean" by 1971 when the Government rid Britain of 105 Soviet "undesirables". But he also posed the question of whether any young KGB recruits could have worked their way up into positions of power in the MI5 by the normal means of promotion and advancement—*Editor.*)

Secrecy in Israel

In no other democratic state, however, is official secrecy as pervasive as it is in Israel. Nor has the international press accepted such censorship so meekly in regard to any other country as it has with Israel. Much of the world never has been told, for example, that virtually all of the reporting of the successive Arab-Israeli wars came through the hands of Israeli censorship and was based solely on what sources Israeli military authorities chose to make available. As a result not only foreign intelligence but the Israeli public never has been told to this day the extent of Israeli military deficiencies in 1973.

What is known of those failures indicates serious problems in organization, mobilization and training—problems familiar to anyone with experience in administration and training of reserve forces. These very common deficiencies suggest that Israel must either make peace with her Arab neighbours or set about building a regular military establishment that could be sustained only with huge foreign subsidies —even beyond those Israel has received all along from the United States. Would the Israeli public support an aggressive foreign policy if it had a full understanding of the military situation? This would not be the first time that censorship in the name of "counter-intelligence" had been used to protect not the security of the nation, but the security of government policies that otherwise would not be supported by the public.

The tendency of intelligence organizations to become a law unto themselves is apparent in the "Lavon Affair" in Israel in 1953, in which Israeli Military Intelligence (Aman) attempted to discredit Egypt by sabotage of American and British property in Cairo. The plot was exposed and Pinhas Lavon, the Defence Minister, was dismissed. Later Lavon was exonerated, Aman apparently having acted without his knowledge or authority.

It is only a short step from such self-initiated foreign adventures to meddling in internal politics. Thus the legendary Israeli intelligence chief, Isser Harrel, has been reported to have "had political police bugging telephones and creating dossiers on opponents on both the left and right from 1948 to 1952". In more recent years, Canadian and French counter-intelligence agencies have been accused by their governments of stepping over that same line— pursuing political or ideological objectives of the security staffs themselves outside of their charter and the law.

As indicated in the discussion of needed US reforms, secrecy can and should be limited to very specific categories of information, mainly to codes, contingency plans, identification of intelligence sources, and weapons performance data in the period prior to deployment. In a day when civilian populations may be in greater danger than the armed forces of a country it is of vital importance that most intelligence be released to the public as quickly as it can be processed. No longer can questions of strategic policy be left to the government. The citizen who values his or her safety must demand to be a full partner. Surely that would seem to be the enduring lesson of the 1975 Vietnam disaster.

That ideological prejudice can be as dangerous as excessive secrecy to production of accurate and timely intelligence is apparent from the American experience and from similar experience in Australia, when a dispute broke out involving the Australian intelligence and security agencies in 1980. According to Robert Moss, a specialist in intelligence reporting, the dispute surfaced when Andrew Campbell, an analyst for the Office of National Assessments (ONA), was forced out of the agency, allegedly because of analyses adverse to the Soviet Union. The pattern that emerged of a left-wing bias within the agency, or at least a tendency to "apologize" for Soviet actions, was strikingly similar to patterns discernible at the same time throughout the Western academic community, including some of the faculties of war colleges and other government agencies. This pattern unquestionably has been a major factor in enabling the Soviet "institutes", discussed in chapter 2, to exploit Western academic and government visitors.

One of Mr. Moss's sources suggested that the way to overcome left-wing bias in the Australian ONA was to return the agency to the supervision of the military authorities. A few weeks spent by that source in the US Army War College Strategic Studies Institute at Carlisle Barracks, Pennsylvania, watching the comings and goings of Soviet and other East European "scholars" as honoured guests, and witnessing the worshipful reports of civilian members of the Institute who visited the Soviet Institute for the US and Canada, would be enough to destroy the illusion that military supervision, in itself, would be an adequate remedy.

The same military people who regard military rank as a sure indicator of knowledge and wisdom transfer that simplistic illusion directly to the holders of civilian academic degrees. Unless the Australian military has maintained a much more hard-headed attitude than have many of their American and West European counterparts, the title "Doctor of Philosophy" usually would be enough to ensure clear sailing for any but a public member of the Communist Party.

In short, military control of national assessments or any other part of the intelligence process is no guarantee of efficiency or purity of purpose. The military has its own bureaucratic and budgetary axes to grind. Given the opportunity to manipulate intelligence to serve those purposes, the military is apt to behave like the puppy that "can resist anything but temptation".

1 ▲

2 ▲

1 A Soviet admiral at a concert in Boston USA, June 17, 1975. At one level such contact is good, but is often bad for security.

2 Much military data is over-classified, but there are blunders—like the release of pictures of this laser trials vehicle.

3 ▲

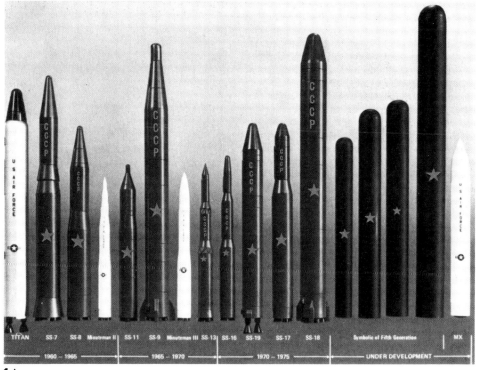

4 ▲

3 Six MIRV re-entry vehicles barrelling in from space onto targets on the Kwajalein Test Range. Over the past 30 years each US advance, such as MIRVs, has been quickly matched by the USSR, suggesting security leaks in the US system.

4 Modern technical means of collecting data have led to a fascination with numbers, with ceaseless counting of weaponry, and consequential diminution of predictive analysis. Graphs, tables and CIA pictures like this have proliferated.

There is simply no substitute for *informed* public surveillance of the intelligence function. Since the individual citizen has neither the time nor the means to maintain constant surveillance, he or she must depend on the press and on some form of official supervision, governmental or quasi-governmental, independent of the intelligence agencies themselves. That sort of delegated surveillance can only be effective if the journalists and the officials who carry it out have a detailed knowledge of what should and what should not be expected of intelligence agencies, and that usually means some sort of experience in the intelligence field. Even here, however, the public must constantly be aware that people who have such backgrounds might have entirely too cozy a relationship with the agencies they are supposed to be watching.

There needs, also, to be greater public awareness of the limitations of technical means of intelligence collection. Evidence presented at a consortium for the study of intelligence in April 1980 (published as *Intelligence Requirements for the 1980s: Counter-Intelligence,* by National Strategy Information Center, New York, 1981), indicates that the non-Communist world was deceived throughout the 1970s about the extent of the Soviet nuclear buildup. Apparently, this was accomplished by falsification and encoding of telemetry and the inducement of deliberate errors in test firings. According to Maj. Gen. George J. Keegan, former chief of US Air Force Intelligence, "with the advent of space surveillance technologies, the [intelligence] community became immersed in the process of . . . . repetitive counting of ICBMs, submarines, and other major artefacts of war. Predictive analysis has declined markedly since the advent of the new collection technology."

Improving analysis

Dr. William R. Harris of the Rand Corporation and David S. Sullivan, a former strategic analyst for CIA, believe that better analysis of available data would have enabled Western intelligence agencies to "read through" the Soviet deception. It is apparent from their remarks, however, and from those of General Keegan and others, that analysis is the weakest part of the intelligence effort, at least in the United States.

Several methods of improving analysis have already been discussed. The West German solution by which analysis, or at least final assessment, is restricted to the country's political leadership has much to be said for it, if a highly experienced political leadership exists.

That certainly was true of Britain in World War II during which, as it is now known, Winston Churchill personally and his cabinet in general consistently reached more accurate assessments than the intelligence analysts.

In terms of strategic planning, the Soviet system has also worked well. Although analysis is conducted in an "information centre" at the very top level of government, final assessment remains in the hands of the Politburo members. As mentioned previously, during the 1970s and into the early 1980s that body represented one of the most experienced groups of political leaders—if you can call them that—in the world. It was not too long ago, however, that this aggregation of the assessment process at the very top of government—then in the person of Josef Stalin—had disastrous results, with respect to Soviet failure to heed British and other warnings of an impending German attack in June 1941.

The existing American system, whereby assessment is spread so widely that no one can be held responsible for anything, plainly serves personal and bureaucratic rather than national needs.

Between these two extremes of responsibility for analysis and assessment concentrated at the top, on the one hand, or spread as something of a smokescreen on the other, lies the British system wherein experienced, identifiable intelligence analysts prepare an assessment and then defend it before a Joint Intelligence Committee composed of the chiefs of the intelligence services and other specialists brought in as required.

We know from the experience of the 1930s that Winston Churchill, *outside* the government, consistently produced a more accurate current and long-range assessment than did the then-fragmented British intelligence services. We know, too, from the examples cited in the first chapter, that the best long-range intelligence always has been

the work of individuals rather than of committees. The current British system with its emphasis on individual rather than committee work, but with severe review by a knowledgeable committee, does seem to offer, therefore, a reasonable amalgam of the hard-earned historical experience.

Still, the Churchillian example of the 1930s suggests that it would be a mistake to rely totally upon one centre of analysis, or even upon competing centres confined solely to the government. It was the creation of an alternate "B" team of analysts by then-CIA Director George Bush in the 1970s that produced the first officially recognized indicators that the permanent CIA "A" team and the civilian academics whose views the CIA analysts accepted were far off the mark.

Somewhere in any government structure, therefore, there should be such a "B" team with access to the same information as the "A" team, but free to reach its own conclusions and to argue for that view in public. Indeed, it was only when the views of Mr. Bush's "B" team became public that any appreciable change began to occur. If, however, both "teams" are drawn from the same academic and social background, and if there is excessive reliance on academic rather than operational background, there is danger that both will "sing from the same book". That argues for a drastic change in intelligence recruitment, as proposed later in this chapter for the CIA.

There is a need in all intelligence staffs for academically oriented people who gain great satisfaction from meticulous cataloguing of information. Some of the best of these are in the British and Japanese services—the latter, perhaps, reflecting British influence in Japan up to World War I. Mostly these people abhor publicity and the *strum und drang* of public debate. They should be able to look forward to a rewarding professional career, for without their work that of the analyst is useless.

For all the reasons cited in this and earlier chapters, the analysts, by and large, should come from operational jobs in or out of government where their judgement has been tested and proven. The analyst who cannot advance and defend his or her position in open, public debate is no analyst at all, so considerable weight should be given to a record of effective performance in such debate. All that suggests a sort of contract arrangement proposed later in this chapter as a remedy for American analytical ills, at least.

But no matter how good the system and no matter how good the people in it the entire intelligence process can be frustrated by a refusal of the people at the top to listen. Who dares to tell an Idi Amin or a Quadaffi that he is courting devastating response from abroad or from within his own country by pursuing wild and brutal policies at home and abroad? Does anyone dare to tell Britain's Prime Minister Margaret Thatcher

1 ▲

1 US Vice-President Bush chairs a meeting of the Administration's Crisis Management Team during a discussion of the problem of technology transfer to the USSR. Fortunately the excesses of the Carter Presidency have now been curbed by legislation.

2, 3 A street scene in Northern Ireland (**2**) as a "wheelbarrow" is sent to examine an abandoned car. British troops in the Province have a clear if unenviable task, which, during the latest phase, has gone on for 14 years. Prime Minister Margaret

Thatcher (**3**) has often visited the operational area, but who dares to tell her the real facts about the situation, and their effect on US-Anglo relations?

4 A large proportion of the KGB's effort is devoted to surveillance of their own armed forces and the civil population—keeping them in as much as keeping foreigners out.

5 Soviet Ryad computers were based closely on US technology, officially delivered, which, with hindsight, can be seen as sheer folly. How much more is obtained illegally?

2 ▲

that Irish-American anger over her policies in Ireland has begun to threaten Britain's key international relationship? Yet US columnist Joseph Kraft warned that just such an influence appeared in the supposed "mix-up" of voting instructions to the US ambassador to the United Nations at a crucial juncture in the 1982 Falklands War.

Important as it is to maintain surveillance of the intelligence agencies by the press and independent official groups, no citizen can afford to delegate and forget. That is, he or she must maintain a healthy interest in what appears about these agencies in the press, on radio and television and in the academic community.

It is also important to realize that however competent the intelligence agencies of other countries may be, only the national intelligence systems of the United States and the Soviet Union have the full range of intelligence collection, analysis and counter-intelligence capabilities. *All* other intelligence agencies in the world depend to one degree or another on one or the other of these giants and in a few strange cases they may be receiving information from both.

This dependence is so great that it is safe to say that all of the smaller intelligence agencies could fail and the effect would essentially be to counterbalance one another with no major influence on the course of human events. But if the intelligence agencies of *either* of the giants were to fail it would shape the entire future course of human history. A misassessment by the intelligence and policy-making system of either the US or USSR could plunge the world into the abyss of nuclear war. That is not true of any other intelligence system or combination of systems, even among the rest of the "nuclear club".

Unfortunately, books, magazines, radio and television — particularly as concerns fiction — have tended to create the impression that both the KGB and the American services (usually lumped together as the "CIA") are near-models of efficiency, good or bad depending on the writer's outlook. Nothing of the sort. Both systems are seriously flawed. Understanding those *weaknesses* is perhaps even more important in understanding those bodies' influence on modern society and events than understanding their *strengths*.

KGB dominated by fear

The most salient characteristic of the KGB is that it is dominated by fear; first and most importantly fear of its own people. That is demonstrated by the fact that at least 15 KGB employees are concerned with surveillance of the Soviet civilian population and armed forces for every one employee directed to foreign intelligence. The fact that some seven decades after the Bolshevik Revolution the Soviet government still is obsessed with fear of "counter-revolution" to the extent that it must deploy this pervasive network of informers and guards of one form or another is far more worrisome than the simple facts of massive Soviet military armament. For, as Flora Lewis of the New York *Times* has warned, that situation is fraught with the danger that the Soviet leadership might bring about a foreign crisis, even war, to forestall internal dissidence. The successive upheavals in Eastern Europe, requiring massive deployments of military force to maintain the stability of the Communist regimes, can only have fed the fears of the Soviet government and its KGB.

It is entirely possible, therefore, that the intelligence assessment that could drive the Soviet government into desperate international action may have nothing at all to do with the information collected by the KGB's foreign intelligence operation, but everything to do with what emerges from the KGB's *internal* surveillance network. The work of non-Communist intelligence agencies, such as Israel's Mossad, in analysing social, economic and political developments within the Soviet Union is, therefore, of crucial importance, for only by such analysis can the non-Communist world be forewarned. This, in turn, would seem to argue in favour of greater efforts on the part of the non-Communist governments in the area of "human intelligence" (HUMINT).

Lt. Gen. Daniel O. Graham, former chief of the US Defense Intelligence Agency, has argued for greater emphasis on HUMINT as a means of identifying Soviet "intentions".

3 ▲

4 ▲

5 ▲

That would require penetration of the Politburo itself either by an "illegal" somehow infiltrated into the top structure of the Soviet government or by recruitment of a Soviet official. The latter may or may not have occurred in the case of Col. Oleg Penkovsky, and some such "defection in place" could occur in the future. The chances of maintaining continuing surveillance by this means, however, are extremely remote. Experience to date indicates that a more reliable, if less spectacular, method would be expansion of the meticulous open research into Soviet institutions and society that has gone on at the University of Edinburgh and at a few other Western academic institutions for many years, supplemented by what can be learned from the continuing flow of Soviet defectors. A gathering of some of the best trained West European specialists in the Soviet armed forces and society into a permanent NATO intelligence staff might also improve matters.

What is *not* needed is more of the sort of "research" by which Western visitors listen reverently to the dons of the Soviet Institute on the US and Canada and its sister "institutes" and then dutifully pipe the propaganda imbibed back into Western academic and governmental channels. It is much less expensive simply to subscribe to the Soviet press and hire someone who reads Russian.

KGB "drowning in detail"

The fear that dominates the KGB and its government is also a major factor in how the Soviet intelligence system processes information gained from throughout the world and the finished intelligence it disseminates.

"Hopefully," says US Admiral Bobby Inman, former Deputy Director, CIA, "we drown them in detail which they're unwilling to trust or believe."

There is considerable evidence, including the everlasting KGB search for evidence of NATO plans for an attack, that something of this sort is occurring. Fear breeds distrust. During World War II (the "Klatt Affair") the Soviets apparently sacrificed tens of thousands of Russian lives to establish the credibility of a "disinformation" programme designed to dissuade Germany from making effective use of a million-man army of Russian deserters willing to fight against the Soviet Communist government. Here again the obsessive fear for Soviet internal security outweighed all other considerations. The Byzantine thought process by which thousands of one's own soldiers can be betrayed to their death by their own government cannot help but distort analysis in what John Barron calls the "bloated, overstaffed, overly centralized, overly bureaucratic and frequently inefficient" KGB structure.

How deep this distrust runs is indicated by the discovery in a recent Soviet espionage operation against Norway and the Norwegian spy had been told by his Soviet mentors to mark unclassified documents as secret because their chiefs in Moscow would not consider anything important unless so marked! If that is the case, it goes a long way to explain why the Soviets seem to reject the enormous amount of open

information available to them disproving both the intent and the capability of NATO to attack the Soviet Union.

Nevertheless credit must be given for the accuracy with which the Soviet system has assessed and exploited political developments in the non-Communist world. Directly in the case of the European anti-nuclear demonstrations of the early 1980s and indirectly through the adroit North Vietnamese exploitation of anti-war sentiments in the United States during the 1960s, the Soviets have demonstrated a capacity to gather accurate information, assess it and make effective use of it where time pressures do not require rapid analysis. In neither case, however, did Soviet intelligence or "disinformation" *create* the circumstances that were being exploited. The European demonstrations were not anti-American or anti-NATO in nature, although the Soviets made every effort to portray them as such. Rather they were the product of a much more deeply seated political process — the significance of which the Soviets may have missed entirely — by which post-World War II Europe was demonstrating that it now has the self-confidence to take over control of its own destiny after 35 years of American dominance. That being the case, American resources tied down since 1945 in the defence of Europe could now be released for employment against Soviet threats elsewhere. Failure of the Soviets to recognize that as the ultimate result of the European demonstrations, indicated now by sentiments expressed in the US Senate, would be an intelligence misassessment of the first order, yet that is exactly the sort of misassessment their ideologically contorted intelligence system is prone to make.

The Soviets almost certainly misread the implication of the 1960s anti-Vietnam War demonstrations in the United States. From the work of Peter Braestrup and Burns W. Roper in *Big Story* and of Col. Harry Summers in a US Army-financed analysis of US strategy, it is apparent that domestic US dissent boiled up from a sensing by the American public that the US Government did not know what it was doing in Vietnam and had no coherent strategy. In short, while there were other contributing factors, it was confusion and irresolution on the part of the US Government — not Soviet or North Vietnamese machinations — that eventually brought about the humiliating American withdrawal. In their subsequent rejoicing over a changed "correlation of forces", supposedly in their favour, the Soviets made it appear that they had misassessed the American failure (as indeed had some Americans and some of America's allies) as a moral collapse leading to the permanent decline of US power and influence.

A more astute analysis of the available information — all of it on the public record — would have shown that the much-decried "Christmas [1973] Bombings" of North Vietnam by President Richard Nixon had the overwhelming support of the American public (who re-elected him 11 months later in one of the most devastating political sweeps in American history), that the American public almost certainly would have supported a full invasion of North

1 ▲

2 ▲

3 ▲

4 ▲

5 ▲

1 Equipment alleged to have been used by Greville Wynne and Colonel Penkovsky, who may have been an "agent in place".

2 Admiral Bobby Inman, former deputy director of the CIA, hopes that the Soviet intelligence services will be drowned in a mass of detail.

3 US bomber during the Christmas 1973 raids on North Vietnam which forced a return to the negotiating table. Despite Press reports, the US public displayed overwhelming support for such determined action.

4 President Nixon is sworn in for his second term after a resounding victory. He knew when and how to take firm action, and was usually an excellent interpreter of intelligence.

5 One of the more spectacular defections of recent years was that of the Polish Ambassador to Washington in 1981, seen here with his wife being comforted by President Reagan. Such high ranking defectors are obviously valuable, but most rewarding of all is the "defector-in-place".

Vietnam, and that from beginning to end of the Vietnam experience *the most successful American politicians were those who indicated a resolve to win.* Here again the Braestrup-Roper and similar analyses show that President Lyndon Johnson lost the confidence of the public only when he gave up after the 1968 Tet Offensive.

The Soviet "correlation of forces" propaganda suggests the same sort of misassessment the German Kaiser made in 1917 and that Hitler and Japan made in 1941, and that Argentina made over the British response to their invasion of the Falklands Islands in the spring of 1982. By their caution, however, in failing to exploit massive military advantage in the Middle East and Northeast Asia the Soviet leadership suggests that the lesson of what happened to Japan in the aftermath of the Japanese attack on Pearl Harbor may not be entirely forgotten.

Assuming that the more careful assessment prevails, is this the product of espionage by the KGB, or is it a product of the overall political experience of a Soviet leadership that has seen much of the history of the 20th Century at first hand? Whatever it is, it is most certainly not the product of what the non-Communist world has managed to *conceal* from the Soviets.

Danger of secrecy

In learning to cope with the KGB brand of intelligence the non-Communist nations must choose between drowning the KGB and its sponsors in detail, in Admiral Inman's words, or attempting to lock up everything that conceivably could be of interest or value to the KGB. Ultimately that would mean locking up the whole of non-Communist society—converting it in the process to something like the very Soviet model most abhorrent to non-Communist societies.

The danger of establishing secret institutions responsible only to themselves in a democratic society has been recognized since the inception of the democratic ideal. Democratic societies today must learn to cope not only with the KGB, but with their own intelligence agencies as well.

In this regard it should be recognized that the US CIA, as presently constituted, is a bureaucratic disaster. Even a favourably disposed critic, Henry H. Ransom of Vanderbilt University, admits that, "CIA carries a seriously burdensome, if not entirely deserved, reputation as the juvenile delinquent of American foreign policy"—and that was written four years *before* the mid-1970s revelations of CIA drug experiments on American citizens, assassination plots and involvement in the Watergate episode.

Supposedly, all of that was interred in history with the resolution of the Watergate crisis. Yet scarcely was a new Administration installed in Washington in 1981 than the Central Intelligence Agency sought and obtained Presidential permission to reinvade the internal security field of the Federal Bureau of Investigation—from which it was supposedly excluded by statutory charter and in which it had perpetrated some of its worst excesses.

Worse yet, there emerged from the "covert action" side of the CIA's Directorate of Operations another of the long series of scandals that have led even more than the excesses of the counter-intelligence staff to the besmirching of the agency itself and of the United States. This is recorded in a long series of articles published by the New York *Times* beginning in 1981, describing the activities of Edwin P. Wilson and other former and supposedly former members of the "covert action" staff in training and equipping Libyan terrorists, providing technicians to support the Libyan invasion of Chad and assisting in the transfer of restricted items of US technology to whomever would buy it, the KGB not excepted. In August 1981, the CIA acknowledged that it had dismissed two employees who were actively supporting Wilson's training school for terrorists. All of this, of course, seriously embarrassed the US Secretary of State who had been telling the world that the Soviets alone were the sponsors of Libyan terrorism.

Of the many appalling incidents described in the *Times* series and confirmed by other news agencies (Wilson's associates acknowledged to CBS News, for instance, that they were selling torture implements) none so clearly demonstrated the extent to which "intelligence" officialdom had escaped normal governmental controls as the dispatch of a US Army Special Forces master sergeant on active duty to assist Wilson, in the belief by the Army that the assignment had been ordered by the CIA. Indeed, it is not altogether certain to this day that the order did not come from a Wilson associate within the CIA. The apparent inability of any investigative agency of the government to get to the bottom of such aberrations and to satisfy the public that the culprits have been identified and punished goes a long way to explaining how the CIA came to be regarded as "notorious".

Worries by West European intelligence specialists that the CIA had become "politicized" were scarcely allayed when a Presidential campaign manager was installed in 1981 as Director of Central Intelligence and when shortly thereafter both the Director and a political associate he had appointed as Director of Operations were called before a Senate committee to explain questionable business dealings. The new Director of Operations resigned and the Director was left with much less than a rousing vote of confidence. Indeed, it was suggested by a senior Senator of the President's own party that the Director resign.

In one of the most stunning rebuffs ever given by the US Congress to a government agency, the US House of Representatives voted on December 10, 1982, to prohibit assistance to paramilitary organizations in Central America seeking to "destabilize" the government of Nicaragua. The action came after a spate of news stories identifying the CIA as at least an indirect supporter and abettor of such movements. The vote in the House was 411 to 0.

It would be pleasant to be able to say that amidst the "empire-building" of the CIA's counter-intelligence staff and the everlasting scandals of the "covert action" staff the analysts of the Directorate of Intelligence

1 ▲
1 William Webster, current FBI Director. According to Executive Order 12333 the tasks of the FBI include not only counter-intelligence within the US but also, under certain conditions, outside it as well, in conjunction with the CIA.

2 ▲
2 An FBI computer operator at work. Is his task still being interfered with by the CIA, even though the FBI, according to Executive Order 12333, is supposed to have responsibility for counter-intelligence?

3 Two members of today's US Special Force. The Special Forces are sometimes used to execute CIA plans. In one incident this even included the Army lending an unwitting master sergeant to assist the notorious Edwin P. Wilson.

4 The Shah of Iran in the Pentagon in 1975. The CIA totally failed to foresee the end of the Shah's rule, "blinded", according to one report, "by the deceptive lustre of the Peacock Throne and the Shah it had placed there".

3 ▲

4 ▲

were quietly working away, producing competent finished intelligence. Unhappily, the record indicates quiet mediocrity, or worse.

In one of the several hearings seeking to establish the propriety of stock holdings by a Director of Central Intelligence, Sen. Daniel P. Moynihan observed that, "I would like to think that you could make a killing in the stock market just having the information that the CIA has about the way oil prices are going in Abu Dhabi. [However, CIA officials] know about as much as *Forbes* [a business magazine] knows."

As indicated in earlier chapters, that is true about much more important subject areas than the stock market. The inadequacies of CIA analyses run as a constant theme through all of the Congressional reviews of the Agency. Nor do CIA apologists attempt to deny such deficiencies.

Indeed, the intelligence "show" staged in March 1982 by the US services to generate public support for Central American policies of the Reagan Administration tended to confirm all that the critics had been saying. Technical collection—pictures of airfields, etc., and intercepted communications—was of a high order. There was almost nothing in the way of evidence to show that this had been correlated with the political and economic information available through the churches, the press, tourists and other "unclassified" sources. Ironically the public and some of their representatives in Congress demonstrated a capability to make such a correlation where the intelligence agencies had failed and within a few weeks generated pressures that forced the government to claim that it is not seeking a new "Vietnam War" in Central America.

Misguided CIA analysts

Even when good work is produced by the lower ranking analysts, CIA Director William J. Casey has indicated, "these analytical insights were strangled in the clearance and coordinating process". Indicators of a Soviet invasion of Czechoslovakia in 1968, of the Yom Kippur War in 1973 and of the Cuban intervention in Angola in 1975 tended to be ignored, says former CIA official Cord Meyer, because of a tendency by CIA analysts to want to believe the best about the Soviet Union and its friends—exactly the state of mind that recently brought about a scandal in the Australian Office of National Assessment (ONA).

Casey, however, may have compounded the problem by placing political appointees in middle-echelon jobs. Congressional critics claim that subsequent analyses, notably of Central American developments, essentially mirror statements those appointees made during the Presidential political campaign in which Mr. Casey was campaign manager. The end product of what the European intelligence specialists call "politicization", of the CIA, therefore, may be CIA analyses that simply support domestic political objectives of the administration in power. It is only a very short step from there to a return to CIA counter-intelligence staff interference in domestic US politics, a potential secret CIA "empire" that awakens nightmares in the minds at home and abroad.

The dangers of assigning political-military operations to an agency created primarily to gather and analyse intelligence are discussed in chapter 1. They are developed in much greater detail in records of the 1970s US Congressional investigations and in books by former CIA officials, in particular *Secrets, Spies and Scholars* by Dr. Ray S. Cline.

Cord Meyer, also a former CIA official, and the Washington columnist Jack Anderson have provided a vivid example, in connection with Iran, of how the operations ("covert action") "camel" that crept into CIA in the 1950s eventually came to dominate and distort intelligence analysis. "As the perceptive reporting of the French newspaper *Le Monde* indicated in the summer of 1978," Meyer records, "it was not necessary to have access to secret agents to understand what was happening [in Iran]."

According to CIA documents examined by two of Jack Anderson's reporters, Eileen O'Connor and Dale Van Atta, French intelligence made an official assessment identical to that of *Le Monde* and provided it to CIA. "But the CIA," says Anderson, "evidently blinded by the deceptive lustre of the Peacock Throne *and the Shah it had placed there* [emphasis added], misread the French intelligence information on Khomeni and concluded that he was merely the puppet of forces beyond his control."

In short, for CIA analysts in the Directorate of Intelligence to have given the French reports the weight they deserved would have meant repudiation of the ultimately disastrous "covert action" launched by the Directorate of Operations in 1953, by which Mossadeq was overthrown and the Shah reinstated. In 1980 the United States paid a heavy price for these internal CIA politics in the unprecedented national humiliation of having its embassy in Teherhan overrun and its staff imprisoned.

In addition to the biases and distortions induced by CIA organizational problems, it seems there is an additional, equally dangerous distorting influence. According to James Schlesinger, former Director of Central Intelligence, "the Intelligence Directorate tends to be in close harmony with the prevailing biases in the intellectual community." There was an assumption by the CIA analysts, says Schlesinger, imbibed from the civilian academic community, that the Soviet Union had the same arms control objectives as the non-Communist countries. The result was that "when the Soviets had actually deployed more than 1,000 ICBMs . . . the National Intelligence Estimates . . . were still saying that they would deploy no more than 1,000 ICBMs." (It is estimated that the Soviet Union fielded 1,398 ICBMs in 1982, according to the Department of Defense—*Editor.*) This assumption of common disarmament objectives, incidentally, was identical to the view pumped back into the US academic community and the US Government itself by people returning from visits to the Soviet Institute on the US and Canada.

These biases, acquired from the civilian academic community and reinforced by indirect Soviet "disinformation", clearly played a part not only in the misassessment cited by Schlesinger, but in the chain of misassessments cited by Senator Huddleston (see chapter 1).

The inadequacies of CIA analysis were acknowledged by both William J. Casey and Vice Admiral Bobby Inman, in testimony before the Senate Select Committee on Intelligence in February 1981. (They are described in much greater detail by distinguished present and former US intelligence officials in a discussion published by the National Strategy Information Center, New York: *Intelligence Requirements for the 1980s: Analysis and Estimates.*) Later, according to Philip Taubman of the New York *Times,* Casey found that "many of his agency's analysts neither know the languages of the countries they watch nor have travelled to those countries."

How could an organization into which billions of dollars have been poured, which possesses, according to Congressional investigators, "some of the most sophisticated information storage and retrieval systems to be found anywhere in the world," and which is able to offer substantially more attractive wages and working conditions than the rest of the US Civil Service, have gone so far wrong? Secrecy, according to the Congressional investigators, is one of the primary reasons.

That should be no surprise to anyone who has had access to US classified libraries over the past 30 years. At least 90 per cent of the documents locked up in those libraries and in thousands of safes elsewhere—all at enormous public expense—have no more business being "classified" than yesterday's newspaper. The system operates, however, as a vast cocoon, protecting the intelligence analyst against the sort of scrutiny to which civilian journalists and scholars are constantly subjected.

A few intelligence analysts, such as Dr. Francis J. Romance of the Defense Intelligence Agency, a distinguished specialist in Northeast Asian affairs, seek out such scrutiny by presenting papers and participating in panel discussions at open civilian academic conferences, but they are very few and far between.

This insulation from the competitive world of ideas is compounded by what the Congressional investigators found to be an almost total absence of quality control. There is no means, the investigators found, to review systematically the work of intelligence analysts in later years and to weed out of the system those analysts found to be repeatedly wrong in their assessments. On the contrary, it seems, whoever tunes his work to internal politics and to prevailing "conventional wisdom" is almost sure to be promoted ahead of the more honest analyst who accepts the risks of long-range assessments that may be at variance with "safe" agency politics or which challenge academic prejudices.

That there are few risk-takers among the CIA analysts and their supervisors is the inevitable product of CIA methods of recruitment, selection and training—now being copied by the Israelis to their great disadvantage.

The standard method of hiring new employees is by recruitment from the college campus. This is followed by a concurrent probationary training and selection process in which the new employee is subjected to intensive scrutiny, including polygraph ("lie detector") tests. In the process, the new employee is required to sign an oath of secrecy, binding for life, by which he or she swears to provide to CIA censors anything prepared for public discussion concerning the agency or its work, no matter how many years after leaving agency employment.

Whatever sense of adventure or desire to be connected with important and interesting events there may be in the CIA's appeal, such attractions are equalled or exceeded by the military and the Foreign Service. Choice of the CIA, therefore, is likely to be based on the more attractive material benefits the agency can offer as compared to any other agency of the US Government.

That process pretty well separates the risk-takers from the non-risk-takers in the intellectual sense. If security and superior material advantages are among the primary reasons for choosing CIA employment, the chances become slimmer every year thereafter that the new recruit will do anything to jeopardize those progressively more valuable benefits.

Next, the polygraph process, used normally in free societies only in criminal investigations, is essentially a dehumanizing process by which the individual's sense of privacy and independence is greatly reduced. The Agency then comes forward to substitute for this partial loss of individuality, reinforcing a dependence that is designed to grow with each year of employment. The new employee is also keenly aware, of course, that the highly personal information elicited during the polygraph process is now in the official files. Anyone who has witnessed the misuse

2 ▲

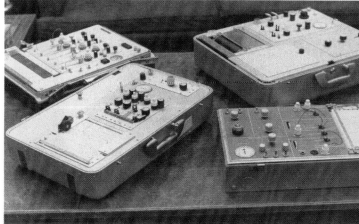

1 ▲

3 ▲

of supposedly confidential information systems by the administrations of Presidents John F. Kennedy, Lyndon Johnson and Richard Nixon should have no illusions about the dangers of potential official blackmail.

In recent years the CIA has made it plain that it will use the oath of secrecy to punish any former employee, even including William E. Colby, a former Director of Central Intelligence, who dares to reveal incompetence or criminal activity; subjects which, of course, are not likely to pass the Agency's censors. Indeed, after what happened to two former CIA authors—Richard Snepp and former CIA Director Colby, both forced, in effect, to pay huge fines for revealing CIA misfeasance and malfeasance, the prospective journalist or scholar who considers employment with the Agency must recognize that the oath is a professional death warrant. Indeed, the only former CIA employees who seem to prosper are people such as Mr Wilson who have made a fortune selling terrorism to the Libyans.

Is it any wonder, then, that National Intelligence Estimates, in the view of US Congressional investigators, tend to be an assemblage of "reinforcing consensus, whereby divergent views of individual analysts can become submerged in a sea of conventional collective wisdom, and doubts or disagreements can simply disappear?"

The weaknesses of these intelligence assessments endanger not only the United States but the entire non-Communist world, for, to one degree or another, all of the small, non-Communist intelligence agencies depend on CIA analyses.

As a corrective, CIA Director William J.

Casey has proposed a closer relationship with journalists, businessmen who travel and work overseas, and with scholars and other groups with extensive knowledge of foreign affairs, such as mission societies. Yet all of these groups have suffered extensively in the past from association with the CIA and have made it abundantly clear that they don't wish to renew the experience. If any reminders were needed, the treatment meted out to Snepp and Colby made it plain that any form of association with the CIA is dangerous.

CIA closed to public

At the same time that he was proposing a freer and more open relationship with knowledgeable non-government groups, Mr. Casey closed the CIA public affairs office in 1981 and announced that, henceforth, the agency would cease publication of unclassified research projects because it took up too much of the analysts' time. The research products, and the briefings provided for newsmen through the Office of Public Affairs, were the agency's only means of demonstrating whether the quality of its work could stand comparison with non-government research and journalism. The intensive pressure from within the agency for a return to total secrecy makes it plain that the agency as it exists today cannot afford comparison with non-agency, non-government work.

As correctives, Dr. Ray S. Cline has recommended that what is now known as the CIA be divested of "covert action" and that it be superseded by an institute capable of competing in the open world of ideas.

The history of the Central Intelligence Agency demonstrates that "covert action" is not only a millstone around the neck of the Agency itself, but a serious continuing embarrassment and impediment to the effective conduct of American foreign policy. In short, "covert action" in any period short of open hostilities has backfired whenever democratic societies have attempted to employ it.

To the extent that there is a genuine wartime need for such activites, it would be sufficient to reconstitute an "Office of Strategic Services" in the US Department of Defense and to restrict its work to research and planning except in periods of formally declared war or national emergency.

Centuries of British experience and the findings of US Congressional investigators that the best of US political and economic intelligence comes from the small State Department Bureau of Intelligence and Research argue for transfer of control of the small US strategic-level espionage function and the overseas counter-espionage function to the State Department. That would put an end to the present intolerably dangerous situation whereby the CIA Station Chief can withhold information from the US ambassador, and circumvent the ambassador as he sees fit in reporting to Washington. That unhealthy relationship is unquestionably a factor in the increasing confusion of US foreign policy over the past several decades and the resulting increasing distrust of American policy and judgement among US allies.

Former CIA Director Schlesinger has warned that the State Department, also, has its own organizational biases, and it is a

4 ▲

1 William J. Casey, CIA Director, told a reporter that "many of his agency's analysts neither know the language of the countries they watch nor have travelled to these countries."

2 A typically peaceful campus scene: potential recruiting ground for CIA agents. The CIA has more PhDs than any other US government agency

3 CIA makes wide use of polygraph tests (lie detectors) in recruiting processes, with machines such as these.

4 A polygraph test in progress. Normally only used in democratic countries for criminal investigations, it has a dehumanising effect.

5 Philip Agee, a former CIA agent, who was deported from Britain and France in 1977, claims that he was being harassed as a result of CIA pressure to try to stop him making more revelations about the agency. All employees take an oath of secrecy on joining and the CIA goes to great lengths to punish any transgressor.

5 ▲

1 This launch manual for Minuteman II ICBMs is correctly labelled "Top Secret", but how many documents are needlessly overclassified?

2 Lieutenant-General James Williams, DIA Director. US Congressional investigators considered that excessive secrecy impeded efficiency of the DIA.

3, 4 The Washington-Moscow Direct Communications Link. If the US President ever has to use the "Hot Line" to the Soviet leader in earnest, when they may have just 15 minutes to make vital decisions which may lead to nuclear holocaust, they will rely entirely on intelligence reports and Assessment. These will have to be good. . . .

◄1
2►

warning that should be heeded. Dr. Cline's proposed institute to be created from residual CIA assets (that is, the Directorate of Intelligence and the Directorate of Science and Technology) would provide a competing centre of analysis. Very little of the work of such an institute need be classified. Indeed, only part of the work of the Directorate of Science and Technology could make any claim to secrecy.

Properly organized and staffed, the creation of such an institute would argue for the cutoff of the large US Government subsidies now paid to an array of "private" research enterprises ranging from the RAND Corporation in California to the Hudson Institute in New York, at a substantial monetary saving. These groups perform, often at exhorbitant administrative costs, the sort of analyses that should be more clearly identified as Government-sponsored assessments. Also, it is even easier than is the case with the CIA for these quasi-private intelligence analysis agencies to escape accountability for value of public funds expended.

Above all, there needs to be a thorough review and revision of the present CIA approach to recruitment.

It is impossible to identify effective or potentially effective intelligence analysts from among students whose judgement is as yet untested by "life". The sorry performance of CIA analysis to date provides ample evidence that the most brilliant of scholars may be totally unable to make common-sense judgements about people —and understanding human conduct is, ultimately, what intelligence analysis is all about.

Indeed, the CIA performance to date is so dismal that it argues for the retirement of the present analytical staff and a totally new beginning, modelled on the far more successful, and vastly smaller, British assess-

ment system dicussed in chapter 2.

Given, also, the ample evidence that searchers after "job security" are the least likely people to accept the risks and competition inherent in good intelligence analysis, recruiting for a new "Institute" should be separated entirely from the civil service system.

A one-time five-year contract with authority to offer a wage substantially above what the desired recruit earns in non-government employment would provide the proposed institute with the means to attract scientists, scholars, journalists and Foreign Service officers who demonstrate in their ordinary employment a high capability for intelligence analysis. Since they would necessarily have access to classified information as a check against the accuracy of their open assessments, such a hiatus from normal employment would be seen as a valuable asset to a career. Maintenance of the present Orwellian atmosphere by which the CIA attempts to mantain "security" would be out of the question with people of the quality needed. That means discarding the polygraph test and the rest of the present "1984" apparatus and reliance on the normal background investigations for all government employees who are given access to classified information.

Since the hiring of people from all of the desired non-government fields would be in an open, forthright manner, and since the work of these people would be highly visible throughout their association with the government, there would be no need for the sleazy methods by which the CIA sought to infiltrate such fields in the past, or for the humiliating, cap-in-hand approach to which it has since been reduced.

People in the Foreign Service or elsewhere in the US Government who are capable of competent intelligence analysis will demonstrate that capability by competitive publi-

cation in such journals as the US Naval Institute *Proceedings*. Identified by that means, they could be recruited for a five-year contract in Dr. Cline's proposed "institute" at a premium over their normal salary.

Deficiencies in the DIA

Although US Congressional investigators rated the military attache system on a par with the State Department as the most productive element of American intelligence they found serious deficiencies in the Defense Intelligence Agency as such. Here again excessive secrecy was seen as a serious impediment to efficient and timely analysis. A similar obsession with secrecy was blamed by a later inquiry for the failure of the raid intended to free American hostages in Iran.

Duplication, compartmentation and the squirrelling away of information all contribute to this problem, by which the product of billions of dollars worth of research and technology becomes trapped in safes and desk drawers, and in minds too small to encompass it.

Intelligence continues to be a less-than-desirable career path in the American military services. This is compounded by the fact that the American services seldom place senior officers of proven operational capability in intelligence assignments. As a result, the US Government continues to be burdened with assessments of major potential conflicts by relatively low-ranking officers who have no experience in major unit operations (i.e., division-level and above).

In DIA as in CIA and, indeed any agency able to resort to the "classified" stamp, secrecy is the great protector of waste, incompetence, duplication and inefficiency generally. No amount of reorganization is

 ◄3
4 ►

likely to remedy this until most of the cloak of secrecy is removed, and until DIA analysts are forced to compete in the open with other, competing centres of intelligence analysis, including those outside the government. As indicated earlier, there are a few analysts in both DIA and CIA who have no fear of such open competition, but they are constantly working against the "security" syndrome.

This situation could be dramatically improved by restricting classification to those very few categories, even in the Defense Department, for which it is truly justified: codes, contingency plans, technology prior to deployment, and sources of intelligence. There is no justification, for example, for classification of the basic Joint Chiefs of Staff intelligence assessment. It is about as exciting as the previous week's issue of *Time* magazine, and usually considerably more out of date. In fact, if it were to be measured out it would be found that most of the day-to-day strategic and policy decisions in all Western governments and in Japan are made on the basis of information supplied through open journalism rather than the official intelligence. The latter is simply too slow in getting around.

In sum, the world's principal antagonists in the "Intelligence War"—the Soviet KGB and the American intelligence "community"—are only marginally effective. The great strength of the KGB is in foreign espionage, whereby it is able to obtain high technology beyond the capability of the Communist nations to produce, and sometimes beyond their capability to use. The strength of the American intelligence services is in their mechanical means of collection, but the potential of that capability is greatly limited by serious deficiencies of analysis.

The great weakness of both intelligence systems is their obsession with secrecy, and

the potential for deception or self-deception that it breeds. Thus, in the words of John Barron, "the Russians have become so addicted to spying that they seem to distrust information unless it is procured by illicit means," as confirmed by the Norwegian incident cited earlier. In the process they fail to understand that all they need to know about non-Communist society is spread out before them on the pages of the daily newspaper, or available to them in very ordinary conversation.

Dominance of the technical over the human factor in the American intelligence services has resulted in the exaltation of "bean counting" over an ability to understand how the objects counted relate to one another and to the rest of the world.

All of this means that neither the Soviet nor the American leadership can depend entirely, or indeed with any degree of certainty on what the official intelligence agencies report to them, except in very limited technical areas.

The President's hunches

For all the billions spent, the situation has not changed a great deal from that described by Harry H. Ransom concerning President Franklin D. Roosevelt's experience in World War II: "The intelligence reports often contradicted each other. The result was that the President had to act as his own intelligence evaluator, or, out of frustration with conflicting estimates, simply had to play his own hunches." Indeed, Winston Churchill, in *The Grand Alliance,* warned of the dangers of unanimous estimates, citing the unamimous assessment of the British services that the Germans would not attack Russia in 1941. Using his own estimate of the raw intelligence, Churchill came to the opposite conclusion and warned Stalin, but to no avail.

If the fateful "first strike" ever is launched, it is likely to be on the basis of a similar personal evaluation, deriving as much from what the chief of state concerned learned in fist fights as a schoolboy as from what he is told by an intelligence agency. This need to be one's own intelligence evaluator extends far beyond the chiefs of state in a democratic society and includes literally every member of that society.

The fact that the judgement of even the best of the intelligence analysts is not always right would seem to suggest that the voter in democratic societies should place greater emphasis than ever before on the experience and training a candidate has had in international security affairs. For if experience to date shows anything it is that there must be a complementary relationship between competent collection and analysis in the intelligence services, on the one hand, and trained international as well as domestic political judgement on the part of political leadership, on the other, if we are to survive.

Quite aside from quality of analysis in or out of the intelligence agencies there is a need for much greater safeguards than now exist on the intelligence agencies. Reform of the KGB cannot be accomplished short of dismantling the entire Soviet system. The dangers resulting from faulty organization, supervision and control of the CIA are sketched here and in much greater detail in the reports of US Senate investigators. Britain, France and Canada have experienced similar problems in recent years, although on a smaller scale. In most instances, excessive secrecy played a major part. More than any other single factor, therefore, a major reduction in the degree of secrecy permitted these agencies is the first and most pressing requirement if we are to cope with the "Intelligence War" without becoming its victims.

Index

Picture credits

Pages 8-9: 1 USN; 2-3 US Dept. of Defense (DoD). **10-11:** 1-2 DoD; 3 Nikon; 4 FFV. **12-13:** 1 DoD; 2 NASA; 3 Lockheed; 4 Itek; 5 DoD. **14-15:** DoD. **16-17:** US State Dept.; 2 Keystone; 3 US Navy(USN); 4 UPI. **18-19:** 1 Salamander; 2 US Nat. Archives; 3 US State Dept. **20-21:** 1-2 USMC; 3 Camera Press; 4 Central Press; 5 USN. **22-23:** 1-5 USN; 6 Camera Press; 7 DoD. **24-25:** DoD. **26-27:** 1 Camera Press; 2 Eshel-Dramit; 3 Keystone. **28-29:** 1-2 Central Press; 3 UPI; 4 DoD; 5 PA. **30-31:** British Ministry of Defence (MoD); 2-3 USN. **32-33:** 1 Keystone; 2-3 IBM. **34-35:** 1-2 DoD; 3 Thomas F. Troy. **36-37:** 1 Cord Meyer; 2-3 Salamander; 4 Tass; 5 Salamander. **38-39:** 1-2 Salamander; 3 CIA; 4 DoD; 5 CIA. **40-41:** 1 USN; 2-4 CIA. **42-43:** 1 US Nat. Archives; 2 DoD; 3-4 US State Dept.; 5 USN. **44-45:** DoD. **46-47:** 1 USN; 2 DoD; 3 Salamander; 4 USN. **46-47:** 1 Camera Press; 2 United States Information Service (USIS). **48-49:** 1 Keystone; 2 DoD; 3 NATO. **50-51:** 1-2 NATO; 3 Boeing; 4 USN; 5 USIS. **52-53:** 1 USN; 2-3 US Air Force (USAF); 4 US Army; 5 DoD. **54-55:** 1 DoD; 2 Camera Press; 3-4 DoD. **56-57:** 1 DoD; 2-3 MoD. **60-61:** 1 Salamander. **62-63:** 1 MoD; 2 Salamander; 3-4 PA. **64-65:** 1 Central Press; 2-3 PA. **66-67:** 1-2 NATO; 3 DoD; 4 Keystone. **68-69:** 6-8 PA. **70-71:** 1-3 CCS Communication Control; 4-8 Keymcd International. **72-73:** 2 Nikon; 3 CCS Communications Control; 4-5 Curtis Peebles; 6 UPI; 7 Popperfoto. **74-75:** 1 NATO; 2 MoD; 3-4 FBI. **76-77:** DoD. **78-79:** 1 Israeli Air Force; 2-4 Eshel—Dramit; 5 DoD. **80-81:** 1 USAF; 2-3 US Army; 4 MoD. **82-83:** 1-2 DoD; 3 US Army. **84-85:** 1 Thomson-CSF; 2 NATO; 3-4 US Army; 5 NASA. **86-87:** 1-2 US Army; 5 GTE Systems. **88-89:** 1 USN; 2 GTE Systems; 3 US Army; 5 Salamander. **90-91:** 1 Beech Aircraft Corporation; 2-3 Grumman; 4 GTE Systems; 5 DoD. **92-93:** 1 DoD; 2-3 US Army; 4 DoD. **94-95:** 1-2 Barre Stroud; 3 US Army; 4-5 USAF; 6 Pilkington Glass. **96-97:** NASA. **98-99:** 1 Novosti; 2-4 USAF. **100-101:** 1-3 USAF; 5 USAF. **102-103:** 1-2 USAF; 3 NASA. **104-105:** 1 NASA; 2 DoD; 3 NASA; 4 TRW. **106-107:** 1 NASA; 2 TRW; 3 DoD; 4 USN; 6 NASA. **108-109:** 1-2 USAF; 3 DoD. **110-111:** 1-2 USN; 3 DoD; 4 USN; 5 USN; 6-7 DoD. **112-113:**

1 USAF; 2-6 DoD. **114-115:** 1-3 DoD. **116-117:** 1-3 DoD. **118-119:** 1-3 USAF. **120-121:** USAF. **122-123:** 1 Imperial War Museum (IWM); 2 USAF; 3-5 IWM. **124-125:** 1 Grumman; 2-4 USAF; 5 Lockheed. **126-127:** 1-2 Itek; 3 Curtis Peebles: 4 Central Press; 5-6 Curtis Peebles; 7 Grumman. **128-129:** 1 Panavia; 2 Northrop; 3 Vinten; 4-6 Northrop. **130-131:** 1 Ford Aerospace; 2 Michael J.H. Taylor; 3 Ford Aerospace; 4-6 USAF. **132-133:** 1-3 British Aerospace (BAe); 4 Israel Aircraft Industries; 5-6 Tadiran Electronic Industries. **134-135:** 1 Eshel-Dramit; 2-4 Dornier. **136-137:** 1 USAF; 2 Northrop; 3 Zeiss; 4-5 FFV; 6-7 BAe. **138-139:** 1-5 USAFE. **140-141:** 1 USN; 2-3 Boeing. **142-143:** 1 Lockheed; 2 DoD; 6-8 DoD. **144-145:** 1 Novosti; 2 Tass; 3 Novosti; 4 DoD; 7 Salamander. **146-147:** US Army; 2 USIS; 3 US Army; 4 Bell Helicopters; 5 US Army. **150-151:** 1 DoD; 2 US Army; 3 Vietnam Embassy. **152-153:** 1 Thomson-CSF; 2 US Army; 3 NATO; 4 MoD; 5 Salamander. **154-155:** 1 MoD; 2 DoD; 3 Salamander. **156-157:** 1-5 US Army. **158-159:** 1-3 US Army; 4 Canadair; 5 US Army; 6 USN; 7 USAF; 8 US Army. **160-161:** 1-4 MoD; 5 DoD; 6 Canadian Forces photo. **162-163:** 1 Panharde Levassor; 3 NATO; 4 Lasergaid Ltd. **164-165:** 1 DoD; 2 MoD; 3 DoD; 4 Salamander. **166-167:** 1 MARS; 2-3 Royal Navy Fleet Photo Unit; 4 Geartest; 5 BAe. **172-173:** 1-5 USN. **174-175:** 1-2 USN. **176-177:** 1 MoD; 2 USN; 3 MoD; 4 Salamander; 5 Hollandse Signaalapparaten BV; 6-10 USN; 11 Thomson-CSF. **178-179:** 6 USN; 7 Société ECA; 8 USN; 11 USN; 12 Sippican. **184-185:** 1-2 Plessey Marine; 3-8 USN. **188-189:** 1 Swedish Navy; 2 Dassault-Breguet; 3 USN; 4 Kawasaki; 5-10 USN. **190-191:** 1 Hughes Helicopters; 2 Tass; 3-4 USN; 5 Royal Navy; 6 USN. **192-193:** Central Press. **194-195:** 1 USN; 2 DoD; 3 CIA; 4 DoD. **196-197:** 1 US State Dept.; 2 MoD-Army; 3 Central Press; 4 MoD; 5 DoD. **198-199:** 1 Central Press; 2 DIA; 3 USAF; 4 USN; 5 US State Dept. **200-201:** 1-2 FBI; 3-4 DoD. **202-203:** 1 US State Dept.; 2 University of Wisconsin-Madison; 3 US Army; 4 FBI; 5 Keystone. **204-205:** 1 USAF; 2 US Army; 3 DoD; 4 US State Dept.

"To carry out a timely response to warning . . . two conditions must
be met: we must not only receive warning, but also take the
decision to respond. The first task has long been recognized; it calls
for strong intelligence capabilities. It is the second task that
has been neglected or misunderstood. We cannot assume that the
enemy, if he actually plans to attack, will necessarily
do us the favor of furnishing warning that is unambiguous.
Military history reminds us that we ought to expect a
massive and skilful effort at deception.
The Soviet Union failed to anticipate the German attack in 1941; the
Soviets, in turn, surprised the Japanese in 1945. Despite the
lesson of Pearl Harbor, we were caught unprepared again in June
1950 by the North Koreans. The Israelis achieved surprise in
1967, only to fall victim to surprise in 1973.
It seems likely that skilful deception could deprive us of clear
warning. Indeed, Soviet military doctrine puts great emphasis on
deception and surprise. Hence we have to change our policy
for reacting to warning. Our forces and those of
our allies must be prepared to respond to warning indicators that
are highly ambiguous . . . Being prepared to respond only to
warning that is unambiguous means being prepared for the kind
of warning we are least likely to get.

Caspar W. Weinberger, United States Secretary of Defense,
addressing Congress, February 8, 1982.